CHARGES
AND ADDRESSES

J. C. Ryle—at his desk in later years.

CHARGES
AND ADDRESSES

J. C. Ryle

THE BANNER OF TRUTH TRUST

THE BANNER OF TRUTH TRUST

3 Murrayfield Road, Edinburgh EH12 6EL, UK
P.O. Box 621, Carlisle, PA 17013, USA

❧

© The Banner of Truth Trust 2021
First published 1903
First Banner of Truth Trust edition 1978
This edition 2021

❧

ISBN:
Print: 978 1 80040 011 5
EPUB: 978 1 80040 012 2
Kindle: 978 1 80040 013 9

❧

Typeset in 10.5/14 Berkeley Oldstyle Medium
at the Banner of Truth Trust, Edinburgh

Printed in the USA by
Versa Press, Inc.,
East Peoria, IL

CONTENTS

N.B. J. C. Ryle's original footnotes are marked by an *asterisk*. All other footnotes have been added by the publisher.

INTRODUCTION

J OHN CHARLES RYLE was consecrated Bishop of Liverpool on June 11, 1880 at the age of sixty-five. Previously a part of the ancient See of Chester, Liverpool had received Parliamentary authority to possess its own bishopric in 1878 and by an Order in Council the new diocese came into being on March 24, 1880. Ryle was thus the first bishop of a city second only to London in importance and, as a sea-port at the mouth of the Mersey, first in the world.

By 1880 the labours for which Ryle is best remembered today— his forceful writings, his commentaries on the Gospels, and his leadership in evangelical thought in the Church of England—were all accomplished facts. From the age of twenty-five he had worked as a pastor and preacher, first in Hampshire (at Exbury, 1841–43 and Winchester, 1843–44) then in Suffolk (Helmingham, 1844–61 and Stradbroke, 1861–80). In March 1880 it seemed that the last stage of his life would be occupied with a new and probably less arduous position, for in that month he was nominated as Dean of Salisbury. Unknown, however, to him, in the weeks immediately following the nomination to Salisbury and before his installation, others were urging that he should be sent to Liverpool. His Protestantism would be congenial to many of the people of Lancashire and, as Benjamin Disraeli, the Prime Minister, wrote to Queen Victoria on April 10, there were other considerations: 'The people of Liverpool are very anxious about their new bishop. The Tories subscribed the whole of the endowment and bought the palace.[1] Lord Sandon[2] says his seat for Liverpool depends upon the appointment being made by Your Majesty's present advisers. The whole city is most anxious that Your Majesty should appoint the present Dean of Salisbury, Canon Ryle.' Disraeli, it should be added, was the outgoing Tory leader—defeated by the Liberals in a general election earlier in the year. The truth is that he no more favoured evangelicals than the Queen herself but it seems that his hurried appointment of Ryle before laying down his office was in revenge for the recent High Church vote for the Liberals who were led by his opponent W. E. Gladstone. Certainly Ryle was, as Dean Church observed in 1889, 'obnoxious to all High Churchmen,' Gladstone included.[3]

In moving to Liverpool, in the North-West of England, Ryle was returning to the region he had always loved. Born in Macclesfield, Cheshire, just thirty-five miles from Liverpool, in 1816, Ryle had intended to remain in that part of England all his days. As a child he had enjoyed a summer at Crosby just north of Liverpool; in early manhood it was to Liverpool he went for ten days every year for military exercises with the Cheshire yeomanry, a regiment in which he had the office of Captain. And cricket, his favourite game, also brought him to the same place in the late 1830s. As the eldest son in an affluent family there seemed to be no reason at that date why his home should not ever be in the county which lay on the southern banks of the Mersey. But all was changed in the month of June 1841. His father's wealth derived from the two banks he owned in Macclesfield and Manchester; the misman-agement of the latter by a subordinate led to its sudden collapse and the Macclesfield branch was dragged down with it. 'We got up one summer's morning with all the world before us as usual,' Ryle remembered in later years, 'and went to bed that same night

---

[1] A Georgian house in Abercromby Square, now used by the University of Liverpool.

[2] Tory Member of Parliament for Liverpool.

[3] For further biographical information see Marcus L. Loane, *Makers of our Heritage, a Study of Four Evangelical Leaders* (1967), and Peter Toon and Michael Smout, *John Charles Ryle, Evangelical Bishop* (1976).

completely and entirely ruined.' The family home was sold, Ryle's gentleman's life over, and he had to move to seek a career elsewhere. Although he was to see in all this the hand of God leading him into the Christian ministry, sadness over his 'exile' from the place of his youth never left him. When fifty-seven years of age he wrote in an autobiographical manuscript, meant for his children, 'Trees are too old to transplant at twenty-five and I was too old ever to take root again in any other part of the world. And ever since I left Cheshire, I have never felt at home, but a *sojourner and a dweller* in a lodging and I never expect to feel anything else as long as I live.'[1]

The opportunity to return to the North-West was indeed as unexpected as his departure but he accepted it readily as his last sphere of Christian ministry: 'I tried to hold the fort for Christ during the past thirty-five years in the comparative seclusion of Suffolk,' he said in May 1880, 'and I hope by God's grace to hold the same fort in the giant city of Liverpool.'

Compared with the town he remembered from the 1830s the city was indeed a 'giant.' No part in Britain had benefited more from the Industrial Revolution. It was virtually the emporium of the British Empire: goods led by cotton and sugar flowed in and the manufactures of Lancashire went out.

In a sermon preached at the time of Queen Victoria's Jubilee in 1887 Ryle drew the comparison with fifty years earlier:

> In our own city of Liverpool, the population in 1837 was only 246,000. It is now, including suburbs, 700,000. The tonnage of shipping at our port in 1837 was only 1,953,894. It is now 7,546,623. The number of ships entering was 15,038. It is now 21,529. In 1837, Liverpool had 9 docks, with a frontage of two miles and a half to the river. There are now fifty docks and basins with a frontage of six miles.

---

[1] J. C. Ryle, *A Self-Portrait, A Partial Autobiography*, edited by Toon and Smout (1975), p. 56. A new edition of this was published by the Trust: Andrew Atherstone ed., *Bishop J. C. Ryle's Autobiography: The Early Years* (Edinburgh: Banner of Truth Trust, 2016).

Increase was also to be seen in the Church of England. When John Newton spent nine years in the port as Tide Surveyor (1755–64) he found no evangelical ministry in any parish church. Through the 18th Century those who were spiritually exercised in Liverpool generally left the Church for Nonconformist or Methodist chapels. In 1837 there were in the city and its suburbs only thirty-six churches and about seventy clergymen. By the 1880s the number had risen to ninety churches and 185 clergy and it is clear that evangelical influence contributed by far the largest part to this growth. In a number of parishes there were outstanding men. Among them were Major Lester who, serving St Mary's Kirkdale from 1855 to 1903, was responsible for the opening of three other churches, and Richard Hobson who in 1864 went to a congregation of five people in a district known as the 'little hell,' yet came to see an average Sunday attendance of 2,000 before he retired in 1901. Hobson had a communicants roll of 811, Sunday School pupils numbering 1,400, and some 1,400 men connected with the church through its various societies.

Notwithstanding the help of men of this calibre Bishop Ryle faced an enormous task in organizing and building the work of a new diocese, covering an area which in a southerly direction stretched almost half-way to Macclesfield. The population of the whole diocese was over one million and for this need he had only 340 clergy. As his 'First Charge' reveals he considered the under-manning of the diocese to be one of his most serious practical problems. How he sought to deal with it and other problems will be revealed in the following pages. For some readers the strategy of a bishop in a Victorian diocese may appear to be a subject of purely historical or merely local interest. But the evangelization of urban populations is one of the most pressing questions of the present day and while the circumstances in which Ryle had to operate no longer exist, his concept of clergy working as a team, his insistence on the importance of the laity, his concern to grasp and convey the facts in a given situation—all these and other matters remain worthy of attention and imitation. An aging man though he was, it is doubtful if any bishop ever gave his clergy and laity clearer spiritual leadership than did the author of these pages. In the year of his installation he said that he did not mean to be 'a milk and water bishop' and he kept his word.

Local administration and evangelism were not, however, the chief problems which Ryle had to face. There were wider spiritual issues, affecting, he believed, both the future of the Church of England and of biblical Christianity itself. He wanted his men to understand the signs of the times, and that not merely in Kirkdale or Huyton or Warrington but in Britain and the Christian world at large. Accordingly he often specified the two greatest dangers which he saw ahead. These were, first, the wish to go back on the Reformation—'to unprotestantize the Church of England'; and, second, the wish to allow universal toleration in matters of theology—'to declare the Church a kind of Noah's ark, within which every kind of opinion and creed shall dwell safe and undisturbed, and the only terms of communion shall be willingness to come inside and let your neighbour alone.'[1] Whether we agree with his assessment of these dangers or not, the fact is that Ryle clearly recognized what have become two of the most dominant influences in the religious and ecumenical thought of the 20th Century.

The reasons why he possessed no sympathy for these ideas are fully documented in these pages. What is not always documented is the pain Ryle knew in opposing these influences in his own diocese. Despite the pressing need for clergy he was prepared to refuse candidates for ordination, and in 1887 he released his own son, Herbert Edward Ryle, from his post as Examining Chaplain on account of the latter's acceptance of the theories of Higher Criticism. Probably nothing troubled him more deeply in his whole episcopate but when he came to Liverpool he had chosen

[1] Introduction to the Third Edition of *Principles for Churchmen* (1884), pp. vii-xxvii.

as his motto for the new See the text, 'Thy Word is truth' (John 17:17) and upon that he stood.

Ryle's work at Liverpool continued until the end of the century. In September 1899 the once granite-like figure of six foot three inches was enfeebled in step, hearing and memory, and he reluctantly reached the conclusion that he must lay down his work: 'I have ventured to hope that I might be allowed to end my days near the Mersey, and to die in harness. But God's thoughts are not as our thoughts.' On Christmas Day 1899, he went, as he had done for twenty years, to St Nathaniel's, where Richard Hobson, his friend, ministered, and at the conclusion of the service, Hobson recalls: 'He reached out his poor hand and drew me to him, saying, "This is the last time; God bless you; we shall meet in heaven." The big tears trickled down his furrowed cheeks.'

The resignation took effect on March 1, 1900. He died in Lowestoft on Sunday, June 10, at the age of eighty-four, and was buried, with a Bible in his hands, at All Saints', Childwall, Liverpool, the following Thursday. 'The graveyard,' wrote H. E. Ryle, 'was crowded with poor people who had come in carts and vans and buses to pay the last honours to the old man—who certainly had won their love.'[1]

It lies outside the scope of this Introduction to attempt to assess what Ryle did as Bishop of Liverpool and records for such an assessment are all too inadequate. The *Liverpool Daily Post* reported a rise in attendance in the Church of England from 54,000 in 1881 to 66,000 in 1891; in the same period Ryle had seen the completion of twenty-seven churches and forty-eight mission halls. His clergy were organized under two archdeacons and in nine Deaneries; in addition he encouraged the enrolment of many auxiliary helpers. There were about fifty licensed Scripture Readers, thirty Bible Women and a Lay Helpers Association of around 580 members. Other statistics will be found later in these pages. Ryle's own judgment at the end of the day, was that 'I have

---

[1] Quoted in *A Memoir of Herbert Edward Ryle*, M. H. Fitzgerald (1928), p. 135.

left undone many things which I hoped to have done when I first came to Liverpool.' Perhaps the surest testimony of all to what his ministry had meant was that large company of 'poor people' who crowded Childwall cemetery on that June morning in 1900. Certainly Ryle himself would have wished for no other tribute than that which he himself had once paid to Hugh Latimer: 'Promotion did not spoil him, nor did the mitre act as an extinguisher of his zeal for the gospel. He was the same in a Bishop's palace that he was in a country parsonage or a Cambridge pulpit; always faithful, always simple-minded, always about his Father's business, always labouring to do good to souls.'

The present volume, first published in 1903, is possibly the rarest of all the many Ryle volumes issued by his publishers. The publishers simply bound up what copies still survived of the Charges and Addresses that had been printed individually as pamphlets when first delivered. Thus, although the date for the published volume was 1903, the contents were, in fact, all printed and issued between the years 1881 and 1898. Consequently the various sections in the original volume appeared in different sizes of type, chapters were not numbered, and the book had neither consecutive pagination nor Index. Probably the number of pamphlets thus collected and bound was very small, hence the extreme scarceness of copies. The present publishers have followed the contents of the original volume with two differences. A pamphlet entitled 'For Kings,' being Ryle's Royal Jubilee Sermon in Liverpool in 1887, has not been included because it can be found among the sermons contained in *The Upper Room*.[1] But Ryle's 'Farewell to the Diocese,' which he wrote on February 1, 1900[2] has been added and it now finds its proper place at the conclusion of this volume. Other changes introduced in this edition concern matters of detail. In the 1903 volume the first three chapters lacked titles and these have been supplied in conformity

---

[1] First published in 1888 and reprinted 1970 and 1977 (Banner of Truth Trust).

[2] It was originally published in the Fourth Edition of *Principles for Churchmen* (May 1900).

with the remainder. Brief explanatory footnotes (marked '—P.') have been occasionally introduced by the present publisher. The Index is likewise new to this edition.

Almost all the contents of this volume were delivered in the context of two different occasions. First were the gatherings of clergy to whom he delivered a Charge at three-year intervals from 1881 to 1893. It will be seen that the primary Charge of 1881 consisted of two different addresses, one delivered in Liverpool and the other in Wigan in the south-west of the diocese: this practice of a double triennial charge he did not continue. The second occasion, marked by eight addresses in this book, was an annual Diocesan Conference, usually held in St George's Hall, in the centre of the city. In some respects these conferences were more important than the charges given at his triennial visitations. For one thing the annual Conference brought together both the clergy and lay workers of the diocese and gave him the opportunity to address both; in addition, the addresses were given at the opening of each conference and there was therefore opportunity for a discussion of his themes in the sessions which followed. It may well be that it was to the Diocesan Conference that Ryle attached the greater significance; at any rate it will be noticed that while his last 'Charge' is dated 1893 he was still speaking at the annual Conference as late as 1898. To the last he stood by his conviction announced in 1881, 'I am sure we all need our spiritual life quickened by intercourse with other servants of our common Master.'

A last word, not only on Ryle's episcopate but on his whole ministry, may fittingly be left to Richard Hobson. In a Memorial Sermon preached on the Sunday after the funeral of his old friend he declared: 'I am bold to say that perhaps few men in the nineteenth century did so much for God, for truth, for righteousness, among the English-speaking race and in the world as our late Bishop.'

INTRODUCTION

Not all servants of Christ are given the same degree of success but all can do no less than aim at the same faithfulness. If the re-issue of this volume serves that end it can fulfil no higher purpose.

The Publishers
September, 1978

1

NO UNCERTAIN SOUND

The first charge to the new Diocese, October 19, 1881.[1]

MY Reverend and Lay Brethren, we are gathered together today on an occasion of much interest and real solemnity. This is the primary visitation of the first Bishop of a new English Diocese. How many visitations may be held, and how many Episcopal Charges delivered before the end of all things, no man can tell. Let us pray that there may be always found in this Diocese a trumpet which shall give no 'uncertain sound,' and a Bishop who shall promote the real interests of the Reformed Church of England.

I ask you to believe that I meet you with a deep sense of my own weakness and fallibility. I have been called unexpectedly to be the chief pastor of a Diocese of vast importance and very exceptional character, a Diocese in which, to use the words of Scripture, 'there remaineth yet very much land to be possessed' (Josh. 13:1). I feel keenly how much is expected of a bishop in these days, and how little in reality he can do—how much the difficulties of his office are increased by our unhappy divisions— and how hard it is for any bishop to do his duty without causing disappointment to some, and giving offence to others. All these things, I repeat, I feel very keenly. But I see no reason for despondency or despair. With prayer, and pains, and faith in Jesus Christ,

---

[1] Delivered at his primary visitation, in the Pro-Cathedral of St Peter, Liverpool, where, with the exception of the following charge delivered in Wigan, each of the visitation charges was given.

nothing is impossible. No doubt there is much to be done by the Church in Lancashire. But he who was the Lord God of Joshua and the Israelites, when they crossed Jordan and entered Canaan, is not dead, but alive. If we have his blessing, and if we have a good understanding between Bishop, clergy, and laity, I have a firm conviction that great results will follow from the formation of the new See of Liverpool, and that in a few years the Church of England will occupy a very different, and an improved position in the West Derby Hundred of this County.

In a new Diocese like ours, accurate statistics are of the utmost importance. We cannot possibly form an estimate of 'things that are wanting' unless we thoroughly understand our position. I make no apology, therefore, in the outset of my Charge, for calling your attention to certain broad facts which we shall do well to remember. There are some very peculiar features in the Diocese of Liverpool, which distinguish it from any other Diocese in the land, and I shall try to set them before you in order.

(1) In a geographical point of view, our Diocese covers a smaller area of ground than any other in Great Britain, with the single exception of London. There are 181,000 acres in the Diocese of London, and 262,000 in Liverpool. It consists simply of the West Derby Hundred of the County of Lancaster, a district so thoroughly intersected with railways that a Bishop residing in Liverpool may reach almost every church in his Diocese in about an hour.

(2) The population of our Diocese is little less than 1,100,000, according to the last census. Nine English dioceses show a larger return: viz., London, Winchester, Lichfield, Rochester, Worcester, York, Durham, and Manchester. In none, however, with the exception of London, is the population per acre so dense and closely packed together. Liverpool and its suburbs alone make up at least 650,000 dwellers in streets out of the 1,100,000. Wigan and its suburbs, Warrington, St Helen's, Southport, Farnworth, Widnes, and Garston supply an aggregate of at least 250,000

more. It is probable that not more than 200,000 of the inhabitants of our Diocese can be found outside towns. In hardly any part of the Queen's dominions has the population increased so rapidly, chiefly from the demand for labour, and consequent immigration in order to meet that demand, during the last decennial period.

(3) The nationalities, employments, and occupations of our large population are curiously diversified. Perhaps there is hardly a district in Great Britain in which you will see such an extraordinary variety of classes. In Liverpool itself you have an enormous body of inhabitants connected with our docks and shipping, and an incessant stream of emigrants from the Continent of Europe to America. You have smoky manufactories and squalid poverty at one end of the city, and within two or three miles you have fine streets and comparative wealth. In Wigan, Warrington, St Helen's, Widnes, and the districts round these places, you have swarms of people employed in collieries, iron foundries, cotton manufactories, glass and chemical works. Around Ormskirk, Sefton, Hale, and Speke, you will see admirable farming. In no part of England, perhaps, will you find such a variety of callings, and all followed with a restless activity. And, though last, not least, in no part will you find such a mixture of the Queen's subjects. Out of the inhabitants of our Diocese, there is reason to believe that at least 200,000 are Irish, and 50,000 Welsh. Of the numbers of the Scotch I have heard no estimate. But I am greatly mistaken if the Scotch element is not very largely represented in such a busy and prosperous community as the great commercial outport of Lancashire and Yorkshire.

(4) The spiritual provision which the Church of England has hitherto made for the 1,100,000 inhabitants of our Diocese appears painfully inadequate. In touching this subject, I would have it distinctly understood that I do not ignore the good work which has been done by our Nonconformist brethren. I thankfully acknowledge the service they have rendered to Christ's cause in Liverpool. Nor can I forget the praiseworthy zeal with which

the Romish Church has provided for its adherents. Still, after every deduction, I think it is impossible to deny that there are myriads of dwellers in our Diocese for whose souls no means of grace are provided, and whose condition urgently demands the attention of Churchmen. If the Established Church of this country claims to be 'the Church of the people,' it is her bounden duty to see that no part of 'the people' are left like sheep without a shepherd. If she claims to be a territorial, and not a congregational Church, she should never rest till there is neither a street, nor a lane, nor a house, nor a garret, nor a cellar, nor a family, which is not regularly looked after, and provided with the offer of means of grace by her officials. Of course she cannot make people value religion, or care for the means she provides. But her aim should be to produce such a state of things, that no one shall be able to say, 'I am no man's parishioner. I am never visited or spoken to: no one cares for my soul.'

How far we are at present from this desirable state of things most of you know as well as myself. The full and complete returns to my Visitation Articles of Inquiry (for which, let me say, I am truly grateful) reveal the painful fact that there are many parishes in our Diocese in which the population has far outgrown the power of any single incumbent to superintend it, and in which there would be abundant work for three or four independent parochial incumbents, if they could be provided. At the present moment we have only 200 incumbents and 140 curates for 1,100,000 people. I venture boldly to say that there is not another diocese in all England in which the disproportion between the demands on the Church and the supply the Church has provided is so startling and so serious. In the Diocese of Norwich[1] you will find 914 benefices and 1,160 clergy for people. Here in the Diocese of Liverpool you have 200 benefices, 340 clergy, and 1,100,000 souls. How glaring is the contrast!

But even the statement I have just made conveys a very inadequate idea of the financial position of the Church in the Diocese

---

[1] Ryle had previously served in parishes in the Norwich Diocese.

4

of Liverpool. In an old diocese like Norwich a large proportion of the benefices are rectories or vicarages, and endowed with tithes or land. In our new Diocese I suppose that there were not altogether twenty-five churches so endowed 200 years ago, and there are not more now. The greater part of our existing churches are comparatively modern, and destitute of anything worth calling an endowment. Their incumbents are entirely dependent on a precarious and varying income, arising from fees, pew-rents, or offertories, and are often most miserably ill-paid. In fact, if such a thing as disestablishment with disendowment were ever to come, I suspect there is no diocese in England where the clergy would suffer less from it than ours! The great majority have neither tithes nor land of which they could be deprived.

The reasons of this extraordinary state of things are not hard to discover. The population of the West Derby Hundred has grown with unprecedented rapidity during the last 180 years. Hamlets have swelled into villages, and villages into towns. Our great seaport on the Mersey has leaped with a few bounds into the foremost position in the Queen's dominions, and, with Lancashire and Yorkshire behind her, seems likely to grow still more. The great development of mining and manufacturing industry in the east side of our Diocese has brought together an immense number of labourers. Both inside and outside of Liverpool there has been a constant influx and immigration of people into the district. But all this time, unhappily, the Church of England, until of late years, has done comparatively little for the souls who were brought together. In days gone by, I am afraid, fortunes were too often made and carried away, while the hands who helped to make them were forgotten and neglected.

The consequences of this want of means of grace are precisely what might be expected by every student of the Bible and human nature. Let alone and left to themselves, great masses of our population appear practically to have no religion at all. No one can read the police reports, or the account of coroners' inquests in our

Liverpool daily papers, without coming across harrowing records of drunkenness, immorality, and crime. No intelligent observer can walk about the more densely peopled quarters of this city, for instance, upon a Sunday, and avoid the painful conclusion that many men and women whom he sees never attend any place of worship. Their dresses, their looks, their whole demeanour supply evidence which cannot be mistaken. For idleness, or gossiping, or visiting, or drinking when public houses are open and drink can be bought, they are ready enough, but not for God's house. It is a sight which is most distressing to every friend of Christianity and morality. From keeping no Sabbath to having no God there is but a flight of steps. But who can wonder? As things are at present, there must be thousands of our people who are completely let alone. If every adult man and woman in Liverpool, who was in good health and able to leave home safely, resolved next Sunday to attend a place of worship, it is quite certain that every church and chapel and mission room in our city would be filled to suffocation, and that myriads would be obliged to return home from want of accommodation!

Such is a brief sketch of the condition of things which confronts the first Bishop of Liverpool. Such are the facts which I ask the Churchmen of this new Diocese to consider, face, and grapple with. I am not aware that I have exaggerated or overstated anything. On the contrary, when I look at the statistics of certain parishes, which I will not name, I believe I have understated my case. Nor shall I waste your time with useless lamentation and fault-finding. I prefer taking it for granted that we all agree that something ought to be done, and the only question is what that something ought to be. Lancashire men, I know, are practical and business-like men. I wish to approach the subject in a business-like way.

At the very outset of our inquiry, I desire to acknowledge with deep thankfulness the large amount of good work which I have found going on in the Diocese of Liverpool under the hands of Churchmen. If anyone, dwelling in a distant part of England and unacquainted with Lancashire, supposes that the Bishop of the newly-created See on the banks of the Mersey found nothing like Church-work going on, no organization, no machinery, no philanthropic Institutions, no religious Societies, I beg to tell him that he is entirely mistaken. The idea that the Church of England in the West Derby Hundred would be found a kind of ecclesiastical wilderness, like a newly-founded Colonial Diocese, is a delusion. Nothing can be further from the truth. Thanks to the diligent care of the Bishops of Chester, who formerly had the oversight of this part of Lancashire, and thanks to the voluntary zeal of resident clergy and laity, I find a large amount of diocesan machinery in excellent working order—machinery which will bear a favourable comparison with that of the oldest diocese in the land. I find ruri-decanal conferences in every deanery. I find the causes of education, of temperance, of Sunday schools, of Foreign and Home Missions systematically and well supported. I find a powerful Scripture Readers' Society, and a Bible Women's Association in Liverpool itself. I find an admirable Sailors' Home. I find nine Hospitals. I find special work going on, by the general co-operation of all professing Christians, for special classes, such as seamen, ship-wrights, waggoners, and cab and omnibus drivers. The orphan, the blind, the deaf and dumb, the street Arabs,[1] and gutter children, even the newsboys, are not forgotten. I find a most useful Diocesan Finance Association. Above all, I find a body of clergy, however small and overworked, and many of them sadly ill-paid, who are, as a body, admirable representatives of the Church of England. All these are facts which I most thankfully acknowledge and would never ignore for a moment. Yet I am sure all whom I address today will agree with me that much remains to be done. And how to set about it, and what to begin with, is the next point to which I propose to direct your attention.

[1] A raggedly dressed child who roams the street.

(1) For one thing, then, the Church of England in our Diocese appears to me to want *a large multiplication of living agents*. When I speak of living agents I mean ordained ministers of the word. In saying this I wish not to be misunderstood. No one can value more than I do the work of Scripture readers and lay agents. The good that they do in their own province is simply incalculable. But if the Church is to be systematically organised in a new district, and placed on a lasting foundation; if a regular congregation is to be called into existence, the sacraments duly administered, and our liturgical services set up; the unit in our calculation must be a presbyter. The dwellers within every new district should be able to feel that they have their own special minister, and that they are his special parishioners. The lay agent may do excellent service by sowing the seed and cutting down the corn. But if the crop is not to rot on the ground, the sheaves must be bound up and stored away in the barn. And this is the presbyter's work. The Scripture reader may gather together recruits, and persuade them to enlist in the King's service. But the presbyter must drill, and train, and discipline them, and show them how to act together, move together, and form an efficient regiment.

My own opinion is most decided, that the Church of England is never in the right position, and can never do her duty as the 'Church of the people,' and do herself justice, until she has no parochial districts, as a general rule, with a population of more than 5,000; and until, for every such parochial district, she has a presbyter in charge. Even 5,000 is a large number if a clergyman is a thorough pastor and a house-going man. But allowance must, of course, be made for a certain proportion of Roman Catholics, and Nonconformists, who are looked after by their own ministers. Once let a clergyman's district exceed 5,000, and I am pretty certain it is almost impossible for him to overtake all his work satisfactorily. As for parishes or districts in which there are 10,000, 12,000, 15,000, or 20,000 souls, with only one incumbent, it is useless to suppose that the clergyman of such

8

districts can possibly know or reach a large proportion of his parishioners.

How frightfully undermanned the Church of England is at present in Liverpool must be evident to anyone on the slightest reflection! Taking it for granted that there are in this great city and its suburbs 650,000 people, there ought to be 130 parochial districts of 5,000 each, and 130 incumbents in charge of these districts. I need hardly remind those whom I address this day, that our present staff of clergymen is lamentably below the figure I have just named. In such a condition of things the Church of England cannot possibly do herself justice, and to expect her to be 'the Church of the people' in Liverpool is simply absurd. You might as well send out of the Mersey a Cunard or White Star steamer, with a crew of only twenty men, all told—officers, seamen, engineers, and stokers—and expect her to cross the Atlantic and reach New York in safety. Our first, foremost, and principal want, I unhesitatingly assert, is a large increase of working clergy.

(2) The second chief want of the Church of England in the Diocese of Liverpool appears to me to be *a greater number of places of worship*. As to the need of more churches in the city of Liverpool itself, a valuable Report was drawn up more than two years ago by a committee appointed by the Bishop of Chester. This Report declared that even then twelve new churches were urgently required, and the proper sites were carefully indicated. Little, however, has been done since the date of that Report, and the necessity is as great now as ever. The population of our huge city seems to grow at the rate of 5,000 a year, and to keep pace with this growth one new church ought to be built every year! At present we have not done anything worth mentioning to make up our lost ground. Let it not be forgotten also that in every large parish a plain roomy mission-room for non-liturgical services, prayer-meetings, and the like, is an indispensable part of the parochial machinery, without which no hard-working clergyman

can ever work comfortably. How many more of these invaluable rooms we want in Liverpool I will not pretend to say; but in point of usefulness, in order to begin and keep up the Church's work, I believe they are even more important than churches.

Whether, in the face of the peculiar wants of our city, we ought not to attempt a special Twelve Churches Fund for Liverpool, is a question which is now very much on my mind, and on which I earnestly desire the advice of all the tried and experienced leaders of good work in Liverpool, both clerical and lay. The money ought not to be an insuperable difficulty, I am certain, if there is only the will. The city which, within five years, has twice raised little less than £100,000—once to found its own Bishopric, and once to found a University—is not unequal to raising another £100,000, in order to make the Church of England in Liverpool commensurate with the wants of the people. The money, I repeat, could easily be provided.

Two things only, I hope, would be kept steadily in view, if such a Twelve Churches Fund as I have suggested were ever set on foot. One is, that in every district where a new church is proposed, there should be an active canvass made of the population, and an earnest appeal made to all holders of property to meet the public fund by a local contribution. People never value a new church so much as when they have helped, as far as they can, to build it themselves. The other thing I would name is the importance of studying economy and practical usefulness, as far as possible, in the construction of all new churches built with public money. Let us make the money go as far as possible, and not waste it in needless external decoration, but aim at making the inside as comfortable as possible. When land is very expensive, it is wise to put the school under the church, as at St Stephen's, Byrom Street. When the district is low in character, and destitute of good houses, a parsonage should accompany the Church. In every case I strongly recommend a large, commodious vestry, for the use of confirmation classes and communicants' meetings.

After all, I desire never to forget that other large and important places in the Diocese need new churches as well as Liverpool. The spiritual wants of several other towns are great and crying. No true friend of the Church of England, I am sure, can ever feel satisfied until more places of worship and more clergy are provided for the population of the whole West Derby Hundred. But I reserve any remarks I have to make on this subject for the visitation I propose to hold tomorrow at Wigan.

The great question yet remains to be answered, How are the formidable wants of our new Diocese to be met? To that question I can only give one reply. We have nothing to depend upon except the voluntary liberality of the laity. For the support of the clergyman of a new district of a certain population; for new curates in mining parishes; and in very exceptional cases for assistant curates in very poor, large incumbencies, we may certainly reckon on obtaining, sooner or later, the help of the Ecclesiastical Commissioners. But for building new churches, and mission-rooms, and for any large increase of clergy, we must depend, I repeat, on the voluntary help of the laity. I do most earnestly hope that this help will be given. If those admirable institutions, the Diocesan Church Aid Society, and the Diocesan Church Building Society, could each command an income of £10,000 a year, the good that might soon be done is incalculable.

How easily the funds needed might be raised if all the Churchmen of the Diocese were alive to their responsibility, and made it a duty to give, may very soon be shown. Few persons have the least idea how small is the number of subscribers to religious objects, and how continually you meet the names of the same noble-minded, large-hearted men in every subscription list you read.[1] There are human mines of wealth in the Hundred of West

[1] *The Secretary of the 'Diocesan Finance Association' informs me that at present there are only 300 lay subscribers to our Diocesan Institutions for Church Building, Church Aid, Education, etc. It appears, moreover, that in this list of 300

1 layman's name appears 7 times.
1 layman's name appears 6 times.
17 laymen's names appear 5 times.

Derby which have never yet been touched. All the churches we need might soon be built, all the additional clergy might soon be provided, if all lay Churchmen would open their eyes, come forward boldly, and realize the luxury of doing good, and, giving money, to advance the kingdom of God. At present that luxury is only enjoyed by a select few. It ought not to be so.

The plain truth is, that in the matter of giving money to Christ's cause, the great majority of English Churchmen are sadly behind the times, and want educating. The Scotch Presbyterians, the English Wesleyans, and the Independents ought to put us to shame. We want more men to come forward as the late noble-minded George Moore did in London, and as some have done formerly in Liverpool, saying, 'I will build a church myself, and will ask no one to help me.' What huge sums are often wasted on luxuries and recreations, and lost for ever! But who ever found the promises fail about 'repayment to him that lendeth to the Lord'? Who ever found, on balancing his accounts at the year's end, that he missed money which he had given to spiritual objects? Who ever came to the Bankruptcy Court by doing good to souls?

After all, though it is only a low motive, rich men should never forget that it is the truest policy and highest wisdom to promote the spread of true religion. Reason itself points out that, in the long run of years, the moral standard of a city or a nation is the grand secret of its prosperity. Gold mines, manufactures, scientific discoveries, docks, roads, eloquent speeches, commercial activity, and democratic institutions are not enough to make or to keep nations great. Tyre and Sidon, Carthage, Athens, Rome, Venice, and Spain and Portugal had plenty of such possessions as these, and yet fell into decay. The sinews of a nation's strength are truthfulness, honesty, sobriety, purity, temperance, economy, diligence, brotherly kindness, charity among its inhabitants, and,

---

15 laymen's names appear 4 times.
23 laymen's names appear 3 times.
67 laymen's names appear twice.
176 laymen's names appear once.

consequently, good credit among mankind. Let those deny this who dare. And will any man say that there is any surer way of producing these characteristics in a people than by encouraging, fostering, spreading, and teaching pure scriptural Christianity? The man who says there is a surer way must be an infidel. Then, if these things are so, the first duty of the wealthy men in every city ought to be to encourage and countenance religion among the people around them in every possible way. Does a man want his poorer neighbours, and those whom he employs, to be steady, provident, truthful, diligent, temperate, honest, moral, and charitable? Does he, or does he not? If he does, he ought to support religion. To punish vice and yet not cherish virtue, to spend public money on paying police, building jails, and yet not to encourage the increase of ministers and the building of churches, is, to say the least, an absurdly inconsistent policy. The more true religion, the better people! The more good people, the more prosperity! The wealthy men of a city who ignore religion, and coolly declare that they do not care whether the inhabitants are Christians or not, are guilty of an act of suicidal folly. Irreligion, even in a temporal point of view, is the worst enemy of a nation or a city.

Of course I am aware that one favourite answer to my plea for more churches is the unhappy fact that there are existing churches which at present are not filled. 'Fill your old churches,' is the cry, 'and then we will build you new ones.' Allow me to say that this is an excuse and not an argument. I am not referring to Liverpool especially, when I say that so long as patrons appoint unfit clergymen who have no gifts suited to their position, and so long as the Church makes no provision for pensioning off invalided or superannuated clergymen, so long there will always be found some empty churches. But empty churches at one end of a city are no reason why we should not build new churches at another. All ministers are not equally adapted to all sorts of parishes and population. Only exercise common sense in the choice of a clergyman, and let him be a man who wisely and lovingly preaches, lives, and works the gospel, and I am certain he will never preach to empty benches. There are many proofs in this Diocese that I am saying the truth. But, alas, when people have little will to help Christ's cause, they never lack reasons to confirm their will! Too many seem to forget that, in the matter of church building, or in any work for Christ, duties are ours, and results are in the hand of God.

(3) The third chief want of the Diocese of Liverpool is one which I feel great difficulty in handling. I refer, of course, to *the need for a cathedral* suited to the size and wealth of our Diocese, and to the importance of the second city in Great Britain. I approach the subject with delicacy. It is a far wider and deeper one than most people suppose. I am constantly asked, 'When are you going to begin your cathedral?' But few seem to realize what the idea involves.

The theory of all cathedrals, no doubt, is an excellent one. Let the principal town of every diocese have a magnificent church, which in architecture and arrangements shall surpass all other churches as much as a Bishop surpasses a presbyter in his official position! Let the services of this church be a model to the whole diocese, and let the public prayer and praise and preaching be a standing pattern of the highest style of Christian worship! Let the management of this church be confided to some grave, learned, and eminent clergyman called a Dean, assisted by three or four other clergymen called Canons! Let these Canons be picked men, selected solely on account of their singular merits, and not for family or political reasons, and famous for deep theological learning, or great preaching power, or wisdom in counsel, or spirituality of life! Let such a choice body as this Dean and Canons be in intimate and friendly connection with the Bishop, be his right hand and his right eye, his counsellors, his helps, his sword, his arrows, and his bow! Let the cathedral body, so constituted, be the heart, and mainspring, and centre of every good work in the diocese! Let its members be well paid, well housed, and have no excuse for not residing in the Cathedral Close the greater part of each year! Let the influence of the cathedral body, as a fountain of spirituality and holiness, be specially felt in the cathedral city! Let its active usefulness be seen in the energetic management of every sort of diocesan machinery for spreading the gospel at home and abroad! Let Deans and Canons be known and read of all men as 'burning and shining lights,' the very cream and flower of Churchmen, and let the cathedral city in consequence become the ecclesiastical Athens of every diocese, the stronghold of Church influence in the district, and the nursery of theological learning! Such, I suppose, is the theory of an English cathedral establishment. Such were the intentions of those who permitted the continued existence of our cathedral bodies at the period of the Reformation. The theory of such a cathedral is excellent. If we had such a cathedral and such a chapter in Liverpool, no one would be more thankful than myself. If anyone would offer to build and endow such a cathedral I would heartily welcome the offer.

But let us consider well what we are talking about. Let us count the cost. We must remember at the outset that in this matter the new Diocese of Liverpool starts at an immense disadvantage compared to every new diocese of modern times. Ripon, Manchester, and St Albans had each a cathedral, or a church fit to be a cathedral, and Ripon and Manchester had each an endowed Chapter. Southwell has a beautiful Minster. Wakefield and Newcastle parish churches are noble buildings, fit to be cathedrals. The Bishop of Truro, no doubt, is building a cathedral. But then the county of Cornwall, which forms his diocese, hardly needs another church to be built in it, and he can easily concentrate all his efforts on his cathedral. Moreover, his cathedral is already endowed with a rich Exeter Canonry.

At Liverpool, on the contrary, we have everything to do from the very beginning. We have not a church in our city which is fit to be converted into a cathedral. We have no site for a new cathedral, except one behind the Gymnasium, in a disused cemetery, which many, perhaps, would dislike; and any other site would cost an enormous sum. The cathedral itself, to be worthy of Liverpool, would cost a quarter of a million pounds before it was finished. The Dean, Canons, and cathedral staff would need to be endowed. Even now the maintenance of our present voluntary cathedral services, on a humble scale, is a very grave difficulty. All these are serious considerations. Are we prepared to face a sum of half a million of money? We might face it, of course; but are we prepared?

Let no one misunderstand me. Let no one fancy I object to a cathedral altogether. Nothing of the kind! If anyone comes forward with a princely offer like that of the ladies who have built Edinburgh Cathedral, or if anyone will do in Liverpool what has been lately done at St Patrick's and Christ Church Cathedrals in Dublin, or at St Finbar's in Cork, I shall be deeply grateful. For anything I know it may be in the heart of someone even now to do this. I only know that my first and foremost business, as Bishop of a new Diocese, is to provide for preaching the gospel to souls now entirely neglected, whom no cathedral would touch. My first work at present is to endeavour to provide more clergymen, and more places of worship, and that, so far as I can see, is likely to fill up the few years of my episcopate.

I leave the want of a cathedral here. I believe the matter will be handled fully at the coming Diocesan Conference. Those who handle it will perhaps throw more light on it than I have done. I lay no claim to infallibility, and may be mistaken. I only ask all who handle it to 'count the cost.'

Before I leave the subject of the wants of the Diocese, I think it would be ungracious and ungrateful if I did not express publicly my thankfulness for many things which I have found here. I have spoken strongly of 'the things that are wanting.' Let me also speak strongly of things that are existing.

(i) I am deeply thankful to find so many clergymen doing solid, good work in the Diocese of Liverpool. I never look for perfection. I suppose that every bishop soon finds that there are ministers and ministers in his diocese—ministers who do little, and ministers who do much. But I doubt extremely whether there are many dioceses in England and Wales where there is so great a proportion of clergymen who are 'workmen that need not be ashamed,' and who are quietly and unostentatiously bearing 'fruit that will remain.'

(ii) I am very thankful for the large number of well-furnished and well-provided churches that I have seen, and the general heartiness and liveliness of the services. I may be allowed to speak of this. I have already preached in more than 90 different churches—nearly half the churches in my Diocese—and my opinion is the result of personal observation. The only thing I have not quite liked has been the extravagantly lavish expenditure, in some cases, on the decoration for Harvest Festivals, when there is so much money needed for many Diocesan objects. These cases are exceptional, I admit; but I must frankly say that I should like to see some limit put to the quantity of decoration. God's house is not meant to be an exhibition of flowers, corn, fruit, evergreens, and ferns, but a place for prayer, praise, and preaching of the word. However, I am willing to suppose that there is such a thing as an excess of well-meant zeal.

(iii) I am thankful for the large number of communicants of the lower classes whom I have seen at some evening communions. I cannot feel the objections that many feel to evening communions. To refuse them in some poor districts would be to repel many wives and mothers from the Lord's Table altogether. For my own personal comfort I certainly prefer receiving the sacrament in the morning. But remembering that the ordinance was originally instituted in the evening, and that our church distinctly calls it the Lord's *Supper*, I fail to see how an evening communion can be positively wrong. That the Church of England can gain and keep the affection of the working classes, when she is properly worked, I have always maintained. I see it proved by the evening communions at which I have assisted in Liverpool.

(iv) I am thankful for the interest I find taken in Church Sunday Schools. Since the establishment of Board Schools[1] for the week days, it is impossible to overrate the importance of Sunday Schools. Without them we should soon have a genera-tion of young people in the land ignorant alike of the Creeds, the Catechism, and the Prayer-book of the Church of England, and utterly unprepared to understand the rite of confirmation. Let me express my earnest hope that the interest in Church Sunday Schools may everywhere deepen and increase, and that those most useful and self-denying persons, the Sunday School teachers, may be encouraged in every way. I believe an efficient body of Sunday School teachers is the right hand of a clergyman.

(v) I am thankful to observe the active and intelligent interest which the laity of the Diocese seem to take in the proceedings of the Church. I have seldom seen a body of churchwardens who appear to come forward and fill their office so efficiently as they appear to do in the churches where I have preached. And I cannot sufficiently commend the invaluable services which many laymen voluntarily render to our Diocesan institutions. All this is as it should be. The laity are 'the Church' quite as much as the clergy. When the laity are passive, sleeping partners, and leave the concerns of the Church in the hands of the clergy, it is a symptom of a most unhealthy state of things in the ecclesiastical body. I trust it may never be so in Liverpool.

For all these things which I have named, for the uniform kindness and courtesy which I have received from all, for the general willingness to meet my wishes which I have observed, I desire publicly, at this my Primary Visitation, to express my deep and hearty gratitude. I came among you with much anxiety, expecting far more difficulties and collisions than I have hitherto

[1] Board Schools were set up after the passing of the Forster Education Act of 1870 during Gladstone's first ministry.

met with. But you have smoothed my course in many ways, and made my path comparatively easy. I thank God, and I thank you.

I must now turn away from subjects of purely local interest, in order to say something about the general position of the Church of England. I do so with considerable reluctance. The great ecclesiastical questions of the day are of such a burning character that a man cannot handle them without coming into collision with somebody's cherished opinions. But a Diocese has a right to expect its Bishop to say what he thinks at his Visitation, and I must not disappoint its just expectations. After all, I suppose there is not a clergyman here who would like his Bishop to be a mere colourless nonentity, without any distinct opinions, or to fill the place of a ship's figure-head, which, however ornamental, adds nothing to the speed or stability of the vessel. I shall, therefore, endeavour to speak out my mind.

Of course we are all apt to exaggerate the importance of our own times. But I venture to think that the present position of the Church of England is more critical and perilous than it has been at any period during the last two centuries. On every side the horizon is dark and lowring. There seem to be breakers ahead and breakers astern, dangers on the right hand and dangers on the left, dangers from without and dangers from within. Whether the good old ship will weather the storm remains to be seen. But I am quite certain that much depends, under God, on the conduct of the crew. If reason and sanctified common sense prevail, we shall live: if not, we shall die.

Concerning dangers from without I shall say little. They arise chiefly from the operations of the Liberation Society. That restless and zealous body, departing widely from the principles of the old Nonconformists, such as Richard Baxter and John Owen, has set itself to promote the disestablishment and disendowment of the Church of England, and to make an end of the union of Church and State. Up to this time, I see no proof that the movement is successful. On the contrary, I have a firm impression that the

Church is even stronger now than it was when the agitation first began.

The plain truth is, that the public mind is not prepared for the state of things which disestablishment would bring about, if conducted to its logical consequences. Of course, if the union of Church and State were dissolved, all Churches and sects would be left on a dead level of equality. No favour or privilege would be granted by the State to one more than another. The Infidel, the Deist, the Mahometan, the Socinian, the Jew, the Romanist, the Episcopalian, the Presbyterian, the Congregationalist, the Methodist, the Baptist, all would be regarded with equal indifference. The State itself would have nothing to do with religion, and would leave the supply of it to the principles of free trade and the action of the voluntary system. In a word, the Government of England would allow all its subjects to serve God or Baal, to go to heaven or to another place, just as they pleased. The State would take no cognizance of spiritual matters, and would look on with Epicurean indifference and unconcern. The State would continue to care for the bodies of its subjects, but it would entirely ignore their souls.

Gallio, who thought Christianity was a matter of 'words and names,' and 'cared for none of these things,' would become the model of an English Statesman. The Sovereign of Great Britain might be a Papist, the Prime Minister a Mahometan, the Lord Chancellor a Jew. Parliament would begin without prayer. Oaths would be dispensed with in Courts of Justice. The next King would be crowned without a religious service in Westminster Abbey. Prisons and workhouses, men-of-war and regiments, would all be left without chaplains. In short, for fear of offending infidels and people who object to the recognition of God by intercessory prayer, I suppose that regimental bands would be logically forbidden to play 'God Save the Queen.'

Now, does the British public wish to see this state of things brought about? I do not believe it for a moment at present. The public knows that, as matters stand now, the Dissenters have liberty to do anything they like, so long as they can find money to do it. They are under no civil or religious disabilities. They may go where they please, build where they please, preach where they please, and worship as they please, without asking anyone's leave. They can do even more than Churchmen can, and have more liberty. A Churchman cannot go into a clergyman's parish, however grossly neglected it may be, and build a new church, without obtaining the incumbent's consent; but any Dissenter can go into that same parish and build a chapel. The public knows that, with all her faults, the Established Church, on the whole, does more good than harm, and that in rural parishes especially disestablishment and disendowment would almost be the death of religion. All these things the public sees and knows; and knowing them, the bulk of Englishmen appear to feel little desire for disestablishment.

For all these reasons I shall not dwell much on the Church's danger from without. Of course it is impossible to say to what extent we may strengthen the hands of our outward enemies by our own suicidal folly. But so long as the Church is true to herself, and to the great principles of the Reformation, so long, I believe, the laity will not allow her to be disestablished. She will be tested by her fruits. The best ally of the Church Defence Society is the clergyman who preaches the truth, lives the truth, works his district, visits his people, and has a kind word, and a helping hand, and a loving heart ready for every man and woman in his parish. The best friend of the Liberation Society is the indolent clergyman, who is content to preach defective sermons to empty benches, who has few communicants, no parochial machinery, no Sunday Schools, no regular visitation of the sick, no knowledge of most of his people, and just leaves everybody alone. The parish of such a man is the surest and best help to the cause of Liberationism.

The principal dangers of the Church of England arise from within. They consist in the strifes, and conflicts, and controversies which rage so furiously within her pale, and threaten almost to tear her to pieces. We know who has said, 'A house divided against itself cannot stand.' It was not so much the army of Titus that destroyed Jerusalem as the internal dissensions of the Jews within the city. I confess I do not fear disestablishment and disendowment half so much as division and disunion among ourselves, and consequent disintegration and disruption.

The chief internal danger of the Church, in my opinion, arises from the continual existence among us of a body of Churchmen who, if words and actions mean anything, seem determined to unprotestantize the Church of England, to re-introduce principles and practices which our forefathers deliberately rejected three centuries ago, and, in one word, to get behind the Protestant Reformation. That there is such a body of Churchmen, that hundreds of them from time to time have shown the tendency of their views by secession to Rome, that for twenty-five years their proceedings have called forth remonstrances and warnings from most of our bishops, that the eyes of all Christendom are fixed on this body and men are watching and wondering whereunto it will grow, that Romanists rejoice in its rise and progress, and all true-hearted Protestants in other lands grieve and mourn—all these, I say, are great patent facts which it is waste of time to prove, because they cannot be denied.

The zeal, earnestness, and self-denial of this body of Churchmen I do not for a moment dispute. But I cannot at all admit that they have any monopoly of these qualifications. Nor can I admit that any quantity of zeal and earnestness confers a licence to introduce 'divers and strange doctrines' and practices into our parish churches, and to overstep the limits laid down in the authorized formularies of the Church of England.

But the point to which I want to direct your special attention is this. It is an unhappy fact that the main subject of contention between the school to which I have referred and their opponents, has been for several years the blessed sacrament of the Lord's Supper. Scores of clergymen have adopted the practice of administering the Lord's Supper with usages which have been almost entirely laid aside for 300 years, usages to all appearance borrowed from the Church of Rome, usages which even Archbishop Laud in the plenitude of his power never dared to enforce, usages which, to the vast majority of thinking men, seem intended to bring back into our Church that most dangerous of all Romish doctrines, the sacrifice of the Mass.

You are all aware that the legality of these new usages in the administration of the Lord's Supper has been made the subject of repeated trials, before the highest Law Courts of the realm. The final result has been that almost all have been pronounced distinctly illegal, and that every clergyman who persists in wearing a chasuble, or burning incense, or having lighted candles on the communion table, or mixing water with the sacramental wine, or elevating and adoring the consecrated elements, is doing that which contravenes the doctrine of the Church of England, is putting a sense on the 'Ornaments Rubric' which the highest Courts of the realm distinctly condemn, and therefore is breaking the law.

But now comes a miserable fact which constitutes the present greatest danger of the Church of England. Some of those clergymen who have adopted these novel usages in the Lord's Supper refuse to pay the slightest attention to the judgments of the Law Courts, or to the admonitions of their bishops. In the face of the *contemporanea expositio*[1] of three centuries, which certainly confirms the interpretation of the Ornaments Rubric given by the Judicial Committee of the Privy Council; in the face of the utter absence of anything in our Communion office to confirm their novel views; in the face of their own solemn vow and promise to obey their bishop; they persist in their own way of administering the Lord's Supper; and for the sake of things which they themselves must allow are *not essential* to it, they seem prepared to rend in pieces the Church of England. And worst of all, in all this, they are aided,

---

[1] That is, the agreed judgment.

backed, countenanced, and supported by hundreds of clergymen who never dream of breaking the law themselves, but seem to regard these law-breaking brethren as martyrs, and as excellent, worthy, and persecuted men, who ought to be let alone! If all this does not constitute a most dangerous state of things, I know not what is danger to a Church. Without some change it will be the ruin of the Church of England.

I hear so many foolish and unreasonable things said about the perilous position of matters, which I have tried to describe, that I think it may be useful to offer a few remarks to all men of practical common sense, which may serve to clear the air, and be useful to some.

(1) I sometimes hear it said, that the ecclesiastical lawsuits of recent times about the Lord's Supper ought never to have been instituted, that law-breaking clergymen might easily have been kept in order by their bishops, and that those who instituted legal proceedings were 'persecutors' and troublers of Israel. How the law *could* be ascertained without a carefully-prepared argument before competent judges I fail to see. What likelihood there was of modern law-breakers paying any attention to episcopal admonitions I leave all calm observers to consider. But as to the hard names and bitter epithets heaped on prosecutors, I regard them with sorrow as unworthy of the lips from which they come. Englishmen who remember that the true doctrine of the Lord's Supper was the very point for which the Marian martyrs went to the stake ought surely not to be surprised if many people are extremely sensitive about the least attempt to bring back the Romish Mass. I for one do not wonder. Thousands of people, I believe, would put up with many ceremonial novelties who would resist to the uttermost any innovations in the Lord's Supper. The words of Bishop Thirlwall,[1] in his last Charge, are worth remembering: 'The persons who instituted these proceedings, though to their adversaries they might appear persecutors, could

---

[1] Bishop of St David's, 1840–75.

24

not but look on themselves as simply acting on the defensive, in resistance to an unprovoked and unlawful aggression, and for the purpose of resisting what to them seemed a tremendous evil' (*Remains* ii. 306). It is easy and cheap work to call names, and revile opponents as 'persecutors.' But the plain truth is, that those who break the law and refuse to obey their bishop are the real persecutors of the Church.

(2) I have heard it said frequently that the interpretation of the Ornaments Rubric, laid down after lawful and deliberate inquiry by the Judicial Committee of the Privy Council, is altogether incorrect, and, therefore, ought not to be obeyed. I have even heard it said, that their last decision was one 'of policy, and not of justice.' I hear such sayings with considerable indifference, and call to mind the old adage, that 'defeated litigants always blame the Court in which they fail.' But broad assertions are not arguments. It is easy for some angry divines to say superciliously that leading English lawyers, of proved intellectual vigour and long experience, are incompetent to handle ecclesiastical subjects, to analyze the language of documents, and weigh the meaning of words in formularies, and that they know nothing about rubrics and Church history, and cannot grasp such matters. But who, I should like to know, will believe all this? The immense majority of thinking men in the House of Lords or the House of Commons, in the Temple or Lincoln's Inn, in the City or the West End, in Oxford or Cambridge, in Liverpool, Manchester, Leeds, Birmingham, or Bristol, will never believe it for a moment, and will think poorly of the sense of those who say such things. As for the unworthy insinuation that eminent English judges of spotless character would ever stain their judicial ermine by deciding ecclesiastical questions in a party spirit, from notions of 'policy rather than justice,' and from impure motives, I will not condescend to notice it. I pity alike the men who can make such insinuations, and the men who can believe them.

(3) Sometimes I hear it said that spiritual questions ought to be left to spiritual men, and that a Court composed mainly of laymen, like the Judicial Committee, is incompetent to try theological cases. This at first sight appears a very plausible idea; but I do not think it will bear the test of calm consideration. No doubt the present Court of Final Appeal, like every Judicial Court composed of men, may have its faults and imperfections, and the Royal Commission now sitting may perhaps suggest improvements. But if the Judicial Committee of the Privy Council is to be set aside in ecclesiastical cases, and a so-called spiritual court set up in its stead, I doubt extremely whether a better court, and one which will satisfy the laity, can possibly be constructed. It is easy to find fault with an institution and pull it down, but it is not always so easy to build a better one. Where are the constituent parts to come from? Who are to be the new and improved judges? I declare I look over the land from north to south, and from east to west, and I fail to discover the materials out of which your 'readjusted' Court of Appeal is to be composed. There may be hidden Daniels ready to come to the judgment-seat of whom I know nothing. But I should be glad to know who they are.

Will you ask the State to sweep away the present Court of Appeal, and compose one of bishops only? I am afraid such a court would never give satisfaction. If there is any one point on which the *Guardian* and the *Record*, the *Church Times* and the *Rock* are entirely agreed, it is the fallibility of Bishops! Each of these papers would tell you that several English prelates are anything but wise and orthodox, and are not trustworthy judges of disputed questions. But if this is the case, what likelihood is there that the whole Church would be satisfied with their judicial decisions?

Will you turn away from the Bishops, and compose your new Court of Appeal of deans, University professors, and select eminent theologians, picked out of Convocation? Again the same objection applies. He that can run his eye over the list of English deans, or the professional staff at Oxford and Cambridge, and then talk of forming out of that list an unexceptionable tribunal, acceptable to all parties, must be a man of faith which is bordering on credulity. As to the 'select eminent theologians,' I have yet to know who is to have the selection. The very divines whom one school of Churchmen would choose are men whom another school would not allow to be sound 'theologians' at all.

The fact is, that the favourite theory of those who would refer all ecclesiastical causes to *clerical* judges, is a theory which will never work. It sounds plausible at first, and looks well at a distance, but it is utterly unpractical. Laymen, and legal laymen, trained and accustomed to look at all sides of a question, are the only material out of which a satisfactory Court of Appeal can be formed. Ecclesiastics, as a rule, are unfit to be judges. We do not shine on the bench, whatever we may do in the pulpit. If there is one thing that bishops and presbyters rarely possess, it is the judicial mind, and the power of giving an impartial, unbiased decision.[1]

(4) I have heard it said sometimes, that the matters for which the recent objectors to decisions about the Ornaments Rubric contend are mere matters of taste. The whole question, forsooth, is one of aestheticism and ornamentation! Why wrangle and quarrel, some say, about such trifles? I wish I could believe this view. Unhappily there is strong testimony the other way. With the party of whom I am now speaking, the whole value of ceremonial consists in its significance as a visible symbol of doctrine. The evidence of leading men before the Ritual Commission, the language continually used in certain books and manuals about the Lord's Supper, all tend to show that the question in dispute is, whether in the sacrament there is a propitiatory sacrifice as well as a sacrifice of praise and thanksgiving, and whether there is a real presence beside that in the hearts of believers. These are not trifles, but serious doctrinal errors, and points on which I am persuaded the bulk of English Churchmen will never tolerate the

---

[1] See appendix, chapter 1, note 1, p. 425.

least approach to the Church of Rome. To use the words of the late Bishop Thirlwall, 'The real question is, whether our communion office is to be transformed into the closest possible resemblance to the Romish Mass' (*Remains* ii. 233).[1]

(5) Last, but not least, I hear it sometimes said that obedience to rubrics ought to be enforced all round, and that it is not fair to require one clergyman to obey the Ornaments Rubric as interpreted by the Privy Council, while another clergyman is allowed to neglect another rubric altogether. This is a favourite argument in many quarters; but I am unable to see any force in it. In matters like these there is no parallelism whatsoever between acts of omission and acts of addition. To place on the same level the conduct of the man who, in administering the Lord's Supper, introduces novelties of most serious doctrinal significance, and the conduct of the man who does not observe some petty obsolete direction, of no doctrinal significance at all, is to my mind contrary to common sense. But, after all, complete and perfect obedience to all the rubrics is simply impossible, and I do not suppose there is a single clergyman in England who observes all. The three first rubrics in the Communion Service are illustrations of what I mean. Moreover, the change of laws and customs, and the large liberty now allowed to a clergyman, have rendered some ancient rubrical requirements obsolete and inexpedient. A certain discretion must be allowed to a bishop in the nineteenth century in deciding what the circumstances of the Church require to be observed. If I ask one clergyman to obey the ruling of the Privy Council about the Ornaments Rubric, and to discontinue the use of the chasuble, the incense, the lighted candles, and the like, I do so because of the immense importance of maintaining Protestant views of the Lord's Supper, and the deep jealousy which prevails among the laity about the appearance of anything like the sacrifice of the Mass. If I decline to ask another clergyman to have matins, and vespers, and saints' day services, in some huge, over-grown,

[1] See appendix, chapter 1, note 2, pp. 425-26.

poor parish in a mining district, or at the North or South end of Liverpool, I decline because I think his time, in the short twelve hours of the day, might be far better employed. He can do far more good by doing things which were flatly forbidden 220 years ago (when our rubrics were last settled), by non-liturgical services in unconsecrated rooms, by Cottage Lectures, by Bible Classes, by Young Men's Meetings, by Mothers' Meetings, by Temperance Meetings, by Prayer Meetings, and other well-known modern means of usefulness. And when men tell me that my balances are unjust, and that it is not fair to interfere with the one clergyman and to leave the other clergyman alone, I hear the accusation with indifference. I believe I am doing that which is best for the Church of England, and most likely to advance her interests.

I leave this weary subject here. For dwelling on it at such length, and trying to discuss it from every point of view, I make no apology. The position of the Church is so critical, and the danger so great, that a Bishop has no right to hold his peace. Without some change of weather, or change in men's minds, or change in the management of the ship, I see nothing before us but the shipwreck of the Church of England. I am often disposed to say with Daniel, 'What shall be the end of these things?' (Dan. 12:8). Let us quietly consider. What are the alternatives?

(1) Shall we give way to the Romanizing party? Shall we try to compel every clergyman in the Church of England to use the chasuble and its accompaniments in the Lord's Supper, and to turn the sacrament into a sacrifice? God forbid! The idea is ridiculous and impossible. You would raise a storm from the Isle of Wight to Berwick-on-Tweed far worse than the storm of the Commonwealth days. When the sun rises in the west and sets in the east, when the Mersey flows back from Liverpool to the Cheshire Hills, then, and not till then, I believe, will the majority of English Churchmen consent to insult the memory of our Marian martyrs, and return to the Romish Mass. They will never consent.

(2) Shall we adopt the notable plan of throwing open the whole question of usages in the Lord's Supper, and allowing every clergyman to administer it with any ceremonies he likes? This, I suppose, is the policy of 'forbearance and toleration' for which many have petitioned, though how such a policy could be carried out, in the face of the last decisions, I fail to see, except by a special act of Parliament. A more unwise and suicidal policy than this I cannot conceive. You would divide every Diocese into two distinct and sharply-cut parties. You would divide the clergy into two separate classes—those who wore chasubles, and those who did not; and of course there would be no more communion between the two classes. As to the unfortunate Bishops, they must either have no consciences, and see no differences, and be honorary members of all schools of thought, or else they must offend one party of their clergy and please the other. This is indeed a miserable prospect! 'Forbearance and toleration' are fine, high-sounding words; but if they mean that every clergyman is to be allowed to do what he likes, they seem to me the certain forerunner of confusion, division, and disruption.[1]

(3) Shall we stand firmly by the last decision of the Law Courts, and refuse to depart from the old paths and old usages about the Lord's Supper with which our forefathers have been content for 300 years? Hard and painful as the conclusion may appear, I see no alternative. My sentence is that we ought so to stand firm, and to abide the consequences, whatever they may be, whether secession, disestablishment, or disruption. '*Fiat veritas, ruat coelum.*'[2] Remember, in saying this, I am no prophet. I do not know that there would be many secessions, or any at all. It is not those who talk most loudly about seceding who secede at last. But supposing that secession and disruption of the Church of England are the results of the policy which I have just indicated, let us just remember how the matter will appear in the future

[1] See appendix, chapter 1, note 3, p. 426.

[2] 'Let the truth be upheld, though the heavens fall.' As usually quoted, '*justitia*' takes the place of '*veritas.*'

annals of history. The record will be as follows: in the latter part of the nineteenth century the Established Church of England was destroyed and rent in pieces because of a contention of two parties within her pale, neither of which would give way. One of the two parties persisted in administering the Lord's Supper with ceremonies borrowed from the Church of Rome, ceremonies not once mentioned in Scripture or the communion office of the Prayerbook, ceremonies decidedly not of the essence of the sacrament, ceremonies condemned by the Courts of Law, ceremonies which had not been used for 300 years. The other party steadily refused to depart from the principles on which the Church was reformed in the sixteenth century, and from the customs which had prevailed since the days of Queen Elizabeth. And as neither party would give way, the public got weary, Parliament stepped in, and the Church was disestablished, disendowed, and rent in pieces. Now what will the verdict of posterity be? I leave it to yourselves to supply the answer.

I have no wish, in saying this, to be a black prophet. I have great faith in our Church's tenacity of life. She survived the expulsion of 2,000 most able clergymen in 1662 by the Act of Uniformity. She survived the secession of the non-jurors, when William III came to the throne. She survived the loss of the Methodist body in the last century. She has survived the departure to their own place of Manning, Newman, Oakley, Faber, the two Wilberforces, and many others in our own day. If she is faithful to Protestant principles, I believe she would survive the secession of the whole 'English Church Union,' if they left us next year! But I cannot bring myself to believe yet that the great majority of the members of that body would actually leave the Church of their forefathers, on account of things which they themselves must allow are not essential to the Lord's Supper. I shall not believe it till I see it.

As to myself, my mind is made up. I mean to abide by the decisions of the Courts of Law, so long as those decisions are not superseded and nullified by Parliament, or reversed. I see no other safe or satisfactory course to adopt. A Bishop who sets himself *above the law*, and ignores its decrees, is launched on a sea of uncertainties, which I, for one, decline to face. I cannot forget, that as a chief officer of the Church, I am specially bound to set an example of obedience to the powers that be, and to acknowledge the Queen's authority in things ecclesiastical as well as temporal.

I came to the position I occupy as Bishop of Liverpool with a settled resolution to be just and fair and kind to clergymen of every school of thought, whether High or Low or Broad, or no party. To that resolution I mean to adhere through evil report and good report. Whenever I see in a clergyman hearty working, consistent living, and loyal Churchmanship, I shall be thankful, and ready to help him, though things may be said in his pulpit and done in his parish with which I do not entirely agree. But my clergy must not expect me to sanction and countenance *transgressions of the law*, and I do entreat them, for the sake of peace, to keep within the limits of the judicial decisions on the great points which have been disputed, argued, and determined in the last few years.

I have long maintained, and still maintain, that every well-constituted National Church ought to be as comprehensive as possible. It should allow large liberty of thought within certain limits. Its *'necessaria'* should be few and well-defined. Its *'non-necessaria'* should be very many. It should make generous allowance for the infinite variety of men's minds, the curious sensitiveness of scrupulous consciences, and the enormous difficulty of clothing thoughts in language which will not admit of more than one meaning. A sect can afford to be narrow and exclusive: a National Church ought to be liberal, generous, and as 'large-hearted' as Solomon (1 Kings 4:29). Above all, the rulers of such a Church should never forget that it is a body of which the members, from the highest minister down to the humblest layman, are all fallen and corrupt creatures, and that their mental errors, as well as their moral delinquencies, demand very tender dealing. The great Master of all Churches was One who would not break a bruised reed or quench smoking flax (Matt. 12:20), and tolerated much ignorance and many mistakes in his disciples. A National Church must never be ashamed to walk in his steps. To secure the greatest happiness and wealth of the greatest number in the State is the aim of every wise politician. To comprehend and take in, by a well-devised system of scriptural Christianity, the greatest number of Christians in the nation, ought to be the aim of every National Church. To these principles, as an English bishop, I mean to adhere.

Comprehensiveness, such as I have described, I believe to be *a peculiar characteristic* of the National Church of England. We have within our pale three widely different 'schools of thought,' the old historical schools, commonly called High and Low and Broad. They are schools which have existed for nearly three centuries, and, unless human nature greatly alters, I believe they will exist as long as the Church of England stands. Our Church has been the Church of Ridley and Latimer and Jewel; of Hooker and Andrews and Pearson and Hammond; of Davenant and Hall and Usher and Reynolds; of Stillingfleet and Patrick and Waterland and Bull; of Robert Nelson and George Herbert; of Romaine and Toplady and Newton and Scott and Cecil and Simeon; of Bishops Ryder and Blomfield, and Jeune, and Thirlwall; of Archbishops Sumner, and Longley, and Whately; of the martyred Bishop Patteson and the late Canon Mozley. What reading man does not know that these divines differed widely about many subjects; about the Church, the ministry, and the sacraments; about the meaning of some words and phrases in the Prayer-book; about the relative place and proportion they assigned to some doctrines and verities of the faith? But they all agreed in loving the Church of England, in thanking God for her Reformation, in maintaining her protest against the Church of Rome, in using her forms of worship, and in labouring for her prosperity. They could pray and praise together. In days of darkness and persecution they drew together, like Hooper and Ridley in Queen Mary's time, and found common ground. We may all have our own special favourites in this list of names. We may greatly prefer some of these men to others. We may think some of them were in error, and did not 'declare all the counsel of God.' But, after all, is there one of them whom we should like to have turned out of our communion? I reply, Not one! With all their shades of opinion, they were 'honest Churchmen,' and there was room in our pale for all. This is what I call the practical comprehensiveness of the National Church, and, as a Bishop, I do not want to see it altered and narrowed.

But while I say all this, I hold that there must be *limits to the comprehensiveness* of the Church of England. There must be certain boundaries and landmarks, for order is heaven's first law. There was order in Eden before the fall. There will be perfect order on earth at the restitution of all things. A Christian Church utterly destitute of order does not deserve to be called a Church at all. A Church, like every other corporation on earth, must have definite terms of membership. It must have a creed, and certain fixed principles of doctrine and worship. Its members have a right to know what its ministers are set to teach.

The member of the National Church of England has a just right to expect one general type of teaching and worship, whether he goes into a parish church in Truro or Lincoln, in Canterbury or Carlisle. Different shades of statement in the pulpit he may find himself obliged to tolerate. But he may justly complain if the doctrine and ceremonial of one diocese is as utterly unlike that of another as light and darkness, black and white, acids and alkalies, oil and water. 'Liberty of prophesying' and free thought, in the abstract, are excellent things. But they must have some limits. Just as in States the extreme of liberty becomes licentiousness and tyranny, so in Churches it becomes disorder and confusion. The Church which regards Deism, Socinianism, Romanism, and Protestantism with equal favour or equal indifference, is a mere Babel, a 'city of confusion,' and not the city of God.

Now I contend that the National Church of England has set up wisely-devised limits to its comprehensiveness. These limits, I believe, are to be found in the Articles, the Creeds, and the Book of Common Prayer. If, therefore, a minister of the National Church maintains and teaches those distinctive doctrines of the Church of Rome which are plainly named, defined, and repudiated in the Thirty-nine Articles, and ignoring the public declaration which he made on taking a living, deliberately teaches transubstantiation, the sacrifice of the Mass, purgatory, the necessity of auricular confession, and the invocation of saints; or if he administers the sacrament of the Lord's Supper with such usages and ceremonies that few persons can distinguish it from the Romish Mass; then, and in that case, I contend that he is transgressing the liberty allowed by the Church of England. He may be zealous, sincere, earnest, and devout, but he is in the wrong place in a Protestant communion. He has stepped over the just limits of the Church's comprehensiveness, and is occupying an untenable and unwarrantable position. By those limits I mean to abide, and my clergy must not expect me to sanction any transgression of them.

I commend these points to the calm consideration of those clergy who may not quite agree with all I have been saying, and may think more liberty should be allowed within our pale. I commend them especially to those zealous young men who think that the true remedy for 'the present distress' is freedom from State control, and disestablishment. I warn such young men to take care what they are about, and to do nothing rashly. There are times when it is better to 'bear the ills we have, than fly to others that we know not of.'[1] A disestablished Church would undoubtedly lay down for its members certain well-defined terms of communion, and require them to be strictly observed, just as our own Established Church does now. In short, disestablishment would give clergymen no more real

---

[1] Quoted from Shakespeare's *Hamlet* 3.1.

liberty than they possess now, and in all probability would soon be followed by disruption, and ultimately by the destruction of the Church of England.

And now let me conclude all with a request which I cannot doubt you will all approve. Let us all resolve to pray more and more for unity. It was a solemn and humbling remark which fell from Lord Macaulay's lips, when he returned from India, and found the strife which began with the *Tracts for the Times*. He said, 'I find Christians wrangling about ceremonies and forms, while millions of heathen in India are bowing down to sacred monkeys and crocodiles and cows.' Let us never cease to plead with him who can make men be of one mind in a house, and let us use more frequently the well-known prayer for unity, which stands in the service for the 20th of June:

> O God the Father of our Lord Jesus Christ, our only Saviour, the Prince of Peace; give us grace seriously to lay to heart the great dangers we are in by our unhappy divisions. Take away all hatred and prejudice, and whatsoever else may hinder us from godly union and concord; that, as there is but one Body, and one Spirit, and one Hope of our Calling, one Lord, one Faith, one Baptism, one God and Father of us all, so we may henceforth be all of one heart, and of one soul, united in one holy bond of Truth and Peace, of Faith and Charity, and may with one mind and one mouth glorify thee; through Jesus Christ our Lord. Amen.

2

FOR DOCTRINAL CHRISTIANITY

A charge at the Primary Visitation in Wigan, October 20, 1881.[1]

M Y Reverend and Lay Brethren, I address you for the first time at a visitation in Wigan under a deep sense of responsibility. For the last three centuries the office of an English Bishop, from Archbishop Cranmer down to Archbishop Tait, and from Bishop Ridley down to Bishop Jackson, has always been one of peculiar difficulty and anxiety. I doubt whether it was ever more so than it is at the present day. Never were there so many knots to untie, and so many problems to solve! It is a day of bitter party spirit, and of scathing newspaper criticism. A Bishop lives under the fierce blaze of public opinion; and he has always the sorrowful feeling that, whatever he may say or do, somebody or other is sure to be displeased.

However, I have a duty to do, and I must do it independently of human praise or blame, 'as to the Lord and not to man.' I claim no immunity from error, and I ask you to put the best construction on what I say. Above all, I ask you to join me in praying, that in this and all my public deliverances I may have meekness and wisdom, may combine decision and firmness with courtesy and toleration, and may be just and fair to all.

About the general statistics of our new Diocese, its acreage and population, its number of incumbents and curates, I shall not waste your time by saying anything. They are all points which you will find fully handled in my first Charge, delivered at Liverpool,

[1] Delivered at the Parish Church of All Saints', Wigan.

and I, therefore, abstain from repetition. In my second Charge I purposely confine myself to the peculiar circumstances of the District in which we are assembled today, its wants, and the best way of meeting them. I also wish to speak of some matters of public interest, which, for want of time, I was compelled to pass over in my first Charge.

There is, however, one point of general Diocesan interest which I think it right to mention before I take up other subjects. The point to which I refer is the exceptionally small number of Rural Deaneries into which our new Diocese is at present divided. For a population exceeding one million, and for 200 incumbents and 140 curates, 340 clergy in all, there are at this moment only six Rural Deans. Some of you, perhaps, are not aware that this is a state of things in which we stand entirely alone. There is not a single diocese in England and Wales which is similarly situated. In Lichfield there are forty-eight Deaneries, in Norwich there are forty-one. In Rochester, a Diocese much like our own, there are nineteen. In St Asaph, with fewer clergy and only 260,000 people, there are thirteen. Even in Chester, with little more than half our population and about the same number of clergy, there are nine. Of course the reason of this state of things is obvious. The West Derby Hundred has increased its inhabitants enormously during this century, and our ecclesiastical arrangements, which answered very well a hundred years ago, are quite insufficient now. But I am bound to say that I consider this small number of Rural Deaneries is a serious defect in our Diocesan organization which wants amending, and I propose to attempt the amendment at an early period. No one, perhaps, but a Bishop, can fully estimate the value of a Rural Dean, as a medium for obtaining information, and for conveying his wishes to the clergy. But a Rural Dean, it must be remembered, is an entirely unpaid officer, and it is not wise or fair to overweight him with incessant demands on his time. And when he has more than about twenty-five benefices in his Deanery, I think he has too much on his hands.

I propose, therefore, to have nine Rural Deaneries in our Diocese instead of six, and to effect the change by dividing each of the three largest Deaneries—North Liverpool, South Liverpool, and Prescot—into two, leaving the other three—Winwick, Wigan, and Ormskirk—almost unaltered. I say *almost* advisedly. I think it quite possible that in some few cases an addition to, or subtraction from, each of the three last-named Deaneries might be convenient, and when a re-arrangement is being made for the whole Diocese, it would be wise to effect any changes that may seem desirable. Our position, in one respect, is very convenient for changes. Our existing Deaneries are not, as in many counties, conterminous with County Hundreds. We have only one Hundred for the whole Diocese, and the boundaries of Deaneries can easily be altered.

In carrying out the change I have referred to, I wish particularly to have the advice and aid of my Rural Deans, and I should feel obliged if they will bring the whole matter before their respective Ruri-decanal Conferences at an early period. Any suggestions they can offer will receive careful consideration. But I feel strongly that the change is absolutely necessary, if our new Diocese is to be officered in proportion to other Dioceses in England and Wales. I trust you will believe that I have not the slightest wish to overload the Diocese with Episcopal officials. But I cannot think that two Archdeacons and nine Rural Deans will form an extravagantly large staff for an English Bishop in a Diocese of more than a million souls. As matters stand at present, if our organization is right, that of other dioceses is wrong; and, *vice versa*, if their organization is right, we need a change.

To all this let me add one more argument. I am very anxious to commence a system of meeting annually the clergy of each Rural Deanery, in a private, quiet, informal manner, for the purpose of spiritual communion, such as cannot be obtained in large, public, official gatherings, and for the promotion of brotherly feeling, mutual confidence, and better knowledge of one another. I know that such private Ruri-decanal gatherings have been found most useful and edifying by other Bishops, and I have no doubt they would do good here. I am sure we all need our spiritual life quickened by intercourse with other servants of our common Master, and perhaps if we saw each other oftener we should understand each other better. But such meetings must be small and quiet if they are to be edifying and refreshing, and I must frankly say that so long as our three largest Deaneries are undivided I should shrink from attempting them.

I turn from this point of Diocesan organization to one of far more serious importance. That point is the spiritual condition of the eastern part of our Diocese of Liverpool, and the best mode of meeting its very peculiar wants. It is a large and wide subject, and demands our best attention.

That the present provision of means of grace made by the Church of England in some parts of this District is totally insufficient, is such a patent fact that I shall not spend time in proving it. You have only to run your eye down the column in our Diocesan Calendar which shows the population of each benefice, and you will see enough, and more than enough, of painful evidence. In the Deanery of Wigan I find Haigh with 7,500 people, Ince with 15,000, Pemberton with 11,000, St Catherine's, Wigan, with 10,000, St George's with 11,000, St Thomas' with 9,000, and Upholland with 6,000. In the Deanery of Prescot I find Eccleston St Thomas' with 12,000 people, Fairfield, Liverpool, with 16,000, Farnworth with 11,000, St Helen's with 18,000, and Widnes with 13,000. In the Deanery of Winwick, I find two parishes in Warrington with 13,000 in one and 9,000 in the other. Even in the Deanery of Ormskirk, which is better off in the matter of churches, I find as many as seven benefices with more than 5,000 souls. In every one of these cases, let me add, I suspect my statement is below the returns of the recent census.

The state of things I have described is most painful and unsatisfactory. Common sense points out that it is physically impossible for the Incumbent of such large parishes as most of those I have named, to overtake the work committed to him, to meet the spiritual wants of his parishioners, and to do justice to himself and the Church of England. If he had the bodily strength of Samson, and the burning zeal of St Paul, it would be impossible. The thing cannot be done. There are but twelve hours in each day, and one Sunday in each week, and if he taxes his energies to the uttermost he can only visit a certain number of hours, and preach a certain number of times. And then, after all, he must continually feel that a great deal of work is left undone. I can assure all my clergy who are placed in such positions as those I have described, that I feel the deepest sympathy with them, and am determined, by God's help, to do all I can, so long as I am Bishop of Liverpool, to lighten their labour and strengthen their hands.

It must, besides, never be forgotten that in many of the large parishes in this district the clergyman's difficulties are not to be measured by the *number* only of his parishioners. It is the peculiar *occupation*, and by consequence the peculiar *character*, of the people which creates most formidable obstacles in his way. The workers underground in coal pits, the labourers employed in the trying atmosphere of chemical and glass works and iron furnaces, by night and by day, need special treatment, and require to be approached in a special way. To suppose that it is enough to build a handsome church, and set up an elaborate liturgical service for these classes, is, in my judgment, a complete mistake. The first thing needed is not buildings, but living men—men ordained, if you can get them, men not ordained, if you can get no other agents; but, in any case, men who have the grace of God and the love of souls in their hearts, and will go in and out among the roughest classes in a friendly manner, and win their confidence.

For, after all, the clergyman of the worst and blackest parish in a district must never allow himself to despair. The darkest-looking and most uncouth collier, or miner, or iron worker, or labourer in chemical works, is a man just like ourselves by nature, and differing only in outward appearance, from the circumstances of his position. Like ourselves, he is open to kindness and sympathy. Like ourselves, he has a heart that can feel sorrow and trouble, and a body liable to sickness and disease and death. Like ourselves, he can often be got at through the simple avenue of attention to wife or children or parents or brothers or sisters or friends. I charge my reverend brethren to keep all this continually in mind. Colliers and iron workers and all their companions of like occupations are flesh and blood, and have souls, affections, and consciences like you and me. They are to be won for Christ, if we go to work in the right way, and have God's blessing. The last day will show that collieries have not only sent up coals for our fires, but have also produced some bright jewels for our Redeemer's crown.

Multiplication of right-minded living agents is the first and foremost remedy that I must always recommend to the incumbents of great colliery parishes. By constant importunate application to those valuable Institutions, the Pastoral Aid, the Additional Curates, and the Diocesan Church Aid Societies, try to get ordained helpers if you can, and lay-agents if you cannot. Encourage and invite every right-minded layman near you to come forward and give you his help. Never, never be afraid of enlisting the aid of the laity. Cast away for ever the old tradition that religious work is to be left to the clergy alone. Boldly make use of 'lay' talent, and you will never be without 'lay' talent to use. Trust the laity, and the laity will trust you. Stir up every Christian man and woman in your congregation, who has a few hours to spare in the week, to give you some voluntary aid. Break up your huge parish into well-organized territorial districts, and give to each helper his own special district. Urge your helpers to get together people wherever they can, in a shed, or a cottage, or a barn, and to give the simplest and most elementary Christian instruction, plain, kindly talk about Christ, simple extempore prayer, and hearty, lively singing. Do this, and persevere in doing it, and I am sure you will not labour in vain. Do this, and persevere in doing it, and, in process of time, the Mission-room, the Church and the regular parochial district will be the happy result, and, what is far better, a harvest of saved souls.

Everything, however, I hope I need not remind you, depends on the message which your living agents proclaim. They must know what they have got to do. If they only go about telling men not to get drunk, not to fight, not to gamble, not to swear, not to break the Sabbath, they may just as well stay at home. If they want to do good, they must tell men to believe as well as repent. They must tell the story of the cross of Christ. They must magnify that grand article of the Apostles' Creed, 'I believe in the forgiveness of sins.' They must make much of that doctrine which fits the empty heart of man just as the right key fits the lock, I mean the doctrine of free and full pardon of sin through faith in the vicarious death of Christ.

This is the glorious doctrine that was the strength of the Apostles when they went forth to the Gentiles to preach a new religion. They began, a few poor fishermen, in a despised corner of the earth. But in a few years, without money to bribe adherents or arms to compel assent, they turned the world upside down. They changed the face of the Roman Empire. They emptied the heathen temples of their worshippers, and made the whole system of idolatry crumble away. And what was the weapon by which they did it all? It was free forgiveness through faith in Jesus Christ.

This is the doctrine which brought light into Europe 350 years ago, at the time of the blessed Reformation, and enabled one solitary monk, Martin Luther, to shake the whole Church of Rome. Through his preaching and writing the scales fell from men's eyes, and the chains of their souls were loosed. And what was the lever that gave him his power? It was *free forgiveness through faith in Jesus Christ*.

This is the doctrine that revived our own Church in the middle of last century, when Whitefield and the Wesleys, and Berridge and Venn, broke the wretched spirit of slumber which had come over the land, and roused men to think. The sermons of these good evangelists, no doubt, were often rough and unpolished. But the matter they contained was 'life from the dead' to myriads of souls. They began a mighty spiritual revolution, without the patronage of Church or State, and with little seeming likelihood of success. They began, few in number, with small encouragement from the rich and great. But they prospered, and produced results for which the ungrateful Church of England has never been sufficiently thankful to this hour. And why? Because they preached *free forgiveness through faith in Jesus Christ.*

This is the doctrine which is the true strength of any Church on earth at this day. It is not orders, or endowments, or liturgies, or learning, or grand cathedrals, that will keep a Church alive. Let free forgiveness through Christ be faithfully proclaimed in her pulpits, and the gates of hell shall not prevail against her. Let it be buried, or kept back, and her candlestick shall soon be taken away. When the Saracens invaded the lands where Jerome and Athanasius, Cyprian, and Augustine, once wrote and preached, they found Bishops and liturgies, I make no question. But I fear they found no preaching of free forgiveness of sins, and so they swept the Churches of those lands clean away. The Churches were a body without a vital principle, and therefore they fell. Let us never forget that the brightest days of a Church are those when Christ crucified is most exalted. The dens and caves of the earth, where the early Christians met to hear of the love of Jesus, were more full of glory and beauty in God's sight than ever was St Peter's at Rome. The meanest barn at this day, where the true way of pardon is offered to sinners, is a far more honourable place than the Cathedral of Cologne or Milan. A Church is only useful so far as she exalts *free forgiveness through Christ.*

This is the doctrine which, of all others, is the mightiest engine for pulling down the kingdom of Satan. When the Kingswood colliers, near Bristol, first heard it from Whitefield's lips, they wept till their black faces were seamed with white lines of tears. The Greenlanders were unmoved so long as the Moravians told them only of the creation and the fall of man; but when they heard of redeeming love, their frozen hearts melted like snow in spring. Preach salvation by the sacraments, exalt the Church above Christ, keep back the doctrine of the Atonement, and the devil cares little. His goods are at peace. But preach a full Christ and a free pardon, and justification by faith, and then Satan will have great wrath, for he knows he has but a short time. A famous divine of the last century said that he went on preaching morality, and nothing else, till he found there was not a moral man in his parish. But when he changed his plan, and began to preach the love of Christ to sinners, then there was a stirring of the dry bones, and a mighty turning to God.

My reverend brethren, I know that these are ancient things. But in days like these it is good to be reminded of them. I am thoroughly persuaded that we want no new doctrine in order to do good to souls. We want nothing but the old paths. Walk in them steadily. Make much of Christ. Pray continually for the quickening influences of the Holy Ghost. Settle it in your minds, that where he is, nothing is impossible. Work on steadily on these lines, and you may live to see miraculous changes. The Lord God of St Paul, the God who raised up flourishing Churches in such dark places as Rome and Corinth and Ephesus, is not dead, but alive. The blackest spiritual wilderness in the colliery districts of Lancashire may yet become a garden of the Lord.

I must now turn from these matters of special Diocesan importance in order to make a few brief remarks on some subjects of more general public interest, which appear to demand the attention of all Churchmen. They are subjects, for the most part, which have come to the surface during the last three or four years. They are subjects which ought to be considered and understood by all public-spirited Churchmen who know the times, and look beyond their own doors. About these subjects you may reasonably expect your Bishop to give his opinion.

(1) I shall speak first about the Burials Act.[1] I need not remind you that it is now the law of the land, and, as such, ought to be willingly obeyed by all loyal clergymen. I shall never conceal my own opinion, that the alleged grievance under the old law was in most parts of England entirely imaginary. In the long course of a ministry of thirty-five years in country parishes, I never met with a single case of a Dissenter who wished a deceased relative to be interred by anyone but the clergyman of the parish. But I will not dwell on this. The law has been altered by the almost universal demand of the laity, and it is childish and ungracious to waste time in useless complaints. I can only counsel all clergymen who have churchyards still used for interments, and are consequently affected by the Burials Act, to allow it to work as easily and pleasantly as possible, and to avoid all friction and collision on the occasion of funerals under the Act. I advise making no difficulties about the use of the parish bier and pall, or the tolling of the bell. Even in the case of Nonconformists dying outside the parish, if their friends wish them to be buried in the parish, I advise the clergyman who consents to allow such a burial (which he is not obliged to do, and should only do occasionally, and with the consent of his churchwardens), to permit such funeral to be conducted with any Christian rights and ceremonies which he would have been obliged to permit if the deceased had died within the parish. I advise this for the sake of peace and charity, though I doubt if it could be demanded as a legal right. The only point which I cannot advise my clergy to concede is the performance of any religious service by a Nonconformist, under the Act, within the walls of the parish church. This is a concession of principle which certainly was not contemplated in either House of Parliament. It would inevitably risk strife and confusion, and would justly give offence to many worshippers in the parish church. I fail entirely to see that the right granted by the Act to use the parish churchyard

[1] Act of 1880. It removed a grievance of the Nonconformists by permitting them to bury their dead in parish churchyards with religious forms selected by themselves, or without any at all.

46

for the performance of a religious service at a funeral, carried with it the right to use the interior of the church.

For the case of persons who die unbaptized, and whose friends wish them to be buried with a religious service by the clergyman of the parish, I strongly advise my clergy to avail themselves of the provision made for such cases in the Act. I advise them to meet the natural feelings of the friends of the deceased by using a service suited to the occasion. The Prayer-book office, you are of course aware, cannot be legally used in such cases. There is, however, a very appropriate form in existence, which has been drawn up by three eminent prelates of our Church, which I shall be happy to sanction in my Diocese. Nevertheless, if any incumbent, at such funerals of unbaptized persons, likes to use a form of his own composition, I shall make no objection, though I recommend him to confine himself to collects taken from the Prayer-book and portions of Holy Scripture.

Before leaving the subject of burials I must seize the opportunity of raising a warning voice about a custom which I am informed is not uncommon in some parts of Lancashire. I refer to the custom of buying and selling what are called 'breadths of ground,' in the churchyard, for the future interment, near their relatives, of persons who are still alive. Now I am advised by good legal authorities, that all such sales of 'breadths of ground' are distinctly illegal, that no one can buy a grave for a person not yet dead without a 'faculty' from the Chancellor's Court, and that no incumbent can make a sale of such a grave which would be in the least binding on his successor. I commend this point to the attention of all incumbents who have parish churchyards. I have reason to believe that this sale of 'breadths' is a fertile source of trouble and strife. Let it then be understood that the custom is illegal, and let me request that henceforth it may be discontinued. Decency and kind feeling point out that a clergyman should direct his sexton, as far as possible, to leave a space near the grave of the husband for the grave of the wife, and, speaking generally, to provide, if it can be so managed, for members of a family being buried near one another. But all buying and selling for future interment, without a 'faculty,' is an unlawful transaction.

(2) I wish to say something, in the next place, about the *Revised Version of the New Testament*, which has justly excited so much interest during the last few months. I regard the work of the Revisers with deep thankfulness, and I believe that all English-speaking Christians ought to feel extremely grateful to them. In saying this, I ask you not to misunderstand me. I am not able to swell the chorus of unmixed praise with which some have received the Revised Version. I cannot admit the correctness of all the new renderings of the Greek text. I think that, with an honest and conscientious desire to be strictly literal, the Revisers have sometimes made needless transpositions of words, and by so doing have not left the sense more plain. I think their English is occasionally more tame and prosaic than that of the Authorized Version, without being more faithful to the original Greek. I fail to see that in their praiseworthy effort to give the full force of the Greek article they have always been quite consistent. But, after all, this is only the opinion of one man, who may very possibly be mistaken. The things I have named are like spots in the face of the sun, and, if they are errors, they can be revised again. Taking it for all in all, the work is a great work, and deserves the thanks of all British Christians. It throws clearer light on many texts of Holy Scripture, and ought to be highly prized and diligently used by thousands.

But the main reason for thankfulness about the Revised Version, which I commend to the attention of my clergy, is the glorious testimony which it bears to the soundness of the whole doctrinal system of Christianity. After ten years of patient and diligent investigation, after careful examination of versions and manuscripts not known 250 years ago, after the united labour of the ablest committee of biblical scholars that could be got together, after all this, the Revised Version comes forth from the crucible without the loss of a single doctrine of our most holy faith; let me rather say with every doctrine more fully established than ever. Who does not know that many of the enemies of Christianity in this land have made the alleged defects of our Authorized Version the chief ground of their attacks on the gospel? 'Give us a new translation,' they have often cried, 'and you will see what will become of your favourite dogmas.' The Revised Version supplies a crushing answer to all these assailants. The New Testament has been translated once more by men whose competency none can dispute. And what is the result? Not a single stone in the fabric of Christian truth has been disturbed! The Trinity, the proper Deity of Christ, the personality of the Holy Ghost, and the atonement, remain just where they were, and are even more clearly brought out than before. For all this, I ask you to join me in thanking, blessing, and praising God. We may boldly say, 'Thy word is truth.' 'Thy word is very pure: therefore thy servant loveth it' (John 17:17; Psa. 119:140).

I cannot pass away from this subject without expressing a hope that none of my clergy will use the Revised Version, instead of the Authorized, in reading the lessons in Church until the practice is formally sanctioned by law. At present, however some may dispute it, the weight of evidence and opinion is most decidedly against it. Let there be no division among us on the subject. Let us not have the Diocese split into two parties—the readers of the new version and the readers of the old. 'He that believeth shall not make haste.' Let us be content at present to use the old version, which, with all its defects, has done such good service for 250 years, until further order is taken by authority. Give the results of the revision, if you please, in your pulpits, by way of commentary. But in the reading desk I strongly advise you to use the Authorized Version.

(3) The third subject about which I propose to say a few words is *the Royal Commission* about the Ecclesiastical Courts, which has been appointed this year. This Commission, you are all aware, was asked for by the Heads of our Church, in order to meet the loudly

expressed dissatisfaction of some persons with the existing Courts of First Instance and Final Appeal. It was thought only fair and reasonable to make a searching inquiry into the constitution and procedure of these Courts, to investigate the working of the Clergy Discipline[1] and Public Worship[2] Acts, and to suggest any reforms or amendments which might remove the dissatisfaction to which I have referred. The whole question is notoriously a vexed and difficult one. In every age of the Church the best mode of dealing with clerical offenders, whether in doctrinal or moral matters, has always proved a hard knot, which has baffled the cleverest fingers. Nevertheless, for the sake of peace, and in the hope of throwing oil on troubled waters, it has been thought desirable to make one more attempt. I trust this attempt will succeed. Nobody, I presume, of any school of thought, would pretend to say that our Ecclesiastical Courts, in their present state, are perfect, and incapable of improvement. What the Report of the Commission will be, of course we do not know at present. We can only wait and hope and pray that the spirit of wisdom and moderation may be given to all the Commissioners. One thing, however, I venture to say. I trust that the punishment for persistent 'contempt of court,' in future ecclesiastical suits, may not be imprisonment. A surer way of enlisting public sympathy on behalf of a defeated ecclesiastical litigant, however mistaken he may be, than to shut him up in prison, could not possibly be devised.

To all who are anxiously awaiting the report of the Royal Commission, let me recommend the importance of cultivating patience and moderate expectations. We must not indulge extravagant hopes. We must not expect the Commissioners to do impossibilities, and to inaugurate an era of halcyon days and perfect peace. If anyone supposes that they will reverse the recent decisions on ritual, or that they will draw up a new and unmistakable Ornaments Rubric, or that they will hand over all spiritual

[1] 1840.
[2] 1874.

questions to spiritual courts, in which laymen shall have no voice, or that they will allow every Bishop to settle disputed matters in his own Diocesan Court without power of appeal to a higher tribunal, or that they will not allow the laity to institute suits against criminous or heretical clergymen, or that they will suggest giving power to Convocation to alter our formularies or decide ecclesiastical questions without the license of the Crown or the sanction of Parliament, or that they will recommend a Court of Final Appeal in spiritual questions in which Bishops and divines alone shall sit and the laity shall have no place at all, or that they will advise allowing all clergymen to do just what they please in Divine service, and even to re-introduce the Romish Mass—if any man in his senses, I say, expects any of these things from the Royal Commissioners, I venture to predict that he will find himself entirely mistaken. The Commission will not exceed its powers. Of three things I am perfectly certain. As long as the Church of England is the Established Church of this realm, the Crown will never give up its supremacy in matters ecclesiastical as well as civil, the Church will never be allowed to act independently of Parliament, and the laity of the Church will never allow the clergy alone to decide ecclesiastical disputes, or to alter the Church's formularies, or to change the Church's laws.

(4) The fourth public subject about which I wish to say a few words is the *Church Defence Institute*, to which the Archbishop of Canterbury has thought it necessary to call attention in a recent letter. The mere fact that the Primate has written this letter is enough to show the importance of the subject, and I need make no apology for taking it up. The Church Defence Institute has been called into existence in order to counteract the unhappy efforts which are being made by the Liberation Society to destroy the connection of Church and State in this country, and to disestablish and disendow the Church of England. The Archbishop recommends us to recognize the importance of the Church Defence Society, and give it our support.

It is matter for deep regret that the necessity for a Church Defence Society should have arisen. If ever there was a time in England when all Protestant Christians ought to be united and avoid quarrels, in the face of aggressive infidelity and active Popery, that time is the present. It is quite certain that disestablishment would do no good to Nonconformists, if the Liberationists could obtain it. They have liberty now to do anything they please. It is equally certain that although disestablishment and disendowment would greatly weaken our Church, and almost destroy it in rural districts, it would hardly touch its power and influence in the towns. It is equally certain that disestablishment would make a breach between Episcopalians and their Nonconformist spoilers which would never be healed. Above all, it is certain that Churchmen would not forsake the Church because she was disestablished, and become Independents, Baptists, Presbyterians, or Methodists. That grand old Communion which, compared with any other single communion in the land, is by far the largest and most influential, would still retain her old influence, and the much-coveted *equality*, of which we hear so much, would be found, after disestablishment, just as far off as ever.

To my own mind the attack of the Liberation Society on the Church of England is one of the most painful features of our time. To cultivate the most friendly relations with all Protestant Nonconformists, and to co-operate with them whenever we can, are, in my eyes, plain and positive duties. I cannot yet believe that the violent language of extreme Liberationists expresses the sentiments of more than a minority of the Nonconformist body. Men often make up by noise what they lack in numbers. I cling to the belief that the vast majority of the Methodists, and a very large proportion of the Independents and Baptists, have no desire to disestablish and disendow the Church of England, and would rather walk in the steps of John Wesley, Adam Clarke, Doddridge, Fuller, Robert Hall, and John Cumming, and leave the Church alone.

However, if the Liberationists will not let us alone, and continue their efforts to disestablish and disendow the Church of England, it is our bounden duty to take the advice of the Archbishop of Canterbury, and to defend ourselves. We must not sit still and allow our parishes to be flooded with unscrupulous statements and grossly incorrect representations, without circulating cheap literature, adapted to the purpose, in reply. With such literature, in the shape of short tracts and leaflets, the Church Defence Institute is ready to supply us. There is no safety in apathy. If others combine, we must combine. If others agitate, we must boldly resist the agitation. If others assert falsehood, we must assert truth.

For in matters like these, we must remember, ignorance is the greatest ally the enemies of our Church possess. To dispel ignorance, and quietly replace it by truth, should be our great aim. Few persons, perhaps, who have not had occasion to look into the subject, can have the slightest conception of the ideas current among some classes about the Church, her revenues, and her clergy. Things are continually said about these subjects which are utterly untrue. For instance, it is utterly untrue that disestablishment would enable the State to save twenty-six millions of annual taxes. The whole endowments of the Church are not six millions a year! It is utterly untrue that the Bishops are rolling in wealth, and the clergy are overpaid. The Bishops have so many demands on their purses that they can hardly make both ends meet, and the clergy, if incomes were equally divided, would hardly have three hundred a year apiece! It is utterly untrue that the clergy are paid by the State, or that the people are taxed to pay the clergy: the State never gave the Church any tithes or lands at all! It is utterly untrue that the Bishops and clergy are 'State-made parsons,' seeing that the State cannot ordain any minister, and the Crown can only nominate as Bishops men who are already ordained. It is utterly untrue that the Church prayers are 'State-made prayers,' seeing that the Prayer-book was compiled by our Protestant Reformers.

It is utterly untrue that the Prayer-book is a mere Popish book; considering that the greater part of it is pure Scripture. All these things are ridiculous untruths, which it is a shame for any man to circulate, and a discredit to any man to believe. I ask Englishmen, when they hear statements such as these, to exercise their own good sense, and to put the simple question, 'Is this really true?' A cause which can only be built on a foundation of gross mis-statements must be in a very unsatisfactory condition.

(5) The fifth and last public subject on which I wish to say a few words is the *unsatisfactory financial position of our great Religious Societies*. By Religious Societies I mean those well-known voluntary Institutions which have been established to enable Christians to promote the spread of the gospel at home and abroad. The support given to these Societies throughout the whole Church of England appears to me far below what it ought to be. The total amount of money given annually to them is less than would be required to build a single ironclad like the *Inflexible*. And yet the support we give to agencies for promoting the spread of Christ's gospel is a fair test of the value we set on it, and the gratitude we feel for it! Surely there is cause here for humiliation, and room for much amendment.

In our own Diocese, I am obliged to say, the state of things in this matter seems far from being right and healthy. There appear to be not a few parishes in which our great Societies receive no support at all. The following statistics are painful, and demand serious consideration. The Society for the Propagation of the Gospel has annual sermons in 93 Churches out of 200, and receives altogether £2,100. The Church Missionary Society has sermons in 77 Churches out of 200, and receives £4,220. The Church Pastoral Aid Society has sermons in 43 Churches out of 200, and receives £1,190. The Additional Curates' Society has sermons in 54 Churches out of 200, and receives £1,500. I lay these painful figures before you with one brief comment. I think you will all agree with me that they are not satisfactory. They are not worthy of Lancashire. They are not creditable to the Church of England in the West Derby Hundred.

I commend the above subject to the attention of the clergy of the Diocese. I am quite aware that we occupy a very exceptional position, compared to other Dioceses, and that without endowments, rates, or old charities, many of our congregations find it extremely difficult to meet the cost of organist, choir, schools, lighting, warming, the pay of officials, and other expenses of public worship. I only say that it appears to me the plain scriptural duty of every individual Christian, and of every congregation, to do something to promote the spread of the gospel at home and abroad. It is far from my intention to prescribe to the clergy what Societies and charities they ought to bring before their parishioners. In these matters I request every clergyman to use his liberty, and act according to his own predilections. But if I am spared to hold another Visitation three years hence, I trust I shall not find a single Church in the Diocese in which there is not one Sunday given annually for collections for Missions abroad, another for Missions at home, and a third for our admirable Diocesan Institutions. There are fifty-two Sundays in every year, and I venture to think that three Sundays out of fifty-two are not too much to ask for the cause of Religious Societies. I trust the suggestion may not be forgotten.

On all the five subjects which I have just mentioned I might easily say much more, if time would allow me. I have purposely touched them very briefly, and must leave them as seeds of thought for the private consideration of all whom I address. I now pass away from them in order to conclude my Charge with some remarks on what I believe is one of the greatest dangers by which Christianity is assailed in our day. The danger to which I refer is the widespread *decay of distinct doctrinal religion*.

Of course I do not forget that the root of the great evil which I deplore is unbelief, and that unbelief is one of the oldest diseases of human nature, and one which, in one form or another, is continually injuring the Church of Christ and ruining souls. I am not surprised at its continued existence. I expect to see it periodically appearing in some new dress, or under some new name, according as the prince of this world finds it expedient to use it for his soul-damaging work. I repeat that I always expect to see a vast amount of unbelief in this pleasure-loving, sensual, proud, money-worshipping world. I see it, and am neither surprised nor afraid.

I am not afraid, for instance, of that coarse, revived infidelity, on the lines of the men of the first French Revolution, which boldly denies the existence of God, and the reality of judgment, and a world to come; which scoffs at the Bible, and dares to place our blessed Saviour on a level with Mahomet and Tom Paine. Such unbelief will never satisfy that universal conscience of mankind, which, from ancient Egypt down to modern Australia, testifies to man's rooted belief in the reality of an unseen world. The advocates of such infidelity have never answered the broad evidence of the Bible being the book that it is, and Christ being the person that he was, and the effects of Christianity on the world, and the continued separate existence of the Jews. I say they have never answered this evidence, and they never will.

Nor yet again am I afraid of the veiled scepticism of some men of science, which confuses so many minds in these latter times. There are scores of highly-educated men, nowadays, you must be aware, who are constantly making statements about things in heaven and earth, about the antiquity of man, about the origin of the human race, which cannot be reconciled with the Bible, if followed to their logical conclusions. Yet those who make these statements will not allow that they are unbelievers! They seem 'willing to wound, and yet afraid to strike.'[1]

Of men of this sort, I repeat emphatically, we need not be afraid. When we cannot reply to their statements, and explain the difficulties they raise, we may safely sit still and wait. 'The

---

[1] Quoted from Alexander Pope's *Epistle to Dr Arbuthnot*.

highest philosophy in some cases,' said Faraday, 'is to keep our minds in a position of judicious suspense.' For, after all, how little do the wisest philosophers know! How extremely limited is the horizon of our minds! How many ideas of modern science are entirely hypothetical! How many general conclusions are drawn most illogically from very slender particular premises! How often something has been brought to light, by the discoveries of travellers, which shivers to pieces the theories of sceptics! I say again, in this day of veiled scepticism we may quietly sit still and wait for more light. 'All human knowledge,' says Professor Rudolf Virchow, 'is only fragmentary. All of us who call ourselves students of nature possess only portions of natural science.'[1]

What, then, is the evil of which I am afraid? I am afraid of an inward disease which appears to be growing and spreading in all the Churches of Christ throughout the world. That disease is a disposition on the part of ministers to abstain from all sharply-cut doctrine, and a distaste on the part of professing Christians for all distinct statements of dogmatic truth.

I ask your attention while I try to handle this subject for a few minutes. The disease before us is 'a pestilence which walketh in darkness,' and threatens to do immense mischief to Christ's cause, because it is not realized and understood. I wish to raise a warning voice, and to show my clergy what reason there is to watch and be on our guard. The hidden enemy within the camp is far more dangerous than the foe outside.

The evidences of this dislike to distinct doctrine of which I speak are so abundant that the only difficulty lies in selection. Unless we are men who having eyes see not, and having ears hear not, we may see them on every side.

I might ask any intelligent man, for example, to mark the vague tone of some English newspapers when they touch religious subjects. He will find that while they are generally willing to praise Christian morality, they too often ignore Christian *doctrine*. I

---

[1] *Freedom of Science*, p. 20.

might ask him to observe the bitterness with which the advocates of School Boards have frequently spoken in the last ten years of what they are pleased to call 'theology,' and how ready they are to shovel it all aside under the vague name of '*sectarianism.*' I might ask him to analyse the most popular fictions and novels of the last forty years, which profess to paint Christians, and to notice how the portrait almost invariably avoids everything like *doctrine*, and exhibits the model Christian like a cut flower at a flower show, a mere bloom without root. I might ask him to look at the anxiety which some liberal speakers are constantly showing, in addressing popular audiences, to sweep away all '*denominational Christianity,*' and to throw aside Creeds and Confessions as old worn-out clothes, which only fetter the limbs of modern Englishmen. In each of these cases let him note one common symptom: that is, a morbid, unreasoning desire to have the fruits of Christianity without the roots, to have Christian morality without Christian doctrine. And then let him deny, if he can, that a *dislike to distinct doctrine* is a widespread evil of our times.

I will then ask any intelligent man to examine the opinions commonly expressed in the talk of private life. You have only to bring up the subject of religion in society, and you will get further proofs still. In many houses, even houses where people make a decent profession of religion, you will find that they make an idol of '*earnestness.*' They do not pretend to know anything about controversies and disputed questions, or to have any opinion as to who is right and who is wrong. They only know that they admire 'earnestness'; and they cannot think that earnest, hard-working ministers can be unsound in the faith. Tell them that any 'earnest,' clever, eloquent clergyman whom they name does not preach the gospel, and they are downright offended. Impossible! Whatever doctrines an 'earnest' man holds and teaches, they think it narrow and uncharitable and illiberal in you to distrust him. In vain you remind them that zeal and laboriousness are useless, if a minister does not teach scriptural truth; and that Pharisees and Jesuits had zeal enough to 'compass sea and land.' They know nothing about that: they do not profess to argue! All they know is that work is work; and that an earnest man must be a good man, and cannot be in the wrong, whatever he teaches. And what does it all come to? They dislike distinct doctrine, and will not make up their minds as to what is truth.

Hitherto we have only seen the evil I am considering in solution, and in its most common and diluted forms. If we want to see it in its more solid and crystallized state, we have only to turn to the preaching and writings of a small but well-known school of *Churchmen* of our days. I will not weary you with a catalogue of the strange and loose utterances which come incessantly from this quarter about inspiration, about the atonement, about the sacrifice and death of Christ, about the incarnation, about miracles, about Satan, about the Holy Spirit, about future punishment. I will not shock you by quoting language frequently used about the Bible by men who seem to regard it as nothing better than an obsolete record of useless mythology, in which you may here and there pick up a few globules of truth. I will not pain you by recounting the astounding theories sometimes propounded about 'the blood of Christ.' Time would fail me if I tried to sketch the leading features of a misty system which appears to regard all religions as more or less true, and in which 'tabernacles' seem to be wanted for Socrates and Plato and Pythagoras and Seneca and Confucius and Mahomet and Channing and Theodore Parker, as well as for Christ and Moses and Elias, all, forsooth, being true prophets, great masters, great teachers, great leaders of thought! I shall content myself with the remark, that *dislike of distinct doctrine* is one prominent characteristic of the leaders and champions of the party to which I refer. Search their sermons and books, and you find plenty of excellent negatives, plenty of great swelling words about 'the fatherhood of God, and charity and light and courage and manliness and large-heartedness and wide views and free thought'; plenty of mere wind-bags, high-sounding abstract terms, such as 'the true and the just and the beautiful and the high-souled and the genial and the liberal,' and so forth. But, alas! there is an utter absence of distinct, solid, positive doctrine. And if you look for a clear systematic account of the way of pardon and peace with God, of the right medicine for a burdened conscience, and the true cure for a broken heart, of faith and assurance and justification and regeneration and sanctification, you look in vain. The words indeed you may sometimes find, but not the realities; the words in new and strange senses, fair and good-looking outside, like rotten fruits; but, like them, empty and worthless within. But one thing, I repeat, is abundantly clear: positive doctrinal statements are the abomination of a certain class of Christian teachers in this day.

The consequences of this widespread *dislike to distinct doctrine* are very serious. Whether we like to allow it or not, it is an epidemic which is just now doing great harm, and specially among young people. It creates, fosters, and keeps up an immense amount of instability in religion. It produces what I must venture to call, if I may coin the phrase, a 'jelly-fish' Christianity in the land: that is, a Christianity without bone, or muscle, or power. A jelly-fish, as everyone knows who has been much by the seaside, is a pretty and graceful object when it floats in the sea, contracting and expanding like a little delicate transparent umbrella. Yet the same jelly-fish, when cast on the shore, is a mere helpless lump, without capacity for movement, self-defence, or self-preservation. Alas! it is a vivid type of much of the religion of this day, of which the leading principle is—'No dogma, no distinct tenets, no positive doctrine.' We have hundreds of ministers, both inside and outside the Church of England, who seem not to have a single bone in their body of divinity. They have no definite opinions; they belong to no school or party; they are so afraid of 'extreme views,' that they have no views at all. We have thousands of sermons preached every year, which are without an edge or a point or a corner, smooth as ivory balls, awakening no sinner, and edifying no saint. We have legions of young men annually turned out from our Universities, armed with a few scraps of second-hand philosophy, who think it a mark of cleverness and intellect to have no decided opinions about anything in religion, and to be utterly unable to make up their minds as to what is Christian truth. They live apparently in a state of suspense, like Mahomet's fabled coffin, hanging between heaven and earth. Their high souls are not satisfied with arguments which satisfied Butler, and Paley, and Chalmers, and M'Ilvaine, and Whately, and Whewell, and Mozley. Their only creed is a kind of 'Nihilism.'[1] They are sure and positive about nothing. And last, and worst of all, we have myriads of worshippers, respectable church-going people, who have no distinct and definite views about any point in theology. They cannot discern things that differ, any more than colour-blind people can distinguish colours. They think everybody is right and nobody wrong, everything is true and nothing is false, all sermons are good and none are bad, every clergyman is sound and no clergyman unsound. They are 'tossed to and fro, like children, by every wind of doctrine'; often carried away by some new excitement and sensational movement; ever ready for new things, because they have no firm grasp on the old; and utterly unable to 'render a reason of the hope that is in them.' All this, and much more, of which I cannot now speak particularly, is the result of that unhappy *dread of distinct doctrine* which has been so strongly developed, and has laid such hold on many Churchmen, in these latter days.

I turn from the picture I have exhibited with a sorrowful heart. I grant it is a gloomy one; but I am afraid it is only too accurate and true. Let us not deceive ourselves. Distinct and positive doctrine is at a discount just now. Instability and unsettled notions are the natural result, and meet us in every direction. Cleverness and earnestness are the favourite idols of the age. *What* a man

---

[1] 'Nihilism' (Latin *nihil*: nothing): a name given by the novelist Turgenev to an extreme form of Socialism, the prelude to Bolshevism, which was very active in Russia in the 1870s.

says matters nothing, however strange and heterogeneous are the opinions he expresses! If he is only brilliant and 'earnest,' he cannot be wrong! Never was it so important for laymen to hold systematic views of truth, and for ordained ministers to 'enunciate doctrine' very clearly and distinctly in their teaching.

After all, have Churchmen any reason to be ashamed of distinct doctrinal statements? Is the wisdom of the nineteenth century so great that we ought to dispense with sharply-cut truth? Is the good old Church of England a dogmatic Church or not? I answer these questions without hesitation. In spite of all the hard words poured on 'dogma' as effete, worn out, injurious to free thought, unsuited to the nineteenth century, and so forth, there remains a catena of acts in support of 'dogma,' which I believe it is impossible to explain away. In short, there is a mass of evidence which cannot be refuted.

(1) First and foremost, we can turn boldly to our Thirty-nine Articles. Is distinct doctrine there or not? I do not forget that many think very little of that admirable Confession of Faith. Some coolly say that 'nobody really believes all the Articles.' Some tell us plainly that they regard the Thirty-nine Articles as a burdensome stone, and an incubus on men's consciences, and that we should do far better to abolish them, throw them overboard, and be content with subscription to the Apostles' Creed. But all this time the law of the land, and of the Church, stands firm and unrepealed, and every incumbent on taking possession of a living is obliged to declare publicly that he will teach and preach 'nothing contrary to the Thirty-nine Articles.' Yet what are these Articles but a wise compendium of dogmatical statements? With few exceptions they are a series of doctrinal assertions, *carefully drawn out of Scripture*, which the Church regards as of special and primary importance. Where, I should like to know, is our honesty, if we shrink from 'enunciating dogma' after pledging ourselves to the Articles? Where is plain faithfulness to our ministerial engagements if we do not teach and preach distinct, systematic doctrine?

As for those clergymen who hold livings, and retain positions in our Church, while they openly contradict the Articles, or deliberately sneer at their statements of doctrine as 'narrow, and illiberal, and unsuited to the nineteenth century,' I can only say that their conduct is most inconsistent and unsatisfactory. I can admire their zeal and cleverness; but I cannot see that they are in their right place in the pulpit of the Church of England. He that is for no distinct doctrine, no Articles, and no Creeds, in my judgment is no true and loyal Churchman.

(2) In the second place, we can turn boldly to the Prayer-book. Is distinct doctrine there or not? That famous book, with all its unquestionable imperfections, finds favour in the eyes of all schools of thought within our pale, and of myriads outside. You rarely meet with anyone, however broad and liberal, however inimical to Creeds and Articles, who quarrels with our time-honoured Liturgy, or would like to see it much altered. Week after week its old familiar words are read all over the globe, wherever the English flag flies, and the English language is spoken. The older the world grows, the more men seem disposed to say, with George Herbert on his deathbed, 'The prayers of my mother, the Church of England, there are none equal to them!' Yet all this time it is a curious fact that an immense amount of dogmatic theology runs through the Prayer-book, and underlies its simple petitions. He that sits down and makes a list, will be surprised to find what a large amount of doctrinal statements the old book contains about the Trinity, about the proper Deity of Christ, about the personality of the Holy Ghost, about the sacrifice and mediation of Christ, about the work of the Spirit, and many other points. They occur again and again in sentences with which we are so familiar that we overlook their contents. Take, for a single instance, the doctrine of eternal punishment. The question has been raised of late whether the Church of England says anything about it in her formularies. Yet all this time the Prayer-book contains three singularly strong expressions on the subject. In the *Litany* one of the first petitions

is, 'From everlasting damnation, good Lord, deliver us.' In the *Burial Service* we say, by the side of the open grave, 'Deliver us not into the bitter pains of eternal death.' Even in the *Church Catechism* we teach children that in the Lord's Prayer they ask to be 'kept from our ghostly enemy and everlasting death.' Once more I say, he that thinks little of distinct doctrine, and yet uses the Prayer-book of the Church of England, is very inconsistent, and is occupying, whether he knows it or not, a most untenable and unreasonable position. I assert, confidently, that the Prayer-book is full of dogmatic theology.

(3) Let us turn, in the third place, to the whole history of the progress and propagation of the gospel from the time of the Apostles down to the present day. I affirm, unhesitatingly, that there never has been any spread of the gospel, any conversion of nations or countries, any successful evangelistic work, excepting by the 'enunciation of distinct doctrine.' I invite any opponent of dogmatic theology to name a single instance of a country, or town, or people, which has ever been Christianized by merely telling men that 'Christ was a great moral Teacher, that they must love one another, that they must be true and just and unselfish and generous and brotherly and high-souled,' and the like! No! no! no! Not one single victory can such teaching show us: not one trophy can such teaching exhibit. It has wrought no deliverance on the earth. The victories of Christianity, wherever they have been won, have been won by distinct doctrinal theology; by telling men of Christ's vicarious death and sacrifice; by showing them Christ's substitution on the cross, and his precious blood; by teaching them justification by faith, and bidding them believe on a crucified Saviour; by preaching ruin by sin, redemption by Christ, regeneration by the Spirit; by lifting up the brazen serpent; by telling men to look and live—to believe, repent, and be converted. This, this is the only teaching which for eighteen centuries God has honoured with success, and is honouring at the present day both at home and abroad. Let the clever advocates of a broad and

undogmatic theology, the preachers of the gospel of earnestness and sincerity and cold morality, show us at this day any English village or parish or city or district, which has been evangelized, without distinct doctrinal teaching, by their principles. They cannot do it, and they never will. Christianity without dogma is a powerless thing. It may be beautiful to some minds, but it is childless and barren. There is no getting over facts. The good that is done in the earth may be comparatively small. Evil may abound, and ignorant impatience may murmur and cry out that Christianity has failed. But, we may depend on it, if we want to do good and shake the world, we must fight with the old apostolic weapons, and stick to 'distinct doctrine.' No dogma, no fruits! No positive doctrine, no evangelization!

(4) In the last place, let us turn to the deathbeds of all who die with solid comfort and good hope, and appeal to them. There are few of us who are not called on occasionally, as we travel through life, to see people passing through the valley of the shadow of death, and drawing near to their latter end, and to those 'things unseen which are eternal.' We all of us know what a vast difference there is in the manner in which such people leave the world, and the amount of comfort and hope which they seem to feel. Can any of us say that he ever saw a person die in peace who did not know distinctly what he was resting on for acceptance with God, and could only say, in reply to inquiries, that he was 'earnest and sincere'? I can only give my own experience: I never saw one! Oh, no! The story of Christ's moral teaching and self-sacrifice and example, and the need of being 'earnest' and sincere, and like him, will never smooth down a dying pillow. Christ the teacher, Christ the great pattern, Christ the prophet, will not suffice. We want something more than this! We want the story of Christ dying for our sins, and rising again for our justification. We want Christ the mediator, Christ the substitute, Christ the intercessor, Christ the redeemer, in order to meet with confidence the king of terrors, and to say, 'Oh death, where is thy sting? Oh grave, where is thy victory?'

Not a few, I believe, who have gloried all their lives in rejecting doctrinal religion, have discovered at last that their 'broad theology' is a miserable comforter, and the gospel of mere 'earnestness' is no good news at all. Not a few, I firmly believe, could be named, who at the eleventh hour have cast aside their favourite, new-fashioned views, and have fled for refuge to 'the precious blood,' and left the world with no other hope than the old-fashioned doctrine of faith in a crucified Jesus. Nothing in their life's religion has given them such peace as the simple truth grasped at the eleventh hour—

> Just as I am: without one plea,
> But that thy blood was shed for me,
> And that thou bid'st me come to thee—
> O Lamb of God, I come.

Surely when this is the case, we have no need to be ashamed of doctrinal theology.

And now, as I leave the subject, let me wind up all I have said with an expression of my earnest hope that all who wish to be honest, true-hearted clergymen in the Diocese of Liverpool will hold fast their Creeds and Articles, will walk in the steps of their forefathers, and stick to the old weapons which they wielded so well and successfully. Let no scorn of the world, let no ridicule of smart writers, let no sneers of liberal critics, let no secret desire to please and conciliate the public, tempt us for one moment to leave the old paths, and drop the old practice of enunciating doctrine—clear, distinct, well-defined and sharply-cut doctrine—in all our utterances and teachings. Let us beware of being vague, and foggy, and hazy in our statements. Let us be specially distinct and clear about such points as original sin, the inspiration and authority of Scripture, the finished work of Christ, the complete atonement made by his death, the priestly office which he exercises at the right hand of God, the inward work of the Holy Ghost on hearts, the reality and eternity of future punishment. On all these points let our testimony be not Yea and Nay, but Yea and Amen; and let the tone of our witness be plain, ringing, and unmistakable. 'If the trumpet give an uncertain sound, who shall prepare himself to the battle?' (1 Cor. 14:8). If we handle such subjects in a timid, faltering, half-hearted way, as if we were handling hot iron, and we had not made up our minds as to what is truth, it is vain to expect people who hear us to believe anything at all.

Let me conclude this Charge with two special words of warning. They are warnings so closely connected with my subject that I dare not keep them back. They are cautions for the times.

(1) On the one hand, I desire to raise a warning voice against *the growing disposition to sacrifice dogma on the altar of so-called unity*, and to give up distinct doctrine for the sake of peace and co-operation. The tide is running strongly in this direction: we must mind what we are about. Peace and unity are excellent things, but they may be bought too dear. And they are bought too dear if we keep back any portion of gospel truth, in order to exhibit to men a hollow semblance of agreement. The divisions of the Church of England are unhappy and dangerous. They are the strength of Liberationism and the laughing-stock of the world. They are an evil omen. God sees them, and is displeased. When children fight about the candle they are often left in the dark. But for Christ's sake let us beware of trying to heal our breaches by lowering our standard of doctrine, and watering our statements of truth in order to avoid giving offence. To skin over a wound externally while mischief is going on inside, is poor surgery, and not a cure. Let our principle be, '*Amicus Socrates, amicus Plato, sed magis amica veritas.*'[1] Let us be kind and courteous to every one, however much we may disagree with him. Let us not forget Luther's maxim: '*In quo aliquid Christi video, illum diligo.*'[2] But never, never let us compromise and give up one jot or tittle of doctrinal truth. Let us boldly 'declare all the counsel of God.'

---

[1] 'Dear to me is Socrates, dear to me is Plato, but truth is dearer still.'

[2] 'I highly esteem him in whom I see anything of Christ.'

Well says Martin Luther: 'Accursed is that charity which is preserved by the shipwreck of faith or truth, to which all things must give place; whether charity, or an apostle, or an angel from heaven.' Well says Dr Gauden: 'If either peace or truth must be dispensed with, it is peace and not truth. Better to have truth without public peace than peace without saving truth.' Well says Gregory Nazianzen: 'That man little consults the will and honour of God, who will expose the truth in order to obtain the repute of an easy mildness.'[1]

(2) On the other hand, at the same time, I desire to raise a warning voice against *the growing tendency to be dogmatical about things which are not necessary to salvation*, to be positive where the Bible is silent, to condemn and anathematize those whom God has not condemned, and to exalt things indifferent and secondary to a level with the primary verities and weightier matters of the gospel. By all means let us be bold, firm, and unbending as steel, about every jot and tittle of Christ's truth; but let us not cultivate the detestable habit of excommunicating every man who does not see everything, in the '*adiaphora*' of worship, exactly with our eyes, who does not support our favourite Societies, who does not conduct his services precisely as we do, who does not work his parish exactly on our lines. Let us always remember it is possible to be too narrow as well as too broad. For Christ's sake let us make allowances for slight varieties of opinion in non-essential matters. Let us not out-ritualize those who are called ritualists in over-scrupulousness and particularity. Let us not squabble about straws when the Canaanite and Perizzite are in the land, or bite and devour one another, like the wretched Jewish factions in the siege of Jerusalem, when the Romans were thundering at the gates. Never, never, I am persuaded, was the old saying of Rupertus Meldenius so worthy of daily remembrance: '*In necessariis sit unitas; in non necessariis, libertas; in omnibus, caritas.*' In the necessary things of religion let there be unity; in things not necessary, liberty; in all things, charity.

[1] *Morning Exercises*, vol. IV, p. 221.

3

LIVERPOOL AND ENGLAND

The second triennial charge to the Diocese of Liverpool,
October 21, 1884.

M Y Reverend Brethren, by the mercy of God we are allowed to meet together again at the second Visitation of the new Diocese of Liverpool. On this occasion, I have thought it best to assemble all the clergy of the Diocese in one place, to address the whole body at one time, and to give up a second day's Visitation at Wigan. In adopting this arrangement, my chief aim has been to consult your convenience. The area of our Diocese is very small, and it is thoroughly intersected by railways. The total number of our clergy is not large, and to the great majority of you, I believe, no meeting place is more accessible than Liverpool. To this let me add that the arrangement follows the precedent of the Diocese of London. In the visitation of that great See, the whole of the clergy meet the Bishop on one day in St Paul's Cathedral.

A triennial gathering like a Visitation is always a solemn season, and the calling over of names ought to raise in our minds solemn thoughts. Our eyes cannot fail to see gaps in our ranks, and some of us perhaps are reminded of the famous picture of 'The Muster-roll' on the morning after a battle in the Crimean War. The incumbents of Walton, Ormskirk, Grassendale, Garston, Prescot, Skelmersdale, Sefton, Ravenhead, St Luke's, St James the Less, and Christ Church, Hunter Street, are no longer with us. Who can tell what gaps there may be before another three years have passed away? May we all be found ready when our turn comes! It is a comfortable thought that the great Head of the Church 'dieth no more,' 'death hath no more dominion over him.' John Wesley's memorial tablet in Westminster Abbey contains a striking saying, 'God buries his workmen, but carries on his work.'

On an occasion like this, a Bishop may reasonably be expected to say something to his assembled clergy about two great subjects. One of those subjects is the special condition of the Diocese over which he is appointed to preside; the other is the general condition of the whole Church, of which his Diocese forms a part. On each of these subjects I propose to say something today.

I. Concerning *our own Diocese*, I shall have to begin with some facts and figures, which I hope you will hear patiently. But it is impossible to form a correct estimate of the spiritual condition of the district in which we live unless we understand the very peculiar position which it occupies, in many respects, compared with other Dioceses in the land. I desire to use great plainness of speech on this point, because of the many unfavourable and unfair criticisms to which the Churchmen of this new See are frequently subjected. I say without hesitation, that there is not a Diocese in England or Wales in which the Established Church has to work under such *disadvantages and difficulties* as the new Diocese of Liverpool.

(1) Our first difficulty consists in the painful *disproportion between the number of our clergy and the number of souls residing in the Diocese.* The West Derby Hundred of Lancashire, which forms the new See of Liverpool, contains a population of little less than 1,200,000. For this immense mass of people we have only 187 incumbents with Parochial Districts. Let this proportion be compared with that of the six Dioceses which exceed Liverpool in population. In York there are 630 incumbents for 1,300,000 people; in Manchester, 490 for 2,300,000; in Ripon, 490 for 1,600,000; in Worcester, 480 for 1,200,000; in London, 500 for 3,000,000; and in Rochester, more than 300 for 1,600,000. Of course, I have used round numbers. Nor is this all. Out of the

187 consecrated churches in our new Diocese, no less than 137 have been built since the year 1800, and are churches practically without endowment, and dependent upon pew rents and voluntary offerings. As to livings well endowed with rectorial tithes or lands, such as you may find by hundreds in some Counties of England, I cannot find twenty in the whole West Derby Hundred. And, to crown all, out of the 187 incumbencies, the income of at least 100 does not exceed £300 a year; and in many cases an incumbent with £300 a year has 8,000 or 10,000 people, or even more, under his charge! I doubt whether there is anything like this state of things in the Church of England from the Isle of Wight up to Berwick-on-Tweed.

(2) Our next difficulty consists in the *very peculiar and exceptional character of our population*. Outside our great city of Liverpool, there is a most singular and remarkable scarcity of resident nobility and large landed proprietors, who, as a general rule, are the chief supporters of the Established Church. A glance at any county map of the West Derby Hundred will show few of those green spots which usually denote the presence of a landed proprietor. Nor must it be forgotten, that at least three of the largest estates in the district are in the hands of old Roman Catholic families. In Liverpool, which comprises half the population of the Diocese, about one half the people are either Roman Catholics, Scotch Presbyterians, or Welsh or English Nonconformists. It is a notable fact, moreover, that few of the wealthy and successful merchants of our great city seem to be rooted and tied down to Lancashire, and that not a few leading families have left Liverpool in the last fifty years for other parts of England, after an honourable success in business. Their names have disappeared on our Exchange, and they are no longer connected with us.

Beside this, it must never be forgotten that Liverpool is the largest seaport in the world, and that many of our people are sailors of all nations, continually moving and changing, here today and gone tomorrow. Moreover, the north and south ends of our great city contain myriads of people connected with the docks, who are almost always in a most destitute condition, living from hand to mouth in very miserable and poor dwellings, and terribly disposed to give way to intemperance, improvidence, and habitual neglect of the means of grace. I might say something besides about the dense colliery population round Wigan, and the thousands employed in the chemical works at St Helen's and Widnes, if time permitted. But I think I am justified in saying that we have altogether in our 1,200,000 souls a mass of people presenting most peculiar difficulties to the Bishop and clergy of our new See. And I say once more that I doubt whether there is anything quite like it in the Church of England.

(3) Our third, but not our least difficulty, consists in the *conspicuous absence of much of the machinery* for carrying on the work of the Established Church with which other Dioceses are supplied. Next to Archdeacons there are no Diocesan officers more useful to a Bishop than Rural Deans. But of these helpers there are only nine in the Diocese of Liverpool. In York there are thirty-one, in London twenty-five, in Rochester nineteen, in Worcester thirty-one, in Manchester twenty-one, in Ripon twenty-four. We have no endowed Dean and Canons, and the services at the Cathedral in the second city in Great Britain are carried on by the voluntary aid of unpaid Honorary Canons, in many cases with great inconvenience to themselves. We have nothing that can be called a Cathedral worthy of the Diocese up to the present day. When Manchester and Ripon Dioceses were formed, there was a Cathedral in each case ready made to hand. At Newcastle there is a parish church of a size and scale fitting it to be a Cathedral. At Wakefield, when the See is formed, there is another parish church far exceeding anything we have in Liverpool. At Southwell there is already a beautiful Minster. In the whole city of Liverpool there is not a single church which could be made into a proper English Cathedral. We have before us the gigantic work of building and endowing a Cathedral in the midst of a huge, crowded city. I

have no doubt the work will ultimately be done; but it is vain to deny that it is a most formidable undertaking, taxing heavily the energy and liberality even of Liverpool, and constituting a very grave difficulty in the face of a new See. In short, our Diocese is thoroughly under-manned and imperfectly equipped, and its first Protestant Bishop is in the position of a captain of some huge steamship who is suddenly called upon to start a voyage across the Atlantic with half the crew, and half the engineers, and half the coals that the ship requires.

Let no one misunderstand me. I do not say what I have said in a spirit of complaint. I find fault with no one. The state of things which I deplore has been chiefly caused by the commercial skill and prosperity of this part of Lancashire, and the marvellous growth of population which has consequently taken place in the last forty years. I admire the zeal, courage, and liberality of those well-known men who laid the foundation of the new Bishopric. I doubt whether Newcastle and Southwell would ever have been founded had it not been for the noble example set them by those who gallantly led the van in Lancashire. But I have mentioned certain facts because many people in England are entirely ignorant of them, and in their ignorance have expected far greater immediate results from the creation of the See of Liverpool than they had any right to expect. Many seem to have thought that, like the Roman general Pompey who boastfully said that he had only to stamp on the ground and an army would rise up, so likewise a Bishop had only to be sent to Liverpool, and in two or three years there would be nothing left defective in the Diocese. For myself, I never expected anything of the kind. I saw the difficulties before me, and came to my post prepared to face them, and to bear patiently the unkind remarks that would be made. Nor have I at this moment the slightest feeling of despondency. Give the Church of England time, and I believe she will yet do as great things in the West Derby Hundred, by the blessing of God, as any Diocese in the land.

One thing only I must publicly regret about the formation of our new See, and that is the omission, in the Act of Parliament which constituted the Bishopric, of any due provision of patronage for the Bishop. Here again I must gently complain that the position of the Bishop of Liverpool is most exceptional. For the relief of aged and infirm incumbents, and for rewarding young clergymen of 'light and leading,' he has only four livings to give away, and four others of which he has the alternate patronage with the Crown. There is not another Bishop on the bench who is in the same position. Even in the newly-formed Diocese of Newcastle, the Bishop has nineteen livings to give away, beside eleven alternately with the Crown. Some of these livings are of far greater value than any of the four which are in the patronage of Liverpool. The See of Chester, which, by the formation of the Bishopric of Liverpool, was relieved of two-thirds of its population and an immense amount of responsibility, at the dissolution of partnership transferred to our See only four livings, and retained the patronage of fifty! I make no comment on this. Patronage is at best an invidious possession. The mistake has been made, and cannot be retrieved except by a general Act of Parliament, which will probably never be obtained. But I do think it right to mention the subject in this public manner, because I wish my clergy to understand how little I am able to do for them.

I now turn with pleasure from the difficulties and black clouds of our Diocesan horizon to the blue sky of our position. We have some blue sky to turn to. Looking back over the last four years, and knowing far more of the ecclesiastical condition of the West Derby Hundred than I did when I first came here, I see many things for which I thank God, and take courage.

(1) First and foremost, I am deeply thankful for the *general courtesy and kindness* with which I have been received by the Churchmen of the Diocese, both clerical and lay. Wherever I have gone, north, south, east, or west, I have met with kindness, consideration, and readiness to assist me and meet my wishes.

An English Bishop in the latter part of the nineteenth century, of course has his own views and opinions. No sensible man would wish him to be a mere figurehead, without any independent mind of his own, and an honorary member of all schools of thought. It is not desirable that he should be. It cannot, therefore, be expected that he will entirely approve everything that every one of his clergy says or does, or that every one of his clergy will entirely agree with him. The Established Church is eminently comprehensive, and allows all her members an immense liberty of thought, so long as they are loyal to her Articles and Prayer-book. There will always be a considerable diversity of opinion and practice among her clergy, within certain limits. From this diversity the Diocese of Liverpool is not exempt any more than other Dioceses in the land. In fact, I think we have a very large share of free thought on theological subjects in the county of Lancaster, as well as on every other subject, and I do not regret it. But, this being the state of things, I must honestly say that I am very grateful for the small amount of friction and collision in our work which I have seen. We have got on much better than I dared to expect, and I trust that our harmonious action will continue and increase. With all our diversities, I believe we are knit together by a common desire to promote the interests of the Church of England, and as time goes on I trust we shall be still more welded together and united. Union is strength, and disunion a prime cause of weakness in a Church. I am very sensible of my own fallibility, and I always feel that all I do might be done far better. But I hope my clergy will believe that I try to do my duty.

(2) In the next place, I am thankful for the large amount of *solid good work* which is going on in a great proportion of the parishes in our Diocese. Of course there are parishes and parishes, and much more is done in some than in others. But when I look at the quantity of Christian machinery which is patiently, persever-ingly, and habitually kept at work by many ill-paid incumbents of unwieldy, overgrown districts in many parts of this Diocese, I

cannot help feeling that we have great cause to praise God, and I should be ungrateful if I did not publicly say so.

(3) In the next place, I am thankful for the *condition and equipment of the great majority of our places of worship* and the manner in which their services are conducted. I have a right to express an opinion about this. Within the last four years I have been enabled to stand in the pulpits of no less than 150 churches, out of the 187 in our Diocese, either for preaching or delivering Confirmation addresses. I speak, therefore, of what I have seen with my own eyes, and observed for myself. I do not hesitate to say that, although we have few grand churches in an architectural point of view, there are very few in which, through the laudable exertions of the clergy and churchwardens, there is anything of which we need be ashamed.

(4) In the next place, I am glad to say the work of *church-building*, in order to meet the crying wants of our huge over-grown parishes, is going on at a much greater rate than most people suppose. In the four years which have elapsed since the See was formed, I have consecrated nine entirely new churches, viz.: St John the Evangelist, Walton; All Saints', Southport; St Luke's, Southport; St Athanasius, Kirkdale; St Cyprian, Edge Hill; St Andrew, Wigan; St Elizabeth, Aspull; St Ambrose, Widnes; and St Gabriel, Toxteth Park; and two others which have been rebuilt, viz. St Andrew's, Maghull, and St Stephen's, Edge Hill; and three chancels added to existing churches, viz. Padgate, Great Sankey, and Upholland. I have also opened by licence three other large churches, viz.: All Saints', Princes Park; St Mary, Waterloo; and St Lawrence, Kirkdale; which will be consecrated as soon as the repair and endowment funds can be raised. Besides this, four other churches, St Agnes, in Liverpool; Cowley Hill, at St Helen's; St Paul's, Widnes; and St Philip's, Southport, are soon likely to be finished. St Bede's, St Polycarp, and St Philip's, Liverpool; St Benedict's, Everton; St Dunstan's, Earl's Road; and a new church at Ince, are likely to be soon commenced. On the whole, I entertain

a strong hope that, by the end of 1885, twenty-three entirely new churches will have been consecrated since our See was formed. Last, but not least, I may add that since I came to Liverpool as many as eighteen or twenty iron rooms,[1] schoolrooms, or mission rooms, have been opened by licence for divine worship and administration of the Lord's Supper in various parts of the Diocese, and not a few unlicensed rooms, of which I cannot speak particularly. The value of such rooms, I am convinced, is immense. They give an opportunity of gathering together hundreds who shrink from a large parish church, but are quite willing to attend a simple elementary service in a room. I take occasion to recommend, in the strongest way, to every clergyman of a large parish the erection of such a room, in order to attract and reach those who at present go to no place of worship. I am sure he will find it an invaluable auxiliary, and not least because it will enable him to secure the Sunday help of gifted laymen.

To sum up all, I see great cause for thankfulness in the material (or bricks and mortar) work which has been done and is doing during the last four years. Much, no doubt, remains undone. The state of things in particular at the North end of Liverpool is painfully unsatisfactory, and there is a pressing and immediate want of, at least, three new churches and parochial districts in the neighbourhood of the Alexandra docks, within the area of St Paul's, North Shore, Bootle, and Seaforth. I have seen with my own eyes, in the last four years, acres of ground in this district covered over with new houses, while nothing has been done by our Church hitherto to supply their inhabitants with places of worship. I earnestly hope that this want may be taken into serious consideration by the clergy, the landed proprietors, and all who are connected with the shipping interest at the North end. There really is need of a great effort being made by the Church in that quarter, and before another triennial Visitation is held I hope that

---

[1] 'Iron rooms' likely refers to a type of prefabricated ecclesiastical building that was made from corrugated galvanised iron which was popular at this time.

something will be done. Unless some energetic steps are taken, thousands of families will soon be lost to the Church of England, or absorbed by other denominations, or added to the roll of non-worshippers.

(5) The *Ordinations* which I have held since I became Bishop of Liverpool afford me much ground for thankfulness. It is a striking fact that, during the four years ending with Trinity Sunday, 1880, the number of deacons ordained for parishes in the West Derby Hundred, which forms our present Diocese, was only seventy-six. The number of deacons whom I have ordained down to the present day, forming another period of four years, has been one hundred and thirteen, showing the large and remarkable increase of thirty-seven in the number of clergy brought to the service of the Church in this Diocese. To this let me add that there were only 131 curates in the Diocese when I came here in 1880, and now in 1884 there are 170. This again is an increase of thirty-nine. These facts, moreover, become even more noteworthy when it is remembered that we have only 187 incumbents, and that many of them are so miserably underpaid that they find great difficulty in providing any curate at all. I have repeatedly said, and I say it again today, that the first want in a large undermanned Diocese like ours is a great increase in the number of living agents. If any wealthy Churchman wishes to do good service to our Church in Liverpool, I believe he could not possibly do better than to say to some incumbent of a large poor parish, 'I will provide £150 a year for five years to endow a new district if you will form one, or to maintain a curate.' There is room for many more clergy in this great city, and for much work to be done.

I cannot leave the subject of ordination, however, without making two remarks, to which I request the special attention of my clergy. For one thing, I wish to say that I have not the least desire to lower the standard of requirements for the office of a deacon, and I cannot sympathize with those who press the Bishops to bring into the ministry men who know little or nothing of Latin,

Greek, Church History, the story of the English Reformation, the Prayer-book, the Church Catechism, or the Evidences of Christianity, and, in short, are only godly men who know the Bible and can talk about the gospel. I think the office of the ministry demands men of a higher standard than this, if it is to command the respect of the laity, and I cannot see the wisdom of what is called an extended Diaconate. Although Ordination is not a sacrament, it is a very solemn thing; and orders ought not to be lightly conferred, whatever the needs of the Church may be. For my part I am entirely in favour of recognizing and calling forward an order of approved Readers, or lay agents. I think they may be a most useful class of men, and I heartily wish there were more of them. Indeed, if it was clearly legal, I would gladly permit such Readers to conduct short religious services in churches at any times when the church was not being used by the incumbent; provided, of course, that they did not administer the sacraments, and that they did nothing which was not fully approved by the incumbent and sanctioned by the Bishop. I have long been of the opinion that we do not make sufficient use of our churches. To erect a huge ecclesiastical building at the cost of £7,000 or £8,000, and then only use it four or five hours on Sunday, and perhaps four or five more during the week, does not appear to me wise or sensible. I long to see our churches turned to account by a class of approved Lay Readers. But I do desire to maintain in this Diocese a well-trained and qualified class of ordained deacons, and of such men I am glad to say the supply at present is far greater than the demand. My other remark is, that I particularly request the incumbents who give titles to curates to remember that a deacon has to be ordained a priest, and not to require of him so much work during the year of his diaconate that he has no time for reading or preparation. It is a painful fact, which I and my chaplains have found out after four years' experience, that when a deacon comes up for priest's orders he seldom does so well and passes so good an examination as he did when he was ordained deacon, and has evidently not had time to keep up his reading.

(6) The Confirmations which I have been enabled to hold annually during the last four years have been on the whole very satisfactory. The number of candidates presented has steadily increased year by year. In the first year I confirmed 4,719, in the second 5,744, in the third 6,310. In the present year about 5,640 have been already confirmed, and my list is not yet completed. The whole result is that I have already administered the ordinance of Confirmation to more than 22,000 young persons since I became Bishop of a Diocese of only 187 parishes. I can find no words to express my deep sense of the value of Confirmation when it is preceded by proper preparation, and followed by proper attention to the spiritual state of those who are confirmed. Though Confirmation is not a sacrament 'ordained by Christ himself, and generally necessary to salvation,' it is one of the most important ordinances which the Church of England has provided for its members. It gives every clergyman a golden opportunity of becoming personally acquainted with the younger portion of his flock at the most critical period of their lives. It enables him to secure an interest in their affections and consciences, and, by God's blessing, to give a bias to the whole future course of their lives. It often secures for him a continual succession of communicants, Sunday-school teachers, and workers in his parish, to take the place of those who are removed by death or change of residence. Let me affectionately charge you, my reverend brethren, never to relax your efforts to make this important ordinance efficient, and to procure as many candidates as possible for its reception. I am quite certain that far more candidates might be presented every year in this Diocese, if the importance of the ordinance was realized in all parishes as much as it is in some. There are still some large parochial districts in which the number of candidates is most painfully small, and more than one, I am afraid, from which I have hardly ever had a single candidate. This ought not so

to be. The clergyman who really wishes to strengthen the Church of England should remember that the right way to do it is to begin with the young, and one of the best ways of enlisting the young is to persuade them to come forward for Confirmation.

(7) I cannot leave this topic without saying a few words on the kindred subject of *Sunday schools*. I am very thankful for the interest taken about Sunday-school teaching in the Diocese at large. I earnestly hope that this interest may never languish, but annually strengthen and increase. I believe we have on the rolls of our Church Sunday schools at this moment, speaking roughly, about 40,000 scholars and 4,000 teachers. I suspect those numbers might be easily increased by a little more exertion. There never was a time when it was so important to provide definite, thorough, dogmatic religious teaching for the children of the Church at least one day in the week. The State having formally refused to recognize or reward religious teaching in schools to which grants are given, the Church must see to it that the scriptural instruction of the young is never neglected in the day school, and that it receives special attention in the Sunday school. I solemnly charge every incumbent in my Diocese to bestow as much care as he possibly can upon his Sunday school, to do his utmost to procure efficient teachers, and to take care that the time at the Sunday school is well spent, and not frittered away by those well-meaning persons who are content to read weak little story-books, and make children smile. Bible and Prayer-book instruction should always come to the front, and clear teaching about the doctrines necessary to salvation should never be lost sight of.

(8) For the efforts made in the Diocese to check *intemperance, and to promote purity* in all the relations of the sexes, and to watch over the welfare of young women, I am again deeply thankful. They are most valuable and healthy movements, and deserve every encouragement from every inhabitant within the district. Steadiness, trustworthiness, morality, regular habits of life, providence, and a high standard of honour, are the backbone of a

nation's prosperity, and no nation ever prospers in which they are neglected. I am certain that the wealthy employers of Liverpool cannot do a wiser or more politic thing than to encourage by money and influence the existing organizations of the Diocese which promote the objects of which I have been speaking.

I cannot now leave the special subjects of our Diocese without mentioning *three points which cause me much anxiety*, and in respect of two of which, at any rate, I think there is great room for improvement.

(1) The first and most painful point is the *conspicuous absence of immense numbers of people in our Diocese from the public worship of Almighty God upon Sundays*. That this is the case in Liverpool has been publicly stated by Mr Gladstone very recently in the House of Commons, and he said, 'that the state of things here was extremely disgraceful.' I am aware that he had Liverpool especially in view, but I am afraid that the state of Wigan, St Helen's, and Warrington is pretty much the same. Now I need hardly say that it is rather unpleasant to have our deficiencies publicly exposed by the Prime Minister of the first country in the world, in the greatest national assembly in existence, and to consider that his words are reported and read in every quarter of the globe. But I will not complain of this. Intentionally or not, I think Mr Gladstone may have done us good service by giving wide publicity to a startling fact. At any rate, I firmly believe that it is likely to set Liverpool thinking. I do not admit that the state of Liverpool is one bit worse than that of London, and other large towns that I could name, in the matter of attendance on public worship. But I frankly admit that things are not at all as they ought to be, and I have said so publicly and privately many a time ever since I became Bishop of this Diocese. There are certain subjects on which it is very hard to make people awake and open their eyes, and if Mr Gladstone's words in the House of Commons help to awaken us in Liverpool, I shall be very much obliged to him. Let me, however, briefly point out what are the true causes of what the Premier calls 'our

extremely disgraceful religious census,' and then point out what in my judgment are the true remedies.

Let me preface what I am going to say by observing that a census of public worshippers in any town on a given day is no fair test of the quantity of religion in the place. I will never concede for a moment that the Christianity of its inhabitants is to be gauged and measured by the number of heads within the walls of churches and chapels. I am convinced that at this moment there are thousands of the working classes of Liverpool, of both sexes, who are never to be found within the walls of any place of worship, and belong to no congregation, and yet are not destitute of all religion, and would be justly offended if you called them heathen. In some cases, from poverty, they have no good clothes, and have an honest feeling that it is not respectful to go amongst well-dressed worshippers until better times come. In other cases they really do not know what place of worship to attend, are never visited, never invited, and are immigrant strangers unacquainted with Liverpool, who could not tell you in what parochial district they live. Beside this, there are not a few who meet together in unlicensed rooms and out-of-the-way places, under the voluntary teaching of good men and women of a missionary spirit; and no census can take account of such assemblies. In considering the matter before us, I think these things ought not to be forgotten.

One primary cause of the small attendance at churches and chapels in Liverpool is the utter inadequacy of the provision made in the city for public worship. It is not too much to say that if all the inhabitants of some of the poorer parishes in Liverpool were to take it into their heads to go to church next Sunday, room could not be found for a tenth part of the worshippers. When the Established church of a Liverpool parish provides only one building for ten or twelve thousand people, and good Protestant Nonconformists provide perhaps only one or two more, the result is sure to be that thousands of people go nowhere upon Sunday, and stay at home. A religious census in parishes of this kind must of course present what Mr Gladstone calls 'an extremely disgraceful result.' The plain truth is, that in the last two or three generations the Established Church has allowed many districts in Liverpool to slip completely out of its fingers, and a population has grown up of people who are practically no man's parishioners. I declare I know no more pitiable condition than that of a Liverpool incumbent at the north or south ends of our city, with eight or ten or twelve thousand working people under his charge, and an income of about £300 a year. Reason and common sense point out that it is perfectly impossible for such a man to reach the greater part of this population. He has only one head, one tongue, two eyes, and two feet, and with all the zeal in the world he cannot possibly reach or visit more than a very limited number of his parishioners. Numbers of them he will never see, and they live and die comparatively 'let alone,' without any fault of his. In such a parish as this who can wonder if hundreds never darken the door of any place of worship, and are practically without God in the world, and without Sunday worship? These are precisely the sort of parishes in which non-worshippers abound, and in which Mr Gladstone says, with too much truth, 'the religious census is disgraceful.'

But if this state of things exists in a green tree, what may we expect to find in a dry? If the incumbent of a parish of eight or ten thousand people, sound in body, right in heart, and willing to work, must sorrowfully confess, after doing all that he can, that many of his parishioners go to no place of worship, what must be the state of a town parish where the conditions are entirely different? What can we expect when the incumbent is old, or infirm, or a chronic invalid, or pressed down by poverty, and has no curate, and no staff of assistants of any kind? What can we expect when this incumbent, however good or well-meaning, has no original fitness for a town parish, no popular gifts? That there are parishes of this description in our Diocese it is vain to deny. What, I say, can be reasonably expected but an empty parish church, and an immense number of parishioners who go to no place of worship at all upon Sunday? To blame such an unfortunate incumbent is unjust and unkind. With an income of about £300 a year you cannot expect him to resign under the Act, and retire on an income of £100 a year. The Church unhappily makes no provision for a superannuation fund for worn-out incumbents. You cannot expect him, out of his limited income, to pay others for doing what he cannot do himself. In short, in cases like these, the system of the Established Church seems entirely to break down, and the parishioners are like 'sheep without a shepherd.' It would be a miracle indeed if the religious census of such a parish as this was not most unsatisfactory and deplorable, or what Mr Gladstone calls 'disgraceful to Liverpool.'

After all, whatever explanations we may offer, we must not shut our eyes to the fact that a town population, in which the majority never seem to worship God, is a most dangerous class, and demands the best attention, not only of all Churchmen, but of all Christians, all philanthropists, and all patriots. The man who supposes that human nature can be safely 'let alone' and not brought under religious and moral influences, must be a very ignorant person. Men and women who never go to a place of worship on Sunday, and are never reminded of God and a world to come, are precisely the class who are most likely to go wrong, and to be intemperate, improvident, quarrelsome, dishonest, a prey to every mob orator and sedition-monger, and a trouble to magistrates, municipal bodies, and Governments. They form the class too often of which Mr Cowen, M.P. for Newcastle, has lately said:

> Society, ashamed and despairing, sweeps them like refuse into dismal receptacles, where, seething in their wretchedness, they constitute at once our weakness and reproach. How to sweeten these receptacles and help their forlorn occupants to help themselves is the problem of the hour. If society does not settle it, it will in time settle society.

The truth is, that men who are left in ignorance of their duty to God are not likely to do their duty to their neighbours. The Bible, whatever some are pleased to say, is the true friend of order, morality, and peace, and people who never hear the Bible read and taught in church or chapel, as I fear is the case with myriads in Liverpool, are the seed-plot for every kind of mischief, and demand the most serious attention of the upper ranks of society. It is cheap and easy work to say that they may be safely 'let alone,' that England is a 'free country,' and that if the working classes do not like to go to church or chapel we cannot help it, and must stand by with folded arms and let them do as they please! I say, on the contrary, that the non-worshipping myriads of our great towns cannot be safely 'let alone,' and that it is not merely the duty, but the interest of the upper classes and employers to use every possible means to remedy the state of things which Mr Gladstone calls 'disgraceful.'

But what can be done to meet the evils of which I have just been speaking? Let us honestly and humbly accept the facts, and look them in the face. What can be done to diminish the ranks of non-worshippers, and to make the religious census of this great city more creditable?

It is useless to suppose that we can at once double the number of our churches, by starting a great building fund, and cure the disease with bricks and mortar. There is not the slightest probability that money could be found for the purpose. You cannot build and equip a church in Liverpool, and provide for site, repair fund and a very moderate endowment, for less than £10,000. There have been noble-hearted men in Liverpool, who, after making their money in the place, have generously built a church without asking the public for a penny. But the number of such men will always be small. Moreover, it must never be forgotten that it is rather doubtful policy to begin by building churches before people are prepared to use them. To expect a working-man, who perhaps has never been inside a church for ten years, to value the excellent service of our Prayer-book, as soon as it is brought near him, is neither reason nor common sense. You might as well expect a man to begin reading a book, when he does not know A from B.

The true remedy for the state of things we deplore, as I have often said both before and since I became a Bishop, is the multiplication of living agents, and an organized system of aggressive evangelization. If we could only provide a territorial division of our large overgrown parishes into districts of about 3,500 people in each, plant an active energetic clergyman in each of those districts, with a Scripture-reader and a Bible-woman to help him, and commission him to work his district in any way he liked, and in any room, providing only that he will use the most elementary means of grace, and not begin with an elaborate liturgical service—if such a man would only go to work as the Apostle St Paul used to do, and visit house after house and room after room with the simple message of the Gospel, telling the story of the Cross, and approaching every one with love, sympathy, and sanctified common sense—if this could be done, I have not the smallest doubt that in five years there would be an immense change for the better in every part of Liverpool, and that our religious census would no longer be called 'disgraceful.' For I never will admit for a moment that the working classes in Lancashire are not to be won to Christ, if the proper means are used. It is false to say that naturally they are a bit more inclined to infidelity or immorality than other classes. They are all descended from the same parents, Adam and Eve, and are all born with the same hearts and consciences as the highest and noblest in the land. But they are what they are, apparently Godless and non-worshippers, simply because they are 'let alone,' never visited, never spoken to, never dealt with lovingly, as Christ dealt with the Samaritan woman. They are a field which, if rightly cultivated, is capable of bearing a rich harvest to the glory of God, the advantage of the place in which they live, and the benefit of the whole nation.

I am entirely unable to see anything unpractical, Utopian, or Quixotic, in the remedial scheme which I have just sketched out, or anything calculated to interfere with the rights and privileges of the incumbents of the Church of England. The scheme has been tried with great success in the Dioceses of London and Rochester, and I fail to see that that which answers in Middlesex and Surrey should not answer in Lancashire. I should never attempt to carry out such a scheme without the aid of a council fairly and impartially chosen. I should never dream of interfering with the rights of any incumbent, or trying to force the scheme upon him. Many of you will remember that the idea was proposed at our second Diocesan Conference, and received no favour at all. But I have seen nothing whatever to alter my opinion since the date of that Conference. No one has attempted to suggest any better means of coping with the evils we deplore; and I repeat this day, if I stand alone in the matter, that I see no surer way to improve the religious census of this great city. One thing, at all events, is very certain. The expense of the plan would be far less than to attempt to build churches. A single new church in Liverpool, as I have already said, costs £10,000. A missionary curate to work up such a territorial district as I have described, with a Scripture-reader and a Bible-woman, could be obtained for £400 a year. And if we got missionary curates of the right sort, at the end of five years many districts would be self-supporting, after an expenditure of about £2,000. I earnestly charge my clergy to look this matter honestly in the face. I can only declare for the last time my deliberate conviction that, without a multiplication of living agents of the right sort, and an organized system of aggressive evangelization, you will never see the religious census of Liverpool improved, or the great defects of our Diocese cured. And if unfriendly critics would remember that no Bishop on earth can make old incumbents young, or invalid incumbents strong, or poor incumbents rich, or provide pensions for worn-out incumbents, there would perhaps be fewer unfavourable remarks made about the position of the Church of England in Liverpool.

(2) I must now mention another point which causes me considerable anxiety. I refer to *the financial condition of our well-known Diocesan Institutions*. They are not receiving the support which they deserve at present, and are in a very languishing condition. Of course, I need not remind you of the purpose which five of these institutions are intended to serve. They are intended to be central fountains of support to which any one desiring to promote church-building, church aid, or education may apply, and obtain grants. The constitution of these institutions was framed with great care and most praiseworthy pains. The committees which manage them, to the best of my belief, are fair, impartial, and well selected. But the subscriptions and contributions of the Diocese are far below what they ought to be, and are really unworthy of the district in which we live. I commend the subject to the attention of all my clergy. I cannot help thinking that more might be done, if each incumbent annually pressed the claims of the Institutions more earnestly upon his parishioners. But there is an evident unwillingness in many quarters to send money out of the parish for Diocesan purposes, and it is plain that we do not yet work together as a Diocese, but as a collection of independent congregations. At any rate, there is great room for improvement, and, as time goes on, I trust the balance-sheets of our various Diocesan Institutions will wear a very different aspect.

One thing, however, must be carefully remembered. The subscriptions and contributions to our Diocesan Societies must not be supposed to represent the total amount of money contributed by Churchmen to Church objects in the Diocese of Liverpool. It would be ridiculous to think so. Within the four years which have elapsed since the creation of the See of Liverpool, no less than seventy-seven faculties have been granted in our Consistory Court, for the repair, alteration, improvement, or enlargement of old or existing churches, at a total cost of no less than £38,137. Beside this, it may surprise some to hear that during the three years which have elapsed since my first Visitation, the money

expended in this Diocese on church building, church enlargement, schoolrooms, and mission rooms amounts to the large sum
of £145,385; and during the same three years no less a sum than
£98,770 has been contributed to Parochial Charities, Diocesan
Institutions, and Home and Foreign Missions. And all this has
been done in a Diocese of only 187 Incumbencies in three years![1]

I think this ought to be known widely, because there is a vast
amount of misrepresentation on the subject, and unfriendly critics
are fond of saying that the Diocese of Liverpool has done nothing
since the Bishopric was formed in 1880. Facts, however, are very
stubborn things, and the fact which I have just mentioned is one
which ought to be known. It speaks for itself. No doubt we do
less than we might do, and less than we ought to do. But when
the total amount raised for curates, Scripture-readers, and Bible-
women, for the cause of temperance, purity, and education, for
church building and school building, for charitable and philanthropic objects, for sailors, for orphans and for reformatories—I
say, when the total amount is reckoned up, it will never do to say
that the Diocese of Liverpool does nothing at all.

(3) The last subject of special Diocesan interest about which
you will naturally expect me to say something, *is the proposed
new Cathedral for Liverpool*, and I am sorry to say it is a rather
thorny and troublesome topic. The subject, you will remember,
has been formally taken up for two years. At our second Diocesan
Conference, a resolution was almost unanimously passed to the
effect that 'Liverpool must have a Cathedral.' Two years have
passed away since the passing of that resolution, and, as the foundation stone of a cathedral has not yet been laid, the dwellers at a
distance may possibly suppose that the matter has been let drop,
and nothing has been done. Nothing could be farther from the
truth than such a supposition. The subject has been taken up,
discussed, and examined with the utmost care by a committee
of leading Churchmen. How many times that committee has

[1] *See appendix, chapter 3, pp. 427-28.

met, and how much anxious discussion has been devoted to the matter, I will not attempt to say. The outside public knows very little about it. Indeed, few persons appear to have grasped and realized the enormous difficulty which confronted the committee at the very outset of its labours. That difficulty consisted in the selection of a site. To find a proper position for a huge, new ecclesiastical building in a large city like Liverpool, is a problem which might well puzzle the cleverest body of men in the world, and no one has a right to be surprised at the delay which has occurred in coming to a conclusion. The value of land in the heart of Liverpool is so great, and the open spaces so few, that a decision has been extremely hard. The plain truth is, that not a single site could be found which was not open to most serious objections; and the utmost the committee could hope to attain was to find the site which was least objectionable, and combined the greatest number of recommendations. The site which was finally decided upon by a majority of the committee, in St John's Churchyard, behind St George's Hall, is undoubtedly not a perfect site. It is easy to point out its defects. But where can a better site be found, except by an expenditure for buying up buildings and clearing ground, which it is frightful to contemplate? It is quite certain that no available site could be named which is so near the three railway stations, and therefore accessible from every part of the Diocese; no site which is so near to Dale Street, Castle Street, Bold Street, the Town Hall, the Exchange, the Clubs, the Hotels, and all the leading places of concourse; and no site which is so likely to be the centre of Liverpool for all time to come. As to the capabilities of the site for the erection of a building worthy of the second city of the empire, I shall not trust myself to give an opinion. I will only say that it has been declared to be such by one of the most experienced architects of the day.

In cases like this, it is utterly useless to expect everybody to be of one mind, however much we may wish it, and if we wait for entire agreement, the new Cathedral will never be built at all.

At present I can only declare my belief, that the committee have honestly done the best they can in the face of much acrimonious criticism, and I believe the day will come when the public will do them justice. The delay no doubt may seem great, and some may point impatiently to the Cathedral of Truro, which appears on the title-page of so many almanacs this year. But really people appear to forget that there is not the slightest parallelism between Truro and Liverpool, beyond the fact that each is the metropolitan city of a Diocese. The difficulties which are found at Liverpool do not exist at Truro, a small city which altogether does not contain so large a population as several of our greater parishes in Liverpool do, while the whole Diocese of Truro is so well provided with churches, that little new church building is required, and the entire attention of the See may be concentrated on the Cathedral.

What the cost of our new Cathedral will be it is impossible at present to say. There is not the slightest desire on the part of the committee to cramp competing architects by specifying any particular sum. I am certain that the one ruling desire of every member of the committee has been to obtain the best and handsomest Cathedral that could be designed. The anonymous charge, too often made, that either I or any of the committee intended to be content with nothing better than a common-place large parish church, is so utterly baseless that I shall not condescend to notice it. We are distinctly assured by our experienced adviser that there is room enough in St John's Churchyard to erect a Cathedral large enough for all practical purposes, and quite as large as some of the oldest and best in England. I presume that no one would wish to erect a Cathedral with a huge, useless Lady chapel at one end or a Galilee porch at the other, and as long as St Paul's, York Minster, Lincoln, Winchester, or St Alban's.

Whether the money which will be required to build and endow our new Cathedral will be forthcoming immediately, I do not pretend to say. There ought to be no difficulty about it. There are families who have realized so much wealth during the last fifty years in Liverpool, that they could easily put down £100,000, and hardly miss it. It would be a grand specimen of Christian liberality, and of fitting gratitude to the Giver of all wealth, if some Liverpool layman would come forward as Mr Guinness did for St Patrick's, and Mr Roe for Christ Church, Dublin, and break the ice, and rouse emulation by some splendid contribution. But I am quite content to leave the whole affair in the hand of him who has all hearts under his control. If we mean to have a Cathedral, our duty is to begin the work, and, if we do not live to see it completed, to believe that those who come after us will place the top stone upon it. For the present, if we have no very grand Cathedral, we have an excellent Cathedral service, and one of which the Diocese need not be ashamed. For this, I think it right and just to say, we are greatly indebted to the care and pains of the Rector of Liverpool. I only wish the Churchmen of the Diocese would understand that our Cathedral service is entirely dependent on voluntary contributions, and would subscribe more liberally to its support.

II. From subjects of purely Diocesan interest, I now turn to the far wider topic of the *general condition of the Church of England*. Our Diocese, we must remember, is only one part of a great body, and it becomes every Churchman to take an interest in the general condition of the great body to which he belongs.

There are undoubtedly many things in the present state of the Church of England, for which we have reason to be most thankful. There is an immense amount of zeal, energy, activity, and work, which did not exist a hundred years ago. The fetters of black tape appear to be broken, and the Church is not in danger of 'dying of dignity,' or rusting out. The formation of new Dioceses, which is still going on; the general desire to meet the wants of all classes of our increasing population, both spiritual, moral, and sanitary; the widespread effort to introduce more elasticity into the arrangements of our services, the awakened readiness of clergy and laity to meet, confer, and discuss the best modes of meeting acknowledged evils; the immense amount of money contributed in the last forty years to the building and restoration of churches; the universal desire to strengthen the things which remain, and to supply the things that are wanting—all these things, I say, are unmistakable facts, and, however misdirected much of the energy may be, we ought to be thankful. Anything is better than idleness, lethargy, and sleep. Silence and immobility are the symptoms of death. With all her faults and shortcomings, our Church is comparatively awake.

In saying all this, I would not be mistaken. I frankly admit that there are many unsatisfactory points on the horizon of the Established Church in the present day, and *not a few black clouds*. I will briefly point out what I mean.

(1) One black cloud is the continued existence in our midst of *a body of Churchmen who appear determined, if words mean anything, to Romanize the Church of England*, to go back behind the Reformation, to reintroduce the Mass and the Confessional into our communion, and, in one word, to revolutionize our Church. I use the words 'appear determined' advisedly. I know well that the members of this body always deny that they have any such intentions as I have described. If this is the case, I can only say that they are most unfortunate in the use of the language continually employed by their organs in the press. That the movement I refer to will ever be successful I do not for a moment expect; I do not believe that the people of England will ever allow the Established Church to go back to Rome. But I do believe that, unless the Romanizing movement I speak of is checked by the active co-operation of moderate men of all loyal parties within our pale, it will ultimately be the cause of disruption and disestablishment. Above all, I believe that unless the laity can be made to understand that the points which have been disputed before the Law Courts are not mere petty questions about ornaments, dresses, music, and decorations, but attempts to subvert the Protestant principles of the Church, and to reintroduce some of the most dangerous doctrines of Romanism, they must not be surprised if,

in a few years, the whole Church of England goes to pieces. The apparent inability of the laity to realize the immense gravity of the questions in dispute, and the common disposition to trifle with them as mere questions of taste, is to my mind one of the most alarming symptoms of our times.

(2) Another black cloud is the growth and progress in our midst of *a party of Churchmen who seem anxious to throw overboard all creeds, articles, and fixed principles*, and, under the specious names of free 'thought,' 'liberality,' and 'broader views of truth,' to do away with the distinctive doctrines of Christianity. I believe the danger from this quarter to be very great. If the old dogmatic paths about inspiration, the atonement, the work of the Holy Ghost, and the world to come, are once forsaken, it is difficult to see what backbone, or nerve, or life, or power is left to the Gospel which our forefathers handed down to us. To the grand old doctrines I have just named we are undoubtedly indebted for any good which Christianity has done in the world, and I have yet to learn that the modern broad principles which are so loudly cried up in this day have ever done any evangelizing work either at home or abroad, or have produced any real, solid, good result in any town or country on earth. But it is vain to shut our eyes to the fact that the leaven of the Sadducees is silently working among us, as well as the leaven of the Pharisees, and that we all need to be on our guard.

I have seen a picture of American Broad Church Theology of such a graphic kind, in an extract from a Chicago paper, that I think it worth while to copy it in the form of question and answer.

1. *What are the Holy Scriptures?*—A useful book to be read discriminatingly—an authority when it accords with our reason—to be believed when it pleases us.

2. *What is man?*—A creature whose antecedents are somewhat doubtful, who perhaps descended from Adam and perhaps not.

3. *What is human depravity?*—Something in man to be got rid of, but nothing serious.

4. *What is the Atonement?*—A moral influence that makes us think less horribly of God than we otherwise would, and that gives us the highest idea of self-abnegation and self-sacrificing love.

5. *What is the future life?*—A state after death in which every man can have another chance.

Such is American Broad Church Theology! I wish I could believe there was nothing like it on this side of the Atlantic.

(3) One more black cloud is the continued *effort of well-meaning but mistaken Liberationists to effect the disestablishment and disendowment of the Church of England.* This is a movement which I always regard with great pain. I believe the promoters of it are utterly ignorant of the little cause they have to complain of the existing state of things, and of the certain disappointment which would be the result of their success. There are no people who are so entirely free from disabilities, and enjoy such a large measure of freedom, as English Nonconformists. They have a perfect plethora of liberty; they may build where they please, preach what they please, worship God in any way that they please, without any one interfering. There is hardly an avenue to distinction in any profession, or to the highest offices under the Crown, which is not open to them as well as to Churchmen. What more would they have? They tell us in reply that they want perfect religious equality! It is truly surprising that they cannot see that, so long as the immense majority of landed proprietors and men of wealth are Churchmen, so long the 'religious equality' they speak of cannot possibly be obtained. A dissolution of the union of Church and State would certainly not procure it. If disestablishment were to come tomorrow, the Episcopal Church, though separated from the State, would still be by far the largest and most influential body in the country, and as such its members would always take a certain precedence in Parliament, in business, in the learned professions, and in every department of social life. However, I suppose it is useless to dwell on this. It is a painful subject,

and I gladly leave it alone. But I leave it with the expression of my deliberate conviction, that while disestablishment would not injure the Church of England in our great towns, it would tend to paganize our rural districts; and while it would confer no advantage on Nonconformity, it would be most displeasing to that Almighty Being by whom kings reign, and on whom our national prosperity depends.

In spite, however, of the three black clouds which I have just mentioned, I must again repeat my conviction that we have very much to be thankful for in the present condition of the Church of England. When we look over the land from north to south and east to west, we must be blind if we do not see many things for which we ought to be very thankful. We have only to look back a hundred years, and compare the England of 1784 with the England of the present day, and the gloomiest pessimist must confess that in many respects there is a vast improvement. It is no longer thought a fine, manly, honourable, and gentlemanlike thing to swear, or to get drunk, or to fight duels, or to break the seventh commandment. The clergy are no longer content to have one service a Sunday, and the Lord's Supper once a quarter, or to preach sermons which are mere moral essays, and in which Christ and the Holy Ghost are not even named. The lower orders are no longer sunk in barbarous ignorance, unable to read or write, and knowing no recreations much better than bear-baiting, bull-baiting, cock-fighting, and the like. Without controversy and beyond doubt, the whole moral standard of the nation is greatly raised, and we ought to be deeply thankful for it. Of course much remains which is most unsatisfactory, both among rich and poor, and there is great room for amendment. Enormous luxury, extravagance, self-indulgence, mammon-worship, gambling, betting, intemperance, and a perfect idolatry of dress and outdoor amusements, are sorrowful marks of our times. But, after all, the state of the nation must be judged by comparison. Our condition, compared with that of a hundred years ago, affords much ground for thankfulness, and among many improvements in the last century I am bold to say that not the least has been the improvement of the Church of England.

There are, however, three points to which I feel it my duty, as your Bishop, to call your attention. For want of a better name, I must call them *tendencies* or proclivities among the clergy, from one end of our Church to the other, which appear to me to demand very serious attention, because they contain in themselves the germs of much mischief. They are tendencies, you will distinctly understand, not peculiar to our own Diocese, but forcing themselves on the notice of observing persons in every Diocese in the land. On each of them I propose now to make a few remarks.

(1) In the first place, I think there is a disposition throughout the Church to *expect too much from legislation about ecclesiastical discipline*. We all remember that a Royal Commission was appointed more than three years ago in order to examine the whole question of our existing Ecclesiastical Courts, and to offer suggestions for their improvement. That Commission devoted itself to its work in a most praiseworthy manner, and presented a very elaborate Report, containing many recommendations, more than two years ago. I am afraid, however, that a large body of Churchmen expected more from the Commission than they had any right to do. Some appear to have thought that it would settle all the disputed points about what is commonly called Ritualism, which have been the subject of so much angry litigation for many years. Some appear to have indulged in the pleasing dream that we were about to have an authoritative interpretation of the famous Ornaments Rubric, and that not a few of the decisions of the Committee of Privy Council were about to be reversed or modified. I need hardly say that there was nothing to justify these expectations, and that the Commission most properly left disputed points entirely untouched, as being *ultra vires*,[1] and confined itself strictly to the inquiry for which it was appointed.

[1] Beyond their powers.

In short, the notorious disputed points are exactly where they were, and I fear that many people have been bitterly disappointed.

But unhappily this is not all the measure of disappointment. Even the recommendations of the Committee for the reform and reconstruction of our Ecclesiastical Courts have not found universal acceptance. However learned and carefully drawn up, they have met with a great deal of unfavourable criticism. Nothing has yet been done to carry out the plans and suggestions of the Commission by an Act of Parliament, and at the end of two years we are pretty much where we were. Of course I do not mean to say that legislation on the lines recommended by the Commission will not be attempted, and I think it not unlikely that a Bill will be brought into Parliament in order to obtain an Act. But will that Bill be carried? This is a very serious question, and he would be a very bold man who would give an affirmative reply with confidence. Nothing can be done in this day without the consent of the House of Commons, and not everything without the House of Lords. The zealous advocates of church independence may not like this, but so long as the Church of England is an Established Church, they must accept the condition of things, and make the best of it.

Now, will the suggestions of the Commission pass the fiery ordeal of the House of Commons, a House which is proverbially jealous of ecclesiastics, and regards any movement which gives the Church more power with great suspicion? Will the House of Commons allow the Bishops to have a veto on proceedings against any criminous clerk? Will the House of Commons entrust a large amount of judicial power to Bishops, who notoriously have their own private opinions on all the disputed points of the day, and can hardly be called impartial judges? Will the lawyers in both Houses of Parliament ever admit that retired Lord Chancellors and learned Judges are not just as competent to decide what the written formularies of the Church meant her clergy to be, to do, and to hold, as any Bishop on the bench? All these are awkward questions, and I marvel at the offhand coolness with which some

Churchmen answer them. They seem to me to forget that we are living in the 19th and not in the 17th century, in the reign of Queen Victoria and not under the Tudors and Stuarts. We have to deal with a reformed House of Commons, and composed of very heterogeneous elements. We live in days when clerical heads are no longer thought to possess a monopoly of learning and wisdom, and no sovereign would ever dream of making a prelate Lord Keeper of the Seals. The days are past when the laity had an unhesitating confidence in the judgment of bishops and clergy. In short, it is my own firm impression that if a Bill is brought into Parliament drawn up on the lines of the Commissioners' Report, it will probably be very roughly handled, and may possibly lead to very disastrous results. I should not be surprised if, like the Public Worship Act, it went into Parliament in one shape and came out in quite another, or else was so completely altered that the promoters would feel obliged to drop it altogether. As a general rule, the less our Church goes to Parliament for help the better.

In the meantime, where are we? And what is our position? A well-known layman told the Reading Congress last year that the Report of the Commissioners had slain and destroyed the Clergy Discipline Act, and the Public Worship Act; and I presume he meant that those two Acts were laid on the shelf and would never be used again. I can see nothing to justify the assertion. On the contrary, at the beginning of this very year the famous Miles Platting decision[1] supplied unanswerable proof that the verdicts

[1] Miles Platting is a suburb of Manchester. In June, 1869, Sir Perceval Heywood, patron of the living, appointed as incumbent the Rev. Sidney F. Green. Six months later the Rev. James Fraser was appointed Bishop of Manchester. In 1871 it was reported to the Bishop that Mr Green was introducing ritualistic practices into his parish and the Bishop wrote to admonish him. In 1874 the Bishop refused to accept as a candidate for holy orders a Mr Cowgill (nominated by Mr Green to the curacy of Miles Platting) because he seemed inclined to sit loose to Church law. In 1877 the Bishop again wrote to Mr Green concerning ritualistic practices which were still being introduced at Miles Platting, and the dispute between the two carried on into 1878 when the Church Association also entered the fray. As Mr Green persistently refused to give way, the matter went to an Ecclesiastical Court over which Lord Penzance presided. The decision went against Mr Green who eventually, in March, 1881, was committed to Lancaster gaol, not for his use of ritual, but for contempt of Court,

of the existing Courts are regarded by Judges as binding on the Church, that a Presbyter who notoriously disobeys the laws laid down by the present final Court of Appeal may lawfully be refused institution by a Bishop, and, in one word, that the old Courts are not dead, but alive! From that Miles Platting decision, we must remember, there has been no appeal.

One thing is very certain: if the present Courts are 'dead,' of which there is not the slightest proof, we are in a state of complete anarchy, and how long this anarchy is to last no man can possibly say. Some persons, I know, are pleased to call the existing state of things 'a period of truce,' and tell us that we have only to sit still and wait, and that everything is in a way to come right at last. I confess that I am unable to see what they are waiting for, and what there is to justify their serene expectations. It is admitted on all hands that nothing whatever can be done to solve our ecclesiastical problems except by an Act of Parliament, and I can only repeat my deliberate conviction that an appeal to Parliament for relief may produce very awkward results. Perhaps I am mistaken, but this, at any rate, is my present opinion.

My advice to all Churchmen at this critical juncture is to give up expecting much from Parliament, and to try to make the best of our present position. Order is Heaven's first law. The way of patience is surely better than the way of disobedience and threats of secession. The decisions on Ritualism which have been given of late years, and which the Judges evidently regard as binding on the Church at present, may not be perfect, and a day may possibly come when greater liberty may be allowed to clergymen

---

for he had stated his determination not to submit to Parliamentary law in matters ecclesiastical. In November, 1882, on the motion of the Bishop, he was released, Mr Green having decided to resign his living. The patron of the living now presented to it Mr Cowgill whom Bishop Fraser had formerly refused to institute as curate, but he refused to constitute him as incumbent on the ground that he declined to undertake not to continue Mr Green's ritualistic practices. The patron then commenced an action against the Bishop, but in December, 1883, judgment was given in the Bishop's favour, after which he proceeded to present and institute a non-ritualistic candidate for the office. The contest now ended. The whole dispute was of profound interest to Bishop Ryle. On this see *The Lancashire Life of Bishop Fraser*, J. W. Diggle, 1889, pp. 397-426.

on some ceremonial points, so long as they are honestly loyal to the Articles to which they declare their assent at their institution. But the day has not come yet, and till it does come I cannot see the propriety of disobeying judgments, merely because we do not like them, or the Courts which pronounce them. Until it does come it is the plain duty of the Bishops to require obedience to the Queen's Courts, and it is not reasonable, just, fair, or kind, to expect them to sanction disobedience.

No doubt it is easy work for some liberal-minded laymen to say that the Church of England is comprehensive, and that every earnest clergyman ought to be allowed to do exactly as he likes without interference. But surely every wise and thoughtful layman must admit that there are limits to comprehensiveness, and that no corporate body can possibly continue in a healthy state in which the first conditions of membership are habitually broken and trampled under foot. It would be an immense blessing to our beloved Church if all her clergy would cease to indulge in vain expectations, and to strain after sanction for novelties in the administration of the Lord's Supper which do not affect the validity of the sacrament and are not necessary to salvation, and if they would be content to walk in the old paths which satisfied such men as Jewel, Hooker, Andrews, Davenant, and Hall. As for those clergymen who habitually persist in doing things which the Queen's Courts have distinctly condemned, I fail to see how their conduct can be justified, and I wonder how any sensible layman can support them. They place their Bishop in a most painful and awkward dilemma. He must either sanction illegality, and pour contempt on his Sovereign's judicial advisers, or else he must sanction the prosecution of some popular clergyman, and at once be branded and denounced as a persecutor by a public which is always ready to support a defendant. What is a Bishop to do? It is a state of things which is gradually becoming intolerable, and unless remedied, threatens to throw the whole Church into confusion.

(2) The second thing which I regard as a dangerous tendency in these times is a *disposition throughout the Church to attach an exaggerated importance to the externals of public worship.* This is a very delicate subject, and it is extremely difficult to handle it without giving offence, and exposing myself to misunderstanding and misrepresentation. But I dare not turn away from it, and I ask your best attention while I try to lay it fully before you.

No intelligent Englishman of common observation can fail to observe that there has been an immense improvement during the last half century in the conduct of public worship in the Church of England. Dirty, slovenly churches; careless, ill-managed ceremonial; neglect of outward decorum; are no longer tolerated in the Establishment, and are seldom to be found except in out-of-the-way corners. Millions of money have been spent within the last forty years in restoring and beautifying old parish churches. Music and singing receive much more attention than they did in the days of our grandfathers. The organist, the choir, and the hymn-book are more thought of than they used to be. The Lord's Supper is administered more frequently than it once was, and not at intervals few and far between. For all this, I for one am sincerely thankful. If the scaffolding of religion is carelessly constructed, it is vain to expect that the building will be carried on in a workmanlike manner.

But now come some very serious questions which I want to have seriously examined. With all this outward show of religion, is there any proportionate increase of internal reality? With all this immense growth of external Christianity, is there any corresponding growth of vital godliness? Is there more faith, repentance, and holiness among the worshippers in our churches? Is there more of that saving faith without which it is impossible to please God, more of that repentance unto salvation without which a man must perish, and more of that holiness without which no man shall see the Lord? Is our Lord Jesus Christ more known and trusted and loved and obeyed? Is the inward work of the

Holy Ghost more realized and experienced among our people? Are the grand verities of justification, conversion, sanctification, more thoroughly grasped and rightly esteemed by our congregations? Is there more private Bible reading, private prayer, private self-denial, private mortification of the flesh, private exhibition of meekness, gentleness, and unselfishness? In a word, is there more private religion at home in all the relations of life? These are very serious questions, and I wish they could receive very satisfactory answers. I sometimes fear that there is an enormous amount of hollowness and unreality in much of the Church religion of the present day, and that, if weighed in God's balances, it would be found terribly wanting.

For after all we must remember that it is written, 'Man looketh at the outward appearance, but the Lord looketh at the heart.' The great Head of the Church has said, 'This people draweth near to me with their mouth, and honoureth me with their lips, but their heart is far from me.' He has also said, 'The true worshippers shall worship in spirit and in truth, for the Father seeketh such to worship him.' If there is one thing more clearly taught than another in the word of God, it is the utter uselessness of formal outward worship, however beautifully conducted, when the hearts of the worshippers are not right in the sight of God. I suspect that the Temple worship in the days when our Lord Jesus Christ was upon earth was as perfectly and beautifully performed as possible. I have little doubt that the music, the singing, the prayers, the dress of the priests, the gestures, the postures, the regularity and punctuality of the ceremonial observances, the keeping of the feasts and fasts, were all perfection itself, and there was nothing faulty or defective. But where was true saving religion in those days? What was the inward godliness of men like Annas and Caiaphas and their companions? What was the general standard of living among the fierce zealots of the law of Moses who crucified the Lord of Glory? You all know as well as I do. There is only one answer. The whole Jewish Church, with all

104

its magnificent ritual, was nothing but a great whited sepulchre, beautiful without, but utterly rotten and corrupt within. In short, the Jewish Church was intended by God to be a beacon to all Christendom, and I am certain that these are days in which its lessons ought not to be forgotten.

We must not be content with what men call 'bright and hearty' services, and frequent administrations of the Lord's Supper. We must remember that these things do not constitute the whole of religion, and that no Christianity is valuable in the sight of God which does not influence the hearts, the consciences, and the lives of those who profess it. It is not always the church and congregation in which there is the best music and singing, and from which young people return saying, 'How beautiful it was,' in which God takes most pleasure. It is the church in which there is most of the presence of Jesus Christ and the Holy Ghost, and the congregation in which there are most 'broken hearts and contrite spirits.' If our eyes were only opened to see invisible things, like the eyes of Elisha's servant, we might discover to our amazement that there is more presence of the King of kings, and consequently more blessing, in some humble unadorned mission room where the Gospel is faithfully preached, than in some of the grandest churches in the land.

There is nothing like testing systems by their results. Let us ask quietly whether there has been any increase of Christian liberality and spiritual-mindedness in the land, in proportion to the enormous increase of attention to external worship. I am afraid the reply will be found very unsatisfactory. In many cases, the money given by a congregation to help missions at home and abroad, and to promote direct work for the salvation of souls in any way, would be found absurdly out of proportion to the money expended on organist, choir, ferns, flowers, and general decoration. Can this be right? And is this a healthy state of things? Does the annual contribution of money for religious purposes throughout England and Wales, in these days of enormously increasing wealth, bear any proportion to the gigantic expenditure on racing, hunting, shooting, yachting, monster entertainments, dressing, dancing, and the general round of recreation? Yet all this goes on in the face of an immense increase of external religion. I cannot think this a symptom of a healthy condition. I shall never forget what an American clergyman said to me not long ago, when I asked him what he thought of the state of Church religion on revisiting England after an absence of some ten years. He told me in reply that while he saw a great increase of music, singing, and ceremonial religion in our public worship, he could not see the slightest increase, but rather a decrease, of true religion among our worshippers. I have a sorrowful suspicion that the American was not far wrong.

I commend the whole subject to the close attention of all my clergy. I am convinced that it demands the notice of the whole Church of England. I leave it with a few words of explanatory caution, which in a day of abounding misrepresentation I wish emphatically to use. If any one supposes that I want to return to the old-fashioned dry and dull worship of former days, he is totally mistaken. Nothing of the kind! God forbid that we should ever go back to the ancient parson and clerk duet, the miserable singing of a bad version of David's Psalms, and the wretched, tasteless music which satisfied most, if not all, of our ancestors. So far from this, I contend that our services are not 'bright and hearty' enough; for I call no service thoroughly 'bright and hearty' until every worshipper repeats all the responses, and takes part in all the praise, and refuses to leave these things to the choir. But what I do long and desire to see is a just proportion of attention to every part of church worship. And I contend that there is never a just proportion until the pulpit receives as much attention from the minister as the reading-desk and the choir, and until the sermon is just as powerful and 'bright and hearty' as the singing.

The preaching of the pure word of God is declared by our Articles to be the first mark of a healthy Church. It is sound doctrine taught and preached, and not ritual, which in every age the

Holy Ghost has used for awakening sleeping human consciences, building up the cause of Christ, and saving souls. The dens and caves and upper rooms in which the primitive Christians used to meet were doubtless very rough and unadorned. They had no carved wood or stone, no stained glass, no costly vestments, no organs, and no surpliced choirs. But these primitive worshippers were the men who 'turned the world upside down,' and I doubt not that their places of worship were far more honourable in God's sight than in after ages was St Sophia at Constantinople or St Peter's at Rome. It was well and truly said that in those ancient days 'the Church had wooden communion vessels, but golden ministers,' and it was this which gave the primitive Church its power. And when religion began to decay, it was said that the conditions were reversed; the ministers became wooden and the communion plate golden. But I want everything in the English Church in the 19th century to be golden. I long to have everywhere golden ministers, golden worship, golden preaching, golden praying, and golden praise. I want everything in the service of God to be done as perfectly as possible, and no part of it to be scamped, slurred over, done carelessly, and left out in the cold. I charge you affectionately, my reverend brethren, to make this your aim in the Diocese of Liverpool. Let the best, brightest, and heartiest services be always accompanied by the best and ablest sermons that your minds can produce and your tongues deliver. Let your sermons be addresses in which Christ's blood, mediation, and intercession; Christ's love, power, and willingness to save; the real work of the Holy Ghost, repentance, faith, and holiness; are never wanting—sermons full of life, and fire, and power; sermons which set hearers thinking, and make them go home to pray. Then, and then only will the Church of England have its just influence in every Diocese, and God will open the windows of heaven and give us a blessing. The very best and most elaborate services are only means to an end, and that end should be the salvation of souls. All is not done when people have heard beautiful music and singing, and seen the most ornamental ceremonial. Are their hearts and consciences better? Is sin more hateful? Is Christ more precious? Is holiness more desired? Are they becoming more ready for death, judgment, and eternity every week that they live? These are the grand ends which every clergyman should set before him in every service which he conducts. He should strive to conduct it with an abiding recollection of the eye of God, the sound of the last trumpet, the resurrection of the dead, and the judgment-seat of Christ, and not with the petty thought, 'Is my service bright, hearty, and well done?' That these may be more and more the aims of every clergyman of the Church of England in the present day is my earnest prayer.

(3) The last tendency of the times which appears to me to require watching is as follows. I think there is a growing disposition throughout the land, among the clergy, to devote *an exaggerated amount of attention to what I must call the public work of the ministry*, and to give comparatively too little attention to pastoral visitation and personal dealing with individual souls. It is a tendency which I regard with much apprehension, and the more so, because I believe it is a snare to many excellent and well-meaning clergymen, and calculated insensibly to mar their usefulness. I wish therefore to say a few words about it.

There is no doubt that there are far more doors of public work open to an English clergyman in the present day than there were in the days that are past. Weekly lectures, weekly Bible-classes, prayer-meetings, communicants' meetings, Sunday school teachers' meetings, young men's meetings, young women's meetings, children's meetings, temperance meetings, purity meetings, committee meetings, mutual improvement meetings, have multiplied enormously within the last twenty years. It sometimes almost takes my breath away to hear the programme of weekly work which some excellent clergymen announce upon a Sunday from their reading-desks, as the parochial bill of fare for the next six days. As I have listened, I have wondered how any one man, with only one body, can keep so many irons hot, and get through such an amount of work, and do every part of it well. And when I hear, as I do occasionally with sorrow, that such excellent men break down in health, I hear it without surprise. I admire their zeal extremely, but I could wish it was tempered with discretion, and I feel doubts rising in my own mind whether they are using their talents with prudence and proper economy. In short, I suspect there are some who would do more if they would do less, and would do a few things with tenfold efficiency if they would not attempt to do more than flesh and blood can possibly grasp. Three powerful, heavy, crushing blows, making everything go down before them, are surely better than six, feebly and faintly delivered.

But the serious point to which I want to direct your attention is this. There are but 'twelve hours in the day,' and it is clearly impossible for any clergyman to fill up his time with public work in addressing, or operating upon, large bodies of people in large parishes, and at the same time to keep up the old-fashioned habit of efficient house-to-house, family, and personal pastoral visitation. And I must earnestly and affectionately entreat my clergy to lay this matter to heart, to review carefully their own systems of employing their time, and to take heed that they make time every week for a due proportion of systematic house-to-house visitation.

To secure the sympathy and personal affection of parishioners is one great secret of ministerial usefulness. Thousands of people care little for eloquent sermons and powerful addresses, addressed to large crowds in which they form nothing better than an insignificant unit. The way to their hearts is to be found by going to their houses, sitting down by their side, taking them by the hand, dealing with them individually as friends, and exhibiting a brotherly interest in their sorrows and their joys, their crosses and their cares, their difficulties and their troubles, and the births, marriages, and deaths of their families. The man whose minister treats him in that way will hear his minister with tenfold attention upon Sunday, and will say to himself, as the sermon goes on, 'This is the kind-hearted person who visited and talked with me last week, and I am ready and glad to hear what he has got to say.' What 'the masses,' as they are called in the present day, want, and value when they get it, is sympathy and brotherly kindness from those that are above them. I firmly believe that one reason why many of the working classes in our large overgrown parishes never go to church, is the want of pastoral visitation which the unfortunate clergyman, with all the demands of a myriad of people upon him, cannot possibly find time to give. If every working man in a great city like Liverpool could be regularly visited at his own home once a month, and talked to by a friendly, loving, wise clergyman, it is impossible to conceive what an immense amount of good would be done. It was a true saying of that wise man, Dr Chalmers, that 'a house-going minister makes a church-going people.'

I must plainly say that I want to see a return to the old paths. We have gone far enough in the direction of public work. We shall do well to go back to the system of our forefathers. They certainly did less public work than we do, but I suspect they did far more in private. Let us not be ashamed to follow their example. Of one thing I am very certain, and I say it with the experience of forty-three years of ministerial life, and after careful observation of the results of work done by others, both in town and country parishes. It is my settled and deliberate conviction that a clergyman of comparatively moderate gifts, who preaches the gospel and gives a large quantity of his time to pastoral visitation and personal dealing with souls, will be found at the last day to have done more for the cause of Christ than a clergyman of far superior gifts, who, although he preaches the same gospel most faithfully, is only seen in the pulpit, and in the lecture room, and on the platform, but is never seen in the houses of his people.

Let me now wind up this over-long Charge with an earnest request that you will all continue instant in prayer for the Church of England at large, and for your own Diocese in particular. Let us all pray that year after year there may be more charity and brotherly love among the members of our communion. Let us not be always looking at the things wherein we differ, but at those wherein we agree. Let High Churchmen try to believe that most Low Churchmen are not necessarily anxious to become Dissenters, and really love the Church and the Prayer-book quite as much as they do. Let Low Churchmen try to believe that High Churchmen are not necessarily half Papists, and have no desire to go over to Rome. Let Broad Churchmen try to believe that men of other schools may be just as friendly to free inquiry, and science, and the exercise of reason, as they are themselves. Above all, let us all give up the habit of thinking every one is party-spirited who does not agree with us, or of flattering ourselves that we are the only persons who hold no party views. The best of us know everything very imperfectly. Half our controversies are mere logomachies,[1] and arise from the different sense we put on words. No school among us has any monopoly of theological light and knowledge. But if we do disagree, let us disagree pleasantly and without bitterness. If we cannot all be of one mind, and see everything alike, and support the same Societies, and work exactly on the same lines, at any rate let it be a settled principle with us to make the best we can of one another, and to work with one another as much as we can. While there is much to deplore and to humble us in this part of the Lord's vineyard, there is yet much for which we ought to be thankful. When I remember Liverpool forty-five years ago, and call to mind how few clergymen there were in this part of England at that date who made any mark on the public mind, and then consider how many there are among the 187 incumbents of this new Diocese who are doing good work which will stand the fire, I do thank God most heartily. I rejoice, and I will rejoice.

I am thoroughly convinced that there never was a time when there was such an immense door of usefulness open to the Church

---

[1] An argument about words.

of England in every direction as there is at the present day, and not least in Lancashire. If every incumbent in the land was faithful to the principles of his own Church, and always, like Sir Henry Lawrence, 'trying to do his duty'; if every incumbent within the three loyal schools of our comprehensive Church was awake, and alive and stirring in the pulpit, the reading-desk, and the parish, and armed with love in his heart and truth on his tongue; if this was the state of things, I believe the Church of England might safely smile at the attacks of all her foes, and shake the nation for good to its very centre. At present too many Churchmen are but half awake, and do not realize how much there is to be done, and how much they might do if they would go to work in the right way. Our forefathers in the 17th and 18th centuries had no such advantages as we have, no such open doors both at home and abroad, no such help from the press and the steam-engine, no such complete liberty of action. But as for us, we stand on vantage-ground, and countless fields are white for the harvest, while, alas! the labourers are few. May I not conclude all by saying, 'Pray ye the Lord of the harvest that he will send forth labourers,' and grant us a true revival. Let us often use that well-known Collect, 'Stir up, O Lord, the wills of thy faithful people; that they, plenteously bringing forth the fruit of good works, may of thee be plenteously rewarded.'

4

OUR POSITION AND
OUR DANGERS

An address given at the fourth Liverpool Diocesan Conference, 1885.

M Y Reverend and Lay Brethren, I offer you a hearty welcome to our Fourth Annual Conference, and I pray that our proceedings may tend to the glory of God, to the benefit of the Church of England, and to the good of our own souls. We have all need to pray. We must not ignore the fact that we are gathered together in very critical times. I doubt whether the ecclesiastical and political horizon of the country has been so dark for many years as it is at the present day. The Established Church of England, I am convinced, demands the watchful attention, the united wisdom, and the unflinching courage of all her faithful children.

In my Address today I shall strictly confine myself to two points. One is the state of our own Diocese, and the other is the general condition of the Church of England. On both these points I have something to say, as your Bishop, which I am unwilling to defer and leave unsaid until my Triennial Visitation. Events of vast moment succeed each other so rapidly in the present age, and carry with them such important consequences, that the consideration of them cannot safely be put off for three years, as they used to be in days gone by. It is rapidly becoming a grave question whether an annual Pastoral address from the Bishop ought not to supersede the old-fashioned Triennial Charge, and whether the

Head of every Diocese ought not to deliver his mind on the topics of the day once every year. I intend to act on this principle in the year 1885.

I. Concerning *the state of our own Diocese* my report must be a chequered one. There is both light and shade in the picture.

There are some things in our condition which are sorrowful and depressing; there are others for which there is cause to be thankful.

(1) The *financial position of our Diocesan Institutions* continues eminently unsatisfactory. In eighty parishes out of our two hundred no collection is made for them. The total income which they receive from annual subscriptions is far below what it ought to be, considering the wealth of the Diocese. At the same time, it must in fairness be remembered that the whole nation is passing through a period of extraordinary commercial depression, and no place perhaps feels this more keenly than Liverpool. Moreover, it is useless to ignore the fact that, in every part of England, Churchmen do not give money so readily to General Societies, to be distributed at the discretion of a General Committee, as they do to objects close to their own doors, with which they are familiar, and in which they have a direct personal interest. I press that fact once more upon your attention. I proved last year in my Charge, by statistics which cannot be overthrown, that while the contributions to Diocesan Institutions in Liverpool appear extremely small, the total sum of money contributed to Church and School and Missionary purposes in our nine Rural Deaneries is very large.

(2) The *spiritual destitution* of many parishes in our Diocese continues to be a cause of great sorrow and anxiety to me. The want of some provision for the retirement of aged and worn-out incumbents in large town parishes is one of the greatest defects in our Church system, and does great harm in every part of England. The number of parochial districts in the West Derby Hundred in which there are eight, ten, twelve, or fifteen thousand people,

with only one Church, one Incumbent, and not always a Curate or a Scripture Reader, and in some of which, consequently, the Church has no influence at all, is very considerable. At present it seems impossible to supply a remedy, while the commercial depression lasts. Moreover, the number of such districts seems to be increasing rather than diminishing. Plant one leg of a gigantic compass at the Town Hall of Liverpool, and then sweep the other leg round a half-circle from Seaforth at the north to St Michael's-in-the-Hamlet in the south, and any thinking man will see at once what I mean when I talk of spiritual destitution. In Bootle, Kirkdale, Walton, Everton, Wavertree, Edge Hill down to the southern boundary of Toxteth, the report is everywhere the same. Miles and miles of £18[1] houses are continually springing up. These houses are occupied as soon as they are built; and the difficulty of providing means of grace for the inhabitants is simply appalling. Without places of worship provided by the Church of England, and without pastoral visitation, it is useless to be surprised if the dwellers in these new districts are lost to our Church altogether, and many never attend any place of worship at all. Until the means of grace and living agents of the gospel are at least doubled, Liverpool will not cease to be branded, blamed, and held up to public notice, as it was last year by Mr Gladstone, in the House of Commons, as a city remarkable for its number of non-worshippers and Sabbath-breakers. Were it not for the invaluable aid afforded by the Church Pastoral Aid Society, and Additional Curates' Society, I should be tempted to sit down in despair. The debt which Liverpool owes to these two Societies is incalculable.

From the shades of the picture of our Diocese, which it is vain to conceal, I gladly turn to the lights, and I am thankful to say that they are not few.

(3) The *building of new churches*, notwithstanding the diminished profits of trade, goes on in a very satisfactory way. I have

---

[1] House rented at £18 per annum (7/ [shillings] per week).

consecrated no less than four churches in the last twelve months, making twelve in all which I have consecrated since I came to the Diocese, viz.:—Maghull; St John, in Walton; St Athanasius, in Kirkdale; All Saints', Wigan; Farnworth; St Cyprian; Aspull; Crossens; St Gabriel's, Toxteth Park; All Saints', Prince's Gate; St Agnes, Sefton Park; and St Chad's, Everton. Besides these twelve, there are four large churches open by licence, and only waiting for the Endowment and Repair Fund to be made up in order to be consecrated. These four are St Mary, Waterloo; St Lawrence, Kirkdale; Cowley Hill, St Helen's; and Widnes. Four other churches are being built, and likely to be finished in the beginning of next year, viz.:—St Bede's, Hartington Road; St Philip's, Sheil Road; St Polycarp's, Everton; and St Philip's, Southport. Three others are about to be commenced immediately: St Dunstan's, Earle Road; St Benedict's, in Everton; and a new church in Ince, near Wigan. From what I know of the promoters of these three last churches, I feel confident that they will soon be built. Besides this, there are already two districts marked out, and temporary churches licensed and in full operation, in Walton. I refer to St Luke's, and St Simon and St Jude's.

All this, I know, is only a talc of bricks and mortar. But it is a talc that means a great deal. Every new church added to the list in our Diocese means a new Incumbent, very often a new Curate, a Sunday School, and a whole train of organized Christian machinery. Every one of the twenty new churches I have named, reckoning up the cost of site, fabric, fittings, warming, architect, endowment, repair fund, and fencing round, represents an average expenditure of at least £7,000 or £8,000, and is a solid proof that the Voluntary system can do something within the pale of the Establishment. Above all, it proves that the Churchmen of our Diocese are not asleep, but awake, and that even in troublous times of commercial depression we are building the walls of our Zion. As Bishop of the Diocese, I feel it a plain duty to express publicly my gratitude to those who have promoted, and are promoting, the church building which I have just described, and I earnestly hope that others may be stirred up to follow their example. Two more large churches and parochial districts are wanted at this moment in Bootle, owing to the immense increase of population caused by the Alexandra docks. Would to God that it might be put into the heart of some one to come forward and offer to build, after the magnificent example of more than one Liverpool family which I could name! There are not a few who could easily do it, and would never miss the money. The pressing want of more clergymen and more means of grace in that district is the greatest blot in our Diocese. A guarantee of £500 a year for five years would soon procure two clergymen to work up two provisional parishes, and with two right men I believe we should soon get two churches.

(4) Another area of light in the picture of our Diocese, to which I have pleasure in directing your attention, is the *annual increase in the number of young persons who are presented to the Bishop for confirmation*. In the first year of my Episcopate the sum total, in round numbers, was 4,700. By the end of the present year I shall have confirmed about 6,700. This return, from a Diocese of only 200 Incumbents, speaks for itself. I am aware that numbers alone do not prove everything, and that the quality of candidates is much more important than the quantity. But the annual increase of which I speak is, at any rate, a plain proof that young persons are more looked after than they once were, and that the clergy of this Diocese are obtaining more influence for good among the junior members of their congregations. About the immense value and importance of the ordinance of Confirmation, and of the previous preparation for it, I can add nothing to what I have frequently said. I believe it to be the right arm of the Church of England, and a means of usefulness second only to preaching and the sacraments. I trust that every year will see a regular increase of the numbers confirmed. There is still room for great improvement, and the presentations from some large parishes are painfully small.

(5) Another bright point in our Diocesan picture is the greatly *increased number of candidates for ordination*, and consequently the growing number of clergymen added to the staff of the Church. In the five years preceding 1880, the number of Deacons ordained for the West Derby Hundred was ninety-two. In the last five years I have ordained 152. I do not, of course, forget that some anonymous writers have thought fit to speak in very slighting terms of the character of the Deacons who obtain titles, and are now ordained in this Diocese. I regard such attacks with complete indifference, as they only exhibit the ignorance of those who make them. I believe the Examining Chaplains of this Diocese are second to none in England in intellectual calibre and capacity for their work, that the standard of attainment required in candidates is not inferior to that of any northern Diocese, and that the examinations are conducted with perfect fairness and impartiality. If any one supposes that all candidates for ordination in this Diocese are accepted and ordained as a matter of course, like Jeroboam's priests, and that no one is ever rejected, I will only remark that he is totally and entirely mistaken. Not a few candidates in the last five years have found that out to their sorrow. No doubt our candidates are not all Cambridge Wranglers and Oxford first-class men, any more than they are in any Diocese; and districts like Lancashire are not so popular with young men as Middlesex, Kent, Surrey, Sussex, Herts, and the sunny South. But if any one means to say that the great majority of our Deacons are below the level of other Dioceses, and are not hard-working, useful clergymen, I tell him he will find it hard to prove what he says. After all, whatever may be said, the broad fact remains that Curates cannot be ordained without titles for orders, and the large annual increase in the number of men ordained here is a clear proof that the Incumbents are taking more pains to add to the number of living agents in their parishes, and that more ministerial work is annually done in the Diocese. For this, as the Bishop of a new Diocese which labours under great disadvantages, I feel extremely thankful.

I could mention other bright points in our position, if time permitted. The solid, steady work done by the Scripture Readers' Society, the Bible Women's Society, the Church of England Temperance Society, the Voluntary Lay Helpers' Society, the Sunday School Institute, and many of the Voluntary Schools in very poor districts, is beyond all praise. It is work done quietly, noiselessly, without any blowing of trumpets or flourishing of banners. The Diocese of Liverpool keeps no trumpeter, and we labour on '*sine vate sacro.*'[1] But it is work which will tell in the long run, and year by year is strengthening the Church of England. From all this, however, I must turn away to a subject of even more pressing importance, and that is the general position of the whole Church of England, of which our Diocese only forms a part.

II. Concerning *the general condition of the whole Church of England* there is much cause for anxiety. It is vain to shut our eyes to the fact that we live in very critical times. Men of all ranks, classes, and shades of opinion seem to agree about this. I know not what you may think, but I am thoroughly convinced myself that the Established Church has arrived at a great crisis in her history, and that it behoves all her children to mind what they are about, to keep their powder dry, and to be ready for any emergency. I shall make no apology for seizing the opportunity which this Conference affords, and for laying before you a few observations which I commend to your special attention. In so doing I shall have to touch some vital questions, and to handle some burning subjects which at any other time I would gladly leave alone. But we have reached a point when I think a Bishop must speak out, or for ever hold his peace. The ship is among breakers, and the captain must not stand on ceremony in the use of language. Events move so rapidly nowadays that he who keeps silence may never have another opportunity of speaking out, and I shall therefore make no excuse for using 'great plainness of speech,' both about our Church's perils and our Church's preparedness to meet them.

[1] Without a holy prophet.

119

Let me begin by reminding you that the Established Church of England is going to be brought face to face with one of the greatest political changes which this country has ever gone through for at least two centuries. I refer, of course, to the recent Act of Parliament[1] by which the Franchise has been greatly lowered, the number of electors to Parliament greatly increased, and the whole power of choosing representatives and creating a House of Commons has been placed in the hands of an immense number of persons who never possessed this power before. Now what will be the consequence of this change? What kind of men will the new representatives be in the third estate of the realm? What kind of legislation may we expect? I cannot find anybody who pretends to give an answer to these questions, or can do more than guess and conjecture. Most wise men seem to agree in thinking that our country is about to take 'a leap in the dark.' Even foreigners are looking on with amazement. One thing only is perfectly certain, and that is, that in these days the House of Commons has all power in its hands. Let me quote the words of a well-known writer not long taken from us. He says: 'When De Tocqueville, the famous Frenchman, was standing in the House of Lords, on the steps of the throne, on the occasion of the opening of a certain Parliament, he watched in silence the gathering of the Peers in their scarlet robes, the entrance of the Ministers in their official uniforms, the appearance of the Sovereign in royal magnificence; but when he beheld the Commons rushing to the bar in their plain unadorned everyday dress, he exclaimed, "*Voila le maitre*" (there comes the master). He seemed to say that the day was come in the nation as in a household, when it is the servants only who appear in livery, while the real master stands above formalities.' That witness is perfectly true. It was true in the days of the shrewd Frenchman. It is much more true in 1885.

---

[1] The Parliamentary Reform Act of 1884 completed universal manhood suffrage, and raised the number of voters in the United Kingdom from about 3 millions to about 5 millions.

And what kind of subjects is the newly-coined House of Commons likely to take up? You have only got to read the newspaper reports of political meetings, and the speeches made by candidates for Parliament, and you will soon get an answer. There is nothing too monstrous or extravagant to be propounded by some aspirants for a seat. The wildest schemes are in the air, and the most sweeping changes are coolly talked of as possibilities, if not probabilities. The desirableness of getting rid of the monarchy, the House of Lords, the landlords, the navy, and the army, is quietly discussed. Preposterous schemes of political economy, under which everybody is to be rich and nobody is to be poor; everybody is to have a certain quantity of land, but nobody is to have much; the rich and the successful in business are to pay all the taxes, and those who are not rich or successful are to pay none; schemes which would infallibly discourage every man from taking pains to get on and prosper, and would ultimately drive all capital out of the country—such schemes as these are deliberately presented to the public ear, and those who propound them get a hearing. It was a wise saying of the 'judicious' Hooker, that the man who tries to persuade people that they are not governed as well as they might be, will never lack hearers. But if the future House of Commons is to contain many members who hold such opinions as those I have just tried to describe, it is perfectly certain that an ancient endowed institution like the Established Church of England will soon be fiercely attacked, and will have to struggle hard for her existence, if indeed she is allowed to exist at all.[1]

But unhappily this is not all. It is folly to shut our eyes to the fact that the Disestablishment and Disendowment of the Church of England already form a subject which is continually brought forward on almost every political platform in the land, from the Isle of Wight up to John o' Groat's House, and from the Land's End to the North Foreland. The Liberationist party, so called, have inaugurated a regular crusade against the Establishment, and one

[1] *See appendix, chapter 4, p. 428.

of the stock questions put to candidates for seats is this: 'Are you prepared to vote for the Disestablishment and Disendowment of the Churches of England and Scotland?' The meaning of that question, in plain English, is this: 'Are you prepared to vote for depriving the Church of her property, for placing the Church of England on a level with all the other Churches and sects in the country, and for entirely dissolving any connection between the State and religion?' To this question I observe many candidates reply, 'Yes.' Many others fence with it, and say it is not a question of practical politics at present. But only a few comparatively say boldly, 'No.' In fact, the subject of Disestablishment is upon us whether we like it or not, and it is high time for every Churchman to open his eyes, and wake up and consider seriously what he is about to do. 'The Philistines are upon thee, O Samson.' The well-known words of Nelson should be remembered, 'England expects that every man will do his duty.'

Now it is useless to tell us that there is no danger, and that we are crying 'Wolf, wolf!' when there is nothing to fear, and no cause for alarm. It is too late for this. A voice has lately spoken to which we cannot afford to turn a deaf ear. In a recent elaborate manifesto, that remarkable statesman, Mr Gladstone, has spoken plainly about Disestablishment as 'a possibility' which we may have to face before many years have passed away. No doubt he has touched the question vaguely and briefly. He has not explained whether he means that the Government of this country shall cease to acknowledge religion. He has not told us whether our future monarchs are to be crowned in Westminster Abbey with prayer or not, and if so, whether that prayer is to be offered up by a Protestant or a Roman Catholic, an Episcopalian or a non-Episcopalian, a Christian or a Jew. But it is quite evident that he contemplates the possibility of Disendowment accompanying Disestablishment, and he darkly hints at 'the vigour' of the Voluntary system. He has not said a word about the justice or honesty of seizing the Church's property, and applying it to secular purposes. Nor has he explained how the clergy in rural districts, already pauperized by agricultural depression, are to live when deprived of the tithes. All these things he has left in the dark. But he has said quite enough to whet the appetite and strengthen the hands of our Liberationist assailants. In short, Achilles has appeared, and come forth from his tent, and lifted up his voice. No man living can tell what this impulsive Statesman may do next. He suddenly turned on the Irish Church, and disestablished it, before some of our Hibernian brethren had time to awake. He may suddenly try to do the same with the English Church, under pressure of influence from beneath. At any rate, he has given us warning, and if we do not beat to quarters, clear the decks, throw lumber overboard, and prepare for action, we are fools or madmen, and given over to judicial blindness. The enemy's ship may be hull-down at present, so that we can scarcely see her royals above the horizon. But the enemy's ship is rising fast, and may be alongside of us sooner than we think.

Concerning the immense amount of harm which Disestablishment and Disendowment would do, if their advocates succeeded, I will not weary you with words. In fact, you all know what my mind is, if you read the papers on the subject which I felt it my duty to send to every Incumbent in this Diocese not long ago. I stand to every sentence which those papers contained, and withdraw nothing. I believe that no man living can realize the amount of damage which Disestablishment would do, not merely to the Church of England, but to the cause of Christ throughout the world, the cause of morality and philanthropy in our own land, and to the cause of unity and peace among English professing Christians. It would shut up two-thirds of our rural churches, or at any rate withdraw two-thirds of the rural clergy from their present position. Stripped of their tithes they could not live; and the population of our country parishes in many cases would be left unvisited, and without means of grace. It would cripple all our Missionary Societies, shut up most of our

Voluntary schools, and dry up many sources of benevolence by which our isolated rural poor are often civilized, humanized, and comforted. If any system has ever proved a dead failure, it is the operation of the Voluntary system in rural districts. And against this immense amount of damage there is next to nothing to set off. Nonconformists, after Disestablishment, will be unable to do anything they cannot do now, for they have already a plethora of liberty to build, and preach, and proselytize as much as they please. Unity and brotherly feeling between Churchmen and non-Churchmen will certainly not be increased by taking away the Church's endowments and pauperizing her clergy. The much-coveted equality between Episcopalians and non-Episcopalians will certainly not be produced so long as Episcopalians comprise within their ranks the immense majority of the upper classes. It would never come unless our Rulers ordered people to 'boycott' all Episcopalians, and made it penal to use a Prayer-book.

And behind all these things there remains a point of far higher and deeper importance. The State will risk incurring the displeasure of Almighty God, on whom alone our prosperity depends, when she deliberately chooses to ignore Christianity, and to have her monarchs crowned without any religious ceremonial, and her Parliaments opened without prayer. Whether our unhappy sister country of Ireland has derived the slightest benefit from the Disestablishment of the Protestant Church is a question which I leave any sensible man to decide. Most men tell me that her internal condition, both socially and politically, has been worse, since the so-called Upas tree[1] was cut down, than it ever was before.

Now, concerning the paramount duty of resisting the Disestablishment movement to the bitter end, I hope we are all of one mind. I know there are some enthusiastic Churchmen here and there who fancy that freedom from State control would

---

[1] Gladstone had formerly compared evils in Ireland to the branches of the (supposedly poisonous) Upas tree of the tropics.

be a real benefit to the Church of England. They have pleasing visions of a free, rich, and powerful Church, no longer fettered by connection with the State, guided by perfect Bishops, no longer interfered with by naughty Parliaments and wicked Courts of law, possessing perfect unity, and able to do a hundred things which it cannot do now. These amiable enthusiasts would soon find, if they had their own way, that a Free Church is a fine thing to talk about, but not so free as it appears. There are other chains and screw-presses beside those of Parliament, secular Law Courts, and the Royal supremacy. The frogs in the fable found King Stork far worse than King Log. When I hear an English Churchman expressing a wish for Disestablishment, I always think of the famous epitaph which said: 'I was well; I would be better; I took physic, and here I am.'

I trust, however, that the vast majority of English Churchmen will turn away from such delusions, and will resolve to do their utmost to prevent the Church of England being disestablished. But I warn my brother Churchmen that we must gird up our loins like men, and prepare for a severe struggle. It will never do to rest supinely on our oars, and let the question drift, and proclaim that 'we never meddle with politics.' I tell the clergyman who talks in that way that, if he does not take care, politics will meddle with him, turn him out of his house, and strip him of his income. I call upon him to remember that it is his primary and bounden duty to spread accurate information about the Church of England, and to furnish his people with correct replies to the gross misstatements that Liberationists are continually making about the Church of England. The number of such misstatements is simply amazing, and they would be ridiculous if they were not calculated to be most mischievous to ignorant minds. It is a shame for any man to circulate them, and a discredit to any man to believe them. The Church has nothing whatever to fear from the most searching examination of her constitution and the amount of her revenues. All she asks is, that people should know the truth about her much-abused connection with the State, and not lightly believe everything that is said, printed, and circulated about it. It was a wise remark of the late Archbishop Tait, when he said, in 1881: 'We must no longer overlook the attempts which are certainly now being systematically made in many neighbourhoods to pervert the judgment and alienate the loyal regard of our people.' It was an equally wise and very practical remark of the present archbishop of Canterbury, only a few weeks ago: 'Every clergyman should consider himself bound by his office to diffuse the truth by books, lectures, papers, conversation, and to ask all Church thinkers, and students, and practical men to help him.' You may depend upon it, if you wish to defend the Church, this must be done, and done without delay. Information, information, information is the first weapon that must be used if we want to defend the Church.

I must turn, however, from this branch of Church Defence to another, which appears to me of equal, if not superior, importance. If we wish to resist the Disestablishment movement successfully, we must set our own house in order. We must resolve that Church Reform shall accompany Church Defence. We must try to rectify known abuses, to stop the sale of livings, to revive ecclesiastical discipline, to simplify our Prayer-book services, to proportion revenues to duties, to provide pensions for aged or infirm clergymen, to organize a system of aggressive evangelization for overgrown or neglected parishes, and to give the laity their rightful place in all the councils of the Church, both great and small. And above all, we must close our ranks, and take care that we have no weak points in our position. You may depend upon it, it is useless to talk of Church defence if we neglect this obvious duty. The famous lines of Torres Vedras would never have kept the French out of Portugal, if the Duke of Wellington had left any part of them open and unde-fended. Our military squares in the Sudan campaign would never have been entered by the Arabs if they had been closed up, and had had no gaps left at the corners. The strongest chain in the world is no stronger than it is at some weak or defective link. Now, have we no weak points in the Church of England? Have we no gaps in our 'square'? I fear that we have some very serious ones, and unless they are rectified we shall suffer greatly in the day of battle, even if we escape defeat. I must say that I should like to see a rather humbler tone among some of our Church defenders, and a greater readiness to confess that our good old Church has some imperfections and defects. Let me try to explain briefly what I mean.

1. The first, worst, and weakest point in the position of the Established Church consists in *its most unhappy divisions*. If we would set our house in order, we must begin there. You need not be afraid that I am going to weary and worry you with controversial details about gestures, and postures, and vestments, and music. I will simply put one great broad fact before you in its naked simplicity, and ask every wise man to judge for himself whether we are not most sadly divided. I find, then, that at the annual meeting of a great religious Society, which was held in London last June of this very year, the President, at the conclusion of a long and carefully prepared speech, used the following words: 'We must strive for union, especially with the great Latin Church from which we were separated by the sins of the 16th century.' I quote these words from the report of the *Church Times*, which was probably revised. The report of another paper differs slightly, and is as follows: 'The restoration of visible unity with the members of the Church abroad, east and west alike, but above all with the great Apostolic See of the West, with the holy Roman Church, which has done so much to guard the true faith—these surely should be our objects, and the objects nearest our hearts.' Whichever report you take, I call that very ominous and painful language indeed. I have no doubt that Lord Halifax, who spoke these words, is a devout and honourable man, though he is not like the Lord Halifax who led the cheering when the Seven Bishops were acquitted in Westminster Hall two hundred years ago. But, of course, we all know that 'the Latin Church' means the Church of Rome, and the 'sins of the 16th century' mean the Protestant Reformation. Now, I find that the

Society which he addressed, the English Church Union, includes among its members no less than 2,600 clergy and 20,000 laymen, and has branches and ramifications from one end of the land to the other. I find, moreover, that the noble President, who used this language, and is, of course, the mouthpiece and representative of these 2,600 clergy, was heard without the slightest objection being made, and I cannot find that his sentiments have ever been repudiated down to the present day. In the face of a fact like this, I ask any one of common sense whether it is possible to deny that our Church is most painfully divided. To shut our eyes, and say, 'We see no divisions,' is the height of folly, and something like judicial blindness. Timid Churchmen may say 'Hush!' but the divisions remain.

I shall not plead guilty to the vulgar charge of narrow-mindedness and illiberality. On the contrary, I have always maintained, and have been bitterly blamed for maintaining, that our Church is eminently comprehensive, and that High, Low, and Broad schools were meant to find room within her pale. But I must contend that there are limits to her comprehensiveness, and those limits seem to me most painfully and dangerously exceeded by the words of the President of the English Church Union. In short, unless the Society disavows them, or explains them away, it is sheer nonsense to say that we are not divided. It is perfectly notorious that there are thousands of English clergymen and laymen who glory in the Protestant Reformation, who abhor the very idea of reunion with the Church of Rome, and who would rather see the Church disestablished than see it give up its Protestant principles. By no ingenious policy of toleration, compromise, or comprehensiveness, can you ever make the members of two such diametrically opposite schools of thought work harmoniously together. There is a yawning gulf between them, and to sing, as we often do,

> *We are not divided—*
> *All one body we.*

is to sing what is not only incorrect, but most painfully untrue.

In short, we are about to join battle with outward enemies, with an army rent by internal divisions; and if we do not come ultimately to grief it will only be by the miraculous interposition of a merciful God. 'The Scripture cannot be broken.' The words of our Lord are just as true now as they were 1,800 years ago: 'A house divided against itself cannot stand.' I leave the matter here for your own private consideration, and your private prayers. If this is not a weak point in our position, I know not what is. It cannot be concealed. Our enemies know it well, and are sure to make capital out of it. We ought to compass sea and land, and leave no stone unturned to obtain more unity. In order to obtain it we ought to be ready to sacrifice many private tastes, and to concede much, provided always that we do not sacrifice God's truth on the altar of a so-called peace. But unless we can heal our divisions we may stave off defeat in the House of Commons for a few Sessions, but sooner or later we shall be beaten.

2. The second weak point in the position of our Established Church is a very serious one. I refer to the widespread spirit of lawlessness and disobedience to authority which prevails throughout our ranks. You need not suppose that I am going to drag you through the thorny jungle of ecclesiastical suits, whether past or present. I am not even going to say who I think has been right and who wrong in any of those suits. I shall simply call your attention to the following undeniable facts. It is a fact that certain practices in the administration of the Lord's Supper have been declared illegal by the Queen's Courts, after careful argument and investigation. It is a certain fact that until the decisions of these Courts are either reversed, or declared null and void by Act of Parliament, they are practically the law of the land. It is a certain fact that if you go to the Temple or Lincoln's Inn, any lawyer would tell you that these decisions, whether good or bad, are binding on all clergymen, and ought to be obeyed. It is a certain fact that in the famous Miles Platting case it was ruled by the Judge that these decisions were law, and from the judgment given on that occasion

there was no appeal. But what is the state of things in every part of England? In the face of the facts I have just mentioned, the very practices which have been declared illegal are habitually carried on by hundreds of clergymen throughout the land, and approved by thousands who do not adopt them. Nor is this all. These very illegalities are tolerated, sanctioned, and not interfered with, and any one who tries to interfere with them is violently denounced and blamed. Now, if this is not 'lawlessness' I know not what is. It is a state of things which is not allowed for a moment in any other profession, in the army or the navy, among medical men, or at the bar. In short, it is complete anarchy and chaos; and discipline is dead. The only rule appears to be that of the times of the Judges, and every clergyman is to 'do that which is right in his own eyes.' As for the unfortunate Bishops, who are bound by their office to see that the Royal supremacy is maintained and the Queen's laws are respected in their dioceses, their position is most pitiable. If they sit still and do nothing, and look on with folded arms, they are blamed. If they allow any steps to be taken to check illegality, they are blamed again. Blamed, did I say? The phrase is euphemism indeed! That word is far too weak to convey an idea of the fierce, violent, insulting language which is poured on the devoted heads of Bishops, by the extreme writers on both sides. Whatever they do they are wrong.

Worst of all, there does not appear to be the slightest prospect of any remedy or change for the better. The very people who tell us that the Law Courts are bad Courts, and their decisions worthless, are making no attempt to get the decisions reversed, or the Law Courts reformed. No Peer, no member of the Lower House of Parliament, brings in a bill for the creation of better Courts, or for the amendment of the Clergy Discipline and Public Worship Acts. The Royal Commission which reported three years ago has proved as completely abortive as the Commission on Ritual. The whole subject seems at a deadlock. The Church appears to go on year after year fumbling, and dawdling, and wrangling, and squabbling, and pamphleteering, and waiting for a 'convenient season,' and nothing is done. '*Rusticus expectat dum defluat amnis.*'[1] The only certain fact that remains is this—the authority of the Queen's Courts is continually set at nought, their decisions are treated as null and void, and the Royal supremacy is practically ignored.

Some good people, I believe, like this condition of things, and consider it healthy and safe. I admire their simplicity, but I differ from them entirely. So long as our present anarchy continues, I am certain it will prove an immense source of weakness when we come face to face with the Disestablishment movement in the House of Commons. The question will naturally be asked whether a Church deserves any favour which sets the Royal supremacy at defiance, or at any rate refuses to attend to the decisions of the Queen's Courts. For it must always be remembered that whether the Courts are good or bad, and whether the decisions are right or wrong, they do represent the Royal supremacy; and the champions of Disestablishment may justly ask, 'Do you mean to deny the Royal supremacy, or do you not?' Our present attitude is sure to make Parliament suspect that we want to make the Church independent of the State, and wish to transfer all power to Convocation, and take it away from the House of Commons. This, we may depend upon it, no British House of Commons will ever allow. The history of Laud's Convocation in 1640 is not forgotten. He that wants our Courts reformed and obnoxious decisions reversed, will find that, sooner or later, he must go to Caesar for authority to do it, and unless Caesar approves, it will not be done. I leave this part of my subject to your private reflection. I only repeat that our present undeniable lawlessness and anarchy will prove one of the biggest gaps in our line of defence in fighting the Disestablishment battle. You may not believe me, any more than Cassandra[2] was believed in ancient days. But it is my deliberate conviction that, if the British

---

[1] 'The Countryman waits until all the water be gone past,' Horace, *Epist.* 1, 2.42.
[2] She repeatedly told her captor Agamemnon of the calamities that awaited him if he returned to Greece from Troy, but he paid no heed to her and was assassinated.

public once grasps the idea that clergymen are a class of men who are chartered libertines, and are to be allowed to defy the law with impunity, you will never prevent Disestablishment.

3. The third weak point in our position is one which I refer to very unwillingly, but I am obliged to do it. I refer to the general apathy and indifference of lay Churchmen about our Church's affairs. The number of laymen who ever come forward and exhibit any interest in ecclesiastical matters, whether in town or country parishes, or in Dioceses, or in Conferences, or in Congresses, is most painfully small. In this respect the comparison between the Church of England and all other Churches which have any life in them is most unfavourable to us. No man can read accounts of the proceedings of the American Episcopal Church, or the disestablished Church of Ireland, of the Canadian or Australian Churches, of the Scotch Presbyterian Churches, or the Methodist, or Independent, or Baptist Churches in our own land, no man, I say, can read these accounts, and fail to observe that in every case the laymen exhibit far more interest in the welfare of their own body than the laity of the Established Church of England do in the welfare of their own Communion. Who does not know that there are hundreds and thousands of hard-headed intelligent laymen in our upper and middle classes who go to church regularly on Sundays, and fill their place in their congregations, and yet never attend a Vestry meeting, never join a Parochial Council, never appear on the platform of a religious Society, and never attend a Diocesan Conference or a Congress? Who does not know, beside this, that too many of them seem determined to push aside all Church questions, however important they may be, and appear resolved not to understand them or be troubled about them? If the clergyman of their parish is only devout, and moral, and amiable, and learned, and hard-working, they seem to think he must be in the right. They forget that all this is no more than might be said of Ignatius Loyola and the Jesuits, and that the grand question about every clergyman ought to be, 'Does he teach God's truth?'

This state of things is a very dangerous symptom in our condition. I suppose it is a remnant of the good old times, when religion was supposed to be the peculiar province of the parson, and the laity seemed to think they had nothing to do but to shut their eyes, open their ears and mouths, and believe whatever the parson told them. But it is high time to awake out of this slumber. It was all very well in the reigns of Queen Anne or the first two Georges. But it will never do in the nineteenth century. If Disestablishment were really to come, there would be a rude break up of this 'Sleepy Hollow,'[1] and the Rip Van Winkles among our laity would find that every one must take an active part in the Church's affairs, or else the Church would melt away and die. We want more men in the navy like Blake, and more men in the army like Havelock and Gordon; more Peers in the House of Lords like Lord Shaftesbury; more men on the judicial bench like Lord Hatherley and Lord Cairns; more members in the House of Commons like William Wilberforce; more statesmen in our Colonies like Henry and John Lawrence; and more bankers and merchants like Thornton and George Moore. At present, I do not believe that four-fifths of the Church laity have at all realized what Disestablishment and Disendowment mean and involve, what an immense rooting up of the very foundations of society would be the result, and what a huge demand would be made on their own purses, unless they were resolved to let the Church of England die altogether. I leave this weak point here, for I have no time to say more about it. In what I have said, you will please to remember that I have been speaking generally about the Church of England. The matter is one in which I firmly believe our own Diocese is better off than many. There are lay Churchmen here who are worth their weight in gold, and are ready to help forward every good work, and without whom this Diocese would never have been formed. I only wish their number was greatly increased. But throughout

---

[1] The name given in Washington Irving's *Sketch Book* to a quiet old-world village on the River Hudson.

the land I am confident that the laity ought to take a more active interest in the Church than they have done hitherto, and show better proof that they really care for its existence. Without this, I am certain the Establishment will not stand many years.

4. Another weak point in our position is one of very grave and deep importance. The whole standard of practical Christianity throughout the land is far below what it ought to be, in spite of a vast show of outward profession. I often think that God is angry with us as a nation because of our national sins, and that one of the sore judgments he is about to send on us is the overthrow of one of our oldest Institutions. It would not surprise me if he were to chastise us, and bring us to our senses by permitting the Disestablishment and Disendowment of the Church of England.

This is an unpleasant subject, and I handle it very reluctantly. But the time is short, the ship is among breakers, and the matter demands very plain speaking. It is such an age for mutual admiration, for complimenting and thanking everybody, and shirking disagreeable subjects, that we are all apt to think too well of our condition, and to shut our eyes to our defects. In short, we are walking in a vain shadow, and gilding and varnishing much that is rotten and defective. Some people, for instance, point to the numerous restorations of cathedrals and churches in the last fifty years, and seem to think that they prove the Church to be in a most satisfactory condition. Others point to the immense increase of what are called 'bright and hearty services,' the improvement in singing and general ceremonial, and the frequent communions, and tell us that they are certain evidences of spiritual life. I cannot see with the eyes of these people. They appear to forget that there never was a grander place of worship than the temple at Jerusalem after Herod's restoration, and there probably never was a more perfect ceremonial than that which was kept up in this temple in the days of our Lord. Yet at that very time both temple and ceremonial were on the brink of destruction. The whole system was like a whitened sepulchre, fair without but rotten within, and in a few years the Romans came and took away both place and nation. 'Let us not be high-minded, but fear.' Notwithstanding the immense change for the better in outward things which the Established Church has exhibited in the last fifty years, it may well be doubted whether there has been any corresponding improvement in inward vital religion and true godliness. If a tenth part of the time and money which have been spent on Church music and ceremonial in the last fifty years had been expended in pressing home on people repentance, faith, holiness, and self-denial, I believe our Church would have been in a far healthier state than she is now. I have read that the famous Italian statesman, Count Cavour, once said: 'Humanity, no doubt, is making progress in arts, sciences, and civilization; but the individual man makes no advance at all.'

I do not forget that we have many excellent Societies for checking evil and doing good, and I am thankful for what they do. But how weak and feeble they are, and how little influence they have over the mass of the nation. Let any thoughtful man take the Ten Commandments, in proof of what I say, and try the practical Christianity of this day by this test, and see what the result will be. Which of all the ten is really reverenced and obeyed as it ought to be? Look at the widespread Sabbath breaking and neglect of public worship which is the habitual custom of millions. Look at the awful revelations of impurity and breach of the seventh commandment which have lately been exhibited to the public eye. Look at the enormous amount of drunkenness and intemperance which still continues in spite of every effort to stop it. Look at the gambling and betting, and perfect idolatry of recreations, which the large-typed columns of almost every daily paper in the land are constantly recording. Look at the extravagant expenditure of money, and self-indulgence of all kinds, compared with the disgracefully small sums given to religious objects. Look at the spread of communism and socialism among the masses, and the cold, sneering agnosticism or infidelity of the upper ten thousand.

Look, last but not least, at the extraordinary bitterness and want of charity with which all controversies, whether political or theological, are continually carried on. The words of the great historian, Thucydides,[1] in which he describes the party spirit of his own day, apply most painfully to our own times. He says:

> No assurances or pledges of either party could gain credit with the other. The most reasonable proposal coming from an opponent was received, not with candour, but suspicion. No artifice was reckoned dishonourable, if a point could be carried. All recommendation of moderate measures was reckoned a mark either of cowardice or insincerity. He only was accounted a safe man whose violence was blind and boundless, and those who tried to steer a middle course were spared by neither side.

Alas! this picture, drawn by a heathen pen, is only too true of our own land, the land in which people call themselves Christians, and profess to believe St Paul's account of charity in the First Epistle to the Corinthians. But let any man, I say, deny the existence of these immense evils if he can. Let him remember that they exist in the face of an Established Church which seems unable to prevent them, and then let him say whether there is not grave cause for anxiety in our camp, and great weakness along our whole line, which may well make us fear for the Establishment in the coming battle. After all, the cool, careless indifference with which most people regard the state of things I have described, is one of the worst symptoms of our condition.

I, for one, am one of those old-fashioned people who believe in God's overruling government of nations. I believe that he deals with them in this world according to their sins, increases or diminishes them, raises or lowers them, according as they deal with him. I look at Nineveh and Babylon and Egypt and Tyre and Carthage and Venice and Spain and Portugal and Mexico and Peru, and I cannot help feeling anxious about our future. Except we repent and amend

[1] *History of the Peloponnesian War*, Book III.9.

our ways, I shall never be surprised if our candlestick is taken away, and our Established Church is broken up amidst a crash of all the ancient and time-honoured Institutions of our land. Every wise and thoughtful man knows that it was the low standard of practical religion and morality which brought on France the tremendous catastrophe of the 1789 Revolution; and if we do not mind what we are about we may possibly come to the same disastrous end.

I shall say no more, and perhaps some of you will think perhaps I have said too much. But I have spoken as I have done from a deep sense of duty, and from a firm conviction that we live in most critical times, and that no man can tell what may happen before our Conference meets in 1886.

I do not despair of the future. God forbid that I should do so. I believe in the Almighty power of God to deliver us, even in the darkest hour. He brought our beloved Church safe through the reign of Elizabeth, though half the clergy in the beginning of that reign were Papists at heart, and secretly cared nothing for the Reformation. He revived us again out of the dust after the Commonwealth days, when the Archbishop of Canterbury had been beheaded, and Bishops and Prayer-books had been clean swept away. He rescued us from the Romanizing designs of James II, and gave the Seven Bishops grace to go to prison rather than sanction popery. He kept us alive in the middle of the last century, when the blindness of our spiritual rulers had shut the Methodists out of the Church. What he has done in time past he may do again. For this let us all agree to pray. A praying, interceding people are the very backbone of a Church.

In any case, let us all resolve to be found at our respective posts, like the gallant Roman sentinel at the destruction of Pompeii in the great eruption of Vesuvius, whose bones tell us to this day that he would not flee, but died where he had been posted. A Church which can number ten millions of people in her ranks ought to make a very good fight, and should take a great deal of killing. We are not dead yet. The old Church of England is an anvil which has broken many a hammer. When the daughter of Sir William Waller, the famous Commonwealth General, was engaged to marry a Churchman, someone expressed his surprise that her father should let her marry a member of a falling Church. The old General replied drily that he observed 'this falling Church had a strange knack of rising again.' So may it be with us! May we be like the bush that burned with fire but was not consumed.

Two duties are immediately before us, and to them let us attend with heart, and soul, and mind, and strength. On the one hand, let us use every reasonable means to spread information, and meet falsehood with truth. On the other hand, let us set our own house in order, and not go to battle with our feet fettered and millstones round our necks. Our watchword and rallying-cry must be, 'Union on the basis of loyalty to the formularies of the Church of England and to the principles of the Reformation.' Of some things we may be quite certain. One is, that the people of England will never allow the Established Church to go back to Rome. Another is, that the Parliament of England will never allow the Established Church to be above the law. The last, but far the most important, is this, that God will never support a Church which is content with a low standard of practical religion.

5

THE OUTLOOK

An address given at the opening of the sixth Liverpool Diocesan Conference, 1886.

R EVEREND and Lay Brethren, I offer you a hearty welcome at the commencement of our Sixth Diocesan Conference. We meet in smaller numbers than I could wish, and I regret to say that none of our Conferences in the last five years has ever been attended by half our members. However, this is a state of things, I believe, which exists in almost every Diocese in the kingdom, and it is useless to complain. So long as these Conferences are purely voluntary associations, whose proceedings possess no binding powers, so long it is vain to expect that all Churchmen will take a deep interest in their meetings and debates.

The subjects about to be brought before you have been carefully chosen, and I think they afford scope for some useful discussion. I take occasion to remind you that the selection of subjects for a Conference is not so easy as some suppose. On the one hand, we do not want questions about which all men are agreed, like themes for little boys at school, such as 'Honesty is a good thing.' On the other hand, we do not want burning controversial questions about which the immense majority of Churchmen have made up their minds one way or the other, and are not in the least likely to change them. What we want to discuss are really practical subjects, about which more light is wanted, and there is a great deal to be said on both sides. If Church patronage, the condition of domestic servants, Church music and singing, and modern preaching, are not subjects of this kind, I am greatly mistaken. At any rate, I think there is room for a great deal more information about them, and I hope we shall get it.

In my own opening address I shall follow the example of most of my brethren on the Episcopal Bench, and seize the opportunity of saying something about the outlook of our own Diocese in particular, and of the Church of England generally. Under each head I have something to say.

I. *The outlook of the Diocese of Liverpool* is, as usual, a very chequered one. Taking a bird's-eye view, as a Bishop, I see many things which are painful and discouraging, and I heartily wish that I did not see them. But I will not complain. I should be ungrateful if I did not publicly acknowledge many causes for thankfulness. There are clouds, no doubt, on our Diocesan horizon, as I have said more than once before. But there is also a good deal of blue sky.

(1) The extremely limited *support given to our Diocesan Institutions* continues to be a very gloomy spot in our Diocesan outlook, and reflects some discredit on the Churchmen of the West Derby Hundred. When I tell the Conference that the total amount of money received in 1885 by our six great Diocesan Institutions was only £3,982, that the whole number of annual subscribers to these Institutions was only 638 in our Diocese of 1,200,000 people, and that out of 200 incumbents 80 never made any collection at all for the support of this important Diocesan machinery, I think you will admit that I have a right to call this an unsatisfactory state of things.

Nevertheless even here there are two sides to the picture. It would be absurd and unfair to measure the liberality of Churchmen by the amount of money given to the Diocesan Institutions. We all know that very large sums are annually contributed for Church purposes which never pass through the hands of the Treasurers of our Finance Association. It is the same in every Diocese throughout the land. As long as human nature is what it is, men will give their money directly to the Church, or School, or Mission-room, or Curate's fund, which is close by their own doors, and they will not put it at the disposal of a Diocesan Committee. A great deal more money is given in our own district in this way, than through the medium of our Office in Commerce Court. It is useless to say, 'This ought not to be so.' We must accept the position, and remember it is one of the many consequences of our unhappy divisions.

After all, the outside critics who are so fond of running down the new Diocese of Liverpool, would do well to remember the princely donations which have been recently given to the cause of the Church by individual Churchmen residing within the boundaries of the new See. Within the last six years, since the creation of this Bishopric, our venerable friend Charles Groves has given £10,000 in one sum towards the building of churches. Mr Horsfall has spent £20,000 in the erection of St Agnes. Messrs. Knowles and Pearson have given £10,000 towards building a church at Ince. An anonymous contributor sent me £2,000 last year in one donation, to be applied to Diocesan purposes. And last, but not least, an honourable lady, whose name I need not mention in this room, has given £20,000 this year for the formation of a Pension Fund for aged and invalided Clergy in the Diocese, after having contributed most munificently to the erection of the three new churches, of St Athanasius, St Gabriel, and St Bede's, in each case about £2,000; after giving a Parsonage to St Athanasius at a cost of £2,000, and a Parsonage to St Paul's, Prince's Park, at a cost of £2,500; and after building and endowing a large and beautiful House of Rest for Incurables. In the face of such facts as these, which are but six years old, they are not to be heard for a moment who tell the world that the Diocese of Liverpool has done nothing in the way of giving money since its creation.

(2) Concerning the outlook of *Church Building* in our Diocese, I see much ground yet unoccupied, while I thankfully admit that much has been done. Fifteen churches built and consecrated

and forming the centre of Parochial districts, four large churches built and opened by licence though not yet consecrated, five new churches founded and in process of building, besides three churches rebuilt, three restored at an expense of £3,000 each, and four enlarged by new chancels, tell a tale which speaks for itself. But when I look at such parishes as St Aidan's, Kirkdale; St Paul's, North Shore; St John the Baptist's, Toxteth Park; or the districts attached to the mother churches of Warrington and St Helen's, or the Bootle quarter, you may well believe that I long to see more done in the matter of Church Building. So long as there is only one incumbent and one consecrated church in a population of 10,000 or 15,000, it is absurd to suppose the Church of England is duly represented, and can make her influence felt. Such districts are the weakness of the Established Church, and supply weighty arguments to Liberationists. Common sense points out that an immense proportion of the dwellers in such districts are like sheep without a shepherd. They know nothing of the clergyman of the parish, and care nothing for a Church which does not seem to care for them. No doubt the immediate remedy such districts require is a supply of plain, cheap mission-rooms, simple elementary evangelistic services, and an increased staff of missionary curates and lay-agents. But after all, these are only temporary stop-gap arrangements. Our ultimate aim should be to break up these overgrown parishes into districts of a manageable size, and to plant in each territory a church, a resident vicar, and a parsonage. I hope and pray that God may yet incline some of our wealthy citizens to come forward, and to build, as some have nobly done, more churches for the great city in which their wealth has been made. At present, however, while I am deeply thankful for the progress we have made in Church Building, I heartily wish the progress was more rapid.

I cannot, however, drop this subject of Church Building without raising a warning voice, and offering some friendly advice to all promoters of new churches. I entreat them, for one thing, to beware of extravagant designs, and to take care that they are not victimized by architects naturally anxious to show their talents. By all means let us have handsome churches, if we can get them, but let us not waste money on bricks and mortar, especially in poor districts. For another thing, I entreat the promoters of new churches to beware of opening them with a heavy debt on them. Nothing, I am certain, so paralyses the minister of a new church as the incessant struggle to pay off a debt. It is like a mill-stone round his neck, and seriously cripples his usefulness, at that critical period, the beginning of his work. Last, but not least, I ask all promoters of new churches to consider more seriously than they sometimes appear to do, the income of their ministers. That question, in poor parishes, where the offertory must always be small, will one day be a very difficult one to solve. A grand Gothic church, with a half-starved Incumbent in the pulpit, is a very sorrowful and unsatisfactory sight.

I cannot leave this branch of my address without mentioning a few things in which I heartily wish I could see a change for the better. I do not forget that 'wishing' is said to be waste of time, but I do want to put my finger on some things about which I long to see alteration and amendment. I will mention them as briefly as possible.

(i) I want to see more done in Liverpool for those two valuable Institutions, the Scripture Readers' and Bible-women's Societies. There is an enormous field of usefulness before each of those bodies, which for want of funds they are quite unable to reach.

(ii) I want to see more done in the Diocese for the Church Aid Society's cause. It is useless to wait till large new churches are built in our overgrown districts. I see no chance of breaking them up, and reaching the people, except by a multiplication of living agents and plain mission-rooms.

(iii) I want to see more done for the cause of seamen in this huge seaport. Far more might be done if the agencies which are specially devoted to their benefit were not hindered by want of funds.

(iv) I want to see more life and zeal for evangelization in our Voluntary Lay Helpers Association. It is easy work to enrol the voluntary helpers in well-worked parishes, and to make out a long list of district visitors, Sunday-school teachers, and the like. But I long to see volunteers offering themselves to go out from their own particular parishes, to assist some of the Incumbents of our large, overgrown districts, where at present there is a dearth of helpers, by visiting from house to house, and aggressive evangelization.

(v) I want to see a much larger number of candidates for Confirmation from some of our large parishes. The number presented to me from year to year in some cases is sadly small, and leaves a painful impression that 'Young Liverpool' is not as much under the influence of the Church of England as Churchmen could wish.

(vi) I want to see legal parochial districts assigned and attached to every church in the city of Liverpool. Few persons, perhaps, are aware that there are large and important churches in this city which at present have no legal district at all. The streets around them are only worked by conventional arrangements, and the incumbents are under no legal obligation to do anything outside the walls of their own churches. Any pastoral work they do is done on the voluntary system, and they are exempt from the requirements of the Pluralities Act. This is a great evil, and I do hope that some day, with a due regard to vested interests, the evil may be remedied. At this moment I believe that St Andrew's, Holy Innocents, St Mary (Edge Hill), St Margaret (Prince's Road), Holy Trinity (Walton Breck), St James (West Derby), St John (Knotty Ash), and St Michael's-in-the-Hamlet, have no legal parochial districts.

I trust you will understand my meaning in naming these wants. I hope I am not a grumbler or complainer, but I long to see the 'things set in order that are wanting.' For an immense amount of good work done in the Diocese, I am deeply thankful. For readiness to meet my wishes, and assist me in every possible way, I shall always be grateful, both to clergy and laity. Few people have the least idea of the enormous difficulties which this new Diocese presents to a Bishop. A population of 1,200,000 with only 200 incumbents, and a population of which at least one-half are Roman Catholics or Nonconformists, a large number of comparatively new Churches most miserably endowed, particularly in the poor districts; the almost entire absence of ecclesiastical prizes to induce first-rate men to settle among us; the want of a great central Cathedral with its Dean and endowed Chapter to make a rallying point for Churchmen on great occasions; the fierce competition of commercial business, which allows so few laymen time to assist the Church's movements, with every good will to do so; the startling proportion of very poor working men and artisans who live without a rich man among them in some of our parishes; all these circumstances added together make an enormous mass of difficulties which are very trying to faith, and to which there is nothing like in any other Diocese in England or Wales. However, I do not despair. I believe that God is with the Church of England in Liverpool, and that there is a bright future yet before us, though I may not live to see it.

So much for the outlook of the Diocese. There is only one point which I have left untouched, and that is the Cathedral. I have said nothing about it, for the simple reason that there is little or nothing to say. You all know that a site has been chosen, which appears, in spite of obvious objections, to be the best site available; an Act of Parliament has been obtained for that site, and plans of a building worthy of this great city have been invited and sent in. We are still waiting for the report of Mr Christian, the President of the Royal Society of Architects, which has been delayed by his illness. What the final result will be, I do not pretend to say. It is vain to expect that any design will ever satisfy everybody, any more than the choice of the site.

One thing at all events is very certain. No Cathedral worthy of Liverpool will ever be built and endowed without an immense expenditure of money, and until the present commercial depression passes away, I suppose it is useless to expect very much money to be given. Nothing of course is impossible. It is the unexpected which often arrives. Some mighty gift or legacy may yet be in the future which may settle the whole question both of the building and the endowment. At present we can only wait and hope.

II. From the outlook of the Diocese I now turn to *the outlook of the Church of England generally*. I feel it a plain duty to say something annually on this point. The days are past and gone for ever when the Bishop's triennial or septennial Charge was thought sufficient for the communication of his thoughts to his clergy. Great events, both political and ecclesiastical, follow each other in such rapid succession in these times, and questions seriously affecting the whole Church are so continually cropping up, and pressing for settlement, that it is not easy to keep our minds abreast with them without constant watchfulness. Whatever affects the Church generally, affects each Diocese particularly. Here in Lancashire we are only part of a great body, and the general condition and health of that body ought always to be interesting to us. I make no excuse therefore for offering a few remarks on certain points in our Church's present condition; and I desire, as your Bishop, to invite your particular attention to them.

What, then, is the real condition of the Church of England in the present day? I find it extremely difficult to answer that question. At a first glance we seem to be in a very satisfactory state. There is a great amount of stir, and bustle, and activity which did not exist fifty years ago. There is undeniably a great show of life. The revival of Convocation, the foundation of Theological Colleges, the institution of Church Congresses and Diocesan Conferences, the formation of six new Dioceses at home, and about seventy in the Colonies, the growth of missionary work at home and abroad, the vast amount of money spent on church building and church restoration, the general readiness to use new means and machinery which would have made our grand-fathers' hair stand on end—all these are broad, undeniable facts in English Church History of the last fifty years which nobody can pretend to deny. But what does it come to after all in the sight of God? How much increase of spiritual life is there behind this great outward appearance of ecclesiastical prosperity? I repeat that I find it very difficult to answer these questions. Deeply thankful as I am for the material advances which our Church has certainly made, and the quantity of ecclesiastical machinery which has been set up, I wish I could feel satisfied that, below the surface, all is right. For this expression of a doubtful feeling I know that some of my friends will call me a gloomy pessimist. There are not a few amiable Churchmen, especially in high places, who can never see anything wrong in our condition. They live in a happy, complimentary frame of mind, and are always putting telescopes to blind eyes when faults are pointed out. I fail to see the wisdom of this excessive optimism about the state of our Church. At all events I see some very black clouds on our horizon which threaten mischief, and I think it a plain duty to call your attention to them. I look at those clouds with great uneasiness. Unless they disperse, we may suddenly find ourselves some day in the crash of some tremendous catastrophe like an earthquake. The sun rose as usual on the day when Sodom was burned by fire from heaven. The eruption of Vesuvius buried Pompeii without any warning. The recent convulsions of the earth in Java and New Zealand were not preceded by premonitory symptoms. The Charleston[1] earthquake earlier this year began in a moment. It may be the same with the Church of England. Let us not be high-minded, but fear.

(1) The first and worst cloud that I see in our Church's outlook is the *widespread disposition to regard religious externalism as a substitute for vital soul-saving Christianity.*

When I speak of externalism, let me explain what I mean. We all know that the outward part of religion has received a large amount of new attention during the last forty years. All over the land it has become the fashion to restore churches, to

---

[1] South Carolina, USA. About seventy people were killed and much property damaged.

get rid of old square pews, to improve the singing and music, to have a surpliced choir, to decorate the church-building in a most elaborate style at great festivals, and, in one word, to adorn, beautify, and improve the whole exterior of Church Christianity. Do I say there is anything sinful or wrong in all this? Nothing of the kind! I abhor everything like slovenliness in the ceremonials of worship. I dislike square pews, and bad music, and bad singing as much as any one. But I do say that I fear an external improvement often takes place in a parish church without the slightest corresponding increase of godliness in the worshippers. No doubt there is far more show and name of religion in our Churches, but it is very doubtful whether there is more vital Christianity, more presence of the Holy Ghost, more heart and conscience work, in the naves of our Churches and the homes of our people. I fear that in hundreds of cases men have rested content with having secured a handsome church and a 'bright and hearty service,' and have forgotten that what God looks at is the hearts of the worshippers, and the quantity of grace to be found among them.

This is a very delicate subject, and I should be sorry to be misunderstood, or to give pain to any one in handling it. But I am obliged to say plainly, that I fail to see that all the outside improvement of the last forty years is accompanied by any corresponding growth of practical holiness in the land. I cannot hear that there is any decrease of gambling, extravagance, or breach of the Seventh Commandment among the rich, or of intemperance, dishonesty, or general immorality among the poor. On the contrary, I hear good judges say that there is positively less repentance, faith, holiness, Sabbath-keeping, Bible-reading, and family religion, in proportion to the population, than there was forty years ago. If this state of things is not a most unhealthy symptom in the condition of a Church, I know not what is.

We may depend upon it that knowledge of Christ, obedience to Christ, and the fruits of the Spirit, are the only tests by which God weighs and measures any Church. If these are absent, he cares not for beautiful buildings, fine singing, and a pompous ceremonial. These are 'leaves,' and he desires to see not leaves only, but fruit. The tree of the Church of England perhaps never had so many leaves on it as it has just now. I wish I could think there was a corresponding quantity of fruit. We must never forget that the Temple service at Jerusalem in the day of our Lord's crucifixion was the most perfect ceremonial that ever was, whether for singing, order, vestments, or general magnificence and beauty. Yet we all know that at this very time the Jewish Church was thoroughly rotten at heart, and after forty years was swept away. Who can doubt that the little upper chamber, where the apostles met on the day of our Lord's ascension, was far more beautiful in God's sight than the temple in which Annas and Caiaphas were the High Priests, and which our Master himself called 'a den of thieves'? I heartily wish that English Churchmen in this day would remember this more than they appear to do. The disposition to make an idol of externals, and to sacrifice the inside of religion to the outside, is, in my judgment, one of the darkest clouds on our ecclesiastical horizon.

(2) The second thing which I see with pain in the outlook of the Church of England at the present time, is the *growing tendency to ignore all distinct doctrine.*

The leading idea of many minds in this day appears to be, that it does not signify much what a man believes or teaches about what are commonly considered the principal verities of the Christian faith. A wave of extravagant liberalism in religion, as well as in everything else, is sweeping over England. Concerning the Trinity, the Divinity of Christ, the atonement, the person and work of the Holy Ghost, conversion, justification, the inspiration of Scripture, the future state, and the like, it seems to be agreed that men may believe as much or as little as they please, and nobody is to find fault. The only question you are to ask is, whether a man is 'earnest, sincere, and zealous,' and if he is, you are not to ask anything more. It is thought very narrow and illiberal to say that any opinion in religion is false, or that anybody is unsound in the faith. Distinct and positive statements about anything in Christianity are thought downright uncharitable. All the old dogmas are to be held in solution, and never to be put forward in a solid, tangible state, or to be put forward in such a foggy, misty manner that, like a half-developed photographic plate, they are never to come out distinct, sharp, and clear. I challenge any one who observes closely the pulpit utterances of this day, or reads platform speeches which touch religion, to deny the accuracy of what I have just said.

Now all this, no doubt, sounds very noble and generous and liberal. It is in perfect harmony with the political tendencies of the age, which all lean in the direction of the principle, that everybody is to be allowed to do what he likes, and to be at liberty to do anything except commit suicide, theft, or murder. Moreover, these ideas save men a great deal of trouble in the way of thinking and inquiry in order to find out truth. But the question still remains to be answered, Can this indifference to doctrine stand the test of cross-examination? Is it really true that there are no limits to the Church's comprehensiveness? If it does not matter what we believe, where is the use of the Bible, Creeds, Confessions, and Articles of faith? We may as well throw them aside as useless lumber. Beside this, does history show that any good work has been done in improving human nature during the last eighteen centuries by any instrumentality except that of distinct and positive doctrine? Did the apostles turn the world upside down by proclaiming everywhere, 'Be earnest, be sincere, be moral, be charitable, and it does not matter what you believe'? Did the early Fathers, or the Continental and English Reformers, work on these lines? Do the missionaries to the heathen abroad, or to those who are practically heathen at home, ever obtain success without distinct doctrinal statements? And, to come home to ourselves at last, is there a man or woman among us who would be content on a deathbed to be told, 'Never mind what you believe; if you are in earnest you will go to heaven'? Questions like these demand very serious consideration.

I commend this whole subject to the attention of all who hear me. I am convinced that it is a very dark spot in the outlook of our Church at the present time, and I apprehend great danger in this quarter. I admit most fully, and have always maintained, that the Church of England is eminently comprehensive, and that all the three great schools of thought, High, Low, and Broad, were intended to have room in her pale. But surely we must stop somewhere. There is such a thing as liberality and 'breadth of thought' gone mad. We all know very well that the first steps to infidelity are to be found in the theory, that all faiths are false, and destitute of foundation. But I confess that the modern notion that all faiths so called are equally good and true, appears to me just as dangerous, and just as replete with mischief, to men's souls.

(3) A third black cloud which I see in the present outlook of the Church of England, is *the almost entire suspension of ecclesiastical discipline.*

It is well known that next to preaching of the word and right administration of the sacraments, discipline has always been considered to be one of the marks of a pure visible Church.

You will find this distinctly asserted in the 28th Homily of our Church. Reason and common sense alike point out that in every large community of persons united together for a particular object, there must be order, and that this order can only be maintained by rules and regulations, which every member of the community is bound to obey. In the army no regiment could be governed if the colonel was not obeyed. In the navy no ship would be safe if the captain had not supreme command. In a firm of merchants no business could be long transacted if every member of the firm did what was right in his own eyes, and the articles of partnership were continually transgressed. It is just the same with a well-ordered Church. When differences and disputes arise about doctrine or ritual, there ought to be some person or body of persons to whom the matter may be referred, and the decision of such person or persons ought to be the final settlement of the affair, and the decision ought to be obeyed. These are obvious truisms, I know, but it is well to state them.

Now what is the present condition of the Church of England in the matter of ecclesiastical discipline? I am not going to discuss who is right and who is wrong on the many controverted questions of the day, which have been the subjects of lawsuits in the last forty years. I only remark that they are not mere trifling questions of more or less 'ornament,' as some people are fond of saying, but something far more serious and deep. However, I certainly will not drag them into our Conference. I simply wish to call your attention to the painfully anomalous position which our Church occupies in the face of Christendom.

At this moment we possess an Ecclesiastical Court for the trial of disputed points under the Clergy Discipline and Public Worship Acts, and from this Court there is an appeal to the Judicial Committee of the Privy Council. In addition to this, we have the Bishop's private and fatherly monitions, which all clergymen swear to obey 'in all things lawful and honest.'

Such is the machinery which the law has provided for our Church. It may be very defective, very clumsy, very dilatory, and very expensive. It might very easily, in my opinion, be improved and amended. The imprisonment of clergymen for contumacy, for example, is a relic of barbarism which ought to be swept away. However, this is the only machinery which the Church possesses at present; and although its faults have been freely pointed out in the Report of the Royal Commission on Ecclesiastical Courts, it still stands, and has not been destroyed. The Report has led to no result whatever, except that of unsettling men's minds. In fact, it has fallen dead, while The Clergy Discipline Act and the Public Worship Act have not been cancelled, abrogated, or repealed. They live still. The decisions of the Courts they constitute are still binding on all the Queen's subjects, and they represent the

Royal Supremacy which, according to the Thirty-seventh Article, the Crown possesses in things ecclesiastical as well as civil.

Now, consider quietly for a moment where we are. A small, but able and well-organized minority of Churchmen refuse to recognize the authority of the existing Ecclesiastical Courts. They refuse to plead before them, they refuse to obey their decisions, they proclaim loudly that these decisions are null and void, and are not binding upon the Church. In short, they set the existing law at defiance, because they think it bad, and the Courts defective in constitution. Of course in a free country they have a right to think anything they please. But I cannot help remarking that most wise men hold that defective laws ought to be obeyed until they are repealed, in England as well as in Ireland, and that the worst state of things is to have no law at all.

As to the Bishop's fatherly monitions, such as the law provides at the time of ordination, licensing, and institution, and every clergyman swears to obey, they are practically useless. A clergyman has only got to tell his Bishop, even when he admonishes him about things non-essential, that his monitions are not 'lawful and honest,' and the unfortunate Bishop is checkmated, brought to a dead standstill, and can do no more.

But this is not all. If any Churchman, anxious to maintain order, proposes to take proceedings in the Ecclesiastical Court for what he believes, rightly or wrongly, are illegal practices in the conduct of public worship, and the Bishop of the Diocese, in the exercise of his discretion, and on the great principle laid down in Magna Carta, that justice must never be denied to a subject, allows him to take these proceedings, at once there arises a storm of dissatisfaction and displeasure against the Bishop and the aforesaid complaining Churchman, of the violence of which few people have the slightest conception. The late Bishop of Manchester,[1] in the Miles Platting case, is an example of what I mean; and I am obliged to say that I have drunk a little of the same cup myself.

[1] James Fraser, 1870–83.

Now I appeal to any impartial Englishman of common sense to say whether this is a healthy state of things. Healthy indeed! It is nonsense to use such a word. It is a state of chaos, confusion, and anarchy! We have Queen's Courts which are not respected! We have decisions which are not obeyed! We have Bishops' monitions about things non-essential set at nought! If all this does not constitute a complete suspension of ecclesiastical discipline, I do not know what can. The most contradictory practices are to be found in our churches about one of the most solemn ordinances of our religion; but it seems impossible to obtain a binding decision as to who is right and who is wrong. Every clergyman does what is right in his own eyes, and the laity ask in vain, 'What is truth about the ritual of the Lord's Supper?'

Last, but worst of all, I cannot see the least symptom of any attempt being about to be made to reform the Ecclesiastical Courts, or to create a new tribunal. If the existing law about Church discipline is bad, by all means let it be altered. But I can hear of no memorial to the Archbishop of Canterbury from that busy minority of Churchmen which objects to the present Court, praying his Grace to obtain powers to create a new tribunal. I cannot hear that those able men, Lord Halifax and Mr Beresford Hope, propose to bring a Bill into either House of Parliament in order to destroy Lord Penzance's Court[1] and erect a better one. In short, nothing is being done, and the delay is annually increasing, hardening, solidifying, and crystallizing our unhappy differences. The result is that we stand before the world in the position of a Church content to have no discipline, and prepared to run the risk of all the painful consequences which will certainly ensue. For evil consequences there certainly will be if the present state of things goes on much longer. Those evil consequences are nothing less than disruption, disestablishment, disendowment of the grandest old Church in Christendom. Come they will, whether we like it

[1] The Court for the trial of disputed points under the Clergy Discipline and Public Worship Acts, presided over by Lord Penzance.

or not, unless something is done. Order is heaven's first law, and a Church which will not have order must not expect to live.

I leave this subject here. I trust I have given many of you some food for reflection. Nothing pains me so much as the inability of Churchmen to see the dangerous position which we occupy from our present want of ecclesiastical discipline, and the enormous damage which it is inflicting on our Zion. I know, of course, that many will tell us that the state of things which I complain arises entirely from the dislike of Churchmen to go to Parliament for a remedy. I will simply remark that it is waste of time to say anything on that point. It is as certain as anything can be certain that the laity of the Established Church of England will never allow Spiritual Courts composed of Bishops and clergy alone to settle disputed points without having a voice in the settlement. We are not living in the days of Tudors and Stuarts, but in the latter part of the 19th century, and the schoolmaster is abroad. It is equally certain that the House of Commons will never allow any Ecclesiastical tribunal to be set up without its sanction and approval. If the Ecclesiastical Courts are to be reformed, we shall be obliged to go to Caesar, and without Caesar nothing will be done.

(4) The last but not the least cloud in the outlook of the Church of England is *the slowness of the Church, as a body, to take up the important subject of Church Reform.*

When I speak of Church Reform, I ask you not to misunderstand me. I have not the slightest sympathy with those who would throw overboard the Creeds, pull the Prayer-book to pieces, or cancel the Articles. Least of all, I have not the slightest sympathy with those who want to go back to the first Prayer-book of Edward VI. On the whole, I am quite content with the Prayer-book as it is, and I do not want to spoil it by tinkering amendments, though some of the additions of the Irish Prayer-book, or of the proposed American Annexed Book, would in my judgment be great improvements. But I am quite willing to let well alone. The reforms I have in view are of a more practical kind, and I will mention some of them.

Convocation stands sorely in need of reform. To say, as the Canons do, that it is 'the Church of England by representation' in the present day, is really going rather too far. The laity need to be brought forward to a more distinct, authorized, and efficient position in everything that concerns the Church. The House of Laymen, no doubt, is a move in the right direction; but it must possess far more power than it does at present if it is to be of much use to the Church. The whole question of Patronage requires thorough improvement, and the sale of advowsons and next presentations to private persons ought to be entirely prohibited. The inhabitants of every parish ought to have some voice in the selection of a minister. We need far more elasticity in the use of our churches, and the employment of gifted laymen in their pulpits on some occasions. The present autocracy of Bishops imposes upon them a far too heavy responsibility. They ought to be assisted by a small Council of picked clergymen and laymen in the consideration of the many difficult questions they have to deal with. For want of such a Council they are always in danger of doing too little or too much, or committing gross errors of judgment. The autocracy of the incumbents of large parishes ought to be restricted. The Bishop and his Council ought to have power to interfere and send a missionary clergyman into a parish of 10,000 or 15,000 people, when it is evident the incumbent cannot possibly look after them himself. The lay communicants of every parish ought to be more frequently consulted by the incumbent in every step that he takes. Few things do more harm than the occasional introduction by a clergyman of practices and ceremonials to which his congregation are not accustomed, without first consulting the laity. I do not want Mr Albert Grey's Parish Councils, but I do want to see the laity brought forward more frequently, and more use made of that constitutional old body the Sidesmen.

I might easily add to this list of reforms, but for want of time I must stop. I know that many will think that my suggestions are needless and quixotical. But I ask any one of common sense to consider whether it is likely that after three hundred years, since the days of Queen Elizabeth, and after the immense advances the world has made in every department of knowledge, there may not be a strong probability that even our good old Church may admit of improvement? It is surely not too much to suppose that the clothes which fitted her three centuries ago are not quite large enough now, and that machinery which has done so much good work may not be altered with advantage, and more adapted to the nineteenth century. Long bows were very useful at Crécy, flint-locks at Waterloo, and wooden three-deckers at Trafalgar. But they are useless now. One thing at all events is very certain. Timely reforms are the best defence of the Established Church against the repeated attacks on her connection with the State, and her tithes and endowments, which are sure to come. If we would only remove all admitted abuses, fill up the gaps in our defences, and strengthen the points that are weak, we need not fear the battle. But it is nonsense to say there are no weak points in the Church of England, and the sooner they are removed the safer she will be.

We live in very perilous times, but I have great faith in the strength and vitality of the Church of England, if Churchmen will only do their duty, unite, and 'set in order the things that are wanting.' We are far stronger than we were in 1747, when the famous Bishop Butler, author of the *Analogy*, refused to be made Archbishop of Canterbury, saying, 'It was too late for him to try to support a falling Church.' We are ten times stronger than we were a hundred years ago, and we might be stronger still if we were not so miserably divided. On one point, at all events, I think we shall all be agreed. We need more of the presence of that Holy Spirit who alone can make men of one mind in a house. For that presence let us all pray night and day. Let a cry go up from every parish of the Diocese: 'Lord, revive thy work among us year by year, and send down upon us more of the grace of the Holy Ghost.'

6

OUR STATE AND PROSPECTS

The third triennial charge to the Diocese of Liverpool,
October 27, 1887.

MY Reverend Brethren, By the mercy of God, we are allowed to meet together once more at the Third Triennial Visitation of the new Diocese of Liverpool. When I came among you seven years ago, I little thought that I should live to address you three times.

The gaps and changes in our ranks during the three years which have elapsed since my last Visitation are rather numerous, considering that there are only 200 Incumbents altogether on our muster roll. Two have resigned and are still living—Mr Brooke of St Bride, Liverpool, and Mr Banner of Roby. Four have resigned and died after resignation—Mr Newenham of Knotty Ash; Mr Wheeler of St Ann's, Liverpool; Mr Carson of St Augustine, Liverpool; and Mr Schonberg of Warrington. Ten have left the Diocese for other positions—Mr Scott of Christ Church, Bootle; Mr Cochrane of St Saviour's, Everton; Mr Pearson of Grassendale; Mr Bower of Woolton; Mr Lory of St Mark's, Liverpool; Mr Macnaghten of Prescot; Mr Neale of St Catherine's, Edge Hill; Mr Dunkerley of St Thomas's, Toxteth; and last, though not least of our losses, Archdeacon Bardsley of St Saviour's, now Bishop of Sodor and Man. Twelve have been removed by death—Mr Read of St Paul's, Liverpool; Mr Power of St Alban's, Bevington; Canon Hume of All Souls, Liverpool; Mr Boulton of Aughton; Mr Bryan of Haigh; Mr Walmdey of Aspull; Mr Crockett of Eccleston; Mr

Gardner of Stanley; Canon Carr of St Helen's; Mr Hassall of St John the Baptist, Toxteth Park; Mr Quirk of Golborne; and Mr Turnbull of St Mary's, Edge Hill.

In short, no less than twenty-seven names have disappeared from the roll of Incumbents which has been called over this day, and no less than 16 are dead who were with us three years ago. This alone is a startling fact, and one which ought to set us thinking. Sixteen deaths out of 200! Whose turn will it be to go next? Who among us all will be here when the names are called over again at the next Triennial Visitation? May we all so number our days, that we may apply our hearts unto wisdom! If called away, may we be found like good servants, with our loins girded and our lamps burning, and ready to meet our Master.

From grave facts like these, which I do not think should be passed over at a Visitation, I shall now turn to the two points which ought naturally to occupy a prominent position in a Bishop's Charge. In the first place, I will speak of our own Diocese in particular. In the second place, I will say something about the Church of England generally. On both subjects, a Diocese has a just right to expect a Bishop to be unreserved, to keep nothing back, and to speak out his mind.

I. Concerning the Diocese of Liverpool, I see *much cause for thankfulness and encouragement.* I say this deliberately, at the end of the first seven years of our separate existence. It is cheap and easy work for dwellers at a distance to point the finger of scorn and call our new Bishopric a failure. But not one in a hundred of our unfriendly critics seems to understand and realize the very peculiar difficulties under which the See of Liverpool has been launched. A brief review of these difficulties may be useful.

(1) First and foremost, few persons are aware that the whole framework of the Church of England in this district, is of comparatively modern origin. Two hundred years ago, I believe, there were not twenty-five churches in the West Derby Hundred, which forms the area of our present Diocese. So lately as fifty years ago, when

our Gracious Sovereign, Queen Victoria, came to the throne, there were only seventy-eight churches in the space of Lancashire now occupied by the Diocese. No less than 120 of our 200 churches have been built, and separate parochial districts formed, within the last half century! Now, to expect the Church of England to be as deeply rooted and as strong in such a territory, as it is in such counties as Cornwall, Notts, Yorkshire, and Northumberland, where scores of old rectories and ancient churches have been before the eyes of people for five hundred years, is unreasonable and unfair. New work can only be consolidated and thoroughly knit together by time. At present we are more like a Colonial Diocese, or a collection of independent congregational chapels, than any Diocese in the land.

(2) In the next place, few people seem to be aware that a very large proportion of the population of our Diocese does not belong to the Church of England, and of course takes no interest in her advancement or prosperity. The county of Lancaster from the time of the Reformation has always been a stronghold of the adherents of the Romish Church. I need not tell you that we have not a few great families in our own district who have retained the faith of their pre-Reformation ancestors to this very day. Beside this, for many years there has been a constant immigration from the sister country in search of high wages and work, and we all know that in the northern parishes of Liverpool, near the docks, Irish Roman Catholics form the great majority of the population, and outnumber all other professing Christians in the proportion of at least three to one. Add to all this the broad fact that you have a very large body of Protestant Nonconformists of all denominations in every part of the Diocese, and not least from Scotland and Wales. Any man with his eyes open will see Dissenting chapels of every kind in every direction. The whole result is, that out of a population of about 1,200,000, within our borders, it admits of grave doubt whether more than a third can be justly classified as Churchmen. One thing at any rate is certain—they know very

little who suppose that the formation of our new See was likely to be welcomed by the great bulk of the inhabitants. You cannot expect men to support and rally round a Church to which they do not belong.

(3) In the next place, few people in England seem to be aware that a very great portion of the wealth of Liverpool is not in the hands of Churchmen. That the second city in the empire, and the first seaport in the world, should be regarded as a rich place is natural enough. But we who live in Lancashire know well that a very large number of the merchants and leading inhabitants of the Diocese belong to Churches outside the Church of England, and cannot reasonably be expected to assist our own Church objects and Church work. The floating idea in many minds that our great city is a vast magazine and storehouse of Church wealth is not justified by facts. Our upper ten thousand are an exceedingly variegated body in the matter of religion, and money is not concentrated in any one set of hands any more than at New York. Even when the new Bishopric was first founded, the sum required by the Act of Parliament was principally made up by a few very large contributions from a limited number of persons. That there is noble liberality in Liverpool for objects in which all can co-operate, the subscription lists of the University and the Royal Infirmary supply abundant proof. But if any dweller in distant parts of England imagines that it is easy to get money for strictly Church purposes in Liverpool, he is mistaken.

(4) In the next place, few people at a distance seem to realize how fearfully undermanned this Diocese is in the matter of clergy. Our population in 1881 was 1,085,000. At the present moment, I believe, it is little less than 1,200,000. And what spiritual provision does the Church of England make for this huge multitude? We have only 200 Incumbents, besides curates, or, upon an average, one Incumbent to each 6,000 souls! Nor is this all. We have not a few parishes with populations of 21,000, 20,000, 18,000, 15,000, 12,000, and 10,000. It is absurd to suppose that the Established

Church is properly represented in such districts, or can keep touch with the people. Real pastoral work in these parishes is impossible, and thousands live and die like sheep without a shepherd, and might almost as well be in a heathen land. And, worst of all, these vast, overgrown parishes are often inhabited by the poorest of the labouring classes, who can hardly earn enough to keep themselves from downright poverty, and are utterly unable to give substantial help to the clergy. Truly the contrast between my old Diocese of Norwich, with 1,050 incumbents and only 700,000 people, and the Diocese of Liverpool, with 1,200,000 people and only 200 incumbents, is terribly painful. Both are Dioceses within the pale of the Established Church of England; but there is a startling difference between their conditions.

(5) In the next place, few people appear to realize the extremely disadvantageous position in which our Diocese is placed by the miserably low endowment of many of its largest parishes. Out of our 200 incumbents, at least ninety-eight, or nearly one half, receive an income of not more than £300 a year, and not a few receive even less. Yet many of these parishes are exactly the most densely populated and the poorest in the whole Diocese. The difficulties of a vicar with the nominal charge of ten or twelve or fifteen thousand souls, and an income of £300 a year, are more easily imagined than described. It is a painful, pitiable, heart-breaking, depressing state of things; and I often wonder that men can be found to fill such posts. So long as such a condition of clerical incomes exists, it is useless to expect first-rate Oxford and Cambridge men to come to our Diocese, whatever anonymous newspaper writers may please to say, or to stay when they come. At best, a title for orders in the north end of Liverpool, or in Wigan, Warrington, Widnes, or St Helens, is not very attractive. But when you add to this the slender chance of promotion to anything worth calling a *living* which stares a curate in the face, you cannot wonder that wranglers and first-class men hesitate to come to Liverpool Diocese! Such men naturally prefer

a post in East London, where they are within reach of College contemporaries who are in business or reading the law, or they embark in some Diocese where the Bishop has patronage with which to reward deserving men, such as, by an unhappy oversight of Parliament, the Bishop of the new See of Liverpool has not got. The whole subject of endowments and clerical incomes deserves more attention than it has hitherto received. It has been too much forgotten that to endow new churches is quite as important as to build them. Clergymen cannot live on air any more than other people, and nothing degrades a minister so much as a constant sense of pecuniary difficulties. If the laity of this Diocese want to get first-rate men into our churches, they may depend upon it they must offer more inducements for first-rate men to come.

(6) In the last place, our Diocese is placed in considerable difficulty by the want of a proper Cathedral, and a body of endowed clergy connected with it. In this respect our new See is worse off than any See in England. The modern Dioceses of Manchester, Ripon, and Southwell found Cathedrals ready for them. The parish churches of Newcastle and Wakefield are large and handsome enough to be made Cathedrals with ease. In Truro, the energetic Bishop, having hardly any new churches to build, has been able to devote himself to the erection of the new Cathedral, which is soon to be opened. In Liverpool, on the contrary, we have not a single church in the whole city which could justly be called a suitable Cathedral.

I frankly admit that I cannot make an idol of a Cathedral, as some people seem to do. I do not think it a primary object in such a Diocese as ours, where more churches and living agents are the first thing wanted. But I should be blind indeed if I did not see that a large Cathedral enables many things to be done which cannot be done without it. For large Diocesan gatherings of any kind, for services and functions connected with Congresses and Conferences, for assemblies of choirs, voluntary lay-helpers, Sunday-school teachers, Societies of young men or young women, and, above all, for popular nave services like those held in St Paul's and Westminster Abbey—for all these purposes a stately ecclesiastical building, capable of accommodating 2,000 or 3,000 people, would be most useful in Liverpool. At present we have nothing of the kind; and whether we ever shall have seems doubtful. It is certain that, to build and endow a magnificent Minster, such as Emerson, Bodley, and Brooks designed, would cost half a million of money; and at present I do not see where this immense sum is likely to be raised. But that the want of a proper Cathedral is in many ways a serious disadvantage to our Diocese, I have no doubt at all.

I wind up the list of our difficulties here, and I make no apology for dwelling on them at such length. They are difficulties which are neither known nor realized by Churchmen who are not acquainted with Liverpool. They are difficulties which ought to be looked at and weighed, if people want to form a just estimate of the condition and progress of our new Diocese at the end of the seventh year of its existence. About that condition I will now supply a few plain facts, and give a brief account of our agencies, machinery, and organization in a summarized form.

(1) When the See of Liverpool was created in 1880, the official staff of the area of the district consisted of one Archdeacon and six Rural Deans. We have now two Archdeacons, and nine Rural Deans, and by the division of the Deanery of North Meols, which is sanctioned and will shortly be gazetted, we shall soon have ten.

(2) We have twenty-four Honorary Canons of our Cathedral, all unendowed, by whom the Cathedral pulpit is supplied every Sunday afternoon.

(3) We have a regular Cathedral service at five o'clock every day; a choir, of which we have no cause to be ashamed; and an afternoon service and sermon at three every Sunday. More than this we cannot manage at present, because St Peter's Cathedral is the parish church of Liverpool, and parochial demands for marriages and baptisms have to be satisfied. For this Cathedral

service we have not at present a single penny of endowment. It is entirely kept up on the voluntary system.

(4) We have 200 Incumbents in the Diocese—a painfully small number for the large population. In 1880 there were 182. We have 194 stipendiary Curates; in 1880 there were only 120. This is an increase of seventy-four Curates in seven years.

(5) We have an organized Church of England Scripture Readers' Society in Liverpool, supplying forty-five Readers, who are doing excellent work in our large parishes.

(6) We have a Mission of thirty-one Bible-women in Liverpool, in order to hold mothers' meetings, and do work which can be better done by women than men.

(7) We have two Church societies for promoting the spiritual welfare of seamen in this the first seaport in the world—the Mersey Mission to Seamen and the St Andrew's Waterside Mission.

(8) We have four Diocesan Institutions—one for Church building, one for Church aid by the provision of missionary curates in large parishes, one for Augmenting and helping small livings, and one for Educational purposes, including a paid inspector of religious instruction in the Diocese.

(9) We have an enrolled and registered Diocesan Finance Association, for the reception and management of all moneys contributed to the Diocesan Institutions, and to any other Religious Societies.

(10) We have a powerful Church of England Temperance Society, with branches and ramifications in every part of the Diocese, which is doing great good.

(11) During the last seven years I have consecrated twenty entirely new churches, and opened by licence two others, which only need an endowment. Three others are being built, and will be completed before long. This makes twenty-five in all. Restoration, or the addition of chancels, at Halsall, Upholland, Ormskirk, Haigh, and St Paul's, Prince's Park, have in each case cost very

large sums of money.[1] It is worthy of notice that no less than forty new churches have been built and consecrated in the little corner of Lancashire forming this Diocese within the last fourteen years.

(12) There are fifty licensed Mission-rooms in the Diocese. In Walton two districts, and in Bootle one, have been regularly assigned to missionary curates, and services are carried on in temporary buildings till churches can be erected.

(13) In the seven years that I have been Bishop of Liverpool I have ordained no less than 217 Deacons. In the seven years before the See was created the number ordained for the same district was only 133.

(14) The number of young persons Confirmed in the first year that I began confirming was 4,700. The annual number is now between 6,000 and 7,000, and these are supplied by only 200 congregations. During the last six years I have held 291 Confirmations, and confirmed 35,458 young persons.

(15) We have a Diocesan Conference, which has met regularly every year since 1881. It differs from all others, I believe, in one remarkable point. It is open to every licensed clergyman in the Diocese, and is only elective for two lay representatives from every parish.

(16) We have in every Rural Deanery a Ruri-decanal Chapter of clergy only, and a Ruri-decanal Conference of clergy and laity combined, each meeting twice annually.

(17) We have a powerful Sunday-school Institute, which is increasingly useful every year, and there are 69,776 scholars in our Church Sunday schools.

(18) We have a Society of voluntary Lay helpers, with 500 enrolled members. Of these, forty-four have been formally admitted as Readers with a special religious service, and have received stamped letters of approval from my hands.

(19) We have a most valuable Pension Fund for the benefit of aged and invalid clergy, for which we are indebted to the noble gift

---

[1] *See appendix, chapter 6, pp. 430-32.

of £20,000 from a well-known lady in Liverpool. At present the income of this fund, which is more than £700 a year, seems likely to meet the wants of the whole Diocese.

(20) We have a large Girls' Friendly Society, which, under the untiring superintendence of Lady Lathom and other zealous ladies, is doing good service to young women.

(21) We have three distinct religious services in the Welsh language in Liverpool—one at the old St David's Church behind the Adelphi, and two in licensed rooms—one at Kirkdale, at the north end of the city, and one at the south end, in St Nathaniel's. This is a matter which has been rather overlooked in past days. We have a large Welsh population in our city, and if we do not provide Church services, we have no right to wonder if our Welsh brethren go to chapels.

(22) Last, but not least, I must testify that the 200 churches of the Diocese, on the whole, as buildings, are in remarkably good order and condition. I may be allowed to speak with authority on this point. I have preached 650 times for my clergy in the last seven years, and have either preached or held Confirmations in no less than 180 churches out of the 200 in the Diocese; and I do not hesitate to say that it is an exception to see a consecrated building in this district which is not clean, well kept, and in good repair. We certainly cannot point to grand ecclesiastical structures, such as you will find in East Anglia. But in point of *condition* I believe our churches are second to none. For this I think we are much indebted to active churchwardens and sidesmen.

I close my account of Diocesan agencies, machinery, and Institutions at this point. Not a few of them I found already existing and in operation when I became Bishop of Liverpool. I claim no credit for them, but have gladly adopted them as part of our organization. The large annual contributions of the Diocese to the Home and Foreign Missions of the Church of England might have been added, and the whole list might easily be lengthened if time permitted. Much of my long statement no doubt applies exclusively to Liverpool proper. But this is natural when it is recollected that one-half the population of the Diocese dwells in our great city. I do not forget that a large amount of good Church work is continually done in Wigan, Warrington, St Helens, and Southport, of which I cannot speak particularly; and perhaps it is more parochial than diocesan. I am also thankful to add that a very large quantity of religious and philanthropic work is continually done in Liverpool by Churchmen and Nonconformists combined. But you will readily understand that in a Visitation Charge I naturally confine myself to the work of the Church of England. And on the whole I think we have no cause to be ashamed of our new Diocese. In short, I am bold to assert that, considering our many difficulties we have much ground for thankfulness. Whatever our enemies may please to say, we are not standing still, but moving. We are not asleep, but awake. We are not dead, but alive.

Of course we are far from perfection. Standing on the watch-tower which a Bishop occupies, and looking over the whole area of our Diocese, I see many things wanting which I long to see supplied.

(1) We want some of our large overgrown parishes wisely broken up and subdivided, and new churches built, and legal districts constituted, with a resident incumbent and his staff in each. The position of such parishes as St John the Baptist, Toxteth Park; St Mary, Kirkdale; St Paul, North Shore; St Mary, Bootle; and the Rectory Parish at Warrington is utterly unsatisfactory. It is absurd to suppose that the Church of England can be properly represented, or her pastoral work kept up, in such enormous districts. No one can wonder that Dissent abounds in them, and that the Church is neither known, nor felt, nor respected by many of the inhabitants.

(2) We want more mission-rooms in many of our large parishes, if we cannot get churches. Good, solid, plain buildings of this kind, accommodating 400 or 500 people, and costing

little compared to a church, are of unspeakable value to an active clergyman, and pave the way by elementary services for churches to be built at some future time. Such rooms as I have seen at Blowick, Southport; All Saints', Hindley; and St Nathaniel's, Liverpool, are examples of what I mean. I commend such rooms as these to the special attention of my clergy. I am sorry to say that the days of £200 a year endowments from the Ecclesiastical Commissioners for every new church with 4,000 people in its district, seem coming to an end, in consequence of agricultural depression. We must no longer reckon on this help, and future churches must be self-supporting. Let us not despair. If we cannot build churches, let us build rooms.

(3) We want far more liberal subscriptions to our Diocesan Institutions. At present their income is disgracefully small, and their usefulness is thereby crippled. No doubt times have been very bad for the last seven years, and there is a great shrinkage in the profits of business. But there is too much reason to believe that myriads of Churchmen both here and all over England never see the positive duty of giving regularly for the promotion of Christ's cause. They appear to think that going to Church on Sunday is the whole of religion. The late Canon Hume used to tell me that he could not find the names of 3,000 persons in all the subscription lists of Liverpool. I do not hesitate to say that this is the weakest point in the character of English Churchmen. They do not seem to understand the duty and privilege of giving money in order to do good. It is a point in which we are far behind English Nonconformists and Scotch Presbyterians. When I find that one-third of the churches in this Diocese have no collection at all for Diocesan Institutions, I am grieved. It is only one among many proofs that the corporate action of the Church of England—a great body with many members—is at present very imperfectly understood in South-West Lancashire. Congregations are too much disposed to think only of themselves, and to forget their neighbours.

I know well that Diocesan Institutions are everywhere unpopular, and are badly supported. But I fail to see how any Diocese can be worked without them. In every Diocese there ought to be a central fund, to which all clergymen wanting help for Church work ought to be able to apply, and through which the richer parishes may help the poorer. The management of such funds cannot, of course, be left in the hands of one school of thought, and all parties ought to be represented on the Committees. My own observation of the annual grants of our wretchedly supported Diocesan Institutions for some years, leads me to the conclusion that they are impartially and fairly administered, and I heartily wish they had larger funds to dispense.

My Reverend Brethren, this matter is a very serious business, and I trust it will not be forgotten and thrown behind your backs. It is gradually becoming a grave question, if our Diocesan Institutions are not better supported, whether they must not be given up altogether and wound up. For the honour of the Diocese, I hope such a discreditable consummation may be avoided. But we really must have more annual subscriptions and Church collections. I hope you will not oblige me to say, when I am asked to occupy your pulpits for some parochial object, 'I cannot give you a sermon if you do not have an annual collection for Diocesan purposes, for one or other of our four great Institutions.'

(4) Finally, we want to see more of the laity coming forward to take part in all the affairs of the Church in our Diocese. It pains me to see how few find time to attend our Committees, to come to the meetings of our Religious Societies, and to take part in our Diocesan Conferences. The demands of business seem to absorb all their days. Yet there never was an era in the history of our Church when she needed the strong sense and the well-balanced minds of her lay sons more than she does now. The affairs of the New Testament Churches were quite as much cared for by the laity as the clergy, and it ought to be the same in the Church of England. It is not a healthy symptom of our condition when it is not so. I

say all this with a sorrowful recollection of our recent losses. Men like Mr Bushell, Mr Groves, and Mr Bailey make gaps, when they are removed, which are not easily filled up. It is a constant prayer of mine that God would incline some of the younger lay Churchmen in Liverpool to come forward and help us more than they do.

However, after all I have now said, I must repeat what I said at the beginning, that on a retrospect of the last seven years, and a calm survey of our progress and condition, the feeling which predominates in my mind is one of deep thankfulness. In the face of many difficulties, and with an uphill battle to fight, much has been done, and much is doing, in our new See. We have as large a proportion of hard-working, diligent clergy, I believe, as any Diocese in England. There is a vast amount of quiet, solid work going on of which the outside world knows nothing, and which is never blazoned and trumpeted in Church newspapers. The mere presence of a Bishop will not work miracles, or convert inefficient clergymen, who have mistaken their calling, into apostles and prophets. But considering what human nature is, and what we have a reasonable right to expect from it, and what obstacles we have to contend with, I believe the new Diocese of Liverpool has abundant reason to thank God and take courage.

II. I must now turn away from our own Diocese, and take up a far wider and more difficult subject. That subject is, the general condition of the great Established Church of England, of which our Diocese forms a part, and with which, for weal or woe, we are bound up. I approach it with a deep sense of its difficulty and importance. We are all apt to think there never were such times as those we now live in; and this is natural. They are the only times with which we are quite familiar. But I am bold to say there never was a period in which there were so many critical and burning questions demanding attention as the present. Our ecclesiastical horizon has very dark clouds in some quarters, and much depends on the activity, wisdom, and moderation of Churchmen in the next five years.

I shall surprise some of you when I begin by saying that, in many points of view, I regard the condition of the Established Church of England as remarkably *cheering, encouraging, and satisfactory*. It is impossible to deny that there is an amount of life, and energy, and activity and zeal, and stir, and 'go,' if I may use a modern term, among Churchmen in the present day, which was utterly unknown fifty years ago. I do not admit for a moment that this change has arisen from the so-called High-Church revival, as some are fond of saying. The large and growing income of the Church Missionary Society this very year shows clearly that there is no decay in the zeal and influence of the Evangelical body. The fact is, that the change is to be seen in every school, and party, and department, and section of Churchmen. All over the land things are utterly unlike what they were half a century ago. The Church of England is no longer asleep, but awake. The energies of her children in some cases may be sadly misdirected, and do much mischief. But her worst enemies must admit that she is moving. She is not quite dead, but very much alive. I will mention a few facts in order to prove the truth of what I say.

(1) First and foremost, I point to the immense amount of money which Churchmen have voluntarily expended in building new churches and restoring old ones during the last fifty years, and notably to the sums expended on our grand old Cathedrals. The total of this money is not less than thirty millions of pounds! Of course it is easy to say that bricks and stones and mortar do not make up religion. No doubt that is true. But it is also true that our grandfathers coolly saw the population growing round them and built no churches at all, while the Dissenters built many chapels. I have read that Bishop Porteus[1] only saw one new church built in the Diocese of London during the whole period of his episcopate. In temporal matters, when merchants and tradesmen begin to enlarge their premises, it does not look like failure and decay.

[1] Beilby Porteus, Bishop of London, 1787–1808.

(2) In the next place, I point to the great and undeniable change in the general character and conduct of the clergy. No doubt there may be false shepherds, and wolves in sheep's clothing, and black sheep in our ranks, just as there are rotten members in every profession; and as long as human nature is what it is, we must expect this to the end of the world. But I confidently assert that the general standard of the clergy as a body is to a certainty better than it was at the early part of this century. Scandalous lives, gross neglect of pastoral duty, perfunctory and slovenly discharge of Church services, sacred buildings closed from Sunday to Sunday, dirty and untidy pews and benches, the Lord's Supper only administered once a quarter, no weekly services, children not gathered into schools, the masses left to the Methodists and Nonconformists without any compunction—all these things were the rule in many English parishes at the beginning of this century. Now, I am bold to say, they are the exception. Will any one deny that this is an immense improvement?

(3) In the next place, I point to the enormous change for the better in the sermons of the clergy of this day, when compared with the sermons which our ancestors were compelled to hear. It is vain to deny that the sermon of the old times was too often nothing better than a moral essay, and from beginning to end of it there was a conspicuous absence of the chief distinctive doctrines of Christianity. The atonement, the work of the Holy Spirit, justification, conversion, repentance, faith, were seldom, if ever, enforced or explained. It is not so now. Most of these mighty verities, even though sometimes stated with questionable clearness, are rarely quite ignored. Nor are they the monopoly of any one school in the Church. You may often hear them in pulpit after pulpit from men who in many points differ widely. Surely we ought candidly to admit that this is an immense improvement.

(4) In the next place, I point to the great increase of parochial work which is regularly done by many clergymen, compared to what was done in days gone by. Week-day services, Bible classes,

meetings of Sunday-school teachers, organized gatherings of young men and young women, temperance meetings, and many other agencies for good, have sprung into existence, and are kept up in every part of the land. I sometimes feel amazed in Liverpool churches, when I hear the long list of engagements for the coming week, which is read out to the congregation, and marvel that so many irons can be found to put in the fire, and all kept hot. But the fact is undeniable, that far more is done in 1887 than in 1800, and I am thankful.

(5) In the next place, I point to the constantly growing desire of the clergy to get together, confer, discuss, take counsel, and pray. As evidences of what I mean, I ask you to remember that Congresses, Conferences, Ruri-decanal gatherings, Retreats, Quiet Days, and the like, are all comparatively modern inventions, and were utterly unknown to our grandfathers, who were content with an occasional quiet clerical meeting. No doubt the gatherings I have mentioned are not always very useful, and sometimes are very dull. But they certainly evidence a state of feeling in the clerical body very different from that of the 'good old times,' when many an Incumbent never stirred out of his parish from January to December, or only met his clerical brethren in order to eat, drink, and play at cards.

(6) In the next place, I point to the increased usefulness of our venerable Cathedrals. I remember the time when they were generally regarded as matchless specimens of architecture, and hardly anything more. People went to see them as they went to see the Elgin Marbles in the British Museum, and admired the wonders in stone and wood and glass which they contained. But what did the Cathedrals do for the cause of Christ and true religion? Little, very little indeed! A few stray sheep in the cold wilderness of the choir on week-days, two or three hundred on Sunday afternoons to hear a good anthem, this was the Cathedral's contribution to the cause of religion in old times! I thank God there is an end to all this. Select picked preachers, lively nave

services, accompanied by a popular service of song, have obtained a new lease of life for the grand old Minsters and Abbey Churches of the land. The man who attends St Paul's or Westminster Abbey on a Sunday afternoon, can no longer say that the Cathedrals are weighed in the balances and found wanting.

(7) In the next place, I point to the astonishing increase of the Colonial Episcopate during the last fifty years. In the midst of vast exertions to promote missions to the heathen and missions at home, the Church of England has found time and money to found new Dioceses in every part of the Colonial Empire, and to plant her Prayer-book and her form of government in every land where the British flag flies, and her children are forming new homes. In the year 1840 there were only ten Colonial Bishops. In the year 1887 there are seventy-three. It goes without saying that Bishops alone do not make a Church, any more than officers make an army, without rank and file. But there is abundant proof that, as soon as a Bishop is sent out to a colony, and a diocese formed, the almost invariable result is a large increase of clergy, means of grace, and congregations. When a great tree begins to decay, one of the first symptoms is the withering and death of the extreme branches. This is precisely what is *not* the case with the Church of England. The colonies supply abundant proof that she is not dead but alive in every part of the globe.

(8) In the last place, I point to the astonishing growth of aggressive evangelistic operations which is to be seen all over the land in the present day. It is only thirty years ago that I had the high honour of taking part in the first mission service, which, I believe, was ever held. It was held for six evenings successively in St Martin's Church, Birmingham, and Dr M'Neile,[1] Dr Miller,[2] and myself were the preachers. That week's effort was regarded as a very dubious experiment, and many predicted failure. But now, at the end of thirty years, Special Missions have become an organized

---

[1] Hugh M'Neile, Canon of Chester, 1845–68.
[2] John Cole Miller; became Incumbent of St Martin's Birmingham in 1846.

institution of the Church of England. They are approved, patronized, and supported by every school of thought. In some Dioceses a mission clergyman is a recognized officer of the Diocese. There are hardly any large towns in which missions have not been held. In short, a determination to carry the Gospel to every class, and to go down to those who will not come up to us, is an unmistakeable sign of the times. If Wesley, and Whitefield, and Berridge, and Grimshaw, had been told a hundred and twenty years ago that the whole Church of England would ever take up aggressive evangelization like our present Special Missions, I can hardly think they would have believed it. But the fact is before our eyes.

I ask your best attention to the list of facts which I have now laid before you. I challenge any one to deny their correctness. They form the ground on which I confidently build the assertion, that there is much that is cheering, hopeful, and encouraging in the present condition of the Church of England. If we are to be disestablished and destroyed, as some think we shall be, at any rate we shall not die sleeping. *Oportet imperatorem stantem mori.*[1] Like the gallant sentinel of Pompeii, we are awake, and shall die at our post.

Let me add to all this, that one of the healthiest symptoms in the Church of England is the general growing desire to reform abuses, and to 'set in order things that are wanting.' Measures have been brought forward, both in Parliament and out of it, for the improvement and strengthening of the Church, most of which deserve the support of all loyal Churchmen, and I think it my duty to make a few remarks about them.

(1) The Bill about Tithes, transferring their payment from occupiers to landlords, appears to me a most important and valuable measure, and one which ought to be thankfully received. I have always held that this arrangement ought to have been made originally, when the Tithe Commutation Act was first passed. It seems impossible to make some farmers understand that the

---

[1] 'In standing at our post of duty it behoves us to be prepared to die.'

payment of tithes lowers their rent, and is a part of the conditions on which they hold their farms. So long as they themselves have to pay the money they think that they are injured and aggrieved. I trust that this measure may soon become the law of the land.

(2) The Church Patronage Bill contains some most excellent provisions, for which most thinking Churchmen have long sighed in vain. The sale of presentations is to my mind a scandal. The sale of advowsons ought only to be allowed under special circumstances, and should be fenced by safeguards. Power ought to be given to a Bishop to refuse the institution of any clergyman nominated to a living who, from age or bodily or mental infirmity, is clearly unfit for his office. Liberty and opportunity ought to be granted to parishioners to show reasons, if they can, why a clergyman nominated should not be instituted, provided always that, if their objections are frivolous and vexatious, they must pay the costs of objection. In my opinion, the weakest and worst point in the original Bill was the proposed Diocesan Patronage Board in every Diocese. I am confident that such a cumbrous Board would not have worked well. In one Diocese, it would have fallen into the hands of some one strong mind. In a second, it would have produced nothing but colourless milk-and-water appointments. In a third, it would have been a scene of perpetual compromise or controversy. I trust we shall never hear of it again. Only let the most patent and glaring abuses of the present system be removed, and then the more patronage is divided and scattered the better. Nothing, I believe, would be a greater misfortune to our Church than to concentrate and accumulate patronage in one set of hands. I would leave it between the Crown, the Chancellor, the Bishops, the Colleges, private patrons, and accredited bodies of trustees. It is the only way to keep up the comprehensive character of the Church of England.

(3) The Bill for permitting the sale of glebe-lands is one which I must honestly say I regard with some doubtful feelings. I hope it might work well, but I am not very enthusiastic about it. I can

quite understand that incumbents of livings endowed with land, and not with tithes, are often placed in a most painful position during the present agricultural depression. They are liable to have their glebe thrown on their hands by the failure of their tenants. They are too often in such cases utterly unable to farm the land, partly from want of capital and partly from want of skill. We cannot wonder that in such livings an Incumbent would like to have the power to sell the glebe, and turn it into hard cash, to be invested in some good and safe security. No doubt there are occasional instances in which the sale might be advantageously effected, and some wealthy landowner might occasionally be ready to give a good price for an addition to his wide domains. But I fear there are very many parishes in which it would be impossible to sell the glebe-land except at an immense sacrifice and a permanent loss of more than half the value of the living, which, if better days come, would be regretted too late. However, it may perhaps be expedient to have a permissive Act. I only maintain that the sale of glebe-lands should always be approached with very great caution, and that a full report of its desirability should be made by competent commissioners residing in the Diocese and close by the parish. To all this let me add my own private impression, that the Ecclesiastical Commissioners, from their long acquaintance with Church property, are the persons to whom the whole transaction should be entrusted.

Turning from the inside of Parliament to outside movements, schemes, and matters which have come into being during the last three years, and are now pressed on the attention of Churchmen, there are four points about which I have something to say, and points about which you have a just right to expect some expression of opinion from your Bishop.

(1) First and foremost comes the newly-created House of Laymen in the Province of Canterbury. I regard that House with great satisfaction, and read the reports of its proceedings with close attention. It is a valuable experiment, and a move in the

right direction. Nevertheless, I cannot expect so much from it as some do. So long as it has no legal status whatsoever, and is not recognized by Queen, Lords, and Commons; so long as it is a mere consultative body, without power to originate anything, or to do anything beside talking and passing resolutions, and this under some little restraint; so long as it is elected in the present fashion; so long I do not think it will gather into its ranks the chief laymen of light and leading in the Province of Canterbury, or excite lasting interest in its proceedings. I repeat, however, that it is essentially a move in the right direction. It is the admission of a great principle, far too long most foolishly ignored, that the laity of a church have a right to be consulted, and ought to have a voice in all its proceedings.[1] The thin edge of the wedge has got in, and a beginning of wise counsels has been made. Whether we shall have a House of Laymen in the Northern Province remains yet to be seen.

(2) Next in importance comes the much-talked of union of the Northern and Southern Convocations. To this, under the present state of things, I am thoroughly opposed, and I trust I shall never live to see it. If the Church of England were ever disestablished like the Church of Ireland, and a brand-new constitution had to be framed, there might be something in the idea. Again, if the Lower House of Canterbury was completely reformed and recast on the model of the Lower House of York, with two clerical representatives from each Archdeaconry, there might be something in the idea. Whether there is much chance of this I venture to doubt. At present the two Lower Convocations are not homogeneous, and till they are, fusion and amalgamation seem to me out of the question. After all, it is a very doubtful matter whether the proposed union would ever work well. The votes of the North

---

[1] *'Till it be proved that some special law of Christ hath for ever secured unto the clergy alone the power of making ecclesiastical laws, we are to hold it a thing most consonant with equity and reason, that no ecclesiastical laws be made in a Christian commonwealth without consent or will of the laity as well as of the clergy.' Hooker, *Eccles. Polity,* Book viii. chap. vi.

would be so entirely swamped and outnumbered by those of the South, that I suspect the huge populations of the North would be dissatisfied. Moreover, if one great Synod was held in London for the whole Church, I predict that the attendance of members from the North of England would be very scanty. The Metropolis is the natural centre of the South of England, and for many reasons members of Convocation gravitate towards it. It is not so with the North. The inhabitants of Lancashire and Yorkshire have their own great centres in Manchester, Liverpool, Leeds, and Sheffield, and do not see the need of continually going to London. It is my impression that one great Synod would fall very much into the hands of a few busy Churchmen in and around London, and the North would be practically left out in the cold. In short, I have a decided opinion that the two Convocations must be content at present to co-operate by delegations, and that any attempt to amalgamate and unite them would be a mistake.

(3) The next public subject about which I shall say a few words is the proposed 'Church House' in London. I feel it my duty not to leave it unnoticed, and I want my attitude towards the scheme not to be misunderstood. The Church House is undoubtedly a brilliant idea, and if carried out would be a graceful memorial of the Jubilee year of Her Majesty Queen Victoria's reign. The building would be most useful to the Convocation of Canterbury, which at present has no suitable dwelling-place. If any Churchman in my Diocese likes to send aid to the proposed Church House, by all means let him do so. I would not lift a finger to prevent him; though I should have thought that London with its four millions might easily have done the work without asking the help of Lancashire. But I must say plainly, that I cannot see what benefit the Northern Province of York would receive from the Church House in London, so long as the two Convocations are separated, and not united. For business purposes we have the offices of the Ecclesiastical Commissioners and Queen Anne's Bounty Board. The great Religious Societies have their own offices, and are not

likely to give them up. For meetings of Bishops, Lambeth Palace is sufficiently large. For what other remaining purposes a northern Churchman can need a London Church House I do not at present see. Beside all this, we want a large sum of money for a Cathedral in Liverpool, and money to build at least a dozen more proposed churches in the Diocese, of which the promoters are brought to a dead standstill for want of funds. Last, but not least, we sorely want a Church House of our own in Liverpool, and I am sure we do not want it quite as much as a Cathedral. A suitable building in a central position in this great city containing the Registry, the Consistory Court, business rooms for my own interviews, offices for the Diocesan Finance Association and all our other Church Societies, a moderately-sized room for Committee meetings, a Church club and reading-room, and the depot of the Christian Knowledge Society—such a building, I believe, would be of incalculable value to our Diocese, and I heartily wish it might be built. At present the business of the Diocese is carried on in cribbed, cabined, confined, and highly-rented offices in a most inconvenient way. In the face of such facts as these, I think you cannot be surprised that I have not seen my way to call upon our Diocese to support the London Church House.

(4) The last public subject which I think it right to touch upon may seem a small one at first sight. But small as it is I dare not pass it over, because it seems to me to contain the germ of much mischief. The subject I refer to is the proposed addition to the Church Catechism which has been lately discussed seriously in the Lower House of Canterbury Convocation. Far be it from me to say that our venerable Catechism is perfect; and I daresay we all think we could improve it. But what I strongly object to is the slightest attempt to pull about anything in the Prayer-book, and to introduce the thin edge of addition, subtraction, mutilation, or alteration. A more fertile source of strife, debate, controversy, and division than the very additions which have been recently launched I cannot conceive. Where are we going to stop? What

next, and what next? Happily the Prayer-book can never be legally altered or added to without permission from the Government and a 'letter of business.' I doubt extremely whether such permission will ever be granted. In the meantime I earnestly hope that the clergy of my Diocese will lend no support to the proposed addition to the Catechism. Let every man explain it loyally and honestly to his parishioners according to his own light. But for the sake of peace, let us not add to the old document, but leave it alone.

I shall now conclude this Charge by calling your attention to two heavy black clouds which appear to me to loom large on our ecclesiastical horizon. I have swept a tolerably large field in my survey of our Church's progress and condition, both inside and outside of our own Diocese. I have brought prominently forward many causes for deep thankfulness, and no one I think can fairly say that I am a pessimist today. But it is useless to ignore dangers, and especially in a great institution like the Church of England. To my eyes there are two very formidable dangers ahead which imperatively require the attention and the prayers of all loyal Churchmen. To be always crying 'Peace, peace, when there is no peace,' and to refuse to touch unpleasant topics, is neither honesty nor charity. It is the conduct of a flatterer and not of a friend. Let me then point out what these two dangers are.

(1) The first danger I see is the *utter paralysis of discipline* in the Church of England.

We all know, and know to our sorrow, that disputes about the ritual of the Lord's Supper have been the plague and trouble of the Church of England for more than twenty years. Differences of opinion about many points there always have been within the Established Church, and no man of common sense expects a rigid cast-iron uniformity of thought and practice among Churchmen. If we cannot be liberal and comprehensive, if we cannot 'think and let think,' we are not in our right place in the Anglican Communion. There will always be High, Low, and Broad schools of thought within our pale. But it is evident that liberty and comprehensiveness must have some limits, and the Lord's Supper is a subject about which Churchmen are reasonably jealous, when they remember that our martyred Reformers were burned because they would not receive the Romish doctrine about that blessed sacrament. We know also that novelties in the celebration of the Lord's Supper have been made the subject of several law-suits in the Ecclesiastical Courts of this country, and have several times been distinctly condemned and declared illegal. Finally, we know that many clergymen regard the judgments of these Courts as null and void, refuse to pay the slightest attention to them, continue to do the very things which they condemn, deny their authority as ecclesiastical tribunals, and decline to obey the admonitions of their Bishop if he supports the Courts, notwithstanding their oath of obedience.[1]

Now this is precisely the state of things which I call *dangerous in the highest degree*, and I think it my duty to direct your attention to it. You will observe that I do not touch the question of right or wrong in these unhappy disputes. I do not say whether the judgments have been good or bad. But I do say that a Church in which the clergy refuse to obey the Church's Courts, Courts which are duly recognized by Queen, Lords, and Commons; Courts which are the only representatives of the royal supremacy—that such a Church is in a most unsatisfactory condition. It is a Church without order and discipline. It is a Church which is in a state of lawlessness, anarchy, chaos, and confusion, and, unless some remedy is applied, must make shipwreck. In short, in matters of discipline we are at present drifting like a ship without a rudder. Unless we mind what we are about, we shall find, by painful experience, that tolerated lawlessness is just as dangerous to a Church as it is to a State.

[1] *'We hold it to be most desirable that the National Establishment should continue to comprise members who are attached to the different schools of thought, so long as every minister whom the Church appoints shall be willing to conform to her standard of doctrine and ritual. But this large comprehension seems to us to render it most desirable, and indeed essential, that in the Church's ministration the officiating minister should not introduce innovations, which are welcome to one party, but are wholly offensive to another.' A. C. Ewald: *Life of Sir Joseph Napier*, p. 334.

The evils of this position of things are simply incalculable. Their name is legion. Party spirit increases in every Diocese. Diocesan Institutions are starved and neglected. One man will not support them because he thinks them too High, and another because he thinks them too Low! Strife, controversy, and theological squabbles about trifles absorb time and attention. Divisions weaken our whole body, and prevent us showing a united front to our enemies. Sceptics and infidels make capital out of our differences, and tell us it is time enough to become believers when we are agreed among ourselves. The advocates of Disestablishment rejoice to see us playing their game so well, and biting and devouring one another. The gulf between clergyman and clergyman becomes wider and wider every year, and ministers of the same Church keep aloof and separate from one another, as if they did not belong to the same communion. At the rate things are going it will soon be impossible for a Bishop to ask candidates for orders any questions about the Lord's Supper! If all this does not constitute danger, I know not what can.

But unhappily this is not all. Throughout England, whenever any clergyman refuses to obey the Courts or listen to his Bishop, the local press is at once inundated with a flood of crude, wild opinions from anonymous correspondents, which reflect little credit on the wisdom of the writers, but do infinite harm to ignorant readers. One man tells the public that every zealous and earnest clergyman ought to be let alone, and to be allowed to preach and practise in his church exactly what he likes. Another man maintains the astounding position that every congregation should be allowed to have any kind of ceremonial it pleases, ignoring the fact that our Church is not an assembly of independent congregations, but a corporate body, requiring a reasonable measure of uniformity in all its members. A third asserts that the famous 'Ornaments rubric' is flatly contrary to the decisions of the Law Courts on ritual matters, but forgets or omits to tell the public that the two greatest lawyers of our time maintained, in a closely reasoned judgment, that this is a complete mistake; that the 'Ornaments rubric' must be interpreted by the light of the 'advertisements' of Queen Elizabeth's day, and that the authority of these 'advertisements' is admitted by the Archbishops of that reign, by Hooker, and by the 24th Canon of our own Church, and endorsed by the findings of three centuries. A fourth protests against the Courts condemning sacrificial vestments and the like, unless they require copes to be worn. But he does not tell the public that copes have no doctrinal significance like chasubles, that they have been disused by common consent for three hundred years, and that the same canons which recommend copes forbid the clergy to wear white stockings. A fifth coolly proclaims that a Bishop's power of 'veto' was never intended to give a Bishop any discretion at all, and that it is a Bishop's bounden duty to prohibit any prosecution of a clergyman, however illegal the clergyman's conduct may seem to be. Crude and wild statements such as these are doing great harm so long as our present paralysis of discipline continues, because they gradually crystallize and solidify until they look like truth. The sooner they are dispersed by the reign of law and order, the better for the Church of England.

Now, if you ask me, as your Bishop, what is the remedy for the present deplorable state of things, I answer the question without hesitation. I see no remedy except legislation. There is a deadlock, and to Caesar we must go. If things have come to such a pass that clergymen will neither obey the Ecclesiastical Courts nor the admonitions of their Bishop, something must be done by Parliament. The distinction between the supremacy of the Crown and the supremacy of Parliament, which some attempt to draw, I fail entirely to see. The Crown must exercise its supremacy through Parliament under the British constitution, and cannot act independently. The Clergy Discipline and Public Worship Acts must either be amended and improved, or else entirely new tribunals must be created by Parliamentary legislation. Courts which no Churchman can appeal to without bringing down on himself furious persecution, Courts whose judgments cannot be enforced without calling out a display of violence, second only to what takes place at an Irish eviction—such Courts are evidently useless. We cannot go on many years longer as we do now. The policy of drifting, doing nothing, waiting, and letting alone, must be given up. It is not in reality the policy of peace. The end of such a policy will be secession or separation.

I am quite aware that the difficulties of Parliamentary legislation about ecclesiastical matters are extremely great. Many shiver and tremble at the very thought of it, and 'fear to launch away.' The surgical operation has been deferred so long, that there is some doubt whether the patient will survive it. But I believe it ought to be attempted. There are seasons when boldness is the highest wisdom. The old saying is strictly true, *Periculum sine periculo raro vincitur.*[1] No doubt the danger of legislation is very great. But in my opinion the danger of doing nothing at all is greater still.

I purposely say nothing about the notable remedy for the present distress which finds favour with some people. I refer to the proposal to have all disputes settled by exertion of the Bishop's paternal authority. I say nothing, because it seems waste of time. Throughout the country the advocates of ceremonial novelties exhibit very little disposition to attend to Episcopal admonitions, however insignificant or non-essential the practices may be which they are requested to discontinue. One of our ablest Bishops has said with truth, 'There is something very one-sided in this cry for fatherliness from the Bishop, when they meet with no filialness from the clergy.'

What the constitution of the new Ecclesiastical Courts may be, in the event of legislation being attempted, of course I do not know. We have had lines laid down by the Royal Commission which may be useful. But the proposed measure will have to pass through the crucible of Parliament, and whether it will emerge in

---

[1] Danger is seldom overcome without incurring danger.

the same state that it goes in is very doubtful. On two points alone I venture a confident prediction. No Parliament, I believe, will ever allow such ritual questions as have been litigated during the last twenty-five years to be finally decided by clerical judges alone, without the aid of laymen. The common objection that lay judges have no right to touch questions of faith or doctrine appears to me unreal and imaginary.[1] The layjudges of the present Court of Final Appeal have repeatedly declared they do not pretend to settle what is religious truth and the doctrine of Scripture. They simply undertake to ascertain the real meaning of certain formularies and rubrics, and to show the sense of the words in which they were drawn up by those who compiled them. My own conviction is, that legally-trained minds are just as competent to do this as clerical minds, and even more so, and I cannot believe for a moment that Parliament will ever sanction ecclesiastical tribunals in which layjudges have not a prominent place. The other prediction I venture to make is that, in any new Church Courts legislation, Parliament will not sanction the Episcopal veto. About that unhappy provision, you all know, I have always held a very decided opinion. A more mischievous arrangement, a more ingenious device for setting a Bishop at variance with one party in his Diocese whenever a complaint of illegality is made, and for creating divided counsels among Bishops, one Bishop allowing suits and another forbidding them—I cannot conceive. I cannot think the veto will survive the ordeal of the House of Commons.

What the result of creating new ecclesiastical tribunals will be, I will not attempt to conjecture. Of course there would be new suits, new arguments, and new decisions. It is not the least likely that those who consider the law of the Church broken by modern novelties in the ritual of the Lord's Supper, will retire

[1] The late Sir Joseph Napier, a man distinguished both as a lawyer and a Christian, declared at Norwich Congress, that the Committee of Privy Council of which he was a prominent member, 'had no jurisdiction to declare doctrine nor to establish it by law. Its province was *jus dicere, non jus dare* (to expound, not to make, the law).'

from the field, fold their arms and sit still. No! they will appeal to the new Courts for justice. And then what will the judgments be? He that will answer that question is bolder than I am. It is just possible that all the old decisions may be confirmed, and the whole body of ritual novelties completely condemned. It is just possible that the old decisions may be reversed, and the whole mass of disputed ceremonial formally sanctioned, and declared to be the binding rule of the Church of England. It is quite possible that a principle of general compromise and toleration will run through all future decisions, and that it will be decreed that every clergyman shall do exactly what is right in his own eyes, and that everybody is right and nobody wrong. Rather formidable possibilities all these! Not one of them that will satisfy everybody! Not one of them that will not endanger the life of the Church of England! But we have reached a point when something must be risked. And I repeat that the present paralysis of discipline, law, and order, is one of the greatest dangers of the Established Church, and a bold attempt ought to be made to remedy it.

(2) The other danger of our Church in the present day is one of a very different kind, but not less serious than the one I have been discussing. It is one which may not strike a careless observer. But for all that I believe it to be real and true.

The danger I refer to is the growing tendency of most preachers in this age to be content with a *low, meagre, defective, and imperfect statement of Bible truth in the pulpit*. I do not for a moment retract what I said at an earlier part of this Charge. I frankly admit that, compared to the sermons of former times, the sermons of this day are greatly improved. But for all that, I am obliged to say that much of the preaching of this generation strikes me as very unsatisfying and unsatisfactory. It is rarely, perhaps, that there is reason to complain of downright false doctrine in a modern sermon. But, somehow or other, there is too often short measure, short weight, and something wanting.

Too often, if not a mere firework, it is a leaden sword, without edge or point, as impotent to wound as it is to heal.

I look at the mighty cloud of verities which I read in the Epistles of the New Testament. I am struck with the clearness, distinctness, decision, sharpness, depth, fulness and boldness with which these verities are placed before the reader. I then turn to the many volumes of modern sermons which are continually flowing from the press, or the sermons reported in religious newspapers. And as I read I am often painfully struck with the timid, faltering, hesitating utterances of modern preachers about such mighty subjects as the inspiration of Scripture, original sin, the Trinity, the Divinity of Christ, the atonement, the personality and work of the Holy Spirit, justification, conversion, sanctification, the reality of the devil, the judgment day, the state beyond the grave, and the enormous difference between spiritual death and spiritual life. Too frequently your modern preacher seems to approach such subjects in a cautious, shaky, trembling, apologetic, uncertain tone, as if he was afraid of offending you, and had not quite made up his own mind, and dared not speak more strongly. I know not whether I make my meaning plain. But after carefully watching the English pulpit for forty years, I am sure there is reason in what I say, and I invite your best attention to the subject. With occasional rare exceptions, I am afraid the sermons of the clergy are too often below the doctrinal standard of the Bible, and intellectually behind the times.

The *causes* of this defectiveness in modern preaching are many and various. Some men are so entirely absorbed in the care of huge parishes, multiplied parochial machinery, and constant little congregational meetings, that they leave themselves no time for deep pulpit preparation, and their sermons are always elementary, thin, and shallow. Others are so thoroughly and conscientiously convinced that music and singing (things hardly mentioned in the Epistles), and the Lord's Supper (only mentioned in one Epistle), are the principal parts of divine service and religion, that they give very little time to their pulpit work. Others are morbidly afraid of the intellectual part of their hearers, the philosophers, so-called, and men of science. They dread being censured and pulled up if they are positive and dogmatical, and they cannot get rid of the fear of man. Others, and they perhaps the greatest number, are eaten up with the mischievous idea that a minister's chief object should be to please people; that he should avoid saying things that might give offence: strong language, strong doctrine, strong reproof, strong exhortation, and should try to make everything as smooth and pleasant as possible. Yet an Apostle said, 'If I yet pleased men, I should not be the servant of Christ' (Gal. 1:10).

The *consequences* of this defectiveness of modern preaching are to my mind very plain and unmistakable. There is no proportionate result of *Christian* victories and conversion-work, considering the immense amount of restless, busy, bustling *Church* work that is annually done. I suppose there never was an age when there were so many religious services and Christian agencies and preachings every week throughout the land. There never were so many special missions both in town and country. But what is the fruit of it all? What quantity of conversions is there? What large additions are being annually made to the number of our communicants? What harvest of souls turned from darkness to light is being reaped? What increase is there of men and women really born again and made new creatures? Alas, I fear there is very little to show. And I have a very strong and growing conviction that the fault is to be found in our pulpits. The Holy Ghost is grieved, and the Holy Ghost withholds his blessing. The Holy Ghost will bless nothing but the truth and the whole truth.

My Reverend Brethren, I leave this branch of my Charge with an earnest request that you will weigh well what I have been saying, and realize that I have good reason for calling your attention to the work of the pulpit. Few, I suspect, are aware that this is probably one of the weakest points in our Church's present condition. There is great room for improvement. There is real want of reform. In every age, during the last eighteen centuries, God has always honoured those ministers most who have most honoured his written word.

In bringing this Charge to a conclusion, I am aware that I have detained you at an unusual length. But I felt that I could not well pass over any subject that I have touched. The field over which I have travelled is wide. The signs of our own times are peculiar. The position of the Church of England is an anxious one. The first seven years of a new Diocese like ours form a very interesting period, and demand special investigation. Last, but not least, my own advancing years remind me that I ought to leave nothing unsaid that I want to say. When a Bishop has passed the stage of threescore and ten, he is bound to remember that each Triennial Visitation may be his last.

In looking back over the seven years of my Episcopate, I find abundant reasons for deep thankfulness. I came among you, clearly seeing that the position I was called to occupy was one of great and peculiar difficulties. I have not found these difficulties greater than I expected. I came, knowing well that every English Bishop in this day must make up his mind to be severely criticized, and that in all his actions, words, and appointments he will always displease somebody. But after living in this city and moving continually under the public eye, I do not feel that I have much cause to complain. So long as human nature is what it is, people will talk, and write, and misunderstand, and misrepresent; and our wisest course is to take it patiently, and hold on our way, turning neither to the right hand nor to the left. There is deep wisdom in the old Scottish proverb about gossip and tittle-tattle: 'They have said. What have they said? Let them say.'

My course since I came to Liverpool has been greatly smoothed by the almost uniform kindness and courtesy with which I have been received by the clergy, as well as the laity, of my Diocese. I came among you a man of very decided theological opinions; and I think it likely that many of you would have preferred a Bishop of a different school of thought. But you have treated me kindly and fairly, and with rare exceptions I have found no difficulty in working with all. I am very sensible that I have said and done things that might better have been left unsaid and undone; and that all I have said and done might have been said and done more perfectly. But I have tried to do my duty, and if I have paved the way for a younger, abler, and more active Bishop, I shall have done something.

My Reverend Brethren, accept the hearty good wishes of your Bishop at the close of his Triennial Charge. 'Be steadfast, unmoveable, always abounding in the work of the Lord, forasmuch as ye know that your labour is not in vain in the Lord' (1 Cor. 15:58). That is a grand text, and one which a clergyman should never forget. There are better days in store for our new Diocese, though my eyes may not see them. There is a great and effectual door before you, and a grand field of usefulness, though there are many adversaries. Work on, and work together as much as you can, and try to think less of the points in which you differ than of those in which you agree. I am firmly convinced, at the end of a long life, that loyal, honest, true-hearted Churchmen of all schools can co-operate in many ways far more than they do, and have much more common ground than they think.

It is my own deliberate opinion that there is a great future before the Established Church of England, if her children know the time of their visitation, continue faithful to the principles of her Articles and Prayer-book, and co-operate heartily on those principles. If the clergy, as a body, will only be satisfied with the ritual which satisfied Hooker and Andrews and Hall and Herbert and Usher and Ken and Beveridge and Pearson and Butler; if the zealous advocates of ceremonial novelties, not essential to the validity of the Lord's Supper, will only abstain from irritating people and creating suspicion until their favourite novelties are formally legalized by some competent tribunal—if all this might be, I believe the old Church of England might 'turn the world upside down,' and gather into her fold a large portion of the Christianity of the land.

Let us, however, distinctly understand that we must cooperate on real Church principles, and that we must not be expected to sacrifice truth for the sake of peace. I believe there are few, if any, clergymen in the Diocese of Liverpool who really wish for re-union with the Church of Rome, and I trust for the honour of Lancashire it will ever be so. With such men, in any part of England, I find it impossible to co-operate, and I charge you with all my heart, and soul, and mind, and strength never to be drawn into their net, and never to assist them. Unity and re-union, no doubt, are fine, high-sounding words. But you may buy gold too dear; and unity bought at the expense of Christ's truth is utterly worthless. Re-union with Rome means the abolition of our Thirty-nine Articles, the complete mutilation of our Communion service, the reception of the Mass and the Confessional, and the base surrender of all the countless blessings of the Protestant Reformation. From such a surrender, from re-union on such terms and conditions, good Lord, deliver us!

Yes, my brethren! when the Church of Rome returns to the pure scriptural doctrines embalmed in our Thirty-nine Articles, it will be time for the Church of England to seek re-union with her. But till that time, I maintain that the Established Church of England had better be disestablished, disendowed, and broken to pieces, than re-united with the Church of Rome. Till that time, let our sentence always be, *Nolumus leges Ecclesiae Anglicanae mutari*.[1]

---

[1] 'We are unwilling for the laws of the Church of England to be altered.'

7

SEEST THOU THESE GREAT BUILDINGS?

'Jesus answering said unto him, Seest thou these great buildings?
There shall not be left one stone upon another, that shall not be
thrown down' (Mark 13:2).

A sermon preached at St Dunstan's Church, Liverpool, 1889.

THESE words, on a first hearing, may startle you, and not
sound like the right text for the day. But I hope to be able to
show that they are eminently suited to the occasion which brings
us together.

Few, I should think, will deny that we are assembled for a very
solemn and interesting purpose. We meet to consecrate to God,
and open for public use by a special service, a new church. I pity
those who find fault with such services, and fail to see their fitness
and propriety. For this great building may stand for centuries,
long after you and I are mouldering in our graves. Think how
many myriads of immortal souls will assemble from year to year
within these walls, think of the numberless sermons which will be
preached and the sacraments which will be administered, think of
the prayers and praises which will go up from these seats, think
of the thousands to whom the means of grace begun today may be
a savour of life and a help toward heaven when this congregation
has left the world—think of all this, as I bring before you a few
thoughts which appear suitable to a consecration service.

The words of the text are a prophecy which was spoken by our Lord Jesus Christ a very short time before he was crucified. They were called forth by the remark of a disciple, who drew his attention to the magnificent buildings of the temple, as our Lord was walking out of it for the last time. That remark at once elicited a most fearful and unexpected reply: 'Seest thou these great buildings? There shall not be left one stone upon another, that shall not be thrown down.' I see here much food for thought.

I. I ask you first to look *carefully at the famous building which formed the subject of our Lord's prophecy, and to consider its history.*

The temple of God at Jerusalem, of which our Lord foretells the complete destruction, was in many respects the most wonderful building on the face of the earth. Built at the first by Solomon, a thousand years before Christ, on Mount Moriah, rebuilt on the same site by Zerubbabel, Ezra, and Nehemiah, after the captivity in Babylon; restored and beautified by Herod just before our Lord began his ministry—there was no more remarkable place of worship in the world when the awful prophecy before you was delivered. In size, no doubt, whether in length, breadth, or height, it was far inferior to many a heathen temple, and many a modern cathedral. In costliness of material, and especially in the quantity of gold used internally, I suspect it was second to none. But in the divine authority of its design, and the priceless typical value of its furniture, the sun never shone on a building reared by man which could be named in comparison with it.

The temple of Jerusalem is the only place of worship ever built on earth of which God himself was the Architect. Before a stone of it was laid we find it written: 'Then David gave to Solomon his son the pattern of the porch, and of the houses thereof, and of the treasuries thereof, and of the upper chambers thereof, and of the inner parlours thereof, and of the place of the mercy seat. ... All this, said David, the Lord made me understand in writing by his hand upon me, even all the works of this pattern' (1 Chron. 28:11, 12, 19). We may admire, if we please, our majestic minsters and cathedrals, and contend for the merits of Gothic or Italian or mediaeval styles, according to our various tastes; but the very best of them is only the design of man. They are all human. Neither William of Wykeham, nor Bramante, nor Michael Angelo, nor Wren, nor Scott, nor Street could say of their grandest works, 'I had the design of this from God.'

Again, the temple of Jerusalem was richly furnished with visible emblems of some of the deepest truths of our holy religion. The mercy seat, the candlestick, the altar of incense, the laver of water, the altar of burnt offering, were all given by God himself to be lively types of good things to come, and to teach us by figures and pictures the glorious gospel of Christ. The finest heathen temples on earth were filled with degrading images of men and women and even beasts, or with vile emblems of which it is a shame even to speak. But the temple in every direction set forth Christ.

Again, the temple of Jerusalem was intimately associated with everything that was most holy in Jewish history. It is the place which God consecrated by his special presence on the day that Solomon dedicated it. 'The house was filled with a cloud, even the house of the Lord; so that the priests could not stand to minister by reason of the cloud; for the glory of the Lord had filled the house' (2 Chron. 5:13, 14). It is the place of which the Lord afterwards said, 'Mine eyes and mine heart shall be there perpetually' (2 Chron. 7:16). It was the place which was honoured by kings and prophets, such as Jehoshaphat and Hezekiah and Josiah and Isaiah and Jeremiah and Amos. It was the place toward which Daniel prayed at Babylon, and Jonah out of the whale's belly. It was the place in which the angel Gabriel appeared to Zacharias, and foretold the birth of John the Baptist. It was the place to which our blessed Lord was carried, when an infant, very soon after his birth, and taken into Simeon's arms. It is the place where he was found at the age of twelve, 'sitting among the doctors, both hearing them and asking them questions.' Finally, it is the place where he often taught and preached during his earthly ministry, until the day when he left it to return no more.

Yet this is the wonderful, holy, and beautiful house about which our Lord pronounced the awful prediction, 'Not one stone shall be left upon another.' Had he spoken these solemn words about the temples of Karnak and Luxor in Egypt, about the temple of Diana at Ephesus, or Venus at Paphos, or Belus at Babylon, with all their superstitions and nameless abominations, we should not have been surprised. But such a prophecy about such a holy place as the temple at Jerusalem is at first sight amazing, astounding, and incomprehensible. A more unlikely and improbable event than its complete destruction could not be imagined.

And yet we know that the prophecy was fulfilled to the very letter. Only forty years after these remarkable words fell from our Lord's lips, the city of Jerusalem was taken by the Roman army under Titus. The beautiful temple was completely destroyed, in spite of strict orders to spare it. The very foundations were ploughed up by Terentius Rufus, a Roman officer, and salt sown on them. Our Lord himself had said, 'Heaven and earth shall pass away, but my words shall not pass away' (Mark 13:31); and so it came to pass.

Let me leave this branch of my subject with one practical remark. Remember, no prophecy of Scripture shall ever fail to be accomplished. Every word predicted under the teaching of the Holy Ghost shall come to pass. The second personal coming of Christ when the times of the Gentiles are fulfilled—the resurrection, the judgment of quick and dead—all these things have yet to come on Christendom, and come they will. To human eyes they may seem unlikely, improbable, or even absurd, so far away that it is waste of time to think about them. They are not what are called 'practical politics.' We shall go on for ever, men think, making money out of cotton, and corn, and coal, and iron, and ships. Tomorrow shall be as this day, and much more abundant. But no! men are utterly mistaken. The coming of the Son of man and the winding up of the affairs of this bankrupt world are events predicted, and events that will certainly be fulfilled. They will break on us suddenly, in an hour when no man thinketh, like the flood in the days of Noah. Our Lord's wonderful words about the destruction of the temple were literally fulfilled, and so will be his words about his own Second Advent.

II. The second thing which I propose to do is to show *the reason why our Lord pronounced the remarkable prediction* which forms the subject of our text.

Questions such as these, I am sure, will arise in some minds— Why did our merciful and gracious Lord speak so sternly and severely about the holy and beautiful house on Mount Moriah? Why were such seats of superstition, idolatry, and immorality as existed at Karnak, and Luxor, and Ephesus, and Paphos spared, and such tremendous denunciations pronounced on the temple of Jerusalem? The answer to such questions is not hard to find, and it is very instructive.

The destruction of the temple predicted by our Lord was entirely owing to the sins of the Jewish Church, the sins both of priests and people. Concerning the nature and extent of these sins something needs to be said.

If we had walked through the streets of Jerusalem, or stood on Mount Olivet, and looked at the glorious building on Mount Moriah, in the days when our Lord was upon earth, I suspect we might have formed a very wrong impression of the real condition of the Jewish Church. We should have seen every ordinance and ceremony of the Mosaic law kept up with the most scrupulous regularity. We should have seen troops of white-robed priests in their courses attending on their duties with the utmost carefulness. The smoke of the daily sacrifice would have ascended from the altar every morning and evening. Psalms would have been daily chanted by well-trained singers. The great feasts of Passover, Pentecost, and Tabernacles would have been most regularly observed. The weekly Sabbath would have been kept most strictly.

In short, we should have beheld an outward show of religion, such as the world never saw before, and has never seen since. He that would like to know what it was should study the late Dr Edersheim's little book on *The Temple, its Ministry and Services in the time of Jesus Christ.*

But what was there behind all this? The most enormous mass of formality and hypocrisy, of lip-service and hollow, heartless worship that ever existed. Our Lord himself describes it in withering language in the 23rd chapter of St Matthew. There was an utter absence of life and reality in the religion of the Church's leaders. They professed to reverence the Scriptures, but made them void by traditions. They compassed sea and land to make proselytes, and then taught them for doctrines the commandments of men. They fasted, and said long prayers, and made broad their phylacteries,[1] but only from ostentation, and to be thought good by others. They made clean the outside of the cup and platter, while inwardly they were filled with wickedness, extortion, and excess. They gave tithe of mint and anise and cummin, while they neglected the weightier matters of the law—judgment, mercy, and faith. The priests were blind leaders of the blind, and showed no one the real way to be saved. They shut up the kingdom of heaven against men, and neither went in themselves nor suffered those that were entering to go in. They made great ado about building the tombs of the prophets, and yet did not know that they themselves were like whited sepulchres, full of dead men's bones and all uncleanness. They appeared outwardly righteous unto men, while within they were full of hypocrisy and iniquity. Party spirit was most bitter and intense, notwithstanding a thin mask of external unity: the Pharisees hated the Sadducees and the Sadducees the Pharisees, and neither party would have any dealings with the Samaritans. Worst of all, with the Old Testament in their hands and the clearest evidence under their eyes, they

---

[1] A small leather box that contains Hebrew texts from the Torah that is worn by Jewish men at prayer to remind them to keep the law.

would not believe that Jesus was the promised Messiah. They rejected him with hatred and scorn, and filled up the measure of their sins by murdering him.

The singularly strong language which our Lord sometimes used about the leaders of the Jewish Church should give us some idea of their guilt and wickedness in his sight. Mercy, kindness, pity, and compassion were the general characteristics of our Lord's words. Yet in one chapter we find him saying eight times over, 'Woe unto you, scribes and Pharisees, hypocrites,' and concluding his address with the fearful words, 'Ye serpents, ye generation of vipers, how shall ye escape the damnation of hell?' (Matt. 23:33). And even of the beautiful temple itself, with its holy of holies, and the ark of the covenant, and the mercy seat, and the daily sacrifice, our Lord declared, 'Ye have made it a den of thieves.'

Nothing, it is evident, is so wicked and offensive in the sight of our Lord Jesus Christ as hypocrisy in religion, nothing so abominable as privileges misused, knowledge not turned to good account, a form of godliness without the power, and high profession without the fruits of the Spirit; without faith, and heart, and holiness of life. It was this state of things that brought down on the temple the tremendous threat, 'There shall not be left one stone upon another that shall not be thrown down.' It was a fulfilment of the words of the prophet Amos: 'You only have I known of all the families of the earth; therefore I will punish you for all your iniquities' (Amos 3:2).

But, after all, we must not forget that the ruin of the Jewish Church does not stand entirely alone. We have only to turn to the pages of Christian Church history, and we shall see abundant proof that there is nothing so displeasing to God as formality and hypocrisy. Where are the churches now to which the apostolic Epistles were addressed—Corinthian, Galatian, Ephesian, Philippian, Colossian, and Thessalonian? Who ever hears of them? Where are the Seven Churches to which the apocalyptic messages were written? Where are the ancient churches in

201

which Ignatius, and Polycarp, and Chrysostom, and Cyril, and Athanasius, and Jerome, and Basil, and Gregory, and Cyprian, and Augustine once lived and laboured? Some of them have been completely swept away by the Saracens, and not a wreck has been left behind. The best of them, if any survive, is like a dried-up fountain, or a ruined lighthouse without a lantern, the mere shadow of its former greatness, and useless to mankind. And what has caused it all? The very same sins that ruined the temple of Jerusalem—deadness, formality, and utter dereliction of duty. Like the Jewish Church, they had ministers and sacraments and ritual and an outward show of religion. They had their bishops and priests and deacons and ascetics and eremites and holy women and liturgies and services and festivals. But, like the Jewish Church, they had neither truth of doctrine among the teachers, nor holy living among the taught, and so their candlestick was taken away. In short, for at least twenty-six centuries it seems to be a great principle in God's dealings with Churches to require practice proportioned to privileges. The measure of men's guilt is the quantity of light they enjoy. Even in Isaiah's time he said to the rulers of Israel: 'To what purpose is the multitude of your sacrifices unto me? Your appointed feasts my soul hateth' (Isa. 1:14). That principle will stand to the end of time. A form of religion without heart is abominable in the sight of God. We are utterly blind if we do not understand that the heart is the principal thing that God looks at in religion. What is apostolic succession of ministers, and what are beautiful liturgical services, or splendid ecclesiastical buildings, or gold, or silver, or marble, or stained glass, to him who made the world, so long as the hearts and lives of professing worshippers are wrong? Like a child who prefers poppies to corn, 'man looks on the outward appearance, but the Lord looks on the heart' (1 Sam. 16:7). The humblest cottage-meeting, where Christ is preached, and the Scriptures honoured, and a few real believers are assembled, is more pleasing in his sight than the grandest cathedral in which the Gospel is never heard, and no work of the Spirit ever goes on.

III. And now, in the third and last place, let me try to show you *the real secrets of a Church's safety and prosperity.*

I dare not leave this point untouched on the solemn occasion which assembles us together. This day we are adding one more noble building to the long list of parish churches which are the glory of our land, the parish churches of our good old Reformed Church of England. How long will this building be permitted to stand? How long will the Established Church itself, attacked as it is on many sides, maintain its position, carry on its work, resist every enemy, live and not die? Let me answer these questions.

If a visible Church is to stand and prosper she must have a full supply of ministers *who do their duty in their pulpits*; ministers who teach and preach scriptural truth, the whole truth and nothing but the truth; ministers who declare all the counsel of God, and keep back nothing that is profitable; ministers who preach Christ, warning every man and exhorting every man in all wisdom; ministers who make it their continual aim, not to please and flatter human nature, but to show men repentance toward God and faith toward our Lord Jesus Christ; ministers who set forth truth in its right proportions, not putting the first things second and the second first, but giving to every part of the gospel message its place and order, and rightly dividing the word of truth concerning Father, Son, and Holy Ghost, and the lives which Christians ought to live.

If a visible Church is to stand and prosper she must have a full supply of ministers *who do their duty as pastors* as well as preachers, ministers who go from house to house, and speak to their hearers at home as well as in the congregation, ministers who make it their business to become the friends and helpers of all their hearers, ministers who do not spend all their week in multiplied church services, but find time to go continually among their people, of all sorts and conditions, of all ranks and classes, to warn the unruly, to comfort the feeble-minded, to support the weak, and to secure the confidence of all by wise kindness and love unfeigned.

If a visible Church is to stand and prosper she must have a full supply of *lay members who know their duty, and do it as well as her ministers*. She must not have a laity who leave all religion to their clergy, and behave like sleeping members of a great concern; who have only to get good, but not to do it; to receive dividends but take no part in business; who have only to sit still, shut their eyes, and allow the parson to manage everything. She must have a laity who are awake, and alive to their position; who know that the rank and file of the army are just as important as the officers; who understand that they are meant to be helpers in every good work, to teach, to visit, to check evil, to be home-missionaries to all around them, and to hold up the hands of their minister in every way, and in every part of his work. Such laymen are the backbone of a visible Church.

Some persons are fond of saying that the Church of England has lost touch with the lower orders, that her services do not suit them, that she no longer possesses their affections, that she cannot reach the masses, that her sun is going down, that she is in danger of perishing for want of churchmen. I do not believe it for one moment, if the Church does her duty. So long as the Church of England is faithful to her Articles and Creeds, so long as she has ministers and lay members of the sort I have tried to describe, so long, I believe, she will not fall. She will hold her ground; no weapon formed against her shall prevail.

Give the Church of England ministers who make the Lord Jesus Christ and his offices and work for our souls the Alpha and the Omega, the chief subject of their teaching. We are all apt to forget that it is quite possible to make an orthodox statement of doctrine, and yet not to *present Christ* to our hearers in the manner and proportion in which he is presented to us in the New Testament. I am struck with the undeniable fact, that most preachers who succeed in getting hold of the working classes, or indeed of any class at all, from the highest to the lowest— whether Whitefield, or Moody, or any other—give a very marked prominence in their sermons to the atoning death, the ever-living intercession, the boundless mercy, the almighty power to save, of that blessed person in whose name Christian worshippers meet together. You have only to read reports of their preaching in order to see proof of what I say. And I will not hesitate to declare my firm belief, that if we would get hold of our congregations, we must make 'Christ crucified and risen again' the sun and centre of our sermons, far more than we have done in the Church of England. It is a lever which shook the world eighteen centuries ago, and is able to shake it now. It is a great magnet which, in every age, from the apostles downwards, has drawn men whom nothing else could draw. And it is a magnet, I am convinced, which has lost none of its attractive influence.

I cannot leave this point without quoting the words of a mighty layman, which deserve attention, a layman of great experience and observation, a layman who in his day has taken great interest in religious questions. The layman[1] I mean was once Prime Minister of England. He said on the 23rd March 1877: 'It is the preaching of Christ our Lord which is the secret, and substance, and centre, and heart of all preaching; not merely of facts about him, and notions about him, but of his person, his work, his character, his simple yet unfathomable sayings—here lies the secret' (*Times*, 23rd March 1877). That witness is true. That great orator never said a truer thing in his life. The sermon full of Christ is the sermon which the Holy Spirit most usually blesses to the souls of all classes.

Give the Church of England ministers who are full of kindness and sympathy themselves, and continually press on their laity to be kind and sympathizing towards all, and not cold and selfish and hard. Oh that there was less idolatry of reason and cleverness

---

[1] William Ewart Gladstone.

and intellect and art and music and singing and fine speaking, and more Christ-like sympathy both in the Church and in the world! This is the medicine which the times require in every branch of society. I believe the late Judge Talfourd[1] hit the nail on the head when he said, in almost his last Charge to a Grand Jury, at Stafford Assizes: 'Gentlemen, the great want of the age is more sympathy between classes.' I entirely agree with him. I think an increase of sympathy and fellow-feeling between high and low, rich and poor, employer and employed, parson and people, is one healing medicine which the age demands. Sympathy, exhibited in its perfection, was one secondary cause of the acceptance which Christ's Gospel met with on its first appearance in the heathen world. Well says Macaulay:

> It was before Deity taking a human form, walking among men, partaking of their infirmities, leaning on their bosoms, weeping over their graves, slumbering in the manger, bleeding on the cross, that the prejudices of the synagogue, and the doubts of the academy, and the fasces of the lictor, and the swords of thirty legions, were humbled in the dust.[2]

And sympathy, I firmly believe, can do as much in the nineteenth century as it did in the first. If anything it will melt down the cold isolation of classes in these latter days, and make our social body consist of solid cubes compacted together, instead of spheres only touching each other at one point, it will be a large growth of Christ-like sympathy.

I believe that vast body of Englishmen whom we are in the habit of calling 'the working classes,' that body which has now got the voting power in its hands and practically rules the country—I believe that body is peculiarly open to sympathy, and the clergyman has peculiar opportunities of showing it. The working man may live in a poor dwelling, and after toiling all day in a coal-pit, or cotton-mill, or iron-foundry, or dock, or chemical yard, or railway

[1] Sir Thomas Noon Talfourd (died 1854).
[2] *The Complete Works of Lord Macaulay*, vol. 5, p. 17.

station, he may often look very rough and dirty. But, after all, he is flesh and blood like ourselves. Beneath his outward roughness he has a heart and a conscience, a keen sense of justice, and a jealous recollection of his rights as a man and a Briton. He does not want to be patronized and flattered, any more than to be trampled on, scolded, or neglected; but he does like to be dealt with as a brother, in a friendly, kind, and sympathizing way. He will not be driven: he will do nothing for a cold, hard man, however clever he may be. But give him a clergyman who really understands that it is the heart and not the coat which makes the man, and that the guinea's worth is in the gold and not in the stamp upon it; give him a clergyman who will not only preach Christ in the pulpit, but come and sit down in his house, and take him by the hand in a Christ-like, familiar way during the week; give him a clergyman who realizes that in Christ's holy religion there is no respect of persons, that rich and poor are 'made of one blood,' and need one and the same atoning blood, and that there is only one Saviour, and one Fountain for sin, and one heaven, both for employers and employed; give him a clergyman who can weep with them that weep, and rejoice with them that rejoice, and feel a tender interest in the cares and troubles and births and marriages and deaths of the humblest dweller in his parish; give the working man, I say, a clergyman of that kind, and, as a general rule, the working man will come to his church. Such clergymen will not preach to empty benches.

I invite the special attention of my clerical brethren to this point. We live in days when public work of all kinds seems every year to absorb more of a clergyman's time. Committees, Bible classes, semi-secular lectures, meetings, frequent services and communions, are rapidly increasing so much that they seem to leave ministers no time for old-fashioned house-to-house work, family work, and winning the confidence of individual souls. I warn them to be on their guard. The absence of house-to-house visitation and friendly, private, personal dealings with families, is one explanation of empty churches. Incessant daily services without this will never fill them, even when every seat in the church is free. A house-going minister is one secret of a church-going people. All the public work in the world, however good, will not compensate for the loss of opportunities for cultivating relations of sympathy between yourselves and your people. Make time for going among them, sitting down with them, holding friendly converse with them, talking face to face, and in the long-run you will find no time so well bestowed.

Men and brethren, the secrets of a Church's stability and prosperity are not mysterious things, like Ezekiel's temple, which it is hard to find out. Show me the visible Church of Christ in which there are such ministers and congregations as I have faintly tried to describe, and I will show you one which will never be overthrown. Infidels and heretics, and other blind though well-meaning foes, may rage around her walls, but they will rage in vain. God is in the midst of her, and God will not let her be destroyed. It shall never be said of her places of worship, 'There shall not be left one stone upon another that shall not be thrown down.' On the contrary, 'The gates of hell shall not prevail against her.'

And now let me conclude this sermon with a few words of practical application.

(1) First and foremost, the text we have considered this day should teach all Churchmen *the great need of increased humility and searching self-examination*. No doubt, the outward progress of the Church of England in the last fifty years has been marvellously great, and we ought to be deeply thankful for it.

The restoration of old cathedrals and churches, the building of hundreds of new churches, the expenditure of more than thirty millions of pounds on these objects—all this has been a remarkable sign of the times. The subdivision of our large dioceses, the multiplication of bishops and clergy at home and abroad, the raised standard of ministerial life, the vast growth of lay agency—all these are striking facts. But what right have we to boast? Are we not apt to forget that Herod's restoration of the temple at Jerusalem, and a rigid attention to the outward forms and ritual of religion, went side by side with an utter decay of all godliness? After all, what are we in the eyes of an all-seeing God, before whom we shall stand in the judgment day? Where is Christ-like love in the land? When the Son of man cometh, shall he find faith in England? Are not his helpers in town and country a petty minority? Has real heart religion increased in England in any proportion to the increase of so-called 'hearty services' and outward and visible profession? What shall we say to the enormous quantity of drunkenness and impurity and covetousness and gambling, and idolatry of sports and amusements, and self-indulgence and Sabbath-breaking and neglect of public worship, which still disgraces our nation? What shall we say to the mass of semi-heathenism and utter disregard of all religion by which our city churches are too often surrounded? What shall we say to the widely prevailing theological bitterness, narrowness, and want of love toward those who cannot pronounce our respective shibboleths? Have we no Pharisees and Sadducees among us? Have we no formal, useless High Churchmen, and Low Churchmen, and Broad Churchmen, and 'no-party' Churchmen among us, doing nothing really for Christ's cause, and only cumbering the ground? Have we no semi-Romanists in our ranks who would gladly put the clock back and get behind the Reformation? Have we no sceptics, who sneer at inspiration and the atonement, and barely conceal their desire to throw overboard half the Bible? Are there not myriads of churchgoing people who shut up their religion from Sunday to Sunday, and never give a thought to the souls and bodies of Christ's poor brethren at their gates? Alas! these are sorrowful questions, and only admit of one answer. Surely we ought to remember the temple of Jerusalem, and learn more humility. Let us not be high-minded, but fear.

(2) In the next place, the occasion which assembles us this day ought to fill our hearts with *deep thankfulness*. Let us praise God that, in a day of much covetousness and indifference to religion,

there are still families to be found in Lancashire who are willing to give of their substance for the building and endowment of noble churches such as that which has been consecrated this day; families who do not migrate and carry away their wealth from Liverpool, and forget the spiritual wants of the great city in which their wealth was made. I am convinced that with such offerings as this church God is well pleased. I am thoroughly satisfied that he who wants to do real and lasting good to a large growing city like Liverpool cannot possibly do better than build and endow a church. The weekly religious services inside a new church are only a small part of the benefit it confers on the district in which it is built. Placed in the hands of a clergyman with heart and head in the right place, it becomes an endless fountain of blessings. Sunday schools, district visiting, temperance agencies, home and foreign missions, Bible-classes, a general increase of the tone of morality, an insensible check to sin in the parish, causing its wheels to drive heavily, a raised standard of brotherly feeling among all ranks—all these and many other blessed results which I have not time to name, are sooner or later the result of a new church. Surely we ought to be thankful for the good work which is happily completed this day.

(3) Last, but not least, let us all pray that the generous example set by the builders of this church may *provoke others to emulation.* The number of parishes in this Diocese with 9,000 or 10,000 or 12,000 people to one incumbent, is still very great. For disproportion of churches to population our Diocese of Liverpool, after all that has been done in the last forty years, still occupies a painful pre-eminence. We have not kept pace with our ever-growing population. We have still only one church to about every 5,000 people. 'There remaineth yet much land to be possessed.' Let us pray night and day that God may put it into the hearts of many wealthy inhabitants of this corner of Lancashire to come forward, like the builders of St Dunstan's, and say, 'I also will build and endow a church. Here am I! Use me! Let me also have the privilege of doing some real solid good before I die!'

210

8

OUR DIOCESE, OUR CHURCH, OUR TIMES

An address given at the opening of the eighth
Liverpool Diocesan Conference, 1889.

REVEREND and Lay Brethren, We are opening this day our Eighth Diocesan Conference, and I offer you a hearty welcome. I trust that our proceedings may be not less useful and interesting than those of preceding meetings. It is vain to shut our eyes to the fact, that no Conference ever attracts the attention of more than a limited number of Churchmen in a Diocese. It must needs be so. So long as a Conference is a voluntary institution, devoid of legal powers, and unable to enforce its resolutions, so long the great majority of Churchmen will take little notice of its debates and discussions. Here in Liverpool we are no worse off than other Dioceses. Indeed, a careful review of the last seven years lands me to the conclusion, that both in the numbers attending, and in the selection of interesting subjects, our Conference is second to none, and in the handling of our subjects by our readers and speakers we have no cause to be ashamed of our platform.

Since we met last year, as you all know, a heavy blow has fallen on my household,[1] after three years of ceaseless anxiety, which obliges me to consider very seriously my position as your Bishop, and to speak plainly to you about it. It is needless to remind you that I have reached an age when a man's 'natural force

[1] Ryle refers to the death of his third wife (April 1889).

211

is abated,' and he can no longer do the things that he used to do. At such an age such a loss as that which I was called, in the wise providence of God, to sustain last April, must needs tell on any one with peculiar power, and I am conscious that it has told on me. In short, I feel the time cannot be very far distant when the work of this Diocese will oblige me either to resign my office, or to obtain the aid of a Suffragan. I will not plead guilty to laziness or love of ease, and if I know my own heart I had rather die in harness than let business fall into arrear, and would rather wear out than rust out. But the oversight of 1,200,000 Lancashire souls, and of a huge city like Liverpool, is no sinecure at the end of this busy nineteenth century. I cannot help sometimes feeling that it needs a younger and more vigorous hand than mine. However, you must understand distinctly that I have not made up my mind, and have formed no decision. God may have something more for me to do. Time, as it rolls on, will open up the path of duty. I only ask you to remember that I know my position, and that I am anxious to do what is best for myself, for yourselves, and for the Church of England in the Diocese of Liverpool, if necessity arises.

I cannot turn away from this subject without expressing my deep thankfulness for the boundless sympathy exhibited towards me in my dark hour of trouble last April, from every part of my Diocese, by all ranks and classes, by all schools of thought among my clergy, by all sorts and conditions of men. Once for all, let me say that it cheered me, sustained me, and raised my estimate of human nature. I received it as a great 'cup of cold water,' which will have its reward. I was grateful: I am grateful: I shall be grateful to my dying day.

Before handling a few points of interest, which I wish to touch briefly, about the condition of our own Diocese and the Church of England in 1889, I wish to say a few words about the arrangements of our Conference, which a slight friction at the close of last year's proceedings seems to make desirable.

An impression appears to exist in some quarters that a Diocesan Conference is an assembly at which any one may get up, at any moment, without any previous notice, and propose a resolution on any subject that he pleases. I think a little reflection will show that such a mode of procedure would never work well. It would risk the possible sacrifice of our two short meeting days to the discussion of trivial, useless, or violently controversial subjects. I can see no better plan than that which we have adopted; the plan, I mean, of requiring all resolutions to be sent to our Standing Committee, to be accepted or otherwise as it seems expedient. I can affirm most emphatically that this Committee acts most fairly and impartially, and has not the least desire to burke the discussion of any reasonable subjects. But the Committee is a trustee for the best disposal of the very limited time of the Conference, and a certain discretion must be allowed to it in arranging our annual proceedings. Even the House of Commons, which sits for six or seven months, not for two days, never allows any resolution or question to be brought forward without previous notice. I think the Liverpool Diocesan Conference may well be content to follow its example.

I. Concerning *the state of things* in our own Diocese, I have a few remarks to make on certain important points, which I will try to place before you as briefly as possible.

(1) Our great cathedral scheme makes no progress. It is on the shelf and sleeps for the present. I say 'sleeps' advisedly: it is not dead, I hope, but sleeps. I admit frankly that the position of the scheme is rather humbling after such a large expenditure of time, talk, controversy, and not a little money, on the subject. I am not surprised that Churchmen at a distance, who do not understand Liverpool, speak rather scornfully of us. But there is no fighting against facts. To purchase and clear a good central site, which all would approve, in a city where land is of fabulous price; to build a cathedral worthy of the second city in the empire; to provide a suitable endowment for a dean, canons, and official staff, beside

daily expenses—all this would cost at least half a million of money. Will any one tell me that it is likely such a sum of money will ever be raised under any Bishop of Liverpool, whether High, Low, or Broad? Nothing, of course, is impossible. Some Lancashire Vanderbilt, or Astor, or Jay Gould, may yet come forward, and put down half a million at once. I only speak of what is likely and probable. The financial experience of the comparatively small Cathedral of Truro, and of the London Church House, and of the difficulty of endowing all new bishoprics, is not very encouraging. Moreover, many new churches are wanted in our Diocese. Many, like our late friend Charles Groves, think that churches are necessities and cathedrals only luxuries. Some of our wealthiest and most liberal and kind-hearted inhabitants are not Churchmen, and cannot of course be expected to help to build a cathedral. All these are great broad facts which cannot be overturned. In the face of these facts I am totally unmoved by the inconsiderate remarks of outside critics about our want of a cathedral. I am not surprised that the scheme sleeps.

(2) The building that I believe our Diocese needs most at this moment is a Church House in some central position in Liverpool. By this I do not mean a grand ornamental structure, but a plain, commodious building, designed for usefulness rather than display. Such a House should contain the Diocesan Registry and suitable offices for the Registrar, making us independent of Chester. It should contain a business-room for the Bishop, for interviews, licensing, and, if necessary, for institutions, with a waiting-room and a room for a secretary. It should contain the offices of the Diocesan Finance Associations, the Scripture Readers' Society, the Church of England Temperance Society, and the Sunday School Society. It should contain a good-sized airy room, or even two rooms, for committees, and for a Consistory Court. It should contain a reading-room large enough to receive the nucleus of a diocesan library of theology, which it is useless to talk of now, and provided with every convenience for writing. The cost of such

a Church House, if we were content with an inexpensive site, ought probably not to exceed £20,000, and the benefit it would confer on the Diocese, I venture boldly to think, would be far greater than any cathedral. The annual rent of our various offices in Commerce Court and elsewhere at this moment is a far larger sum than most people suppose. If God should not put it into the heart of some wealthy Churchman to come forward and help us, I sometimes think a Syndicate might find it a good investment to build such a Church House as I have described, and let us hire it at a fixed rent until we can purchase it by a sinking fund.

(3) Church-building, I am thankful to say, continues to make very satisfactory progress. St Dunstan's at the south end of Liverpool, and St Leonard's at the north, are gratifying proofs that the generation of large-hearted, generous lay Churchmen is not yet extinct in Liverpool. Mr Harrison's church at Stanley, and Mrs Turner's at St Chrysostom's, Everton, are rapidly following the two I have already mentioned. New churches have also been commenced at Formby, at St Peter's, Warrington, at Haydock, at North Meols, and St James's, Birkdale. St Lawrence, Kirkdale, and St Philip, Sheil Road, are ready for consecration, but are still, unhappily, waiting for an endowment and repair fund. In the new districts of St Matthew, Bootle, St Luke, and St Simon and St Jude, Walton, we have still nothing but temporary places of worship, quite inadequate to the wants of the population. In each of these three districts I trust we shall at no distant date see a permanent church. Another new church seems greatly needed in Kensington Fields, and I heartily wish some one would take up its erection. However, I have said enough to show that church-building in our new Diocese has not yet come to a standstill. Small as the area of our Diocese is compared to Manchester, at least thirty new churches will be added to it in the first ten years of its separate existence.

(4) The annual increase of Mission Rooms, or Church Rooms, is another most satisfactory item in the condition of our Diocese.

The rooms already built at St Nathaniel's, St Michael's-in-the-Hamlet, St Cleopas, Litherland, Hindley, Grassendale, Roby, Skelmersdale, and Christ Church, Everton, and being built at St James's Toxteth, and St Cyprian, Edge Hill, will greatly strengthen the hands of the incumbents in the parishes I have named. I repeat my formerly expressed opinion, that the value of these rooms cannot easily be overrated. They enable a clergyman to give short, elementary, non-liturgical services, such as the Apostles used to hold. They enable him to obtain the help of gifted and qualified laymen to hold such services, when he cannot hold them himself. Both these things are impossible in consecrated churches by reason of the Act of Uniformity. They can be built at a quarter of the expense of a regular church, while at present the financial condition of the Ecclesiastical Commissioners makes it useless to build any church in a poor district, unless some one comes forward to provide an endowment. Above all, they meet the wants of a large body of our working classes, who now go nowhere at all, and certainly will seldom begin their religious life by going to a long liturgical service which they cannot understand. The objection sometimes made that mission-room services do not lead people to Church, and only increase Dissent, I do not admit to be valid. Even if it was, I had much rather see people going to mission rooms than going nowhere at all. The plain truth is, that a miserable cast-iron want of elasticity has long been the bane of the Establishment. A great Church like ours ought never to be ashamed to meet the wants of all sorts and conditions of men, and to provide true scriptural means of grace, of one kind or another, for every rank and class of the community. I will leave this subject with one particular hint to the promoters of mission rooms. That hint is to be very careful about the terms of their *trust-deeds*, and to see that they are drawn up with an eye to the future, and a wise provision against possible contingencies. Neglect on this point may be the cause of much future trouble.

(5) The Commission of Inquiry which I appointed last Conference, in consequence of a resolution moved by our friend the present Dean of Norwich, is likely to prove very useful. Its Report will supply us with a manual of information about the 'things that are wanting' in our Diocese. Accurate statistics are the first steps towards reforms, and such statistics the Report of the Commission will provide. There are facts about the city of Liverpool, containing more than half the population of the Diocese, of a most extraordinary kind, crying loudly for a change, of which few people are aware.

It is a fact that there are some large and important churches here which have no regular districts attached to them. Their incumbents are not legally responsible for any pastoral work, and they do what they do voluntarily and by conventional arrangement. I will instance St Luke; St Andrew; St Mary, Edge Hill; St Michael's-in-the-Hamlet; St Mary, Bootle; and Walton Breck.

It is a fact that there are districts which nominally belong to the Rectors of Walton, West Derby, and Liverpool, which lie at such a distance from the Mother Church that they are practically 'no man's land.' Walton, for example, embraces both St Mary, Bootle, and St Michael's-in-the-Hamlet.

It is a fact that there is more than one church which, by the absorption of shops into warehouses, the opening up of new streets, and the consequent diminution of population, is no longer wanted, and ought to be taken down and rebuilt elsewhere.

It is a fact that there are some parishes in Liverpool, and specially at the north end, with large populations of eight, ten, or twelve thousand souls, in which, at first sight, new churches are greatly wanted. But inquiry will show that in these parishes three-fourths or four-fifths of the inhabitants are Roman Catholics, and that at present more churches are not wanted.

It is a fact, on the other side, that there are many districts, both in Liverpool and in Wigan, Warrington, St Helen's, Widnes, and Pemberton, where the number of professing Churchmen is far greater than one incumbent can look after, and there is a grievous want of more means of grace and more pastoral superintendence, if the Established Church is really to keep her position as 'the Church of the people.'

On all these points I believe our Commission will throw a searching light, and lead to useful results. At present I am afraid many people in our Diocese are living without any spiritual visitation either from clergymen or nonconformist ministers, and die and are buried without a word being said to them about their souls. This last evil, no doubt, could be met by Christian liberality and evangelization. The evils mentioned earlier can only be reached by a special Act of Parliament. To speak plainly, we want a 'Permissive Act for the City of Liverpool,' giving power to the Ecclesiastical Commissioners, with the consent of the Bishop, the patrons, and the incumbents, and with a due regard to vested interests, to assign legal districts to every church in Liverpool, Walton, and West Derby; to annex neglected districts to the nearest church; to pull down and remove churches no longer wanted; and to provide for the ultimate extinction of the present liberty to be married at a distance from the district in which the parties reside and are known, and the ultimate settlement of the question of marriage fees. None of these things can be done without an Act of Parliament. Dean Lefroy's Committee has no power whatsoever to do them, and can only report and recommend. But if its Report only shows the things that are wanting, sets Liverpool Churchmen thinking, and finally leads up to such a Permissive Act of Parliament as I have tried to describe, the Committee will have done good service, and I publicly give its members my thanks for the trouble they have taken.

Into the contents of the Report it is impossible for me to enter now. It is a long, full, and exhaustive document, which requires careful reading. I propose to send a copy to every incumbent in the Diocese, and to many leading lay Churchmen. There are, however, a few remarkable facts which I will bring before the Conference at once.

218

(i) The Report shows that the population of our Diocese just now is about 1,203,000, and that of this number 261,000 are Romanists and 257,000 Nonconformists, leaving 663,000 to the Church of England.

(ii) The Report shows that for this 663,000 the Church of England at present provides 196,000 seats (162,000 in churches and 34,000 in mission rooms).

(iii) The Report shows that of these 196,000 seats no less than 144,000 are free, and only 52,000 rented.

(iv) The Report shows that during the nine years since the Diocese was formed, twenty-six new churches have been built and consecrated, three new chancels have been built, four churches have been built and are not yet consecrated, and seven new churches are being built at this moment.

(v) The Report shows that beside the 199 consecrated churches in the Diocese, there are no less than 198 mission rooms used for public worship.

(vi) Finally the Report shows that nothing is more wanted in the Diocese than a Sustentation Fund for the assistance of the clergy in poor parishes, when the living is either insufficiently endowed or has no endowment at all. Such a Sustentation Fund might easily be grafted on our valuable Benefices Augmentation Institution.

These six points I commend to your special attention, when the Report comes into your hands.

For the many figures in the Report nothing more can fairly be claimed than approximate correctness. I understand that the returns from some quarters are rather imperfect and defective. But I believe every effort has been made to secure general accuracy.

(6) The last point in the state of our own particular Diocese which I must touch is the well-worn subject of our Diocesan Institutions. I will not weary you with many words about them. They hold their own position, I am glad to say; but I repeat emphatically that they receive far less pecuniary support than

they deserve, and consequently do far less than they ought to do. It is much the same, I am told, in most Dioceses. People will not give to central common funds, but to objects under their own eyes, and close to their own doors.

To suppose, as some unfriendly critics say, that the income of our Diocesan Institutions represents all the money given annually for church purposes in our Diocese, is simply ridiculous. I have good reason to know that tens of thousands of pounds are given every year to the cause of Christ within the boundaries of the West Derby Hundred, which the public never hears of, and which never passes through our office in Commerce Court. I hope for better days. I can only repeat my old opinion, that the Diocesan Institutions, the Scripture Readers' Society, and the Bible Women's Society, ought to receive five times as much money as they do now. Their present financial condition reflects little credit on the Churchmen of Liverpool.

II. Concerning *the general state of things in the whole Church of England at the present day*, I shall now, as usual, make a few remarks. You have a right to know what your own Bishop thinks about many important topics which are annually cropping up and attracting notice, and I think it a plain duty to speak about them without reserve.

It goes without saying that there are many *bright points* on our ecclesiastical horizon which our forefathers never saw or dreamed of a hundred years ago, and much good going on among all schools of thought which it would be dishonest and ungrateful not to acknowledge. Our worst enemies must admit that the Established Church is no longer asleep but awake, and that there is a spirit of stir and activity in our ranks from one end of the land to the other. Bishops, presbyters, deacons, deans, canons, and rural deans, are all doing ten times as much work as they did last century. The drones in the Anglican hive are a diminishing quantity, and may some day become an extinct species, like the dodo.

The creation and endowment in the last fifty years of seven new Dioceses at home and of seventy in the Colonies; the expenditure of some thirty millions of money in building and restoring churches; the immense increase of contributions to Missionary Societies both for foreign and home objects; the popular services in our long neglected cathedrals; the training colleges for candidates for holy orders and for teachers; the thousands of Church schools built in every Diocese; the creation of Congresses and Conferences; the revival of Convocation; the organized aggressive evangelization by special missions; the efforts made to provide for the spiritual wants of soldiers, sailors, emigrants, and young men and women; the largely multiplied administration of the Lord's Supper, and the greater attention to confirmation—all these are broad facts in the history of the Anglican Church of the nineteenth century which he who runs may read. Whether for good or for evil, there is movement everywhere.

However, not everything new is good. Some of the proposals of the zealous friends of progress in the present day appear to me of rather doubtful expediency. Zeal for reforms and for the amendment of defects is an excellent thing no doubt. But there is such a thing as a 'zeal not according to knowledge,' and certain schemes and plans of improvement which have been lately put forward by well-meaning Churchmen, and are now being discussed, appear to my eyes to be of that kind of zeal. I will name a few of them, and tell you what I think.

(1) I doubt the wisdom of that large increase of Dioceses which some desire, who talk of doubling or trebling the number of our Bishops. You may go too far in that direction, and destroy the independence of incumbents by a grand-motherly kind of system, under which Rectors and Vicars would never be let alone. There is a limit to the number of new Dioceses required. You may have them too small as well as too large. You may be over-officered and over-bishoped. One worthy reformer, for instance, has coolly proposed to cut our own Diocese into two, and to have

one Bishop for the city of Liverpool, and another for the districts outside. This I call riding a good idea to death. A Bishop in the nineteenth century, with railways, telegraphs, the printing press, and the penny post, can do a hundred times as much work as a Bishop in the Primitive Church ever did.

(2) I doubt the wisdom of the frequent proposals to extend and enlarge the diaconate, and to confer holy orders on a lower order of men. The plan, if adopted, would lower the standard of ministerial qualifications. To this I am entirely opposed. I speak after the experience of nine years' ordinations, and I say that the standard is quite low enough already. It would never answer to have two sorts of deacons side by side. The thing needed is to bring forward the laity. There is a rich mine of strength in that quarter, which has been far too much neglected hitherto by the Church of England.

(3) I doubt the wisdom of the attempt to add anything to our Church Catechism, in order to provide more definite teaching about the Church. A more ingenious addition to our unhappy strifes, controversies, and bones of contention, I cannot conceive. He that supposes Canterbury and York Convocations could ever draw up a set of questions for children about the Church, which all Churchmen would accept and approve, must have a very strange view of human nature in England.

(4) I doubt the wisdom of the proposed 'Draft Prayer Book Bill about Additional Services and Rubrics.' The object of that Bill appears to be to enable certain ecclesiastical measures to be got through Parliament without discussion, if, after 'lying on the table' for forty days, no objection to them is raised. I must say that this appears to me a 'very large order,' and fraught with danger. I question whether any reformed House of Commons would ever allow any measure affecting the Established Church to be withdrawn from its consideration. I question the prudence of talking about a Bill to alter or add rubrics. That expression may mean a very great deal of mischief. The words of Lord Cross about

this Bill at the recent Carlisle Conference are worth notice. He said that if the advocates of this measure 'meant to interfere with doctrine and ritual, they would pull the Church about their ears.'

(5) About another recent proposal I not only doubt the wisdom, but have the strongest objection to it. That proposal is to revive in some shape the monastic system, and to introduce into our large parishes Brotherhoods of men bound by vows of poverty, chastity, and obedience. Of course there is not the slightest objection already to two or three curates living together in a Clergy House provided by the incumbent, and, if they agree well, it is a comfortable arrangement, of which we have more than one example in our own Diocese. But the system proposed for adoption appears to be another thing altogether, and in my opinion is open to very grave objections. I object to introduce the system of vows over and above the vows of baptism. If the vow of *poverty* means that these new Anglican monks are to work for nothing, I doubt if there will be many of them! Where is this new supply of qualified young men to be found who will do Church work for nothing or next to nothing? If the vow of *chastity* means perpetual or even temporary celibacy, I doubt if Protestant Churchmen will care to see the new order among them. What the vow of *obedience* means, I do not at present understand. If the monks are to obey the clergyman of the parish, it is only what every licensed curate is bound to do now. If they are only to obey the bishop and to be independent of the incumbent, there is risk of constant friction and collision, and a complete break up of the parochial system. Last, but not least, monasticism is a needless return to a machine which however well meant at first, has been tried and found wanting, and was deliberately rejected by our Church at the Reformation.

There are other modern proposals of which I might speak, if time permitted, but I think it better to pass them by, and to conclude with a few remarks on two *black clouds* which threaten to obscure the whole horizon of the Church of England.

(1) One of those clouds is the continued want of unity, or rather the increase of the 'unhappy divisions' of Churchmen. I see them with sorrow, but not with surprise. So long as the *Ornaments Rubric* remains in its present disputed condition; so long as the Ecclesiastical Courts are disapproved and disobeyed, and those who disapprove them will not make any effort to obtain better tribunals; so long as imprisonment of clergymen for contumacy disgraces the law of England; so long as that huge anomaly, the episcopal veto, is allowed to continue—so long I have ceased to expect unity, order, or discipline within our pale. For anything I can see, we are likely to go from worse to worse, until we break up altogether. There are some handwritings on the wall which it needs no Daniel to interpret, and I heartily wish all loyal Churchmen would awake and look at them. A house divided against itself cannot stand.

I think it possible that some of you may not see clearly why I lay such stress on the four points I have just named, as primary causes of our 'unhappy divisions.' Let me try to explain my reasons.

(i) I believe the Ornaments Rubric, as it stands, is an enemy to peace, because you cannot get Churchmen to agree about its interpretation. One man says it means one thing, and another says it means another. It is an obscure and clumsy statement, which ought to be swept clean away, and replaced by an intelligible rule, stating plainly the maximum and minimum of Anglican ritual, granting a reasonable amount of liberty to every clergyman, but not allowing anyone to do just what he likes.

(ii) I believe that imprisonment of *clergymen for contumacy* is a disgrace to ecclesiastical law, and a penalty only worthy of the dark ages. However mistaken a clergyman may be, imprisonment makes him a martyr, and enlists public sympathy on his side. If the sentence of a competent Church Court in a question of doctrine or ritual is not obeyed, the only punishment should be suspension or deprivation.

(iii) I believe that the continuance of the *Episcopal veto* does great mischief. I agree with one third of the Royal Commissioners on Courts, that it ought to be given up. It is far too great a power to be placed in the hands of one fallible individual. It is a most invidious power, which no Bishop can exercise without offending one party or another in his own diocese, and without risking flat contradiction to the decisions of his brother Bishops. Finally, it is diametrically opposed to one of the first principles of Magna Carta, which declares that the ruler shall 'never refuse justice.' Among the laity, I am convinced that the veto is a fertile source of grave dissatisfaction.

(iv) Last, but not least, I believe we shall never have peace until there is some *reform of our Ecclesiastical Courts*. At present a large body of clergymen, whether rightly or wrongly, regard them as incompetent, and pay no respect to their decisions. More than five years ago a Royal Commission reported that they were defective, and made suggestions for the creation of better tribunals. But from that time to this nothing whatever has been done. The old Courts have been discredited and damaged, and new ones have not been created; and the result is that for doctrinal and ritual disputes the Church has practically no law at all! This must be wrong. Why those who dislike the present Courts make no effort to obtain reform I do not pretend to explain. I only remark that if they are waiting in hope that they will some day get purely spiritual Courts in which the laity will have no seat or voice, I am certain they will be disappointed. The English Bishops are no more infallible judges than the Bishops of Rome. I am convinced that the House of Commons will never sanction such Courts until the Church is disestablished and disendowed. Even if Disestablishment were to come, I am convinced that the lay members of our Church would never allow the clergy *alone* to settle disputed questions of doctrine and ritual, any more than the laity in America, Australia, or Ireland. It is too late. The English laity will never submit to be priest-ridden again. They will insist that their voice shall be heard.

Of course, I am aware that all the four points I have mentioned are debatable and disputable, and admit of something being said on both sides. I do not for a moment suppose that you will all agree with me. I only want you to see that when I spoke of division and want of unity as a black cloud on our ecclesiastical horizon, I did not speak without cause.

Before passing away from this branch of my address, I think you may perhaps expect me to say something about two subjects which have greatly agitated the minds of Churchmen during the last year. Of course, I refer to the two ecclesiastical lawsuits commonly known as the St Paul's Reredos case and the Lincoln Prosecution. But I must disappoint you. The two cases are still *sub judice*[1] and undecided, and I think it is my plain duty to say nothing whatever about them.

(2) The other black cloud, or rather fog, which seems sweeping over our heavens, is the increasing laxity of opinion both about doctrine and practice among all professing Christians, which is a most painful sign of the times. As to *doctrinal* religion, multitudes all over England appear to see no difference between truth and error, and not to care what a minister holds or teaches about the Inspiration of Scripture, or the Work of Christ, or the Atonement, or the Personality of the Holy Ghost, or the world to come, provided he is clever and earnest. Everybody is right, and nobody is wrong: everything is true, and nothing is false! A leading speaker at the recent Cardiff Congress spoke of the Thirty-nine Articles, and Pearson *On the Creed*, as 'old-fashioned books, which he supposed it would raise a smile to mention as standards.' And I cannot see from the report that any one objected to this statement. The popular sermon in this day is far too often a mere exhibition of intellectual fireworks, very pleasant to the many hearers who only like temporary excitement, and dislike any preaching which pricks their consciences and makes them uncomfortable, but utterly destitute of distinct doctrine; and powerless to move hearts

---

[1] Under judicial consideration (legal term).

226

or affect lives. In short, a 'downgrade' theology is spreading and is popular everywhere, and earnestness and cleverness are the idols of the day. As to practical religion, the Ten Commandments seem to be forgotten, except the sixth and the eighth. The shocking indifference constantly exhibited about fornication and adultery, and the total disregard of the Sabbath among myriads of all classes, both rich and poor, are melancholy evidences that I speak the truth. All this is very sad. There is a God in heaven who sees all that is going on, and takes account. There is a judgment day, and a world behind the grave. What will the end be?

Let me entreat my brethren in the ministry, both as their Bishop and an elder brother, to understand the times, and to be bold and faithful witnesses for God's truth. Yes, witnesses! You cannot convert men, and give them eyes to see or hearts to feel. The Holy Ghost alone can do that. But you can be witnesses. Stand fast, both in public and in private, even if you stand alone. But you will not stand alone. I thank God there are hundreds of godly lay Churchmen who will stand by you to the last.

Stand fast in the old belief that the whole Bible from Genesis to Revelation was given by inspiration of God, and that the historical facts recorded in the Old Testament are all credible and true. Do not be shaken by the vague assertions and big swelling words of those who sneer at everything supernatural, and talk about 'the laws of nature, the discoveries of science, and the results of modern criticism.'

(i) As to the *facts mentioned in Genesis*, we may be content to stand by the side of Christ and the apostles. They repeatedly refer to them in the New Testament as real, genuine, authentic, true history. Were they likely to be deceived? Did not they know? The very supposition is blasphemy. I think we may rest satisfied with our old-fashioned views. We may safely continue to believe that Noah, Abraham, Isaac, and Jacob were real persons, and that the events mentioned in Genesis were not myths, or pleasing romances, but really took place.

227

(ii) As to the '*laws of nature*,' which modern philosophers tell us cannot be reconciled with the supernatural things mentioned in the Bible, we must remember that it is not at all certain that we know *all* the 'laws of nature,' and that higher and deeper laws may yet be discovered. At any rate they must own that some of the existing laws were not known until Newton's *Principia* brought them to light two centuries ago. But surely, if that is the case, we may fairly assume that many other laws may yet be found out, and that many problems which we cannot solve now will be solved hereafter. Carlyle's *Sartor Resartus* contains some striking remarks on this subject, which I recommend to the attention of all who have time to read.

(iii) Of the '*discoveries of science*' it may be truly said that 'we know in part.' About light and heat and force, about steam and gas and electricity, about chemistry and optics and mechanics, about medicine and anatomy and surgery, about geology and mineralogy and astronomy, about all these things, no doubt, we know much more than our grandfathers. But you may depend there is a great deal more to be learned. At present I cannot find that the discoveries of science really contradict the Scriptures. Even when they have appeared to do so, further discoveries have often solved the difficulty, and made all things plain. In the meantime it is wiser to remember the great Faraday principle, and to cultivate a 'judicious suspense,' when we find knots we cannot untie. When men like Sir George Gabriel Stokes, President of the Royal Society, are found advocating the divine authority of the Bible on public platforms, the friends of the grand old book need not be afraid of science. In saying what I have just said, I should not like to be misunderstood. Remember that I have not the slightest sympathy with those weak-kneed Christians who seem to think that science and religion can never harmonize, and that they must always scowl and look askance at one another, like two quarrelsome dogs. On the contrary, I shall always hail the annual discoveries of physical science with a hearty welcome. For the continual progress of its students by experiment and observation, and for their annual accumulation of facts, I am deeply thankful. I only fear that, in their zeal, they are sometimes apt to forget that it is most illogical to draw a general conclusion from a particular premise, to build houses of theories without foundations. I am firmly convinced that the words of God's mouth, and the works of God's hands, will never be found really to contradict one another. When they *appear* to do so, I am content to *wait*. Time will untie the knot.

(iv) As to the *results of modern criticism*, whether German or British, it will be time enough to consider them when the critics are all of one mind. At present they are hopelessly disagreed, and we may safely wait. We need not be frightened when some men coolly tell us that Moses and David and Solomon never wrote anything at all, or prune away book after book out of the Bible, as if they would improve and reduce the dear old book into a skeleton. We can afford to wait. Well and wisely says Bishop Ellicott, himself no mean critic:

> There are no 'well-established results of biblical criticism,' save those old and fundamental truths which modern thought is trying to explain away and to modify. There has been indeed no lack of unverified assertions that from time to time have claimed to be established results; but true biblical criticism knows them not. Nay, they are already becoming antiquated by the very science on which they have been supposed securely to rest (Gloucester Diocese Conference, 1888).

Stand fast in the maintenance of the grand old dogmatic truths which have been the glory of the Church of England for the last three centuries, the truths which were first drawn from the Scriptures and then embalmed in her Creeds, Articles, and Prayer-book. Beware of watering them down in order to suit the taste of modern times. Worldly men may say that they are effete, worn out, and not fitted to the nineteenth century. Ask them in reply to show you any other religion which is doing real good to mankind. Semi-sceptics and half-and-half Christians may say that they cannot get over the many difficulties of revealed religion. Tell them in reply that the difficulties of unbelief are far greater than the difficulties of faith. Challenge them boldly to show anything which supports souls in the day of bereavement, on the bed of sickness, or in the hour of death, except old-fashioned dogmatic Christianity.

Stand fast in the maintenance of a high standard of practical religion, and never be ashamed of regarding the Ten Commandments as the Christian's best rule of life and test of true faith. Resist every attempt to change our old English Sunday into a Continental one, and to injure the working classes by throwing open picture galleries and museums on Sunday. So long as the fourth Commandment is part of the Decalogue, and is read every week in our most solemn ante-Communion Office by the clergy, and so long as the people are desired to pray that God would 'incline their hearts to keep this law,' as well as the sixth and eighth—so long the feet of defenders of the old English Sunday stand on very firm ground.

I will detain you no longer. I have already trespassed too long on your attention. But the evening of my life draws near, and I am not likely to have many more opportunities of addressing the Diocese collectively. 'The time will come,' said St Paul, 'when men will not endure sound doctrine' (2 Tim. 4:3). I fear that time draws very near. But I trust there never will be a day when the Churchmen of Lancashire will loose their hold on the truths of the Gospel, and cease to 'contend earnestly for the faith which was once delivered to the saints' (Jude 3). If it were my last word, I would say, as dying Sir Henry Lawrence said in the cantonments of Lucknow: 'Never, never, never surrender!'

9

HOLD FAST

The fourth triennial charge to the Diocese of Liverpool,
November 4, 1890.

A BISHOP'S Triennial Visitation is in one point of view a very
solemn occasion. The roll-call which precedes the Charge
brings forward the grave fact that we are all passing away, and
that our own names will one day disappear from the Clergy
List of our Diocese. The changes of the last three years among
members of our body are neither few nor unimportant. The
removal of such well-known men as Archdeacon Jones, Canon
Hopwood, and Canon John Stewart makes gaps in our ranks
which are not easily filled up. But I cannot forget some of the
last words of the late Bishop Lightfoot,[1] as he approached the
end of his career:

> Men may come and men may go; individual lives float down
> like straws on the surface of the waters till they are lost in the
> ocean of eternity; but the broad, mighty, rolling stream of the
> Church itself—the cleansing, purifying, fertilising tide of the
> river of God—flows on for ever and ever.[2]

That this stream in our Diocese may become every year
wider, deeper, and more powerful, whoever among us is removed
before next Visitation, is my heart's desire and prayer.

In the Charge which I am now going to address to you, I
purposely refrain from saying anything about our own Diocese. I

---

[1] J. B. Lightfoot, Bishop of Durham 1879–89 (d. 1889).
[2] Address to the Durham Diocesan Conference, October 1889.

have already handled that subject at such length at the opening of our Annual Diocesan Conference last month, that I can add nothing more today. I shall confine myself exclusively to matters affecting the whole Church of which we form a part. I propose to speak my mind with the utmost plainness about certain points of peculiar importance in the present day, and to charge you with all affection, as your Bishop, to take care that you 'discern things that differ,' and 'hold fast that which is good.' I have resolved to do so, partly because I have reached an age when I cannot expect many more opportunities of addressing you collectively, and partly because of the dangerous character of the times in which we live. In the year 1890 the trumpet of an English Bishop ought to give no uncertain sound.

Perhaps we are poor judges of our own times. If we had lived in the era of the Long Parliament, when Archbishop Laud and Charles the First were beheaded, we should very likely have thought the world was coming to an end. Yet the horizon of our own times, politically, socially, and ecclesiastically, clouded by unequalled violence in parliamentary parties, by unequalled strife between labour and capital, and by unequalled absence of discipline among Churchmen—this horizon, I say, is so black that it demands the gravest attention of all sensible patriots and Christians. With abounding temporal prosperity, we seem, as a nation, to be sitting on the edge of a volcano, and at any time may be blown to pieces, and become a wreck and a ruin.

Worst of all, the air seems filled with vague agnosticism and unbelief. Faith languishes and dwindles everywhere, and looks ready to die. The immense majority of men, from the highest to the lowest, appear to think that 'nothing is *certain* in religion,' and that it does not signify much what you believe. Even in our Universities, the tendency to multiply the 'dubia,' or doubtful things of Christianity, and to diminish the 'necessaria,' the essentials, appears to grow and increase every year. All the foundations of faith are out of course.

In times like these, I shall make no apology for charging my Clergy to beware of losing, insensibly, their grasp of Christian truth, and holding it with slippery and trembling fingers. I ask them, therefore, to hear me patiently this day, while I try to set before them a list of cardinal points on which I think it of essential importance to 'hold fast that which is good.' Of course I do not expect you all to agree with some of the things I am going to say. Far from it! A wise Bishop lays no claim to infallibility. But at any rate you will not be left in ignorance of your own Bishop's opinions.

I. First and foremost, let me charge you *to hold fast the great principle that Christianity is entirely true, and the only religion which God has revealed to mankind.*

You may think it strange that I begin with such an elementary proposition as this. But our lot is cast in an age of abounding rationalism, scepticism, and, I fear I must add, downright infidelity. Even among those who have not cast off all faith, some tell us there is a good deal to be said in favour of Buddhism and Mahometanism. Never, perhaps, since the days of Celsus, Porphyry, and Julian, was the truth of revealed religion so openly and unblushingly assailed, and never was the assault so speciously and plausibly conducted.

In reviews, magazines, newspapers, lectures, essays, novels, and sometimes even in sermons, scores of clever writers are incessantly waging war against the very foundations of Christianity. Reason, science, geology, anthropology, modern discoveries, free thought, are all boldly asserted to be on their side. No educated person, we are constantly told nowadays, can really believe supernatural religion, or the plenary inspiration of the Bible, or the possibility of miracles. Such ancient doctrines as the Trinity, the Divinity of Christ, the Personality of the Holy Spirit, the Atonement, the obligation of the Sabbath, the necessity and efficacy of prayer, the existence of the devil, and the reality of future punishment, are quietly put on the shelf by many professing leaders of modern thought, as useless old almanacs, or contemptuously thrown overboard as lumber! And all this is done so cleverly, and with such an appearance of candour and liberality, and with such compliments to the capacity and nobility of human nature, that multitudes of unstable Christians are carried away as by a flood, and become partially unsettled, if they do not make complete shipwreck of faith.

The existence of this plague of unbelief must not surprise us for a moment. It is only an old enemy in a new dress, an old disease in a new form. Since the day when Adam and Eve fell, the devil has never ceased to tempt men not to believe God, and has said, directly or indirectly, 'Ye shall not die, even if you do not believe.' In 'the latter days' especially, we have warrant of Scripture for expecting an abundant crop of unbelief: 'When the Son of Man cometh, shall he find faith on the earth?' 'Evil men and seducers shall wax worse and worse.' 'There shall come in the last days scoffers' (Luke 18:8; 2 Tim. 3:13; 2 Pet. 3:3). Here in England scepticism is that natural rebound from semi-popery and superstition, which many wise men have long predicted and expected. It is precisely that swing of the pendulum which far-sighted students of human nature looked for; and it has come.

But, as I tell you not to be surprised at the widespread scepticism of the times, so also I must urge you not to be *shaken in mind by it*, or moved from your steadfastness. There is no real cause for alarm. The ark of God is not in danger, though the oxen seem to shake it. Christianity has survived the attacks of Hume and Hobbes and Tindal; of Collins and Woolston and Bolingbroke and Chubb; of Voltaire and Paine and Holyoake. These men made a great noise in their day, and frightened weak people; but they produced no more real effect than idle travellers produce by scratching their names on the great Pyramid of Egypt. Depend on it, Christianity in like manner will survive the attacks of the clever writers of these times. The startling novelty of many modern objections to revelation, no doubt, makes them seem more weighty than they really are. It does not follow, however, that hard knots cannot be untied because our fingers cannot untie them, or that formidable difficulties cannot be explained because our eyes cannot see through or explain them. When you cannot answer a sceptic, be content to wait for more light; but never forsake a great principle. In religion, as in many scientific questions, said Faraday, the famous chemist, 'The highest philosophy is often a judicious suspense of judgment.'

When sceptics and infidels have said all they can, we must not forget that there are three great broad facts which they have never explained away; and I am convinced they never can, and never will. Let me tell you briefly what they are. They are very simple facts, and any plain man can understand them.

(1) The first fact is *Jesus Christ himself*. If Christianity is a mere invention of man, and the Bible is not from God, how can infidels explain Jesus Christ? His existence in history they cannot deny. How is it that without force or bribery, without arms or money, without flattering man's pride of reason, without granting any indulgence to man's lusts and passions, he has made such an immensely deep mark on the world? Who was he? What was he? Where did he come from? How is it that there has never been one like him, neither before nor after, since the beginning of historical times? They cannot explain it. Nothing can explain it but the great foundation-principle of revealed religion, that Jesus Christ is very God, and that his Gospel is all true.

(2) The second fact is *the Bible itself*. If Christianity is a mere invention of man, and the Bible is of no more authority than any other uninspired volume, how is it that the book is what it is? How is it that a book written by a few Jews in a remote part of the earth, written at distant and various periods without concert or collusion among the writers; written by members of a nation which, compared to Greece and Rome, did nothing for litera-ture—how is it that this book stands entirely alone, and that there is nothing that even approaches it, for high views of God, for true

views of man, for solemnity of thought, for grandeur of doctrine, and for purity of morality? What account can the infidel give of this book, so deep, so simple, so wise, so free from defects? He cannot explain its existence and its nature on his principles. We only can do that who hold that the book is supernatural, and is the book of God.

(3) The third fact is *the effect which Christianity has produced on the world*. If Christianity is a mere invention of man, and not a supernatural, Divine revelation, how is it that it has wrought such a complete alteration in the state of mankind? Any well-read man knows that the moral difference between the condition of the world before Christianity was planted, and since Christianity took root, is the difference between night and day, the kingdom of heaven and the kingdom of the devil. At this very moment I defy any one to look at the map of the world, and compare the countries where men are Christians with those where men are not Christians, and to deny that these countries are as different as light and darkness, black and white. How can any infidel explain this on his principles? He cannot do it. We only can who believe that Christianity came down from God, and is the only Divine religion in the world.

Whenever you are tempted to be alarmed at the progress of infidelity, look at the three facts I have just mentioned, and cast your fears away. Take up your position boldly behind the ramparts of these three facts, and you may safely defy the utmost efforts of modern sceptics. They may often ask you a hundred questions you cannot answer, and start ingenious problems about geology, or the origin of man, or the age of the world, which you cannot solve. They may vex and irritate you with wild speculations and theories, of which at the time you cannot prove the fallacy, though you feel it. But be calm and fear not. Remember the three great facts I have named, and boldly challenge them to explain them away. The difficulties of Christianity no doubt are great; but, depend on it, they are nothing compared to the *difficulties of infidelity*.

II. In the next place, let me charge you *to hold fast the authority, supremacy, and Divine inspiration of the whole Bible.*

About the authority of that blessed book I need not say much. I am speaking *ad clerum.*[1] I am addressing men who have answered the solemn questions of the Ordination Services, and subscribed the Thirty-nine Articles. By so doing you have declared your belief that the Scriptures are our Church's rule of faith and practice. The clergyman who preaches and teaches anything which flatly contradicts the Bible, appears to me to forget his own pledges and subscriptions, and to deal unfairly with the Church of which he is a minister.

About the inspiration of the Bible I feel it necessary to speak more fully. It is, unhappily, one of the chief subjects of controversy in the present day, and one about which a Diocese has a right to know what its Bishop thinks.

The subject of inspiration is *always important.* It is the very keel and foundation of Christianity. If Christians have no Divine book to turn to as the warrant of their doctrine and practice, they have no solid ground for present peace or hope, and no right to claim the attention of mankind. They are building on a quicksand, and their faith is vain. If the Bible is not given by inspiration throughout, and contains defects and errors, which would invalidate any legal settlement or will, it cannot be a safe guide to heaven. We ought to be able to say boldly, 'We are what we are, and we do what we do, and teach what we teach, because we have here a book which we believe to be, altogether and entirely, the word of God.'

The subject without doubt is a *very difficult one.* It cannot be followed up without entering on ground which is dark and mysterious to mortal man. It involves the discussion of things which are miraculous, supernatural, above reason, and cannot be fully explained. But difficulties must not turn us away from any subject in religion. There is not a science in the world about which

[1] 'To clergymen.'

questions may not be asked which no one can answer. It is poor philosophy to say we will believe nothing unless we can understand everything! We must not give up the subject of inspiration in despair, because it contains things 'hard to be understood.'

One cause of difficulty lies in the fact that the Church has never defined exactly *what inspiration means*, and consequently many of the best Christians are not entirely of one mind. I am one of those who believe that the writers of the Bible were supernaturally and divinely enabled by God, as no other men ever have been, for the work which they did, and that, consequently, the book they produced is unlike any other book in existence, and stands entirely alone. Inspiration, in short, is a miracle. We must not confound it with intellectual power, such as great poets and authors possess. To talk of Shakespeare and Milton and Byron being *inspired*, like Moses and St Paul, is to my mind almost profane. Nor must we confound it with the gifts and graces bestowed on the early Christians in the primitive Church. All the apostles were enabled to preach and work miracles, but not all were inspired to write. We must rather regard it as a special supernatural gift, bestowed on about thirty people out of mankind, in order to qualify them for the special business of writing the Scriptures; and we must be content to allow that, like everything miraculous, we cannot entirely explain it, though we can believe it. A miracle would not be a miracle, if it could be explained! That miracles are possible, I do not stop to prove here. I never trouble myself on that subject, until those who deny miracles have fairly grappled with the great fact that Christ rose again from the dead. I firmly believe that miracles are possible, and have been wrought; and among great miracles I place the fact that men were inspired by God to write the Bible. Inspiration, therefore, being a miracle, I frankly allow that there are difficulties about it which at present I cannot fully solve.

The exact manner, for instance, in which the minds of the inspired writers of Scripture worked when they wrote, I do not pretend to explain. I have no doubt they could not have explained it themselves. I do not admit for a moment that they were mere machines holding pens, and, like type-setters in a printing-office, did not understand what they were doing. I abhor the 'mechanical' theory of inspiration. I dislike the idea that men like Moses and St Paul were no better than organ-pipes, employed by the Holy Ghost, or ignorant secretaries or amanuenses, who wrote by dictation what they did not understand. I admit nothing of the kind. But I do believe that in some marvellous manner the Holy Ghost made use of the reason, the memory, the intellect, the style of thought, and the peculiar mental temperament of each writer of the Scriptures. How and in what manner this was done, I can no more explain than I can the union of two natures, God and man, in the person of our blessed Lord Jesus Christ. I only know that there is both a Divine and a human element in the Bible, and that, while the men who wrote it were really and truly men, the book that they wrote and handed down to us is really and truly the word of God. I know the result, but I do not understand the process. The result is, that the Bible is the written word of God; but I can no more explain the process, than I can explain how the water became wine at Cana, or how five loaves fed five thousand men, or how the Apostle Peter walked on the water, or how a few words from our Lord's lips raised Lazarus from the dead. I do not pretend to explain miracles, and I do not pretend to explain fully the miraculous gift of inspiration.

The position I take up is, that while the Bible-writers were not 'machines,' as some sneeringly say, they only wrote what God taught them to write. The Holy Ghost put into their minds thoughts and ideas, and then guided their pens in writing and expressing them. Even when they made use of old records, chronicles, pedigrees, and lists of names, as they certainly did, they adopted, used, and compiled them under the direction of the Holy Ghost. When you read the Bible, you are not reading the unaided, self-taught composition of erring men like yourselves, but thoughts and words which were suggested by the eternal God.

The men who were employed to indite the Scripture 'spake not of themselves.' They 'spake as they were moved by the Holy Ghost' (2 Pet. 1:21). He that holds a Bible in his hand should remember that he holds not the word of man, but of God. He holds a volume which not *only contains, but is God's word.*

In saying all this, I would not be mistaken. I only claim complete inspiration for the original languages in which the books of the Scripture were written. I admit fully that transcribers and translators were not infallible, and that occasional mistakes may have crept into the sacred text, though wonderfully few. When, therefore, some critics object to a word or a verse here and there, reason would that we should bear with them patiently, and agree to differ. Difficulties about the meaning of many places in the Bible, apparent discrepancies, obscure passages, no doubt, there always will be. But the book, as a whole, contains nothing that is not true.

But unhappily the battle of inspiration does not end here. A school of men has risen among us, who boldly deny the inspiration of large portions of the Old Testament. The book of Genesis, for example, is declared by some to possess no Divine authority, and to be only a collection of interesting fictions. I can find no words to express my entire disagreement with such theories. I maintain firmly that the Old Testament is of equal authority with the New, and that they stand or fall together. You cannot separate them, any more than you can separate the warp and woof in a piece of woven cloth. The writers of the New Testament continually quote the words of the Old Testament as of equal authority with their own, and never give the slightest hint that these quotations are not to be regarded as the word of God. The thrice-repeated saying of our Lord, taken from Deuteronomy, 'It is written,' when tempted by the devil, is deeply significant and instructive (Matt. 4:5-10).

But this is not the whole of my objection to these modern theories. I contend that attacks on Genesis in particular involve most dangerous consequences. They tend to dishonour our

Lord Jesus Christ and his apostles. That they appear to regard the events and persons mentioned in Genesis as real, historical, and true, and not fictitious, is clear to any honest reader of the Gospels and Acts. Now, how can this be explained if Genesis is, as some say, a mere collection of fictions? You cannot explain it except on the supposition that our Lord and his apostles were ignorant, and did not know as much as modern critics do, or else that they secretly suppressed their knowledge in order to avoid offending their hearers. In short, they were either fallible or fallacious, deceived or deceivers. God forbid that we should adopt either one conclusion or the other!

I frankly confess that my whole soul revolts from these modern teachings about Genesis. When I read that our Lord Jesus Christ is 'One with the Father,' that 'In him are hid all the treasures of wisdom and knowledge,' that he is 'the Light of the world,' my mind cannot conceive the possibility of his being ignorant, as latter-day theories about Genesis certainly imply, however fully I admit the 'Kenosis' of his Incarnation. That blessed Saviour to whom I am taught to commit my soul, in the very week that he died for my redemption, spoke of the Flood and the days of Noah as realities! If he spoke *ignorantly*, with Calvary in full view, it would shake to the foundation my confidence in his power to save me, and would destroy my peace. I abhor the idea of an ignorant Saviour! From all distrust of any part of the Bible may you ever be delivered. How any English clergyman can read a lesson from Genesis in church, if he does not believe its inspiration, I cannot understand. And how after this he can gravely ascend the pulpit, select a text from Genesis, preach a sermon on the text, and draw lessons from it, when he does not believe in his heart that the text he has chosen was given by inspiration, this, I say, is one of those things which fill my soul with amazement, and make me tremble for the ark of God. Well and wisely has this age been called 'an age of downgrade theology.' The man who only admits a partial inspiration of the Bible, has been justly compared to one with his head in a fog and his feet on a quicksand. From theories like these may you ever be preserved!

I take occasion to say that I decline to admit the correctness of the translation of 2 Tim. 3:16, which is given in the *Revised Version*. I stand firmly by the *Authorized Version* of the text, in company with Chrysostom and Bengel, and I maintain that the translation of this verse given by the Revisers is a strained, harsh, and unnatural rendering of the Greek words. The translation 'all scripture' is amply justified by 'all flesh' in Luke 3:6.

III. In the next place, let me charge you *to hold fast the old doctrine of the sinfulness of sin, and the corruption of human nature.*

I can find no words to express my sense of the vastness and importance of this subject. It is my firm conviction that a right knowledge of sin lies at the root of all saving religion. The first thing that God does when he makes man a new creature in Christ is to send light into his heart, and show him that he is a guilty sinner. The material creation in Genesis began with 'light,' and so also does the spiritual creation. I have an equally firm conviction that a low and imperfect view of sin is the origin of most of the errors, heresies, and false doctrines of the present day. If a man does not realize the extent and dangerous nature of his soul's disease, you cannot wonder if he is content with false or imperfect remedies. I believe that one of the chief wants of the Church in the nineteenth century has been, and is, clearer, fuller teaching about sin.

Sin, I need not remind any Bible reader, consists in doing, saying, thinking, or imagining anything that is not in perfect conformity with the mind and law of God. 'Sin,' as the Scripture saith, is 'the transgression of the law' (1 John 3:4). The slightest outward or inward departure from absolute mathematical parallelism with God's revealed will and character constitutes a sin, and at once makes us guilty in God's sight. The Ninth Article of our Church declares that sin is, the fault and corruption of the nature of every man that naturally is engendered of the offspring of Adam; whereby man is very far gone (*quam longissime*, is the Latin) from original righteousness, and is of his own nature inclined to evil, so that the flesh lusteth always contrary to the spirit; and, therefore, in every person born into the world, it deserveth God's wrath and damnation.

Sin, in short, is that vast moral disease which affects the whole human race, of every rank and class and name and nation and people and tongue, the plague of rulers and statesmen, the divider of Churches, the destroyer of family happiness, the cause of all the miseries in the world.

Now I am obliged to declare my conviction that the extent and vileness and deceitfulness of sin are a subject which is not sufficiently brought forward in the religious teaching of these last days. I do not say it is ignored altogether. But I do say that it is not pressed on congregations in its Scriptural proportion, and in harmony with the two grand Confessions of our Prayer-book. The consequences are very serious.

One result, I am persuaded, is the immense increase of that *sensuous, ceremonial, formal kind of Christianity*, which has swept over England like a flood in the last forty years, and carried away so many before it. I can well believe that there is much that is attractive and satisfying in this system of religion, to a certain order of minds, so long as the conscience is not fully enlightened. But when that wonderful part of our constitution is really awake and alive, I find it hard to believe that a sensuous, ceremonial Christianity will thoroughly satisfy us. A little child is easily quieted and amused with gaudy toys and dolls and rattles, so long as it is not hungry; but once let it feel the cravings of nature within, and we know that nothing will satisfy it but food. Just so it is with man in the matter of his soul. Music and singing and flowers and banners and processions and beautiful vestments and confessionals and man-made ceremonies of semi-Romish character may do well enough for man under certain conditions. But once let him awake and arise from the dead, and he will not rest content with these things. They will seem to him mere solemn triflings and a waste of time. Once let him see his sin, and he must see his Saviour, in order to obtain rest for his soul. He feels stricken with a deadly disease; and nothing will satisfy him but the Great Physician. He hungers and thirsts; and he must have nothing less than the bread of life. I may seem bold in what I am about to say, but I fearlessly venture the assertion, that one half of the semi-Romanism of the last forty years would never have existed, if English people had been taught more fully and clearly the nature, vileness, and sinfulness of sin.

I believe the likeliest way to cure and mend this defective kind of religion is to bring forward more prominently, and expound more frequently, the Ten Commandments as the true test of sin. They really seem to me to have fallen into the rear of late, and, with the exception of the sixth and eighth, to receive less attention than they deserve. It is an awkward fact that, in consequence of early administrations of the Lord's Supper, the ante-communion service at our full morning worship is so often omitted, that many persons rarely hear the Decalogue at all! Let us try to revive the old teaching in nurseries, in schools, in training colleges, in universities. Let us not forget that 'the law is good if a man use it lawfully,' and that 'by the law is the knowledge of sin' (1 Tim. 1:8; Rom. 3:20; 7:7). Let us bring it to the front once more, and press it on men's attention. Let us expound and beat out the Ten Commandments, and show the length and breadth and depth and height of their requirements. It is the way of our Lord in the Sermon on the Mount. It was the way of great divines like Bishops Andrews and Leighton and Hopkins and Patrick, whose works on the Commandments are classics to this day. We should do well to walk in their steps. We may depend upon it, men will never come to Christ, and stay with Christ, and live for Christ, unless they feel their sins, and know their need of a Saviour. Those whom the Holy Spirit draws to Christ are those whom the Spirit has convinced of sin. Without real conviction of sin, men may seem to come to Christ and follow him for a season, but they will soon fall away and return to the world.

I commend this point to your private consideration. I suspect that the prevailing desire to make things pleasant to hearers, and the fear of giving offence by plain speaking, have much to say to the neglect of the law in this day. But the testimony of the Bible is clear: 'By the law is the knowledge of sin' (Rom. 3:20; 7:7). The words of the late Bishop Lightfoot are most deeply true: 'The consciousness of sin is the true pathway to heaven.'

IV. In the next place, let me charge you *to hold fast the great foundation-principle of Scripture and our Church, that forgiveness of sins is only given to man through the atoning death of Jesus Christ on the cross.*

This is a deep and solemn subject; but there is such an immense amount of strange doctrine floating in the air about it, that I dare not pass it over. It seems to me to lie so near the roots of the Gospel, that it is my duty not to be silent.

So far as I can understand—and I am not sure that I do—the theory of many appears to be that it is the incarnation rather than the sacrifice—the human nature that Christ took on him rather than the death he died which is intended to be the chief ground of hope for our souls. It seems to be held that the blood which 'cleanseth from all sin' is not so much the life-blood which Christ shed when he died, as the blood of human nature of which he became partaker when he was born into the world, and by partaking ennobled all Adam's race, and made salvation possible for fallen man. As to the old doctrine that the blood which flowed on Calvary was the ransom paid for our souls and the price of our redemption from the punishment due to our sins, it seems to be thrown aside by many like an obsolete dogma, unworthy of these latter days. Some even sneer at it as 'blood theology,' and tell us that Christ's death was only the death of a great martyr, and a grand example of perfect submission to God's will, but not a propitiation for sin.

Now I know not what some of you may think of the theory I have tried to delineate; but I must plainly say that I cannot for a moment admit that it is true, and will bear the test of calm examination. The subject is one about which I dare not call any one master.

(1) I cannot reconcile the theory with scores of *plain texts in the New Testament*, in which the forgiveness of sins, salvation, justification, reconciliation, redemption, deliverance from wrath to come, and peace with God, appear to be inseparably connected with the sufferings and death of Christ, and not with his life. The expression in Romans, 'We shall be saved by his life' (Rom. 5:10), is sometimes quoted as a reply to what I am saying. But that text does not mean anything but Christ's life of intercession, and it is like the words in Hebrews: 'He is able to save to the uttermost ... seeing that he ever liveth to make intercession' (Heb. 7:25). When Moses and Elias appeared in the Transfiguration, the one subject they were heard speaking about was our Lord's 'decease,' and not his life (Luke 9:31). When the saints in Revelation are shown to us in vision as singing a new song before the throne, the theme of it was, 'Thou wast slain, and hast redeemed us to God by thy blood' (Rev. 5:9).

(2) I cannot reconcile the theory with the uniform language of our *authorised formularies* on the subject of Christ's death. The Te Deum, the Litany, the Office for the Visitation of the Sick, the Communion Service, all contain expressions about the precious blood and death, which point to our Lord's vicarious sufferings on Calvary as the object on which Christians should especially look in all their thoughts when they look to him for salvation. Redemption by death appears to my eyes to turn up everywhere. The well-known Homily of Salvation confirms this view most fully, to say nothing of other Homilies.

(3) I cannot reconcile the theory with the uniform teaching of the *Old Testament dispensation* about the way of access to God. The great principle which, like a red line, runs through the whole

Mosaic ceremonial, is the absolute necessity of sacrifice. Day after day, all the year round, and especially at the Passover, the Jew was taught by emblems and figures that 'without shedding of blood' there was no safety for the soul, and 'no remission of sins.' If the Mosaic system was meant to keep before the mind of Israel, by types and figures, the great future sacrifice of the Lamb of God on Calvary, and redemption by his blood, I can quite see its reasonableness. But if the vicarious death of Christ was not to be the main purpose of his coming into the world, the incessant slaughter of innocent animals on Jewish altars for fourteen hundred years appears to my eyes an unnecessary waste of animal life, inconsistent with God's mercy towards all his creatures, and admitting of no satisfactory explanation.

(4) Last, but not least, I cannot reconcile the theory with the unvarying *language of our Prayer-book* on the subject of the Lord's Supper. In that holy ordinance, St Paul tells us that we 'show the Lord's death till he come' (1 Cor. 11:26). His *death*, observe, not his life! Hence our Catechism tells every child that this blessed sacrament was ordained 'for the continual remembrance of the sacrifice of the death of Christ.' The Communion Office in one place speaks of Christ's 'meritorious cross and passion, whereby alone we obtain remission of our sins.' In another it bids us give hearty thanks 'for the redemption of the world by the death and passion of our Saviour Christ.' In a third it tells us that God did give 'His only Son Jesus Christ to suffer death upon the cross for our redemption, who made thereby his one oblation of himself once offered, a full, perfect and sufficient sacrifice, oblation, and satisfaction for the sins of the whole world.' If these remarkable expressions do not point to the death of Christ rather than his life, his crucifixion rather than his incarnation, as the object of faith and the one ground of man's hope for his soul, I do not know what Prayer-book words mean.

I may not dwell longer on this solemn subject. If time permitted, I might remind you how the 'story of the cross' and the blood has always been found the most effective weapon in the mission field all over the globe. But the limits of a Charge will not allow me. If others are content to turn away from the 'old paths' of redemption by blood and substitution, and to rest on a vague hope that, *somehow or other*, they will be saved by Christ's incarnation, I am not their judge. Give me rather for my faith the standing-place of the noble army of martyrs and the goodly company of Reformers, namely, the blood and passion of Christ. I dare not launch forth into a world unknown on any other plank but this. To use the words inscribed on an old Kentish tombstone:

> *Christ's death is my life;*
> *My death to life the portal;*
> *Thus through two deaths*
> *I'll reach one life immortal.*

V. Let me charge you, in the next place, *to hold fast sound and scriptural views of the work of the Holy Ghost.*

Faith in the Holy Ghost, we must always remember, is as truly a part of Christianity as faith in Christ. Every child who repeats the Church Catechism is taught to say, 'I learn to believe in God the Holy Ghost, who sanctifieth me and all the elect people of God.' Furthermore, the work of the Holy Ghost, though mysterious, will always be known by the fruits it produces in the character and conduct of those in whom he dwells. It is like light which can be seen, and fire which can be felt, and wind which causes noticeable results. Where there are no fruits of the Spirit, there is no presence of the Spirit. Those fruits, I need not tell you, are always the same, conviction of sin, true repentance, lively faith in Christ, and holiness of heart and life.

Now I believe this kind of truth about the work of the Holy Ghost needs strongly to be pressed on congregations in the present day. I am afraid there are myriads of professing Christians throughout the land, who really know nothing about the Holy

Ghost, except the declaration of belief in him in the Creed. They seem to think that as baptized members of a great ecclesiastical corporation, they possess all the privileges of members. But of the work of the Spirit on their own individual hearts, of conversion, repentance, and faith, they know nothing at all. They are spiritually asleep and dead, and unless they awake are in great danger. To arouse such persons to a sense of their unsatisfactory condition, to stir them to see that if there be any Holy Ghost, they ought to know something of him by inward experience, and never rest till they feel this. This is work which I am convinced every clergyman ought to keep continually in view, and I entreat you to do so this day. Not only preach Christ, but take care that you also preach the Holy Ghost.

But I may not stop here. There are other classes of Christians besides those to whom I have just referred, who need sound scriptural teaching about the work of the Holy Ghost. Let me explain what I mean. I suppose no intelligent Churchman can fail to see that there has been of late years an immense increase of what I must call, for want of a better phrase, *public religion* in the land. Services of all sorts are strangely multiplied. Places of worship are thrown open for prayer and preaching and administration of the Lord's Supper, at least ten times as much as they were fifty years ago. Services in cathedral naves, meetings in large public rooms like the Agricultural Hall and Mildmay Conference Building, mission services carried on day after day and evening after evening, Holiness meetings, Higher-life conventions—all these have become common and familiar things. They are, in fact, established institutions of the day, and the crowds who attend them supply plain proof that they are popular. In short, we find ourselves face to face with the undeniable fact that the last quarter of the nineteenth century is an age of an immense amount of *public religion.*

I am not going to find fault with this. Let no one suppose that for a moment. On the contrary, I thank God for the revival of the old apostolic plan of 'aggressiveness' in religion, and the evident spread of a desire 'by all means to save some' (1 Cor. 9:22). I thank God for shortened services, home missions, and evangelistic movements like that of Moody and Sankey, and Mr Aitken.[1] I thank God for any organized effort to raise the standard of holiness in the land. It has long been, and is, terribly low. Anything is better than torpor, apathy, and inaction. 'If Christ is preached, I rejoice, yea, and will rejoice' (Phil. 1:18). Prophets and righteous men in England once desired to see these things, and never saw them. If Whitefield and Wesley, and Rowland, and Grimshaw, and Berridge had been told in their day that a time would come when English Archbishops and Bishops would not only sanction mission services, but take an active part in them, I can hardly think they would have believed it. Rather, I suspect, they would have been tempted to say, like the Samaritan nobleman in Elisha's time, 'If the Lord would make windows in heaven, might this thing be?' (2 Kings 7:2).

But while we are thankful for the increase of *public* religion, we must never forget that, unless it is accompanied by *private* religion, it is of no real solid value, and may even produce most mischievous effects. Incessant running after sensational preachers; incessant attendance at hot, crowded meetings protracted to late hours; incessant craving after fresh excitement and highly-spiced pulpit novelties—all this kind of thing is calculated to produce a very unhealthy style of Christianity; and, in many cases, I am afraid, the end is utter ruin of soul. For, unhappily, those who make *public* religion everything, are often led away by mere temporary emotions, after some grand display of ecclesiastical oratory, into professing far more than they really feel. After this, they can only be kept up to the mark, which they imagine they have reached, by a constant succession of religious excitements. By and by, as with opium-eaters and dram-drinkers, there comes a

---

[1] Rev. W. Hay M. H. Aitken, Incumbent in Liverpool, 1891, founded the Church Parochial Mission Society, 1876.

time when their dose loses its power, and a feeling of exhaustion and discontent begins to creep over their minds. Too often, I fear, the conclusion of the whole matter is a relapse into utter deadness and unbelief, and a complete return to the world. And all results from having nothing but a *public* religion! Oh that people would remember that it was not the wind, or the fire, or the earthquake, which showed Elijah the presence of God, but 'the still small voice' (1 Kings 19:12)

I desire to lift up a warning voice on this subject. I want to see no decrease of *public* religion, remember; but I do want to promote an increase of that religion which is private between each man and his God, and that religion which is most beautifully exhibited at home. I want to see more attention paid to those passive graces which are the truest evidence of the work of the Spirit. To be religious among the religious, and spiritual among the spiritual, all this is comparatively easy. But to adorn the Gospel, and be Christlike, in the midst of a large family circle of unconverted and uncongenial relatives; to be always patient, gentle, loving, kind, unselfish, good-tempered; this is the grandest fruit of the Holy Ghost. We want more of this kind of religion. The root of a plant or tree makes no show above ground. If you dig down to it and examine it, it is a poor, dirty, coarse-looking thing, and not nearly so beautiful to the eye as the fruit or leaf or flower. But that despised root, nevertheless, is the true source of all the life, health, vigour, and fertility which your eyes see, and without it the plant or tree would soon die. Now, private religion is the root of all vital Christianity. Without it we may make a brave show in the meeting or on the platform, and sing loud, and shed many tears, and have a name to live, and the praise of man. But without it we are dead before God.

Our forefathers had far fewer means and opportunities than we have. Full religious meetings and crowds, except occasionally in a large room or in a field, when such men as Whitefield or Wesley or Rowland preached, these were things of which they knew nothing. Their proceedings were neither fashionable nor popular, and often brought on them more persecution and abuse than praise. But the few weapons they used, they used well. I have a strong impression that they had among them more of the presence of the Holy Ghost than we have. In quantity of religious profession we have far surpassed them; in quality, I fear, we are sadly behind. With less noise and applause from man, they made, I believe, a far deeper mark for God on their generation than we do, with all our conferences, and meetings, and mission rooms, and halls, and multiplied religious appliances. Their converts, I suspect, like the old-fashioned cloths and linens, wore better and lasted longer, and faded less and kept colour, and were more stable and rooted and grounded than many of the new-born babes of this day. And what was the reason of all this? Simply, I believe, that they gave more attention to *private* religion than we generally do. There was more deep, solid work, quiet work of the Holy Ghost, among them. There was more private Bible reading and private prayer. They walked closely with God, and honoured him in private, and so he honoured them in public. Oh, let us follow them as they followed Christ! Let us exhort our people to go and do likewise. Let us honour the Holy Ghost more than we have done.

IV. Let me charge you, in the next place, *to hold fast the old doctrine of our Church about the two sacraments*.

You must not suppose that I am about to discuss the thorny questions which are connected with the Baptismal Service and the ritual of the Lord's Supper. Nothing of the kind! The one only point which I am going to press on your attention is the importance of always teaching the necessity of a right reception of the sacraments. We must not only receive them, but receive them *rightly*.

You must all be aware that extravagant views of the effects of Baptism and the Lord's Supper have been in every age of the Church the most fertile source of mischievous superstition. Such is the intensity of man's natural tendency to formalism in religion, that myriads have always clung to the idea that these two sacraments necessarily confer grace, independently of faith, in those that receive them, and that they work on the soul in a kind of physical way, if I may so speak, like medicines on the body. The high-flown rhetorical language of the Fathers about them did immense harm in the early ages. The Church of Rome has stereotyped and crystallized the error, by the decree of the Council of Trent, which says: 'Whosoever shall affirm that grace is not conferred by these sacraments of the new law, by their own power (*ex opere operato*[1]), but that faith in the Divine promise is all that is necessary to obtain grace: let him be accursed.'[2] Thousands of English Churchmen, wittingly or unwittingly, seem to maintain practically the same view as the Church of Rome, and to attribute to the mere outward administration of the two sacraments of Baptism and the Lord's Supper a kind of invariable influence and power, no matter how, or with what feeling, intention, heart and spirit, they are used.

Now, to these extravagant views of the effect of the sacraments, I unhesitatingly assert that the Church of England gives no countenance at all. The Twenty-fifth Article declares plainly about both sacraments, that 'in such *only* as worthily receive the same they have a wholesome effect or operation; but they that receive them unworthily, purchase to themselves damnation.' The Twenty-eighth Article says: 'To such as rightly, worthily, and with faith receive the same, the bread which we break is a partaking of the body of Christ, and likewise the cup of blessing is a partaking of the blood of Christ.' The Twenty-ninth Article says: 'The wicked, and such as be *void of a lively faith*, although they do carnally and visibly press with their teeth the sacrament of the body and blood of Christ, yet in no wise are they partakers of Christ: but rather, to their condemnation, do eat and drink the sign or sacrament of so great a thing.'

[1] *Lit.* 'from the work performed.' The view that the sacraments yield their benefits by the mere outward act of administration.

[2] J. M. Cramp, *A Text-Book of Popery*, London 1851, p. 155.

I do hope my Clergy in this day will stand firm on this subject. There is, I am afraid, a sad disposition to give way and recede from scriptural and Church of England truth in this direction. Partly from a fear of not honouring the sacraments enough, partly from the pressure of modern teaching, there is a strong tendency to exalt Baptism and the Lord's Supper to a place never given to them in Scripture, and especially not in the pastoral Epistles. Let us set our foot down firmly on the wise and moderate principles laid down in our Articles, and refuse to go one inch beyond. Let us honour sacraments as holy ordinances appointed by Christ himself, and blessed means of grace, though most shockingly neglected, I grieve to say, by many churchgoers who never go to the Lord's Table. But let us steadily refuse to admit that Christ's sacraments convey grace '*ex opere operato*,' the external act, and that in every case where they are administered, good must of necessity be done, no matter how or by whom they are received. Let us refuse to admit that they are the principal '*media*' between Christ and the soul—above faith, above preaching, above prayer, and above the word. Let us maintain, with the judicious Hooker, that 'all receive not the grace of God, who receive the sacraments of his grace.' Above all, let us never encourage any one to suppose he will receive any benefit from the Lord's Supper, unless he comes to it with the qualifications laid down at the end of the Church Catechism, 'with repentance for sin, and lively faith in Christ, and charity toward all men.' St Paul says there is such a thing as 'eating and drinking unworthily' (1 Cor. 11:27) in the Lord's Supper. To press men to become communicants who neither repent nor believe, is no kindness, and does more harm than good.

VII. In the next place, let me charge you *to hold fast the old doctrine of the Church of England about the sanctity and right observance of the Sabbath Day.*

I name this point because our old English Sunday appears to me to be in great danger. We live in perilous times. Partly from the spread of infidelity, that old enemy of the Lord's Day; partly from the morbid love of liberty, and letting every one do as he likes; partly from the exaggerated love of pleasure which marks this age; partly from the facilities afforded by railways for Sabbath travelling, of which our fathers knew nothing, and got on well enough without them; partly from one cause and partly from another, the devil is just now getting more help in his campaign against the Lord's Day than he has done since the Reformation. You may see what I mean in the persistent attempts frequently made to throw open places of amusement, aquariums, libraries, theatres, museums, picture galleries, and the like, under the plausible pretence of 'affording recreation to the working-classes'! All such attempts, I maintain, ought to be firmly and vigilantly resisted. They are the first steps towards a Continental Sunday, and a general flood of Sabbath desecration, Sunday shop-opening, and Sunday delivery of letters in London. I would not have you give way to such attempts. 'No surrender!' should be our cry. Let us fight to the last plank for the old English Sunday. Give up the outworks, and the citadel will soon fall.

That laymen of high position and education, noblemen, philosophers, and scientific lecturers, should assist the attempt to break down the standard of Sunday observance, is matter for deep regret. I can only suppose that they do it in ignorance. If they would only study hearts and consciences and death-bed feelings half as much as they study political economy, or stones and plants and beasts and geology and astronomy and light and chemistry and the secrets of earth and air and sea, I believe they would not act as they do. I pity and pray for them. 'They know not what they do.'

But how any clergyman holding office in the Church of England, and reading the Fourth Commandment every Sunday to his congregation, can lend his aid to movements which must infallibly prevent the Sabbath being kept holy, if they succeed, is one of those mysteries of the nineteenth century which pass my understanding. I am amazed, pained, troubled, grieved, and astonished.

The good that the best clergyman does at his very best in a fallen world is small. But he that expects to do good by introducing a Continental Sunday into his parish, exhibits, in my judgment, however excellent his intentions, great ignorance of human nature. He is cutting off his right hand, and destroying his own usefulness. Whatever may be the bad habits of the working-classes in large parishes, they will never be cured by organizing modes of breaking the Fourth Commandment. We should call that statesman a poor lawgiver who sanctioned petty larceny in order to prevent burglary; and I call that clergyman an unwise man, who, in order to stop drunkenness and its concomitants, is prepared to throw overboard the Sabbath Day. Surely to sacrifice one commandment in order to prevent the breach of another, is neither Christianity nor common sense. It is, in my opinion, 'doing evil that good may come.'

The best practical way of resisting the attack made on the Sabbath in the present day, is to supply the working-classes with plain instruction on the subject, and to open their eyes to all its bearings. I make no apology for urging my brethren in the ministry to do this continually.

Tell the working-classes never to be taken in and deluded by those who want the sanctity of the Lord's Day to be more publicly invaded than it is, and yet say they are 'their friends'! However well-meaning and fair-spoken such persons may be, they are not real friends. They are in reality their worst enemies. They are taking the surest course to add to their burdens. They do not mean it, very likely, but in reality they are doing them a cruel injury.

Tell the working-classes that if English Sundays are ever turned into days of play and amusement, they will soon become days of labour and work. It is vain to suppose that it can be avoided. It never has been in other countries. It never would be in our own land. Once established the principle that libraries, picture galleries, aquariums, museums, and crystal palaces, are to be thrown open on Sundays, and you let in the thin edge of the wedge. The enemy would have got inside the walls. The sacredness of the day of rest would be gone. Shops would soon be opened. Farmers would insist on cultivating the land, or getting in hay or corn on Sundays. Factories would go on working. Contractors would press forward their operations.

Tell the working-classes that if they ever lose their old English Sabbath, they will soon find that they have lost their best friend. Tell them that those who want to secure them a little more time for rest and relaxation should not try to take that time out of Sunday. Let them take a little piece out of one of the six working days, if possible, but not a bit out of the day of God. Tell them that as the world has got six days for its business, and God has only left himself one for his, it is only fair and right that the world should give up some of its time before we begin robbing God of his.

After all, there is a world to come, a life after death, an eternity either in heaven or hell. We must all die at last, and stand before the judgment-scat of Christ, when we rise again. Never, never let us cease to maintain and proclaim these great realities, whether men will hear or whether they will forbear. Never let us forget that the value we put on the Lord's Day, and the manner in which we spend it, are some of the most useful and searching tests of our fitness to die, and our readiness for heaven.[1]

VIII. Let me charge you, in the next place, *to hold fast the teaching of Scripture and the Prayer-book about the state of man after death.*

This is a very solemn and painful topic, and flesh and blood naturally shrink from its contemplation. But so many strange doctrines are floating in the air about the whole subject, that I dare not refuse to consider it. The language of the Bible and the Liturgy about 'judgment to come' and the future punishment

---

[1] *In September 1889, the French Government, anxious to take steps to win back 'the lost Sabbath,' called an International Congress to consider what could be done to secure the Sabbath for France. Delegates attended from England, Germany, United States, Switzerland, Belgium, Italy, Norway, Austria, Brazil, and many other countries. M. Leon Say, the Minister of Commerce, presided, and forty-eight resolutions were passed, all in favour of the Sabbath Day.

of those who die impenitent, appear to me so distinct, that I do not see how it can be explained away. Those who object to the doctrine of future punishment, talk loudly about love and charity, and say that it does not harmonize with the merciful and compassionate character of God. But what saith the Scripture? Who ever spoke such loving and merciful words as our Lord Jesus Christ? Yet his are the lips which three times over describe the consequence of impenitence and sin, as 'the worm that never dies, and the fire that is not quenched.' He is the person who speaks in one sentence of the wicked going away into 'everlasting punishment,' and the righteous into 'life eternal' (Mark 9:43, 48; Matt. 25:46).[1] Who does not remember the Apostle Paul's words about charity? Yet he is the very Apostle who says the wicked 'shall be punished with everlasting destruction' (2 Thess. 1:9). Who does not know the spirit of love which runs all through St John's Gospel and Epistles? Yet the beloved Apostle is the very writer in the New Testament who dwells most strongly, in the book of Revelation, on the reality and eternity of future woe. What shall we say to these things? Shall we be wise above that which is written? Shall we admit the dangerous principle that words in Scripture do not mean what they appear to mean? If so, where are we to stop? Is it not far better to lay our hands on our mouths and say, 'Whatsoever God has written must be true.' 'Even so, Lord God Almighty, true and righteous are thy judgments' (Rev. 16:7).

The language of our Prayer-book on this deep and awful subject is very remarkable. Almost the first petition in our matchless Litany contains this sentence, 'From everlasting damnation, good Lord, deliver us.' The Catechism teaches every child who

---

[1] *'If God had intended to have told us that the punishment of wicked men shall have no end, the languages wherein the Scriptures are written do hardly afford fuller and more certain words than those that are used in this case, whereby to express a duration without end; and likewise, which is almost a peremptory decision of the thing, the duration of the punishment of wicked men is in the very same sentence expressed by the very same word which is used for the duration of happiness of the righteous.' Archbishop Tillotson *On Hell Torments.* See Matthew Horbery, *Scripture Doctrine of Eternal Punishment,* 1744, vol. ii, p. 42.

learns it, that whenever we repeat the Lord's Prayer we desire our Heavenly Father to 'keep us from our ghostly enemy and from everlasting death.' Even in our Burial Service we pray at the graveside, 'Deliver us not into the bitter pains of eternal death.' Once more I ask, 'What shall we say to these things?' Shall we teach our congregations that even when people live and die in sin, we may hope for their happiness in a remote future? Surely the common sense of many of our worshippers would reply, that if this is the case, Prayer-book words mean nothing at all.

I lay no claim to any peculiar knowledge of Scripture. I feel daily that I am no more infallible than the Bishop of Rome. But I must speak according to the light which God has given to me, and I do not think I should do my duty if I did not raise a warning voice on this subject, and try to put the clergy of my Diocese on their guard. Six thousand years ago, sin entered into the world by the devil's daring falsehood: 'Ye shall not surely die' (Gen. 3:4). At the end of six thousand years, the great enemy of mankind is still using his old weapon, and trying to persuade men that they may live and die in sin, and yet at some distant period may be finally saved. Let us not be ignorant of his devices. Let us walk steadily in the old paths. Let us hold fast the old truth, and believe that, as the happiness of the saved is eternal, so also is the misery of the lost.[1]

(1) Let us hold it fast *in the interest of the whole system of revealed religion*. What was the use of God's Son becoming incarnate, agonizing in Gethsemane, and dying on the cross to make atonement, if men can be finally saved without believing on him? Where is the slightest proof that saving faith in Christ's blood can ever begin after death? Where is the need of the Holy Ghost, if sinners are at last to enter heaven without conversion

---

[1] *'There is nothing that Satan more desires than that we should believe that he does not exist, and that there is no such place as hell, and no such things as eternal torments. He whispers all this into our ears, and he exults when he hears a lay man, and much more when he hears a clergyman, deny these things for then he hopes to make them and others his victims.' Bishop Christopher Wordsworth, *Sermon on Future Rewards and Punishments*, p. 36.

and renewal of heart? Where can we find the smallest evidence that any one can be born again after death, and have a new heart, if he dies in an unregenerate state? If a man may escape eternal punishment at last, without faith in Christ or sanctification of the Spirit, sin is no longer an infinite evil, and there was no need for Christ to die on Calvary.

(2) Let us hold it fast for the sake of holiness and morality. I can imagine nothing so pleasant to flesh and blood, as the specious theory that we may live in sin and yet escape eternal perdition; and that, although we 'serve divers lusts and pleasures' while we are here, we shall somehow or other all get to heaven hereafter! Only tell the young man who is 'wasting his substance in riotous living,' that there is a heaven at last, even for those who live and die in sin, and he is never likely to turn from evil. What does it signify how he lives, if there is no 'judgment to come'? Why should he repent and take up the cross, if he can get to heaven at last without trouble?

(3) Finally, let us hold it fast *for the sake of the common hopes of all God's saints*. Let us distinctly understand that every blow struck at the eternity of punishment, is an equally heavy blow at the eternity of reward. It is impossible to separate the two things. No ingenious theological definition can divide them. They stand or fall together. The same language is used, the same figures of speech are employed, when the Bible speaks about either condition. Every attack on the duration of hell is also an attack on the duration of heaven.[1] It is a deep and true saying, 'With the sinner's fear our hope departs.'

I turn from this part of my Charge with a strong sense of its painfulness. I feel keenly, with Robert M'Cheyne, that 'it is a difficult subject to handle lovingly.' But I turn from it with an equally strong

---

[1] *'If the punishment of the wicked is only temporary, such will also be the happiness of the righteous, which is repugnant to the whole teaching of Scripture; but if the happiness of the righteous will be everlasting (who will be equal to the angels, and their bodies will be like the body of Christ), such also will be the punishment of the wicked.' Bishop Christopher Wordsworth, *Sermon on Future Rewards and Punishments*, p. 36.

conviction, that if we believe the Bible we must never give up anything which it contains. From hard, austere, and unmerciful theology, Good Lord, deliver us! If men are not saved, it is not because God does not love them, and is not willing to save them, but because they 'will not come to Christ' (John 5:40). But we must not be wise above that which is written. No morbid liberality, so called, must induce us to reject anything which God has revealed about the next world. Men sometimes talk exclusively about God's mercy and love and compassion, as if he had no other attributes, and leave out of sight entirely his holiness and his purity, his justice and his unchangeableness, and his hatred of sin. Let us beware of falling into this delusion. It is a growing evil in these latter days. Low and inadequate views of the unutterable vileness and filthiness of sin, and of the unutterable purity of the eternal God, are fertile sources of error about man's future state. Let us think of the mighty Being with whom we have to do, as he himself declared his character to Moses, saying, 'The Lord, the Lord God, merciful and gracious, long-suffering and abundant in goodness and truth, keeping mercy for thousands, forgiving iniquity, and transgression, and sin.' But let us not forget the solemn clause which concludes the sentence: 'And *that will by no means clear the guilty*' (Exod. 34:6, 7). Unrepented sin is an eternal evil, and can never cease to be sin; and he with whom we have to do is an eternal God.

IX. In the last place, let me charge you *to hold fast the great Protestant principles on which the Church of England was reformed three hundred and fifty years ago, and to resist firmly all attempts to promote reunion with the Church of Rome.*

There was a time when it would have been needless for a Bishop to offer such advice to his clergy. But times have strangely altered. No intelligent observer can fail to observe that the tone of public feeling in England about Romanism has undergone a great change in the last sixty years. There is no longer that general dislike, dread, and aversion to Popery, which was once almost universal in this realm. The edge of the old British feeling about Protestantism seems blunted and dull. Some profess to be tired of all religious controversy, and are ready to sacrifice God's truth for the sake of peace. Some look on Romanism as simply one among many English forms of religion, and neither worse nor better than others. Some try to persuade us that Romanism is changed, and not nearly so bad as it used to be. Some boldly point to the faults of Protestants, and loudly cry that Romanists are quite as good as ourselves. Some think it fine and liberal to maintain that we have no right to think any one wrong who pays taxes and is in earnest about his creed. And yet the two great historical facts, (1) that ignorance, immorality, and superstition reigned supreme in England four hundred years ago under Popery; (2) that the Reformation was the greatest blessing God ever gave to this land—both these are facts which no one but a Romanist ever thought of disputing fifty years ago! In the present day, alas! it is convenient and fashionable to forget them. In short, at the rate we are going, I shall not be surprised if it is soon proposed to repeal the Act of Settlement as too narrow and illiberal for the nineteenth century, and to allow the Crown of England to be worn by a Papist.[1]

The *causes* of this melancholy change of feeling are not hard to discover.

(1) It arises partly from the untiring zeal of the Romish Church herself. Her agents never slumber or sleep, whatever English Churchmen may do. With unwearied zeal they compass sea and land to make one proselyte. With a watchful pertinacity, worthy of a better cause, they leave no stone unturned, in the palace or the workhouse, to promote their cause. (2) It has been furthered immensely by the proceedings of a zealous, well-meaning, but sadly mistaken party within the Church of England, which has given many converts, like Newman and Manning, to the Church of Rome. The novel teaching and

[1] See appendix, chapter 9, pp. 432-35.

ritual of modern days have gradually familiarized people with every distinctive doctrine and practice of Romanism—the real presence, the mass, auricular confession and priestly absolution, the sacerdotal character of the ministry, the monastic system, and a histrionic, sensuous, showy style of public worship. The natural result is that many simple people see no mighty harm in downright genuine Popery. (3) Last, but not least, the spurious liberality of the day we live in, helps on the Rome-ward tendency. It is fashionable now to say that all sects should be equal, that the State should have nothing to do with religion, that all creeds should be regarded with equal favour and respect, and that there is a substratum of common truth at the bottom of all religion, whether Buddhism, Mahometanism, or Christianity! The consequence is, that myriads of ignorant folks begin to think there is nothing peculiarly dangerous in the tenets of Papists any more than in the tenets of Methodists, Independents, Presbyterians, or Baptists, and that we ought to let Romanism alone, and never expose its unscriptural and Christ-dishonouring character.

The *consequences* of this changed tone of feeling, I am bold to say, will be most disastrous and mischievous, unless loyal Churchmen can be aroused to see their danger. Once let Popery get her foot again on the neck of England, and there will be an end of all our national greatness. God will forsake us, and we shall sink to the level of Portugal and Spain. With Bible-reading discouraged, with private judgment forbidden, with the way to Christ's cross narrowed or blocked up, with priestcraft reestablished, with auricular confession set up in every parish, with monasteries and nunneries dotted over the land, with women everywhere kneeling like serfs and slaves at the feet of clergymen, with men casting off all faith, and becoming sceptics, with schools and colleges made seminaries of Jesuitism, with free thought denounced and anathematized—with all these things the distinctive manliness and independence of the British character will gradually dwindle, wither, pine away, and be destroyed; and England will be ruined.

And all these things, I firmly believe, will come, unless the old feeling about the value of Protestantism can be revived.

I warn all who hear this Charge, that the times require you to awake and be on your guard. Be ready, with all diligence, according to your ordination vow, to 'drive away all erroneous and strange doctrine contrary to God's word.' Hold firmly, if you please, the old loyal High Church principles of Andrews and Hooker and Ken and Taylor and Barrow and Stillingfleet and Bull and Beveridge, if you conscientiously prefer them. But, like those great divines, resist Romanism, and beware of any religious teaching which, wittingly or unwittingly, paves the way to it. I beseech you to realize the painful fact that the Protestantism of this country is gradually ebbing away, and I entreat you, as Christians and patriots, to resist the growing tendency to forget the blessings of the English Reformation.

For Christ's sake, for the sake of the Church of England, for the sake of our country, for the sake of our children, let us not loose our moorings, and drift back into the waters which our fathers wisely left three hundred and fifty years ago. They separated from Rome for just and sufficient reasons, as Bishop Jewel has shown in his matchless, though little-read, *Apology*. Those reasons remain to the present day unshaken and unrefuted. Nine times over, your own Thirty-nine Articles condemn, in plain and explicit language, the leading doctrines of the Church of Rome; and these Articles are still binding on every minister of the Church of England. Then let us resolve to have no peace with Rome till Rome abjures her errors, and is at peace with Christ. Till Rome does *that*, the vaunted reunion of Western Churches, which some talk of, and press upon our notice, is an insult to the Church of England.

I must now bring this over-long Charge to a conclusion. I am afraid it will appear to some a mere dry statement of fossilized theological points, unworthy of the nineteenth century. Be it so. I am content to wait. The dark days of sorrow, the sick-bed, the death-bed, and above all the day of judgment, will teach us all in a few years whether the old-fashioned theology which men are so fond of decrying in 1890, is a thing to be despised. I will wind up all with a few practical words about our present and our future duty.

(1) As *to the present*, it is vain to deny that our beloved Church is placed in a most dangerous position by our 'unhappy divisions,' and the conspicuous absence of any attempt to heal them. Year after year the gulf between discordant parties within our pale seems to yawn wider and grow deeper, and some violent catastrophe appears ultimately inevitable. So long as that wretched puzzle, the Ornaments Rubric, which is interpreted in two diametrically opposite ways, remains in the Prayer-book; so long as the existing Ecclesiastical Courts are thought by many conscientious clergymen worthless and incompetent, and their decisions are ignored and disobeyed without any interference; so long as those who think the Courts incompetent decline to take any steps to have better Courts created; so long as it appears to be held, even by many in this Diocese, that no clergyman is ever to be called to account whatever he may teach and do, and every one is to do what is right in his own eyes; so long as that barbarous law remains unrepealed by which conscientious clergymen declared guilty of contumacy in doctrinal suits, may be sent to prison—so long, I say, as this miserable state of things continues, the present condition of the Church seems at first sight hopeless. A house divided against itself cannot stand; and sooner or later we shall be disestablished, disendowed, and broken up. But I said 'seems' hopeless advisedly. When I read how wonderfully God kept our Church alive in the days of Queen Mary, in the times of the Long Parliament, and during the deathlike apathy of the last century, I refuse to despair. Nothing is impossible. Our present duty is to hope and pray and work on and wait. He that healed lepers and raised the dead can heal and revive the Church of England.

(2) As to *the future*, I lay no claim to the gift of prophecy, and I shall certainly not attempt to offer counsel as to the line of duty in certain hypothetical cases. 'Sufficient unto the day is the

evil thereof' (Matt. 6:34). It will be time enough to make up our minds when a crisis arrives. After all, it is the thing unexpected which often comes to pass.

In any case, as long as we live, I trust we shall always cultivate the habit of treating Churchmen of other schools of thought than our own, with kindness, courtesy, and respect. Let us give them credit for being as much in earnest as ourselves, though we may think them sadly mistaken. Let us believe that many Churchmen with whom we now disagree, may be, and often are, real Christians, in spite of all their errors. Their hearts may be right in the sight of God, though their heads seem to us very wrong. However erroneous we may consider their views, we must charitably hope that they are in the way of life and travelling toward heaven, and will be 'saved by the grace of God, even as ourselves.' However much we may believe they mar their own usefulness by their imperfect statement of truth, we must not rashly pronounce them godless and graceless, lest we be found condemning those whom God has received. To speak plainly, it never will do to brand people as unconverted heretics and children of wrath, because they differ from us about the effect of the sacraments, or about ritual, or about the precise nature of inspiration. Firmly as we may cling to our own views of such subjects, we must carefully remember that it is possible to hold the Head, and stand on the Rock under a great cloud of error.

In any case, let us not lightly forsake our mother, the Church of England. So long as the Church of England sticks firmly to the Bible, the Articles, and the principles of the Protestant Reformation, so long I advise you strongly to stick to the Church. When the Articles and Prayer-book are altered or thrown overboard, and the old flag is hauled down, then, and not till then, it will be time for us to launch the boats and quit the wreck. At present, let us stick to the old ship.

So long as we preserve our Articles, Creed, and Prayer-book whole and unaltered, how can we better our position by secession? Where shall we enjoy such liberty, though now we may not have things all our own way, whether High or Low or Broad? To whom can we go? Where shall we find better prayers? In what communion shall we find so much good being done, in spite of the existence of much evil? No doubt there is much to sadden us; but there is not a single visible Church on earth at this day doing better. There is not a single communion where there are no clouds, and all is serene. 'The evil everywhere are mingled with the good.' The wheat never grows without tares. But, for all that, there is much to gladden us—more good preaching than there ever was before in the pulpits of the Establishment, more good work done both at home and abroad. Then let us all work on, and fight on, and pray on, and stick to the Church of England, and make the best of our position. The Churchman who walks in these lines, I believe, is the Churchman who 'understands the times,' and does his duty.

I now close what may possibly be the last Charge I may ever be allowed to deliver, with St Paul's words: 'I commend you to God, and the word of his grace, which is able to build you up, and give you an inheritance among all them which are sanctified.' 'Watch ye; stand fast in the faith; quit you like men; be strong. Let all your things be done with charity' (Acts 20:32; 1 Cor. 16: 13, 14).

10

BROTHERHOODS

An address given at the Hull Church Congress, 1890.

O N one point I entirely agree with Archdeacon Farrar.[1] I admit
without reserve that the condition of a vast proportion of
the lower orders in many of our large overgrown parishes, both
morally and socially, is simply deplorable. It is useless to shut
our eyes to it. I dwell in Liverpool, the second city in the Queen's
dominions, and I know what I say! There is a state of things in
some quarters of all our great cities, within a short walk of grand
Town Halls and Palaces, which cries to heaven against England,
and is enough to make an angel weep.

The class of whom I speak, remember, are not infidels or
reasoning sceptics, like many of the upper ten thousand in our
Clubs and Squares. Nothing of the kind! The mental position of the
immense majority is utter *indifference* to all religion. They are not
touched either by church or chapel. They drift on without Christ,
without God, and of course without any moral standard. They are
rightly called 'the dangerous classes' by our French neighbours; and
no wonder. For they are a standing danger to Church, and State, and
social order. They have nothing to lose by a general scramble, and
are always ready to become the prey of those talking meddlers who
delight in setting labour against capital, to encourage discontent,
and to make a living out of the ignorance of their fellow-creatures.
These dangerous classes have stirred the heart of Archdeacon
Farrar; and I sympathize with him entirely.

[1] Frederic William Farrar, appointed Archdeacon of Westminster in 1883.

I believe, however, that there is nothing in the condition of these huge masses of English humanity which cannot be reached, if we use rightly the right means. There is nothing more incurable in the religious and moral state of the men and women who compose them than there was at Rome in the days of Tiberius, Nero, and Caligula. There is nothing worse than there was in London last century, as we may learn from Hogarth's pictures. There is nothing for which the old Gospel of Christ, rightly administered, is not an amply sufficient remedy. We need neither Robert Elsmere, nor a revised Book of Sports, nor a Continental Sunday. We shall obtain no solid lasting results from a vague restless altruism, or music, or dancing, or pictures, or theatricals. These things may touch the skin of the evil; but they do not reach hearts. We need nothing new, nothing but the old story of the cross, the blood, the love, the power of our Lord Jesus Christ. These men and women whom we want to moralize, and civilize, and Christianize, are made of the same flesh and blood as ourselves. Like us they have hearts and consciences. If Christ and the Holy Ghost have done good to you and me, I maintain that we should never despair of any 'rank, sort, or condition' of men, however fallen and degraded they may at present appear to be. The old Gospel is not worn out, and what it has done it can do again.

But it is needless to say that the value of a remedy depends very much on the manner in which it is used. Does the Church use the best and most effective machinery for bringing the gospel to bear on the vast crowds of our non-worshipping population? Archdeacon Farrar contends that she does not, and wishes us to try a new engine in the shape of Brotherhoods. Here is the point at which, with all respect for his zeal and able advocacy, I am obliged to part company with him and his supporters. I maintain that wherever the existing machinery of the Church of England is rightly worked we want nothing more. Our present system, in right hands, is not a failure. We do not want Brotherhoods in order to reach the masses. In short, my objection is twofold. I contend that in well-worked parishes this well-meant new machine is not needed; and that in no parish would it ever comfortably work.

The statement I have just made requires fencing with a few words of explanation. If the patrons of large working-class parishes choose to make unwise appointments and put round men in square holes; if they appoint quiet prosy men destitute of popular gifts, as good as gold, but as heavy; if they appoint men who are only preachers and not pastors, men whose whole time is devoted to the composition of pulpit fireworks, mere homiletic orators, on Sundays incomprehensible and on week-days invisible; or men who can think of nothing but music, singing, and liturgical services in church—if *this* is the representation of the Church of England, I admit frankly that you will not reach the masses. The great gulf which the Archdeacon and I alike deplore will not be bridged.

But give me a clergyman who really knows Christ, and has the Holy Spirit, a thorough pastor as well as a preacher; a man of decided positive opinions, and not one of those unhappy clergymen who say that nothing is certain in religion, that it does not matter what a man teaches, if he is only in earnest; a man who takes care to have plain, hearty, bright, simple meetings for worship in mission rooms as well as prayer-book services in church; a man who can preach in a street without a surplice, as well as in a pulpit; a man who will go in and out of every alley in his district and talk simple Gospel to half-a-dozen ragged folks in a dirty cellar as heartily as to five hundred well-dressed people in a church; a man of fire, and love, and sympathy, and tact, and patience, and sanctified common sense, if not a giant in intellect and book-learning. Give me a clergyman who has not only the regulation staff of curates, district visitors, Scripture readers, Bible women, and Sunday School teachers who visit their classes at home, but also scores of communicants who voluntarily help

Christ's cause, and think it a privilege and a duty to be always carrying on a work of aggressive evangelism. Give me a clergyman of this style in a large working-class population (and there are such to be found) and I see no need of a Brotherhood. I see no place for the new machine, and I do not believe such a clergyman would care to have it. I believe he would tell you, 'I want nothing new. Our old machinery is quite sufficient.'

I do not say that such a clergyman as I have described will do impossibilities, if you are senseless enough to give him a parish of 15,000 or 20,000 people. I do not say that he will convert, or reach, or moralize every man or woman in any parish. I do not expect the Millennium before the Lord comes. But I do say that he will make a deep mark, and will prove that the lowest strata of our people can be got at by our old machinery, and that Brotherhoods are not needed at all.

There are, however, in my opinion, three heavy special objections to this scheme of Brotherhoods, which I will proceed to state as briefly as possible.

(1) My primary objection is the extreme improbability of *a sufficient supply* being found of qualified persons to form them. You cannot bombard a fortress without gun-powder, or make bread without flour. The number of men who are entirely independent of professional income is at all times very limited, and if the members of the Brotherhoods are not to be paid, I am convinced there will be very few of them, except perhaps in London. If they are to be paid I do not see wherein they differ from curates and lay-agents. However I will not dwell on this point. I will assume that the men can be found.

(2) My next objection is that I cannot imagine how Brotherhoods can be made to fit in with our existing *parochial system*, and be worked without incessant risk of friction, collisions, heartburnings, and scandalous quarrels. If the members of the Brotherhood are clergymen, are they to be licensed to the Bishop to work independently of the Incumbent under the

Bishop's directions, or are they to be licensed to the Incumbent, and become a supplement to his existing staff of curates? If on the other hand they are to be laymen, I should like to know who is to select them, who is to judge of their qualifications, who is to mark out and superintend their daily work, and in what respect they are to be more useful than our present Scripture readers and lay agents. Under all these heads I see a large crop of difficulties. The parochial system of the Church of England will never work successfully if you try to put the reins in more than one set of hands. You might as well have two captains in a ship. Rectors and Vicars are not angels and seraphim, but flesh and blood. They have their feelings like other men, and are not fond of interference with their own plans and official position. Give a right-minded Incumbent as many more living agents as you please, and he will find something for them all to do. Call them Brotherhoods, if you like, and let them all live together, if they wish to do so. But for peace sake let them all work under the Incumbent's directorship.

(3) About *vows* I could say much. But time will not allow me fully to discuss this disputed subject. I must frankly say that I have a strong dislike to the multiplication of them. I am content with the vows of baptism and confirmation, required of all members of our Church, and I want no more. The light of Church history in the first fifteen centuries makes me regard any apparent attempt to revive monasticism with deep suspicion. Orders of men and women have too often been founded under the banners of avowed poverty and celibacy, and have ended most disgracefully. Experience does not favour 'will-worship' and self-imposed asceticism. Such things have a great 'show of wisdom,' and are very taking for a season with ignorant and shallow Christians. But they only 'satisfy the flesh.' If men professing to be converted, and true believers in a crucified Christ, cannot be chaste, self-denying, and obedient without solemnly registering a vow, I must plainly say I think they are not likely to do much good. At present I see scores of curates and Scripture readers doing most excellent work

as men simply licensed, with no vows at all. If the members of the proposed Brotherhoods cannot do like work without vows—I think it will be a public confession that they are an inferior order of men.

But, after all, I must plainly tell the Congress that the roots of our 'present distress' about the unreached classes are far lower than is commonly supposed. They will not be touched by Brotherhoods or any other brand-new machinery. The true solution of the problem is to arouse our lay communicants all over the land, and awaken them to a sense of their responsibilities and duties. This is the true alternative. We want a revival among our communicants quite as much as among our non-worshipping classes. We have been too long blind and asleep on this matter. Let me explain what I mean.

I assert then, without hesitation, that at present the laity of our Church are not where they ought to be in the direct work of Christ, and the furtherance of Christianity in the land. There is a sad gulf between the Church of the first century and that of the English Church in the nineteenth century. A mischievous habit of leaving all religion to the parson of the parish has overspread the country, and the bulk of lay Churchmen seem to think that they have nothing to do with the Church but to receive the benefit of her means of grace, while they contribute nothing in the way of personal active exertion to promote her efficiency. The vast majority of church-goers appear to suppose that when they have gone to church on Sunday, and have received the Lord's Supper, they have done their duty, and are not under the slightest obligation to warn, to teach, to rebuke, to edify others, to promote works of charity, to assist evangelization, or to raise a finger in checking sin, and advancing Christ's cause in the world. Their only idea is to be perpetually receiving, but never doing anything at all. They have taken their seats in the right train, and are only to sit quiet, while the clerical engine draws them to heaven, perhaps half-asleep. If an Ephesian or Philippian or Thessalonian lay Churchman were to rise from the dead and see how little work most lay Churchmen do for the English Church, he would not believe his eyes. The difference between the primitive type of a lay Churchman and the English type is the difference between light and darkness, black and white. The one used to be awake and alive, and always about his Master's business. The other is too often asleep practically, and torpid, and idle, and content to leave the religion of the parish in the hands of the parson.

No one, I suppose, will think of denying that the Churches to which the Epistles of the New Testament were written, were in a far more lively condition than our own Church in the present day. They had no printed books, no endowments, no cathedrals. But they turned the world upside down, emptied the heathen temples, confounded the Greek and Roman philosophers, increased in numbers and influence every year. And what was the reason of it? I answer that the prominent position occupied by the laity in these primitive communities was the grand secret of their undeniable strength, growth, prosperity, and success. There were no sleeping partners in those days. Every member of the ecclesiastical body worked. Every one felt bound to do something. They needed no Brotherhoods; for all were brothers. All the baptized members, whether men or women, if we may judge from the 16th chapter of the Epistle to the Romans, took a direct active interest in the welfare and progress of the whole ecclesiastical body. They were not tame, ignorant sheep, led hither and thither at the beck of an autocratic sacerdotal shepherd. The best regiment in an army is that in which officers and privates take an equal interest in the efficiency of the whole corps. It is the regiment in which the officers trust the privates and the privates trust the officers, as they did when they fought through that eventful night at Rorke's Drift in the Zulu war.[1] It is the regiment in which every private is intelligent, and behaves as if the success of the campaign depended on him. It is the regiment in which every private knows his duty, and is honourably

[1] January 1879. A British force of 103 men successfully held a 'laager' against a host of Zulus.

proud of his profession, and would fight to the last for the colours even if every officer fell. Such a regiment was a Primitive Church in apostolic days. It had its officers, its bishops, and deacons. It had orders, due subordination, and discipline. But the mainspring and backbone of its strength lay in the zeal, intelligence, and activity of its laity. The Epistle to the Philippians was addressed to the saints, 'with the bishops and deacons.' Oh that we had something of the same sort in the organization of the Church of England! We should have no need then of Brotherhoods.

With the deepest feeling of affection for the Church of England I cannot avoid the conclusion that in the matter of the laity its system is at present defective and infra-scriptural, and hence this well-meant scheme of Brotherhoods. I cannot reconcile the position of the English lay Episcopalian in 1890 with that of his brother in any apostolic Church eighteen centuries ago. I cannot make the two things square. To my eyes it seems that in the regular working of the Church of England almost everything is left in the hands of the clergy, and hardly anything is assigned to the laity! The clergy settle everything! The clergy manage everything! The clergy arrange everything! The laity are practically allowed neither voice, nor place, nor opinion, nor power, and must accept whatever the clergy decide for them. In all this there is no intentional slight. Not the smallest reflection is implied on the trustworthiness and ability of the laity. But from one cause or another they are left out in the cold, passive recipients and not active members, in a huge ecclesiastical corporation; sleeping partners and not working agents in an unwieldy and ill-managed concern. In short, in the normal action of the Church of England, lay Churchmen have been left on a siding. Like soldiers not wanted, they have fallen out of the ranks, retired to the rear, and sunk out of sight. The effect at the present day is that the English laity are far below the position they ought to occupy, and the English clergy are far above theirs. Both parties, in short, are in the wrong place. The clergy have too much to do and the laity too little, and the whole result is that the masses are not reached.

I know not whether the present state of things can now be remedied. But I never like to admit that it is too late to win a battle, and I cannot admit that matters will be at all mended by Brotherhoods. I should like every parochial Incumbent to make a point of teaching every communicant that he is an integral part of the Church of England, and is bound to do all that he can for its welfare—to visit, to teach, to warn, to exhort, to edify, to help, to advise, to comfort, to support, to evangelize; to awaken the sleeping, to lead on the enquiring, to build up the saints; to promote repentance, faith, and holiness everywhere, according to his gifts, time, and opportunity. He should educate his people to see that they must give up the lazy modern plan of leaving everything to the parson, and must be active agents instead of sleeping partners. On this point, I believe John Wesley was the first man who understood the wants of this country in the last century. The old Methodists beat Churchmen hollow. With them every new member was a new home missionary in their cause, and the first question asked, as soon as he was enrolled, was 'What are you going to do?' The blind stupidity with which John Wesley was treated was a disaster to our Church. We ought to have taken a leaf out of his book. Never will things go well with the Church of England until every individual member realizes that he has a duty to do to Christ and his Church, and keeps that duty continually in view.

My reverend and lay brethren, the times are critical, and this is our day of visitation. In our Established Church it will never do to try to man the walls with officers, and let the rank and file sit idle in their barracks. Clergy and laity must learn to work together. We must have not only an apostolical succession of ministers, but an apostolical succession of laymen, if our Church is to stand much longer. Give us a church in this condition, and we need no Brotherhoods.

11

THE PRESENT CRISIS

An address given at the annual Liverpool Diocesan Conference, 1892.

R EVEREND and Lay Brethren, I am allowed to meet you once more at our Annual Diocesan Conference, and I trust that our proceedings will not be less interesting or useful than they have been on former occasions. I am not convinced, after the experience of eleven years, that our arrangements admit of much improvement. I read with watchful curiosity the reports of other Conferences, and I venture to think our own will bear comparison with any. An assembly which only meets for two days in a year can ill afford to waste time, and the plan of devoting most of our time to four well-selected subjects rather than to a multitude of somewhat small and unimportant resolutions, is to my mind the wisest and best.

I shall proceed at once, according to my former practice, to say a few things about matters in our own diocese, and in the Church generally, about which you may reasonably expect some information and some expression of opinion from your bishop. I shall touch them both rather briefly, because I want to direct your attention to a subject of far wider importance than the condition of any one diocese, or any one branch of Christ's visible Church. That subject is the so-called 'Higher Criticism of the Old Testament.'

I. Concerning *matters in our own diocese*, the annual report, as usual, is a chequered one. There are many clouds on our horizon, but there are also not a few bits of blue sky. On the blue side I place first and foremost the gratifying success of the attempt to establish a Sustentation Fund for supplementing annually the very poor incomes of many incumbents in our diocese. The kind response which this tentative movement met with from many generous laymen has cheered me exceedingly, and enabled my Committee to gladden the hearts of not a few underpaid clergy. I am satisfied that the scheme is a move in the right direction, and I trust it will continue to prosper more and more. To all who have assisted me I publicly return my sincere thanks. I believe many more laymen would support the scheme if they knew of its existence, and I am persuaded that, with a little more exertion, the annual income of every benefice might be easily raised to £250 or £300 a year. I can see no reason why the Sustentation principle should not succeed in Lancashire as well as it does in Scotland, while the possibility of raising a huge capital sum, enough to endow all the poorer livings with the interest from it, appears to me utopian, and farther off than ever, with Disestablishment looming large in the distance. Of other bits of blue sky I could say a good deal if time permitted. The continued and increased support given by the diocese to the Church Missionary Society, the Scripture Readers' Society, and the Mersey Mission to Seamen; the very large number of candidates for confirmation, considering that we have only two hundred churches in the diocese; the steady progress of church and mission-room building, though much remains to be done, as, for instance, in Walton and Kensington Fields; and though last, not least, the continued energy with which the cause of Temperance is kept up, notwithstanding the heavy loss it has sustained by the removal of my own dear friend, its invaluable champion, Mr Clarke Aspinall—all these are causes for deep thankfulness, and I think it my duty as your bishop to bring them to the front. Few outsiders have the slightest idea of the difficulties by which the infancy of a new diocese like Liverpool is surrounded, and I should be ashamed of myself if I did not publicly thank the clergy and laity, as well as thank God, for all the assistance I have received since I came among you.

On the cloudy side of our diocesan horizon there are some things which it is painful to be mentioning annually, but useless to conceal. I am aware that any bishop is blamed as a pessimist who does not paint everything in rosy colours, and keep back the 'things wanting' in his diocese. My conscience will not let me do so, and I am sure that it is bad policy. In commercial matters it never answers to 'cook the accounts.'

In Church matters, to know our defects is one step towards mending them. It is vain to deny that huge masses of our population never attend any worship at all, that not a few of our churches are more than half empty, that some of our church schools in poor districts are in danger of extinction, and require immediate and liberal assistance, that our Diocesan Institutions are most miserably supported and yet blamed for not granting money which they have not received, and that in some parishes the number of confirmees and communicants is far smaller than it ought to be. All these, no doubt, are painful facts, and it is useless to shut our eyes to them. On the contrary, it is our highest wisdom to open our eyes as wide as possible, to look steadily at them, and use every means to improve our condition. After all, I believe that we have no great cause to be ashamed. We know our own weak places in this diocese, and they trouble us. Very likely if we knew the inner status of other dioceses, we should find that they are not much better off than ourselves, and for a very large proportion of hard-working clergy, I am certain that our district will bear comparison with any in the land.

I heartily thank the two hundred incumbents of my diocese and their curates for all they are doing. I know your immense difficulties—1,200,000 people in the diocese,—6,000 to each incumbent, a disproportion not to be found in any other part of the land I know, and I feel deeply for you. But remember the words of the 1st chapter of Joshua, 'Be strong and of good

courage.' Go on, and persevere, and never give way to despondency or 'weariness in well-doing.' St Paul at Ephesus and Corinth
was far worse off than you are, and had far less help from man.
But he always pressed on, though faint, yet pursuing. Use every
kind of aggressive evangelisation. Double and redouble regular,
patient house-to-house visitation. Gather together young men,
and deal kindly and genially with them. Invite in all matters the
aid of your steady, godly laymen, and let them see that you think
them as much a part of the Church as yourselves. Lift up the Lord
Jesus Christ in your pulpits, in all his offices, as lovingly, plainly,
and in as simple Saxon as you possibly can. Keep up a steady fire
on all the besetting sins of the day and place where you live. Fire
straight and fire low at Sabbath-breaking, intemperance, betting,
and gambling, and let them have no rest. Continually urge on
your communicants a high standard of practical holiness in daily
life. No evidence of Christianity like that! Above all, water all
your work with prayer for the blessing of the Holy Ghost, and let
your path to the throne of grace be never overgrown with weeds.
Give yourselves wholly to these things, my dear clergy, and I am
sure that your labour will not be in vain in the Lord.

II. About matters which concern *the Church of England
generally,* and of course affect ourselves, I shall not say much.
There are two, however, which demand special notice, the new
Clergy Discipline Act, and the recent Privy Council Judgment in
what is called 'The Lincoln Case.'[1] About each of these you will
naturally expect to hear my opinion, and I will tell you frankly
what I think.

(1) The Clergy Discipline Act does not excite in my mind any
great measure of enthusiasm, because I never thought the old Act
was very defective, provided it was properly worked, and sensible

[1] Dr Edward King appointed Bishop of Lincoln in 1885 was accused of unlawful
ritualistic practices by the (Protestant) Church Association, and tried in 1889 by a
court of six bishops over which the Archbishop of Canterbury presided. Later on
appeal the case went before the Privy Council. The result was 'substantially a great
victory for the ritualists.'

and judicious Commissions of *prima facie* inquiry appointed. I speak with some experience of its operation in more than one part of England, and long before I was your bishop. However, if the new Act makes proceedings against clergymen for moral offences more simple, more inexpensive, and more expeditious, I shall be extremely thankful. Happily, these cases are very rare. But when they do occur, the harm that they do to the Church of England and the cause of religion is incalculable. It will indeed be a crowning mercy if in future they can be dealt with speedily, not kept long before the eyes of the public, and, as soon as possible, buried in oblivion. The anxiety displayed by many, while the Bill was under debate, to reserve to the bishops the privilege of pronouncing the sentence of deprivation, was an anxiety which, I confess, I never shared, and I do not think it improved the Bill. The gravest defect, to my eyes, is the retention of the episcopal veto, that most ingenious device for obliging a bishop to offend either one party or another in his diocese. However, I know that in this matter I stand very much alone.

(2) The recent Privy Council Judgment in the Lincoln case is a far more important subject than the Clergy Discipline Act, and I must ask your special attention to a few remarks I am going to make about it.

I do not for a moment propose to examine the contents of the Judgment, and discuss it point by point. It would be useless to do so, and scarcely respectful. In common with many others, I cannot admit the soundness of its reasonings and interpretations, and the correctness of its conclusions. Nor am I able to believe that the famous ritual points in dispute have no doctrinal significance, when I know that their principal advocates never admit this for a moment.[1] However, the Judgment is the decision of the

---

[1] *The leading article of the *Times* newspaper on the Privy Council Judgment contains the following sentence:

'There is a sense of *unreality* in the effort to treat as neutral or colourless acts which we all know to be, in the view of a party in the Church, *technical symbols and unequivocal doctrinal signs.*'

highest Court of the realm, and at present that decision cannot be reversed, though some future Judicial Committee may possibly reverse it. As a law-abiding Englishman and a believer in the Royal supremacy, I submit, though I cannot approve or admire. I shall not therefore trouble you with arguments. I shall simply point out to you what I believe the consequences of the Judgment will be, both present and future. This, after all, is the practical point.

(i) About the *present and immediate consequences* of the Judgment I have no doubt at all. It will not produce peace and unity, as some expect, although it puts an end to ecclesiastical prosecutions. Thoughtless laymen, who probably never read the Thirty-nine Articles, know little about theological controversies, and fancy that our Church differences are only about unmeaning outward trifles, may possibly not understand this. But I do marvel at the innocent simplicity of many good men, who are dreaming that henceforth there will be no more strife, and that we shall be a kind of happy family, everybody in the right, and nobody in the wrong! They forget that while they are sitting still under their own vines and fig-trees, and crying 'Peace, peace,' there are others inside our Church who never sit still, and may rudely disturb them one day. My own belief is, that our 'unhappy divisions' will be widened, deepened, crystallized, and increased, and that harmonious co-operation between parties within our pale will become more difficult than ever. Peace is a precious thing, but it must be peace with honour, and not peace at any price. Liberty and toleration, no doubt, are fine, fashionable, high-sounding phrases, but they must have some limits. It was under the specious plea of liberty and toleration that King James II put forth his famous Declaration of Indulgence, by which he intended to bring back Popery into the realm, but thereby lost the confidence both of Church and Dissent, as well as his own crown.

I hold very strongly that the Established Church of this free country ought to be as tolerant and comprehensive as possible, and to allow large liberty to its clergy. But whether the very wide toleration of the recent Judgment is likely to bring in a general reign of peace among Churchmen, I take leave to doubt extremely. I ask you to consider calmly the history of the things which the recent Judgment declares to be *not illegal* in future, but permissible, in the administration of the Lord's Supper. They are things not even mentioned in the Communion Office of our Prayer-book. They are things of no small importance. Most of them had a place in the first Prayer-book[1] of Edward VI, compiled at a time when the English Reformation was not completed. They were deliberately and purposely left out and omitted when Edward's second Prayer-book[2] was brought out, as appearing to favour the Romish Mass. They were not re-admitted in the Prayer-book drawn up and used in Queen Elizabeth's time, and finally were not re-introduced and brought back, when the Prayer-book was last revised in the days of Charles II. In the face of these facts, I cannot wonder that the recent Judgment offends and pains many Churchmen who are content with the Prayer-book as it is. They consider that it is a step backward behind the Reformation, and that it seems to bring back into our Communion Office things rejected long ago. I cannot therefore help thinking it is more likely to increase division than to promote peace.

The plain truth is, that a Church in which two opposite views of such cardinal subjects as the Lord's Supper and sacerdotalism— the very keys of the great Romish controversy—are formally declared to be not illegal, is not a Church in which the clergy can work very cordially and comfortably together, and its thinking laymen will gradually separate into two camps. We may sing as loud as we please—

> *We are not divided,*
> *All one body we;*

but we cannot make the words a reality. Two pilots in one ship, two drivers in one carriage, two stewards in one household, are

[1] *1549.
[2] *1552.

285

obviously incompatible. I see no prospect of perfect peace. On the contrary, I think we have reached a crisis which demands the exercise of the utmost courtesy and forbearance on all sides, if the old machine is to work at all. Never was it more needful to cultivate charity, good temper, consideration, and kindness of language in communication with other schools. May we all try to do so in the Diocese of Liverpool! If men cannot help differing, let them try to differ pleasantly, and avoid those 'grievous words' which are sure to give offence. So doing, there may be some lengthening of our tranquillity, and, though it may strain our Church to the uttermost, we may possibly live on.

(ii) About the *future and distant consequences* of the recent Judgment, I shall speak with some hesitation, for two very grave reasons.

For one thing, much will depend on the line of conduct about to be adopted by that active and persevering body of Churchmen who, for many years, have honestly avowed their desire to set back the clock of the Reformation, and to unprotestantize the Church of England. They have now practically obtained legal sanction for some of their cherished views, and it remains to be seen what they are going to do next. If this body is determined to press on, and never rest till it has procured formal sanction for more and more liberty, toleration, and concession—for chasubles, incense, adoration of the elements, prayers for the dead, the confessional, and a close imitation of the mass—then I can soon tell you what the consequences will be. I am no prophet, but I confidently predict there will be troublous times.

For another thing, much will depend on the treatment received by those loyal Churchmen who conscientiously disapprove the recent Judgment, and by the Evangelical body generally. Such men, no doubt, are not required to alter one jot of their doctrine and ritual, or to leave their old paths. More than this, as honest Churchmen, and men thoroughly attached to the principles, Prayer-book, and Articles of our Church, they have a right to expect to be treated with perfect fairness and impartiality. But if, after this Judgment, any foolish attempt is made in any quarter to trample on them as a defeated or silenced minority; if they are continually harassed and irritated by interference with their liberty, and indirectly pressed to give up their favourite Societies; if they are frowned upon because they decline to discontinue evening communions, or adopt the eastward position; if they are always charged with denying sacramental grace because they hold firmly the doctrine of the Twenty-fifth and Twenty-ninth Articles about the effect of the sacraments; if they are incessantly taunted as Puritans because they prefer Jewel and Hooker to Archbishop Laud; if these things are incessantly pushed to the front, and not dismissed wisely to the rear, as they ought to be—once more, I say, I can soon tell you what the consequences will be. There will be very troublous times.

Remember carefully that I am only speaking of the distant consequences of the Judgment under certain contingencies. I do not know, of course, whether those contingencies will arise. It is quite possible that the advanced and extreme section of Churchmen may think it prudent to lie on their oars and seek no further concessions at present. It is also possible that the dominant majority within our pale may think it wise to adopt a policy of conciliation towards the minority. But these are uncertainties, and it is impossible to say what a few years may bring forth. However, I am quite certain, since the Judgment appeared, that there are breakers ahead, and that our dangers are far greater than most people suppose, and that not the least of these dangers is the gradual approach of Disestablishment. For saying this you may think me an alarmist. But when the Prime Minister of this great country speaks gravely of the 'Disestablishment and Disendowment' of an integral part of the Church of England as possibilities, and myriads of the masses to whom we have given political power swallow greedily all his words, it is high time for the Church to set her house in order, to number her forces, and to prepare for a deadly struggle. Now, I ask, where are we in view of this coming struggle? Are we ready for it? Are we united? Are we prepared to stand shoulder to shoulder, as the 42nd did on the field of Quatre Bras?[1] I wish I could give satisfactory answers to these questions. But at present I cannot. If the party of progress is allowed to drive on unchecked, and to thrust into our Communion Office one Romish innovation after another, until Church worship becomes a Babel of discordant teachings, it is useless to expect that we shall present a united front to our foes when the fight begins. That solid minority of Churchmen who cling tenaciously to the principles of the Reformation, and are content with the Prayer-book as it is, would stand aloof, I fear, in the day of battle, and cause great gaps in our ranks, which the Church could ill afford. For a Protestant Establishment, I believe, they would fight to the last. For a semi-popish Establishment I doubt if they would strike a blow. I know they are a minority among the clergy, and always have been since the days of the Stuarts. But I am not sure that they are a minority among the laity, and in any case a minority contending for great religious principles (like Ulster) is not to be lightly esteemed. Sooner or later, if things go on as they have done in late years, I predict this minority will see little use in defending the Church of England. Then, with a democratic House of Commons, the end will soon come. Weakened by some secessions of impatient men, and by incessant internal dissensions, the Church will not be able to stave off Disestablishment and Disendowment. Then will come disruption, and the grand old ship will be wrecked by the 'unhappy divisions' of her own officers and crew. I only hope that, 'some on boards, and some on broken pieces of the ship,' you will all get safe to land.

I will not dwell longer on this painful subject. But, as an old man soon likely to go off the stage and join a better Church in a better world, and as one who has carefully watched the progress

---

[1] A place of encounter between the armies of Napoleon and Wellington a day before the Battle of Waterloo (1815).

of ecclesiastical events for fifty years, I think it a plain duty to warn you about the possibilities which are before you and your children. There is no reason for panic and despair.

The fate of the Church is in the hands of Churchmen. If they are true to her first principles, I believe she will never fall. We never know what a day may bring forth. There is One in heaven who kept our Church alive in the days of Grosseteste[1] and Wycliffe, in the reign of Queen Mary Tudor, in the times of Laud and Charles I, and in the blind era of 1662, when two thousand able ministers were foolishly driven out of our pale, and the foundations of English Dissent were laid. He lives and reigns, and orders everything on earth, and can make light arise out of seeming darkness. For the time present let us wait patiently on him, and ask him to give wisdom to our rulers, and sanctified common sense to our clergy, and not to deal with our nation according to its sins.

III. I turn now to a theological subject of world-wide importance which is exercising the minds and shaking the faith of many professing Christians in the present day. I refer to what is commonly called *The Higher Criticism of the Old Testament Scriptures*. This subject just now is forced on our notice continually, in books and pamphlets, in lectures and sermons, in newspapers and periodicals, at Conferences and Congresses. Whether we like it or not we cannot shut it out. Like the frogs in the plague of Egypt, it creeps in everywhere, and its novelty makes it especially attractive to the half-educated and the young.

I propose to make a few plain remarks on this very grave subject. It is filling our horizon with clouds, and as an old watchman I dare not hold my peace. My remarks will be almost all in one direction. About many branches of the controversy I shall say nothing at all. I leave them to others who have more leisure than a Lancashire bishop can have. I only wish to dwell on one point, which seems to me to have been somewhat overlooked, and to have received far less attention than it deserves. That point

[1] Bishop of Lincoln (died, 1253).

is, the immense *improbability* of all the schemes and theories of 'Higher Criticism.'

I use that word 'improbability' with strong emphasis. All sensible men know that on many subjects probability is our only guide. 'To us,' says that mighty reasoner, Bishop Butler, 'probability is the very guide of life.'[1] I think the criticism of the Old Testament is a case in point. The whole subject is dark and mysterious, and we cannot draw conclusions about it with absolute certainty. There is a huge gap or chasm which we have no bridge to cross, and must fill up as we can with scanty materials. The manuscripts of the books of the Old Testament have long disappeared. There is no contemporaneous literature supplying information about them. The Septuagint, or Greek translation of the Old Testament, was never even partially brought out until a hundred years after the completion of the book of Malachi, and at least twelve hundred years after the death of Moses. The book called the Old Testament is now much more than two thousand years old—a vast length of time, which our minds cannot grasp and realise much more than the distance between the fixed stars and the earth. It is a book which was written many centuries before printing was invented, and long before most of the cities of Europe existed. About such a field of inquiry I am content to consider what is probable. I leave dogmatic positiveness to others, and I see rather too much of it in the present day. I often think of the words addressed by Oliver Cromwell to the General Assembly of the Church of Scotland (August 3, 1650): 'Sirs, I beseech you in the bowels of Christ, think it possible you may be mistaken.'

I begin by saying that I am one of those old-fashioned Christians who believe implicitly in the plenary inspiration of all the books of the Old Testament Scriptures, from Genesis to Malachi. I admit frankly that in the historical books the writers were taught and permitted to incorporate lists of names and pedigrees from existing documents, and to use materials made

---

[1] *The Analogy of Religion* (1756), Introduction.

ready to their hands, under divine direction. I have, of course, no doubt that Moses at the end of Deuteronomy did not write the account of his own death and burial, and that it was added by some unknown inspired penman, in all probability by Joshua or Samuel. I grant that some incorrect readings may have crept in here and there in copying unprinted Hebrew books. But that the *traditional* view of the Old Testament, such as Josephus gives us, about the authorship of the several books, the dates at which they were written, and the reality of the events and persons mentioned in the historical portions, that this view, speaking generally, is the only true and safe one, I firmly maintain. I know that it is surrounded by many difficulties. But are there not countless difficulties both in the heavens above us and the earth under our feet? Surely there must needs be many difficulties about the origin and contents of a book given by inspiration of God! The saying of Origen, quoted by Bishop Butler, in the Introduction to his *Analogy*, should never be forgotten: 'He who believes the Scripture to have proceeded from him who is the Author of nature, may well expect to find the same sort of difficulties in it as are found in the constitution of nature.' I admit that the safe preservation and transmission of the inspired books through many centuries can only be accounted for by the miraculous interposition of God. But I am one of those who believe in miracles, and I regard the Bible as a miraculous book. Great, therefore, as the difficulties of the old traditional view of the Old Testament undoubtedly are, I hold that it is far the most probable and the most safe view, and I advise my brethren not to forsake it lightly. I stand firmly by the old faith of the Church, and refuse to give it up until I can find a better.

On the other hand, I entirely decline to accept the leading principles of the advocates of the 'Higher Criticism' of the Old Testament, about the authorship of its books, the dates at which they were composed, and the historical reality of the persons and events named and mentioned in them. I reject, as utterly incredible, the strange, but painfully common idea that Old Testament history is nothing more than 'a huge halo of legendary matter surrounding a small nucleus of truth.' I believe that one person, and not three or four, wrote and compiled all the first five books of the Bible, and that person was Moses. I believe that all the wonderful events related in these books did actually take place, such as the Fall, the Flood, the dispersion after the building of Babel, the destruction of Sodom and Gomorrah, the plagues of Egypt, the crossing of the Red Sea, and the subsequent facts and miracles recorded in Exodus. I have no doubt that there were such persons as Adam and Eve, and Cain and Abel, and Abraham and Lot, and Isaac and Jacob, and the twelve patriarchs, and that they really lived on earth, and said and did the things attributed to them in Genesis. I entirely repudiate the modern theory that the Pentateuch in its present form was never compiled till the times of Ezra and Nehemiah, and that many of the facts therein recorded, and especially in the first eleven chapters, are mere myths, fables, and legends, imagined or invented, and utterly destitute of solid and divine foundation. And if I am asked why I take up this ground, I answer, that the theories I repudiate appear to me to involve *infinitely greater difficulties than the old traditional views* which I maintain. I will state as briefly as possible what those difficulties are, and will confine my remarks to modern theories about the first five books of the Old Testament.

(1) My first difficulty is this. I want to know how it is that the views of 'Higher Criticism' about the authorship, date, and contents of the Pentateuch are of such *entirely modern origin.* It is admitted that they were never heard of before they were propounded by the Swiss physician Astruc, who lived 1684–1766. From the time of Josephus for nearly seventeen hundred years, I can read of no one who ever thought of denying that Genesis, Exodus, Leviticus, Numbers, and Deuteronomy were books written by the hand of Moses and by no other hand, and I can read of no one who ever doubted that the facts recorded in these books were historically true. The early Primitive Churches, the

Greek and Latin Fathers, the Schoolmen of the Middle Ages, the Roman and Greek Churches, the Reformers, the Puritans, the old Anglican Churchmen, all, all have been of one mind about this subject. However wide and deep their differences may have been on other points, they have all maintained that Moses was the author of the Pentateuch.

The 'Higher Critics' of the last hundred and fifty years have taken up entirely new ground. They ask us to believe that for seventeen centuries the students of Holy Scripture have lived and died in comparative blindness. During that long period the Old Testament has been constantly perused and prayer-fully searched by thousands and myriads of devout and learned men. Living in days when there were few books, and still fewer openings for religious usefulness, they probably spent far more time over the Bible than most Christians do now. Nor can it be said that all the Bible readers for these seventeen hundred years were weak-minded, unlearned, and unable to understand deep questions. It would be simply ridiculous to say so. Look at such men as Jerome, Origen, Chrysostom, and Augustine, among the Fathers; as Thomas Aquinas, Peter Lombard, Albertus Magnus, Bonaventura, among Schoolmen; as Luther, Calvin, Melanchthon, Brentius, Zwingli, Peter Martyr, Bucer, Bullinger, Gualter, Beza, Musculus, Chemnitius, Gerhard, Paraeus, among Continental Protestants; as Cranmer, Tyndale, Ridley, Jewel, Whitgift, among English Reformers; as Hooker, Andrews, Whittaker, Pearson, Hall, Davenant, Willet, Rainolds, Usher, Stillingfleet, Hammond, Bull, Waterland, Barrow, Hody, among Anglican divines; as Owen, Goodwin, Baxter, Manton, Charnock, Poole, among Puritans— look at these men, I say, and tell me if they were men of weak and inferior intellect. Surely, I think, any one well-read in theological biography must admit that this list contains the names of men who were just as hardheaded, as deep-thinking, and as capable of forming a sound judgment as any theologians that ever lived. On many questions they differed widely. But on one point they were entirely agreed. Not one of them ever maintained that the Pentateuch was not written by Moses, and Moses alone. This is a discovery that was made a hundred and fifty years ago!

In short, we are asked to believe that the students of the last century and a half have found out things which were hidden from the intellectual giants of the previous seventeen hundred years! This is my first difficulty, and I cannot get over it. It seems to me to contain an enormous improbability.

(2) My second difficulty is this. I find no satisfactory proof that the advocates of modern Old Testament criticism have a more thorough *knowledge of the Hebrew language* than the learned men who lived before them. It is needless to say that this is precisely one hinge on which the great controversy of the day turns. We are told continually by the leaders and friends of the new school that minute examination of the words, style, and language of the Pentateuch affords indisputable internal evidence that it could not have been written by the hand of one and the same person, and during one and the same life, and that considerable portions of Genesis and Exodus are nothing better than old myths and legends, of utterly uncertain authorship. If you doubt the truth of these startling assertions, you are told that your doubt arises from your ignorance of the Hebrew language, and that if you were a better Hebraist you would see the wisdom of modern Old Testament criticism. At present you cannot be expected to see it, any more than a babe. You are not competent to have an opinion, and ought to sit still and hold your tongue.

However, a very serious question remains behind, to which at present I see no answer. Let it be granted for a moment, though it is not proved, that there are no first-rate Hebrew scholars in the world except the advocates of 'Higher Criticism,' and that the opinions of other living Hebraists are comparatively of little value. But by what right do the modern critics claim to know more about Hebrew than those who studied that holy dead language more than one hundred and fifty years ago? Such men as Reuchlin,

James I's Old Testament translators, Ainsworth, Hugh Broughton, Fagius, Pellican, John Lightfoot, Gataker, Tremellius, Buxtorf, Mercer, Arias Montanus, Pagnini, Vatablus, Houbigant, Walton, all these were notoriously familiar with Hebrew, and deep lifelong students of the language in its minutest words, letters, jots and tittles. Yet none of them ever found out that the Pentateuch was not compiled till the time of Ezra! They all lived and died in the belief that Moses, and Moses alone, was the author of the first five books of the Bible under God's inspiration, and that all the statements of those books are 'the word of God.' Were all these men mistaken? What would they say now? They are dead long ago, and cannot defend themselves. It is cheap and easy work to underrate them in 1892. But most of them left behind them reputations of no mean authority as Hebrew scholars, and made a great mark in their day. I respect the zeal and diligence of modern critics both at home and abroad. But their fundamental theories appear to me to require belief in a huge mass of improbability. Until they can prove that Ainsworth, Broughton, and their companions were comparatively ignorant of Hebrew, and did not understand that holy language so well as the professors of Germany, Oxford, and Cambridge in these latter days, I cannot accept their 'Higher Criticism.'

(3) My third difficulty is this. I cannot reconcile the views of modern Old Testament critics with the *use which our Lord Jesus Christ continually made* of the Old Testament Scriptures in the Gospels, and with his mode of speaking about events, persons, and things in the Pentateuch, and specially in the book of Genesis. This, after all, in my opinion, is the crucial test of the whole matter in dispute. What did the Eternal Son of God, when he was 'manifest in the flesh,' say, and apparently think, about the Old Testament? In what light did he regard it? What authority did he attach to it?

I answer these questions without hesitation. It appears to me that, throughout the Gospels, the Lord Jesus always regards the Old Testament Scriptures as in every part 'the word of God,' devoid of any defect, error, or imperfection, the only rule of faith for God's Church, the only test of truth. I believe that such sentences as 'Search the Scriptures,' 'What is written in the law?' 'How readest thou?' were continually heard in our Lord's teaching. (I believe it, though of course I cannot prove it.) It has been well said by an American divine, 'We have no evidence that our Lord Jesus Christ ever read any other book than the Old Testament Scriptures. But of them his teachings are full: he lived in them. There appears with him throughout the Gospels an unquestioning acceptance of the Jewish canon, of the law, the prophets, and the Psalms.' As to the law he said, 'Not one jot or tittle shall pass away till all things shall be fulfilled' (Matt. 5:18). As to the prophets, he began his ministry at Nazareth by reading a passage from the 61st chapter of Isaiah, and saying, 'This day is this Scripture fulfilled.' Daniel, whose authority is disputed by many, he endorsed as 'Daniel the prophet' (Matt. 24:15). As to the Psalms, he quotes them frequently. A text from the Psalms was the last word which came from his lips on the cross (Psa. 31:5; Luke 23:46). And of the 110th Psalm, which some modern critics assign to the era of the Maccabees, he says distinctly that David spoke its words 'by the Holy Ghost' (Mark 12:36). Finally, it is a remarkable fact that Deuteronomy, the part of the Old Testament which some tell us was compiled after the Babylonian captivity, is the very book which he quotes three times in resisting the temptation of the devil, and so stamps as a book of peculiar value and authority.

I cannot detect the shadow of a hint that our Lord did not think the whole Pentateuch was written by Moses. Repeatedly he quotes from it, and speaks of Moses as the author of Exodus, Leviticus, Numbers, and Deuteronomy (Luke 20:37; Matt. 8:4; Mark 10:3). He calls Exodus 'the book of Moses' (Mark 12:26). He says distinctly, 'Moses wrote of me. If ye believe not his writings, how shall ye believe my words?' (John 5:46, 47). Repeatedly he speaks of events described in Genesis as real historical events, and persons mentioned in Genesis as real historical persons. Any well taught Sunday scholar can tell us that Jesus Christ speaks of the institution of the Sabbath, marriage, and circumcision, of the Flood, the ark, the destruction of Sodom, of Satan as a 'liar from the beginning,' of Abel, Noah, Abraham, Isaac, Jacob, Lot, and Lot's wife. In every case his language is that of one who has before his mind records of indisputable authority, which he handles with unhesitating confidence. He appears to my eyes to see the hand of only one author from the beginning of the Pentateuch to the end, and that author he taught his hearers was Moses. If the theories of modern Old Testament critics are true, there is at any rate a remarkable absence of support for them in Matthew, Mark, Luke, and John.

Of course I do not forget that many 'Higher Critics' maintain that our Lord did not really believe in his own mind that Moses wrote the Pentateuch, or that the events narrated in Genesis actually took place. They say that, in order to avoid giving offence, he adopted the traditional views of his hearers, and accommodated himself to their ignorant legends. A more improbable solution of a difficulty I cannot conceive! If ever there was a teacher who was above flattering his hearers or accommodating his language to their prejudices, that teacher was our Lord. 'Ye err,' he says, 'not knowing the Scriptures' (Matt. 22:29). Eight times over he says to the scribes and Pharisees in one chapter (Matt. 23), 'Woe unto you, hypocrites.' Once he says, 'Ye serpents, ye generation of vipers, how can ye escape the damnation of hell?' (Matt. 23:33). Once he says, 'Ye are of your father the devil, and the lusts of your father ye will do' (John 8:44). Will any one tell us that such a Teacher as this was ever likely to accommodate himself to his hearers, and to speak of things as facts which he knew were not facts, and men and women as real persons who he knew never existed at all, in order to please and satisfy his audience? Let those believe it who can. To my mind, such an attempt to explain our Lord's language requires us to believe the utmost improbabilities.

I do not forget that some other 'Higher Critics' of the Old Testament try to explain the difficulty before us by alleging that our Lord Jesus Christ's knowledge was limited, that he was ignorant on some subjects like other men, and was capable of erring about the authorship of the Pentateuch, and the facts and persons mentioned in Genesis. This is an explanation which I must decline to accept, and which I regard as dangerous in the extreme. I admit that our Lord was really and truly man, and that from his birth he 'increased in wisdom and stature' like other men (Luke 2:52). But that his knowledge was imperfect and limited when he came to full age, like the knowledge of any other man who was merely a fallen child of Adam, I cannot believe for a moment. For we must remember that he was always God as well as man, and that in his marvellous and mysterious person, 'The Godhead and manhood were joined together, never to be divided' (Second Article). To suppose that at any time during the three years of his earthly ministry he could speak ignorantly of *past things*, and teach things that were not really true, appears to my eyes a serious error, and a step in the direction of Socinianism. My soul revolts from the very idea of a fallible Saviour, Redeemer, Priest, and Judge! At this rate our Lord was merely the greatest of human prophets, but nothing more, and not 'God manifest in the flesh.' Once concede that he was fallible in any part of his teaching, and I do not see where you can draw the line. No one could now pronounce positively when he spoke ignorantly and when not; and a mist of uncertainty descends on all his words. That in the mysterious counsels of the eternal Trinity it was *appointed* that the Son, during his earthly ministry, should not know, as a thing to be revealed to the Church, the precise date of his own Second Advent and the end of the world, I can believe, and I think with reverence that I see wisdom in the appointment (Mark 13:32). He says, 'The Father which sent me gave me a commandment what I should say, and what I should speak' (John 12:49). But that he ever stated anything inaccurate I cannot for a moment believe. If he was, he could not be the infallible Teacher of the Church and the 'Light of the world.' As to the text and language of the Hebrew Scriptures, I can hardly conceive that Christ did not understand it better than any German or English professor that ever lived. At any rate, I think no one would dare to dispute his knowledge after his resurrection. It was after his resurrection we read that, 'Beginning at Moses and all the prophets, he expounded to them in all the Scriptures the things concerning himself' (Luke 24:27). If 'Moses' in that place does not mean the Pentateuch, I do not see what it can mean. After all, if he who was born of the Virgin Mary was the second person of the Blessed Trinity, who appeared to Abraham, as the Angel of the Covenant, the very day before the destruction of Sodom, it appears to me incredible that afterwards, 'in the days of his flesh,' he was ignorant of the events of Abraham's time. To ask me to believe that he did not know events which he had *seen nineteen centuries before*, is to ask me to believe a great improbability.

(4) My fourth difficulty is this. I cannot reconcile the theories of modern critics of the Old Testament with the *supremacy and sufficiency of Holy Scripture*. If these theories are true, there is an end of the old cardinal principle of Christianity, that the Bible is the rule of faith and practice. It goes without saying that for centuries the volume called the Bible has been regarded by most orthodox Christians as the authorized test of truth and error, and the source of all true religion. To me and many others it is God's mouthpiece to a dark and fallen world, and the final Court of Appeal in religion which never makes any mistakes. The only question asked about anything which we have been called upon to believe as spiritual truth has been simply this. Is it in the Bible? If it is there, it is worthy of credit, and ought to be received; if it is not there, it has no right to demand our assent. The preacher, the Bible-class teacher, the Sunday-school teacher, throughout the land, all ask you to believe what they say, and accept it, because they find it written in a book which they tell you is 'God's word

written, the word of God.' A plain text of Scripture settles everything. Our own Thirty-nine Articles refer to the Bible in this point of view no less than nineteen times.

But what are we to say to all this, if the theories of 'Higher Criticism' are correct? If some parts of Scripture are the uncertain compositions of uninspired men; if Genesis, for instance, is only a patchwork of contributions from four or five different hands; if its historical parts are mere legends, fables, and myths, destitute of any divine authority; the preacher, the lecturer, and the Sunday-school teacher are all deprived of their chief weapon. They will be obliged to say to their hearers, 'The things that we tell you may possibly be true, but we are not certain that they are.' At this rate the chief use of the Bible appears to my eyes to be destroyed. The old book is dethroned from the high position which it held as the pure word of God, by being mixed up with things which are the mere uninspired words of fallen man. Who shall decide, if we once admit the thin edge of uncertainty, what portions of the Old Testament are the infallible 'oracles of God,' and what are the fallible writings of the erring and corrupt children of Adam? Which of the historical parts of Genesis are real history, and which are mere baseless myths and legends of no authority? These are questions to which I believe no one can supply an answer. I do not know whether the clerical advocates of 'Higher Criticism' ever preach from such parts of Genesis as the story of the Fall, or of the Flood, or of the Tower of Babel. If they do, I should like to know whether they tell their congregations that they are teaching them lessons from the inspired 'word of God.' If they object to do so, I want to know where they are going to stop, and on what authority they can ask their hearers to believe the story of Abraham, Isaac, and Jacob. If you reject one part of Genesis, you can be certain about no part at all.

After all, I come back to my first position. I maintain that a book cannot be a rule of faith to a Church if it contains defects, errors, flaws, imperfections, inaccuracies, and untruths. It may contain a large measure of true and interesting matter, but it certainly cannot be called the infallible 'word of God.' I abhor the idea of a *fallible* Bible almost as much as the idea of a fallible Saviour. If the Bible is anything at all, it is the statute-book of God's kingdom, the code of laws and regulations by which the subjects of that kingdom are to live, the register-deed of the terms on which they have peace now and shall have glory hereafter. Now, why are we to suppose that such a book will be loosely and imperfectly drawn up, any more than legal deeds are drawn up on earth? Every lawyer can tell us that in legal deeds and statutes every word is of importance, and that property, life, or death may often turn on a *single word*. Think of the confusion that would ensue if wills, and settlements, and conveyances, and partnership deeds, and leases, and agreements, and Acts of Parliament were not carefully drawn up and carefully interpreted, and every word allowed its due weight. Where would be the use of such documents if particular words went for nothing, and every one had a right to add, or take away, or alter, or deny the validity of words, or erase words at his own discretion? At this rate we might as well lay aside our legal documents altogether! If God's statute-book is not inspired, and every part and jot and tittle of it is not of divine authority, God's subjects are in a very pitiable position! 'Higher Criticism' takes away the old rule of faith, the old test of truth and error, and gives them in its place a volume replete with guesses and conjectures, with doubtful points and uncertainties.

Well and wisely says the Bishop of Colchester, in an able article in *The Contemporary Review for June* 1892: 'The first and most obvious consequence of extreme rationalistic views is that, as far as the Old Testament is concerned, we shall have no Bible left. A collection of books so untrustworthy, so riddled through and through with spuriousness and deception, can no longer be reverenced as Holy Scripture! They can no longer be regarded as containing a revelation!'

(5) My fifth and last difficulty is this. I cannot understand how a book containing so many flaws, inaccuracies, and imperfections; a book of such doubtful authorship in many parts as the Bible, according to 'Higher Criticism,' is alleged to be—I cannot understand how such an imperfect book can have *done such an enormous work as the Bible certainly has done in the world.* This single volume, translated into all the principal languages on the face of the globe, has been accepted by millions of men and women for many years as true throughout, and has been regarded as an unerring teacher of soul-saving religion, and a sure and trustworthy guide to eternal life. This is the volume which alone, unaided by churches, ministers, sacraments, or schools, kept Christianity alive for twenty years among thousands of converted heathen in Madagascar, when all foreign missionaries and teachers had been forcibly expelled from the country.[1] This is the book whose doctrinal statements and single texts have been for the last three centuries the spiritual food and comfort of myriads of immortal beings. They have lived holy lives under its instruction, and gone down to the grave in peace, resting entirely on its statements, and believing every part of its contents. I think no one will dare to deny this.

But where are we placed if we accept the assertions of 'Higher Criticism'? We are asked to believe that large portions of this volume called the Bible are of such uncertain authorship that they cannot be honestly called 'the word of God.' We are asked to believe that large portions of the Pentateuch were not written by Moses, if any part at all, and that David only wrote one Psalm, and that not the 110th. We are asked to believe that Genesis is a compilation of writings from several hands, and that many of its historical statements are mere traditions of uncertain origin, or myths and legends utterly destitute of any solid foundations. As to the books of Daniel and Jonah, we are to regard their contents as nothing better than ingenious inventions of the nature of fables. All this, and much more which I might add, we are asked

---

[1] From 1837. Queen Ranavalona was the persecutor.

to believe on very slender and inconclusive evidence, while those who ask us to believe their theories are often divided among themselves.

Now, I appeal to the common sense of all into whose hands this Address may fall. Is it at all *probable* that the book which, however poorly translated, as it sometimes is, has obtained, and still maintains, such an immense influence over the hearts, heads, and lives of millions of mankind in every part of the globe, can be a book containing many imperfections, many doubtful statements, and many positive untruths? Is it likely and *probable* that God would employ such a book as this? That it may be badly translated sometimes, I admit. That the fallen human agents whom he employs to use it should be imperfect I can quite understand. But that the whole volume he puts in their hands as a weapon to work with, should be so imperfect as 'Higher Criticism' declares it to be, requires more credulity than I possess to believe it. To my eyes it is a grave improbability.

Of course I have only attempted to touch one side of a very large subject. I frankly admit that the advocates of 'Higher Criticism' can ask a hundred questions about the Old Testament, which, in common with other supporters of the old-fashioned traditional view, I am quite unable to answer. But I firmly maintain that the difficulties of their system are far greater than the difficulties of ours, and that the argument from *probability* is decidedly on our side. Nor can I refrain from saying, that the writings of the whole school appear to me to contain a large quantity of wild conjectures, proofless assumptions, illogical assertions, and self-contradicting statements. To all who wish to go more deeply into the subject, I strongly recommend Bishop Christopher Wordsworth's 'Introduction to Genesis,' at the beginning of his *Commentary on the Whole Bible*.

It is vain to deny that the whole subject of inspiration has always been, and will always be, a very mysterious one. I greatly admire the wisdom of our own Church of England in abstaining from dogmatism about it. I expect there will be shades of differences among us as long as the world stands. Most truly has Dean Burgon said,

> You cannot dissect inspiration into substance and form. As for the thoughts being inspired, apart from the words which gave them expression, you might as well talk of a tune without notes, or a sum without figures. No such dream can abide the daylight for a moment. No such theory of inspiration is even intelligible. It is as illogical as it is worthless.

How and in what precise manner the Holy Spirit worked on the minds of those who wrote the Bible, I for one would never attempt to explain. Minds cannot be anatomized like bodies, or inspected like physical objects with the microscope. I certainly do not believe that inspired writers, like reporters, only wrote down what they had seen with their own eyes, or heard with their own ears, or been told by other people. I hold that, after a miraculous manner, the Holy Ghost suggested matter to be written down by those whom he inspired, and also suggested the words and language in which that matter should be clothed. But in all this the mental process is a deep miracle which I do not pretend to explain, any more than to explain how Lazarus was raised from the dead. I only know that the result is a firm conviction in my soul, that the whole book has something about it utterly unlike any other book in the world, and is rightly called 'the word of God.'

I humbly confess that when I sit down to read the Scriptures I always expect to meet 'some things hard to be understood.' Sometimes I feel that I do not know who wrote this or that book in the Bible, or when it was written, or why such and such things were written in it, or what they all mean. But then I fall back on the thought, that this is part of a miraculous book given by inspiration. This is God's word, and what I know not now I shall know hereafter. To use the words of Hooker, 'The little thereof which we darkly apprehend we admire; the rest, with religious ignorance, we humbly and meekly adore' (*Eccles. Polity*, Bk. I. ch.

2.5). I agree entirely with Augustine when he says: 'If I meet with anything in the canonical books of Scripture which seems to me at variance with the truth, I do not doubt but that either my copy of that book is faulty, or that the translation of it which I am using has missed the sense, or that I myself have failed to understand the true meaning of the writer' (Augustine, *Epistle to Jerome*, 82). It is a wise remark of old Thomas Fuller in his *Commentary on the Book of Ruth*, 'Even as a man that hath a piece of gold, which he knows to be the right weight, and sees it stamped with the king's image, careth not to know the name of the man who minted or coined it; so we, seeing the book to have the superscription of Caesar, the stamp of the Holy Ghost, need not to be curious to know who was the penman thereof.'

I conclude all with a striking passage from Gaussen, the Swiss divine:

> One trembles when, after beholding the Son of Man commanding the elements, stilling the tempests, and despoiling the tomb, and solemnly declaring that he will, on an appointed day, return to judge, by this book, the quick and the dead— one trembles to see a poor accountable mortal, seated in a professor's chair, and handling the word of God as he would handle Terence or Thucydides, retrenching, adding, praising, blaming; lopping off whole chapters as containing mistakes, inconclusive arguments, rash assertions, and the like! Yet in a few years the learned professor and his pupils will all be in the tomb, while not a particle of the divine book will have passed away, and when the Son of Man shall descend from heaven, by this book shall they all be judged.

I will not detain the Conference any longer, and I wish I could have made my address shorter. But we meet in peculiar times, and the burning questions I have tried to handle cannot be dismissed in a few brief sentences. Of course I do not expect you all to agree with me. But I hope you will all believe that I have told you frankly and honestly what I think. We only 'know in part,' and I lay no claim to infallibility.

12

STAND FIRM

The fifth triennial charge to the Diocese of Liverpool,
November 10, 1893.

W E meet together today at my fifth Triennial Visitation. It is
a solemn and heart-searching occasion. Three years make
gaps in our ranks, and the names of some honoured brethren have
disappeared from our roll, which were read out in this Cathedral
in 1890. We also shall follow them when our work is done. God
can do without us. The words on John Wesley's memorial tablet
in Westminster Abbey should never be forgotten: 'God buries his
workmen, but carries on his work.'

But while three years make many gaps, they also make
much history, and in this hurrying age great events follow one
another with startling rapidity. In the last triennial period not a
few burning subjects have come to the front, which imperatively
demand the attention of all thoughtful Churchmen. They are
subjects which affect the whole Church of England, and not the
Diocese of Liverpool alone. To these subjects I now propose to
direct your minds today. You have a right to know my opinions
about them. A Bishop was never meant to be a mere figure-head,
and an honorary member of all schools of thought. He ought to
have decided opinions, and on suitable occasions to express them.
You may not agree with me on some points that I shall handle, but
at any rate you shall know what I think.

I. I shall speak first about *Our Unhappy Divisions*. Their existence it is impossible to deny. Whether we like to acknowledge them or not, they are seen, known, and observed by millions outside our pale. The infidel, the Romanist, the Scotch Presbyterian, the English Nonconformist, all have their eyes upon us, and, if they do not understand our formularies, they do understand that our Church is a very divided body.

There is nothing which need surprise us in a certain amount of divisions among professing Christians. As long as human nature is what it is, it is useless to expect all men to see all things in the same light. This has been the condition of the Church in every age, from the days of the apostles; and the history of our own Reformed Church for three centuries supplies not a few examples. Hooper and Ridley in Edward VI's time; Whitgift and Cartwright, Travers and Hooker, in the reign of Queen Elizabeth; Laud and the Puritans under Charles I; the Savoy Conference Bishops and the Nonconformists under Charles-the-Second; Hoadly and Law in the early Georgian era; the rejection of the Methodists in the last century; all tell the same melancholy story. There is nothing new in religious divisions, and our Church has seen and outlived many of them. They have been, and will be, as long as the world stands. There will be no perfect Church until our Divine Head comes again.

Nevertheless, I am obliged to say that our divisions in the present day appear to me far more serious than any we have ever had to face in the Established Church since the era of the Reformation, and to threaten very dangerous consequences. Causes of difference which at one time only existed in solution, are now crystallized and solidified. The gulf between opposing schools of thought seems wider and deeper. It is impossible to repress the anxious thought, what will the end of these things be? That thought will arise in many minds.

Of course, I do not forget that myriads of unthinking people suppose that the present divisions of Churchmen are entirely about trifles and petty matters of ritual detail—a little more or less music! a few more or less flowers! a few more vestures, and gestures, and turnings, and postures! This is all the difference they can see between one clergyman and another. Why should they be divided? Why not work harmoniously together, if they are both earnest men? Superficial judgments like this are the great misfortune of our times. An immense number of laymen cannot or will not see that our 'unhappy divisions' arise almost entirely from discordant opinions about the Lord's Supper. But, surely, the importance of that blessed sacrament can hardly be overstated. History tells us it is the very ordinance about which our martyred Reformers laid down their lives at the stake. If the clergy of this generation are entirely divided about the Lord's Supper, the laity may not understand it, but they may be sure our Church is in very evil plight.

It is useless to shut our eyes to plain facts, when the ship is really in danger, and there are breakers ahead. Are we really much divided? Are our differences very serious? Let us see. I shall not shrink from naming some notorious points which appear to me to demand attention, and supply sorrowful proof that our divisions are real.

(1) One section of our clergy, and probably the majority, maintains that the Lord's Supper is a sacrifice. Another, and probably the minority, maintains, with equal firmness, that it is not, and should only be called a sacrament.

(2) One maintains that the Communion table is an altar, and should be always treated as such. Another maintains that it is only the Holy Table.

(3) One maintains that the minister at the Lord's Supper is a sacrificing priest. Another maintains that he is only an officiating presbyter, though called a priest, and that there is no authority for sacerdotalism in the New Testament or the Prayer-book.

(4) One maintains that the officiating minister should celebrate, and consecrate the elements with his face to the east,

and his back to the people. The other maintains that he should stand at the north end with his face to the south.

(5) One maintains that the Lord's Supper ought never to be administered in the evening. The other maintains that there is no objection whatever to evening Communion, where the circumstances of the congregation make it desirable.

(6) One maintains that the Lord's Supper does good, more or less, to all who receive it, and that as a general rule all persons should be urged to become communicants. The other maintains that it only does good to believing and worthy communicants, and to those who are destitute of lively faith does no good at all, but rather harm.

(7) One maintains that the Lord's Supper should always be received fasting, and after confession to a clergyman. The other regards both these additions to the sacrament with deep aversion, as not warranted by Scripture or the Prayer-book.

(8) One maintains that there is a real objective presence of Christ's body and blood under the forms of the consecrated bread and wine. The other maintains that there is no real presence whatsoever, except in the hearts of believing communicants.

Now, I shall not for a moment attempt to argue these disputed points, or to say, on this occasion, who is right and who is wrong, whatever my own private opinions may be. I shall not pretend to say what is, and what is not, legal. We seem to have reached days when ecclesiastical law about doctrine and ritual is practically dead and buried, and every clergyman, like Israel in the time of the Judges, does, and teaches 'what is right in his own eyes.' I only place before you plain facts which nobody can deny, and ask you to observe what an immense cause of weakness these divisions must be, and are, to the Church of England. When a clergyman on one side of a street or road administers the Lord's Supper in one way, and his neighbour a few hundred yards off in another way, there is a terrible lack of unity. It may well be said to the Church whose ministers are so divided, 'Be not high-minded, but fear.'

A church which can live with such discordant elements in her bosom is a miracle of vitality.

Some tell us, I know, that if we are quiet and hold our tongues, everything will come right. The bud of unity is growing, and will soon bloom into a perfect flower! I confess I see no symptom whatsoever of this, and indeed things seem to me, since the Lincoln decision,[1] to look worse rather than better. Some tell us that the Church of England is eminently comprehensive, and that we must expect many divisions and differences. No doubt this is true. But, surely, there must be limits to our comprehensiveness! Some consider that the minority of the clergy should always give way to the majority, and meekly adopt its views of the Lord's Supper. I am quite certain that the present Protestant minority will do nothing of the kind. They will stand firm in the old paths, supported by a very large body of the laity, and any general attempt to prohibit such a thing as evening Communion, or to enforce the eastward position, or to bring back, and legalize in our service, the defective First Prayer-book of Edward VI, or to sanction auricular confession, would blow the Established Church to pieces.

I admit that in a large Church like our own, there will always be some shades and varieties of opinion. Our National Church is rather like our National Army, which contains several various forces, each firmly convinced of its own peculiar importance. In time of peace the Guards chaff the Line, and the Line the Guards; the Cavalry makes light of the Artillery, and the Artillery of the Cavalry; the kilted Highlanders think little of the Rifle brigade or the Welsh Fusiliers, and the Irish regiments think themselves best of all. But let the stern realities of war once begin, and a British army be sent to a foreign shore; let the campaign really commence and the enemy be met on the field of battle; let the word be given to advance across the Alma, or charge up the valley of death at Balaclava, or storm the Redan, or force the Khyber Pass; and where

---

[1] The judgment given by E. W. Benson, Archbishop of Canterbury, in 1891, concerning the case of Dr Edward King, Bishop of Lincoln, who had adopted Romanizing practices.

will you find more real union, and brotherly feeling, and readiness to stand shoulder to shoulder, than in the army of our Queen? And so I hope it might possibly be in our National Church. There may be many traitors among us, sceptics and Romanists who are useless and untrustworthy, and ought to go to their own place. But for all this there is a considerable amount of substantial agreement within our pale. In spite of all her apparent differences, and conflicting Schools of thought, the National Church has some strong elements of cohesiveness, and contrives to satisfy and keep together a very large proportion of the people of this land. But a *modus vivendi*[1] in a church, as well as in the Army, can only work by rigid observance of impartiality. The General of an army who favoured one branch of his forces more than another would never succeed very well in war. The Heads of a Church who ostracize and frown on any one school of thought, and smile on another, will look in vain for unity. Here is a great problem, and I know not how it is to be solved. I only ask you to ponder the solemn words of our Lord Jesus Christ: 'Every kingdom divided against itself is brought to desolation, and a house divided against itself shall not stand' (Matt. 12:25). And he says: 'My word shall not pass away' (Matt. 24:35).

I leave the whole subject of our 'unhappy divisions' at this point. I cannot square the circle, or produce perpetual motion, and I cannot undertake to untie the huge knot I have tried to describe and set before you. We are drifting, drifting, drifting, as a Church, and in imminent danger of shipwreck. I can only offer you fatherly counsel, and ask you for the sake of peace to receive it. If you must needs have divisions I entreat you to cultivate courtesy and kindness in all your dealings with one another. Let us agree to differ pleasantly if we must differ. Let us not refuse to work together as far as we can. Education, sanitation, philanthropy, common morality, supply a vast extent of common ground. To men of one School I offer the following advice: do

[1] Mode of living.

not be in a hurry to secede from the Established Church because things are not going on according to your mind, so long as the Articles and Prayer-book remain quite whole and unaltered. The list of things permissible and not illegal may be sadly increasing. But stand firm so long as nothing new is required or forced on you, and you are allowed to work on your old lines. The way of patience is better than the way of secession. I am old enough to remember the secessions of Baptist Noel and Capel Molyneux. I believe they both lived to see that secession was a mistake. To men of an opposite school I offer the following advice: Try to be satisfied with the advantages you have obtained in late years. Do not press on violently for more permissions, more concessions, more ritual novelties, which will only provoke fresh conflicts and create a storm. Very likely you may all reject my counsel. But one thing is very certain, if we cannot lessen 'our unhappy divisions' there is only one conclusion before us. That conclusion is the disruption and complete breakup of the Established Church of England. Our candlestick will be taken away, and we shall be left in the dark.

II. The second subject about which I propose to speak is hardly less important than my first. I refer to—*Higher Criticism*. It is needless to say that I speak of the modern and startling views of the authority, the dates, the construction, the historical veracity, of large portions of the Old Testament Scriptures, which have been brought before the public during the last few years.

I handled this subject at considerable length in my opening address at the Diocesan Conference last year. I shall not dwell much on it now. On that occasion I declared my inability to accept the theories of 'Higher Criticism' on account of *their enormous improbability*. Since that time I have found no reason to alter the opinions I expressed. I acknowledge most willingly the learning, the cleverness, the diligence, the reverent tone of most of the champions of this new school of thought. I have no doubt they think they are doing God's service. But I cannot shut my eyes to the tendencies—the unmistakable tendencies—of the whole system of 'Higher Criticism.' It is my deliberate opinion that it is calculated to shake the faith of millions, and to strike a heavy blow at the two great foundation truths of Christianity. One of those foundations is the supremacy and sufficiency of Holy Scripture. The other is the perfect divinity of our Lord Jesus Christ.

Let us turn first to Scripture, and consider the position that 'God's word written' occupies in Christianity. I need not remind you of the old cardinal principle of our holy religion that the Bible is the true rule of faith and practice, a sure guide for belief while we live, and a sure guide of hope when we die. It goes without saying that for centuries the volume called the Bible has been regarded by orthodox Christians as the authorized test of truth and error, and the source of all true religion. To me and many others it is God's mouth-piece to a dark and fallen world, and the final Court of Appeal in religion, a Court which never makes any mistakes. The only question asked about anything which, from our childhood, we have been called upon to believe as spiritual truth, has been simply this, 'Is it in the Bible?' If it is there, it is worthy of credit, and ought to be received; if it is not there, it has no right to demand our assent. The preacher, the Bible-class teacher, the Sunday-school teacher, throughout the land, all ask you to believe what they say, and to accept it, because they find it written in a book which they tell you is 'God's word written, the word of God.' A plain text of Scripture settles everything. Our own Thirty-nine Articles refer to the Bible in this point of view no less than nineteen times. The book, no doubt, contains many things hard to be understood, and many deep things which we cannot explain, but nothing incorrect or untrue. And it is a book utterly unlike any other book in the world. It is a book given by inspiration of the Holy Ghost.

But what are we to say to all this, if the theories of 'Higher Criticism' are correct? If some parts of Scripture are the uncertain compositions of uninspired men; if Genesis, for instance, is only a patchwork of contributions from four or five different hands, if some of its historical parts are mere legends, fables, and myths, destitute of any divine authority—the preacher, the lecturer, and the Sunday-school teacher are all deprived of their chief weapon. They will be obliged to say to their hearers, 'The things that we tell you may possibly be true, but we are not certain that they are.' At this rate the chief use of the Bible appears to my eyes to be destroyed. The old book is dethroned from the high position which it has hitherto held as the pure word of God, by being mixed up with things which are the mere uninspired words of fallen man. Who shall decide, if we once admit the thin edge of uncertainty, what portions of the Old Testament are the infallible 'oracles of God,' and what are the fallible writings of the erring and corrupt children of Adam? Which of the historical parts of Genesis are real history, and which are mere baseless myths and legends of no authority? These are questions to which I believe no one can supply an answer. I maintain firmly that a book cannot be a rule of faith to a Church if it contains defects, errors, flaws, imperfections, inaccuracies, and even untruths. It may contain a large measure of true and interesting matter, but it certainly cannot be called the infallible word of God.

Let us turn next to our Lord Jesus Christ, and consider how the theories of Higher Criticism must affect our estimate of his person and infallibility. They appear to me to land us unavoidably in a most painful and difficult position. Most of us have been taught to believe that we have a Divine Saviour of perfect knowledge, and incapable of saying what was not true, or making any mistake. We have thought him not only a perfect Redeemer, but a perfect Prophet and Teacher. But we are now asked to believe that he sometimes spoke of persons as real persons who never existed, and events as real historical events which never took place. In short we are invited to believe that Jesus Christ, when he was on earth, was a person of *limited knowledge*. This is a theory which I must decline to accept, and must regard as dangerous in the extreme. I admit that our Lord was really and truly man, and that from his birth he 'increased in wisdom and stature' like other men (Luke 2:52). But that his knowledge was imperfect and limited when he came to full age, like the knowledge of any other man who was merely a fallen child of Adam, I cannot believe for a moment. For we must remember that he was always God as well as man, and that in his marvellous and mysterious person, 'The Godhead and manhood were joined together in one person, never to be divided' (Second Article). To suppose that at any time during the three years of his earthly ministry he could speak ignorantly of *past things*, and teach things that were not really true, appears to my eyes a serious error, and a step in the direction of Socinianism, though I am sure the advocates of Higher Criticism would abhor the very idea. Now, I must say that my soul revolts from the very idea of a fallible Saviour, Redeemer, Priest, Prophet, and Judge! At this rate our Lord was merely the greatest of human prophets, but nothing more, and not 'God manifest in the flesh.' Once concede that he was fallible in any part of his teaching, and I do not see where you can draw the line. No one could now pronounce positively when he spoke ignorantly and when not, and a mist of uncertainty would descend on all his words. That in the mysterious counsels of the eternal Trinity it was *appointed* that the Son, on one single occasion (Mark 13:32), during his earthly ministry, should not know, as a thing to be revealed to the Church, the precise date of his own Second Advent and the end of the world, I can believe, and I think, with reverence, that I see wisdom in the appointment. He says himself in one place, 'The Father, which sent me, he gave me a commandment what I should say, and what I should speak' (John 12:49). But that he ever stated anything in error I cannot for a moment believe. If he did, he could not be the infallible Teacher of the Church, and 'the Light of the world.' From a fallible Bible and a fallible Saviour, Good Lord, deliver us!

I leave this painful subject here. Time, perhaps, will throw more light upon it, and make Christians more of one mind. At present I cannot withdraw my opinion that an acceptance of the conclusions of Higher Criticism has an unmistakable tendency to lower a man's view of the two foundations of revealed religion, the Bible and Christ.

I can only advise all my clergy, who want counsel on the subject of Higher Criticism, to cultivate a very cautious attitude of judgment. Beware of taking up loose and confused views of the doctrine of inspiration. Stand firm on the grand old text, 'All Scripture is given by inspiration of God' (2 Tim. 3:16). The translation of the Greek of that verse which the *Revised Version* has given us, is in my opinion most awkward and unnatural. The old is better. Do not be carried off your feet by the first clever new book you come across, and especially if you have never examined this branch of study before. Do not mistake assertions for proofs, suggestions for solid arguments, and hypothetical conjectures for logical conclusions. There are two sides to most questions; mind you look at both. Never give up great principles on account of petty, flashy objections, which at first sight look unanswerable, but soon melt like snow. Above all, never forget the wise saying of the great philosopher Faraday: 'On all disputable points try to preserve your mind in a state of judicious suspense.'

III. The next subject to which I shall invite your attention is—*The Increasing Desecration of our English Sunday.*

This is a subject which every Englishman ought to consider seriously in the present day. I can find no words to express my own sense of its importance. I am persuaded that one half of English Christianity is bound up with the maintenance of the 'old English Sunday.' Whether we shall be able to maintain it remains to be seen. The enemy is coming in like a flood, and if we would 'hold the fort,' we must gird up our loins and fight. There are two points in the lines of revealed religion which the great enemy of souls seems to be attacking with special enmity in these days, one doctrinal, the other practical. One of these two is the Priestly office of Christ, and the other is the obligation of the Fourth

Commandment. We must defend these two points to the last. 'He that hath no sword, let him sell his garment and buy one' (Luke 22:36).[1]

I am aware that many thoughtless people in this thoughtless age sneer at the Sabbath as an effete Jewish institution. By so doing they only exhibit their own ignorance of the Bible and human nature. They do not see that the Sabbath is an institution as old as creation, and was 'made for man' long before the Decalogue. It was made to keep man in touch with God, and is an unmixed good for all classes.

(1) The Sabbath is good for man's *body*. We all need a day of rest. On this point all medical men are agreed. Curiously and wonderfully made as the human frame is, it will not stand incessant work without regular intervals of repose. The gold-diggers of California soon learned this fact. Reckless and ungodly as many of them probably were, urged on as they were, no doubt, by the mighty influence of the hope of gain, they still found out that a seventh day's rest was absolutely needful to keep themselves alive. Without it they discovered that in digging for gold they were only digging their own graves. I firmly believe that one reason why the health of hard-working clergymen so frequently fails, is the great difficulty they find in getting a day of rest. I am sure, if the body could tell its wants, it would cry loudly, 'Remember the Sabbath Day.'

(2) The Sabbath is good for man's *mind*. The mind needs rest quite as much as the body. It cannot bear an uninterrupted strain on its powers. It must have its intervals of leisure to unbend and recover its force. Without them it will either prematurely wear out, or fail suddenly like a broken bow. I have been credibly informed that the testimony of old Mr Wilberforce, the famous statesman and philanthropist, on this point was very striking. He declared that he could only attribute his own power of endurance to his regular observance of the Sabbath Day. He remembered that he had observed some of the mightiest intellects among

[1] At this point Bishop Ryle repeated verbatim the warnings given in his fourth triennial Charge: see pages 254-55.

his contemporaries in Parliament fail suddenly at last, and their possessors come to melancholy ends. And he was satisfied that in every such case of mental shipwreck the true cause was neglect of the Fourth Commandment.

(3) The Sabbath is good for *nations*. It has an enormous effect both on the character and temporal prosperity of a people. I firmly believe that a people which regularly rests one day in seven will do more work, and better work, in a year than a people which never rests at all. Their hands will be stronger, their minds will be clearer, their power of attention, application, and steady perseverance will be far greater. What two nations on earth are so prosperous at this day as Great Britain and the United States of America? Where shall we find on the globe so much energy, so much steadiness, so much success, so much public confidence, so much morality, and so much good government as in those two countries? Let others account for all this as they please. I say, without hesitation, that the grand secret of it all has been the observance of the Sabbath. Great Britain and the United States, with all their sins, are the two most Sabbath-keeping nations on earth. They have given up seven years of good working days in the last fifty years to keeping the Lord's Day holy. But have they lost anything by it? No, indeed! None speaks more decidedly on that point than Lord Macaulay. The two Sabbath-keeping nations are the most prosperous nations in the world. Sabbath-keeping, no doubt, appears to lose a nation a seventh part of its time, and is a tax on its income. But it is undoubtedly the best tax we pay!

(4) Last, but not least, the Sabbath is an unmixed good for man's *soul*. The soul has its wants just as much as the mind and body. It is in the midst of a hurrying, bustling world, in which its interests are constantly in danger of being jostled out of sight. To have those interests properly attended to, there must be a special day set apart. There must be a regularly recurring time for calmly and quietly examining the state of our souls. There must be a day to test and prove us, whether we are prepared for an eternal

heaven. Take away a man's Sabbath, and his religion soon comes to nothing. As a general rule, there is a regular flight of steps from 'no Sabbath' to 'no God.'[1]

IV. The last subject, but not the least, to which I wish to direct your attention is the proposed *Disestablishment and Disendowment of the Church in Wales*.

It is needless to tell you that the Welsh Church, as it is commonly called, is an integral part of the Church of England. You cannot attack one without attacking the other. And the point I wish to press on your consideration is the positive duty of buckling on our armour and getting ready for a fight which is evidently coming. It is useless to say that Disestablishment is not a question of 'practical politics.' It was so once, and it is a terribly practical question now; and if that Statesman who disestablished the Church of Ireland[2] continues to live, it will be more practical still.

In handling this great and pressing subject I shall say nothing about legal points. Parliament is omnipotent in this day, and if Parliament resolves to disestablish and disendow the Church of England, we must submit, however indignant and disgusted we may feel.

I will assume that the deed is done, and that all Churches and sects in Great Britain are placed on a dead level of equality. No favour or privilege would be granted by the State to one more than another. The State itself would have nothing to do with religion, and would leave the supply of it to the principles of free trade and the action of the voluntary system. In a word, the Government of England would allow all its subjects to serve God or Baal, to go to heaven or to another place, just as they please. The State would take no cognizance of spiritual matters, and would look on with Epicurean indifference and unconcern. The State would continue

---

[1] At this point the Bishop repeated the warnings given in his fourth Triennial Charge; see pp. 256-57.

[2] W. E. Gladstone (in 1869).

to care for the *bodies* of its subjects, but it would entirely ignore their *souls*.

I will now point out to you what the practical consequences of this revolutionary legislation would certainly be. I think it important to approach the subject from this side. Many thoughtless people, I suspect, have not the least idea of the length and breadth of the harm which Disestablishment and Disendowment would do in this country. They point to the Colonies and the United States of America and ask us to observe how well people get on there without any union of Church and State. I am not convinced that things go on so pleasantly in those countries without Established Churches as many suppose, either in towns like New York, or in the great Western States. At any rate I think it a plain duty to point out what I believe would be the consequences of Disestablishment and Disendowment in old England.

(1) The injury which *the Church* would receive is very great indeed. Deprived of her present endowments it would be necessary to diminish the number of her rural clergy by at least one half, to consolidate half the livings, and put an end to half the services! The voluntary system in rural districts is notoriously an entire failure. None know that better than the ministers of Nonconformist country chapels. It would tax the energies of a disestablished Church most heavily to keep up an Episcopal ministry outside the towns. It would immensely cripple the power of the Church of England to do much for the evangelization of the heathen abroad, and the general spread of the gospel at home. 'Sustentation funds' would absorb three-quarters of the Church's attention; and we should find it hard enough to maintain our position, and much harder to extend our lines. Last, but not least, Disestablishment would almost certainly lead to divisions, schisms, and possibly disruption in the Episcopal body. We should all become more narrow, and less liberal and comprehensive in our views. Of course this goes for nothing with some Christians, who seem to think that divisions and schisms are very nice things,

and that the multiplication of sects is the nearest thing to heaven upon earth! I content myself with repeating the words of our Lord Jesus Christ, 'A house divided against itself cannot stand.' The more divisions among Christians the greater the weakness, and the smaller the influence of Christianity! To promote an increase of division among English Christians is the surest way to help the Church of Rome, the agnostic, and the infidel.

I will not waste words on those who tell us that the English clergy, after Disestablishment, would preach better, and write better, and speak better, and work better than they do now, and that, like wild elephants, we should all be made tamer and more useful by starving. Anybody can make assertions like these; but assertions are worth nothing when they are contradicted by plain facts. I do not see that the American Episcopalians over the water, who have no connection with the State, are a bit better preachers and workers than the clergy of the English Establishment. Above all, I do not see that English Nonconformist ministers, as a body, are at all superior, in preaching or in working, to the clergy of the English Established Church.

In short, the assertion of the advocates of Disestablishment, that this movement would do the Church of England good, and not harm, appears to me utterly destitute of foundation. It would inflict on us immense damage. An ounce of facts is better than a pound of theories. Free Churches are very fine things to talk about, and look very fine at a distance; but matters are not always serene inside.

(2) While, however, Disestablishment would greatly cripple and injure the Church of England, I fail to see that it would do any good *to the Dissenters*. I believe that it would neither increase their numbers, nor raise their influence, nor add to their power in town or country.

Would Disestablishment *destroy* the Church of England, and take the great rival of Dissenters completely out of the way? Would it leave the Dissenters a clear field, and throw the whole population into their hands? It would do nothing of the kind!

Unless the House of Commons resolves to proscribe the use of the Liturgy to make it penal to be an Episcopalian, to confiscate the property of Churchmen on the principles of French Communism, and to imprison or shoot clergymen who work harder than others—unless the House of Commons does this, the Church of England will never be killed by Disestablishment. Dissenters would soon find that the old Church, when Disestablished, was not dead, but very much alive.

Disestablishment would not even ruin the Church *financially*. The pew-rents and offertories would still remain: Parliament could not take them. The endowments of the last two centuries would still remain: Parliament, on the reasonable principles of the Irish Act,[1] would not touch them. The life-interests of the Bishops and Clergy, on the same principles, would still remain. A judicious system of life insurance or commutation, such as wise lay Churchmen, accustomed to financial matters, could soon devise, would turn those life-interests into a very large capital for investment, if safe investment could be found. In short, though sorely crippled and impoverished, the Church of England would not be ruined. We could still get on, and would get on, though many of us might have to reduce our expenditure very largely. The Liberationists would soon discover, after spoiling and impoverishing us as much as they could, that we were not quite bankrupt. We should maintain our position, in spite of our poverty, and not die.

Disestablishment would not affect the influence of the Church in *great towns* in the slightest appreciable degree. The tithe-receiving clergy in rural districts would doubtless lose half their income by life insurance or commutation, and be sorely hampered. But most of the clergy in our large cities, such as London, Liverpool, Manchester, Birmingham, Leeds, and Sheffield, who generally depend on pew-rents, Easter offerings, and offertories, as a body, would be almost as well off after Disestablishment as they were

[1] 1869.

before. 'The great towns govern the country,' we are continually told. Yet in most great towns the Church would be as powerful as ever!

Disestablishment would not make the bulk of Englishmen *forsake the Church of England*, and become Baptists, Independents, Presbyterians, or Methodists. It would not fill the chapels and empty the churches. It would not make the aristocracy, or the upper and middle classes, or a large part of the working-classes, burn their Prayer-books, desert Episcopally ordained ministers, and fall in love with extempore prayer. Not a bit of it! The vast majority of Churchmen would stick to bishops, rectors, vicars, curates, liturgical worship, and the old paths of the Church of England, closer and tighter than ever. They would make more of their poor old Church in her adversity than they ever did in her prosperity. They would love her better, and open their purses more liberally, when they saw her in plain attire, than they ever did before. In point of number of adherents I verily believe Disestablishment would soon prove a dead loss to Dissenters, and not a gain.

Last, but not least, Disestablishment *would not give more liberty* to Dissenters, or enable them to do any thing which they cannot do now. No Christians on earth have such a plethora of civil and religious liberty as the English Nonconformists have in the present day. They have far more freedom than Churchmen! They can build chapels anywhere, preach anywhere, gather congregations anywhere, worship in any way, and serve God in any way, no man forbidding them: while Churchmen are checked and stopped by laws and restrictions at every turn. What in the world could Dissenters do more, if the Church was disestablished tomorrow? I cannot for a moment suppose they would ask leave to shoot or hang all the clergy, to 'improve us off the face of the earth,' to confiscate the cathedrals and parish churches, and to compel the millions of English men and women who now go to church to go to chapel, on pain of fines or death. But, short of this, I know of nothing they cannot do now. They have free liberty to make all Englishmen Dissenters, *if they can*; and what more do they want? The dissolution of the union of Church and State would do the Dissenters no good at all.

(3) Great, however, as the injury would be which Disestablishment would do to the Church, it is my firm conviction, that it would do *far greater injury to the State.*

Reason itself points out that the moral standard of a nation's subjects is the grand secret of its prosperity. Gold mines and manufactures and scientific discoveries and eloquent speeches and commercial activity and democratic institutions are not enough to make or to keep nations great. Tyre and Sidon and Egypt and Carthage and Athens and Rome and Venice and Spain and Portugal had plenty of such possessions as these, and yet fell into decay. The sinews of a nation's strength are truthfulness, honesty, sobriety, purity, temperance, economy, diligence, brotherly kindness, charity among its inhabitants. Let those deny this who dare. And will any man say that there is any surer way of producing these characteristics in a people than by encouraging and fostering pure scriptural Christianity? The man who says there is must be an infidel. Does a State want its subjects to be provident, truthful, diligent, temperate, honest, moral, and charitable? Does it or does it not? If it does it ought to encourage, and not to ignore, religion. To punish vice and yet not cherish virtue, to spend public money on building jails and yet not encourage Christianity, is, to say the least, an absurdly inconsistent policy. The more true religion the better subjects! The more good subjects the more prosperity! The Government which ignores *religion*, and coolly declares that it does not care whether its subjects are Christians or not, is guilty of an act of suicidal folly. Irreligion, even in a temporal point of view, is the worst enemy of a nation.

After all, I am one of those old-fashioned people who believe in a God. I believe in him not only as the God of creation, but as the God of providence, the God who governs the world, the God who hears and answers prayer. Believing all this, I will never admit that it signifies nothing whether a Government recognizes Christianity or not, and that it matters little whether a country has an Established Church. I set my foot down firmly on the great principle, 'Them that honour me I will honour, and they that despise me shall be lightly esteemed' (1 Sam. 2:30). I apply that principle to nations, and I believe it will always hold good. The Act of Parliament which disestablished the Church of England might do great damage to the Church, but I am quite sure it would do far more damage to the State. We should lose much, but the State would lose a great deal more. As a patriot and an Englishman, I would stand firm and maintain the union of Church and State for the sake of my country.

What may be before us no man can tell. But in an age like our own, an age of restlessness, an age of liberality falsely so called, an age of popularity-hunting, an age of sensationalism and surprises, an age of idolatry of the mob, an age of contempt for old things merely because they are old, an age of spasmodic feverish zeal for new things merely because they are new, an age of change for the sake of change, an age of laziness and apathy among the defenders of the old things, and of earnestness and perseverance among the advocates of the new—in such an age I shall never be surprised if Disestablishment comes. When it does come, I believe it will inflict such an amount of damage on the State as the mind of man can hardly conceive. I declare I had far rather see the Episcopal Establishment upset, and the Methodists, Presbyterians, Baptists or Independents made the Established Church of England, than see the State ceasing to recognize God.

In what manner God would punish England, if English Governments cast off all connection with religion, I cannot tell. Whether he would punish us by some sudden blow, such as defeat in war, and the occupation of our territory by a foreign power; whether he would waste us away gradually and slowly by placing a worm at the roots of our commercial prosperity; whether he would break us to pieces by letting fools rule over us and allowing Parliaments to obey them, and permitting us, like the Midianites, to destroy one another; whether he would ruin us by sending a dearth of wise statesmen in the upper ranks, and giving the reins of power to communists, socialists, and mob-leaders; all these are points which I have no prophetical eye to see, and I do not pretend to determine. God's sorest judgments, the ancients said, are like millstones; they grind very slowly, but they grind very fine. The thing that I fear most for my country is gradual, insensible dry-rot and decay. But of one thing I am very sure. The State that begins by sowing the seed of national neglect of God, will sooner or later reap a harvest of national disaster and national ruin. If Disestablishment comes, it will do no hurt to the true Church of Christ, the body of real believers: *that* it is beyond the power of man to harm. It will do little comparative injury to the visible Episcopal Church of England: though impoverished and crippled in many ways she will still live, and not die. But it will do boundless harm to the State, and in the end will prove the ruin of all our greatness. For our dear old country's sake let us stand firm and resist Disestablishment.[1]

I bring my charge to a conclusion at this point. I have felt it my duty to call your attention to four very important subjects—Our unhappy divisions, Higher Criticism, the growing desecration of the Sabbath, the probable approach of Disestablishment. I commend all four to the serious consideration of all my clergy. They are not pleasant subjects, but they knock at the door, and imperatively demand admission to our minds, and I hope they will receive it. At any rate they supply food for thought.

There are several other deeply important subjects which I had intended to handle. Among these are the painful increase of gambling, and drunkenness, the extremely critical position of many of our Church Schools, the dearth of distinctive doctrinal

---

[1] The Welsh Church Disestablishment Act was passed in 1914, but its operation was suspended until six months after the close of the World War.

teaching in Board Schools, the huge social difficulties arising from strikes and lock-outs, and the collision of capital and labour. But I have no time today for such wide fields of discussion, and, however unwillingly, I must leave them alone.

It is very possible that this may be the last Triennial Charge I shall ever be allowed to deliver. A Bishop at seventy-seven cannot expect his life to be much prolonged. For all your kindness to me, during the thirteen years of my Episcopate, accept this day my hearty thanks. I wish I could have done more for the Diocese than I have done. But I think I can say, 'I have tried to do my duty.'

I should have been glad if this last Charge had been delivered under brighter prospects. But it is vain to conceal from ourselves that our horizon is dark on every side, dark ecclesiastically, dark politically, dark commercially, dark socially. What shall the end be? Is the tide never going to turn? Is the sun never going to rise? I cannot wonder that this text comes across many minds: 'Men's hearts failing them for fear, and for looking after those things which are coming on the earth' (Luke 21:26).

I conclude with a few sentences of a sermon preached by Edward Reynolds, Bishop of Norwich, in the reign of Charles II. They are so curiously applicable to our own days that I cannot forbear from quoting them:

> We live in failing times; we have found men of low degree vanity, and men of high degree a lie. We have trusted too much in Parliaments, and they have been broken, in princes, and they have given up the ghost. Our ships have been broken, our trade broken, our estates broken, our government broken, our hopes broken, our Church broken, nothing but our hearts and our sins unbroken. Well, it hath been our sin and our folly to trust in broken reeds, in perishing and dying comforts. Let it at last be our wisdom and our faith to trust in the living God, and by repentance and humiliation to remove our sins. Then no other impossibilities can obstruct the passage of mercy to us.[1]

---

[1] Edward Reynolds, *Works*, vol. 5, p. 180.

These are striking words. We may remember with thankfulness, that the sun did rise again, and the tide did flow, after Bishop Reynolds left the world. So may it be with us. Let us not sit down in despair, but each in our own place stand firm, work, fight, watch, hope, and pray.

13

WHAT IS WANTED?

The opening address at the fourteenth Liverpool Diocesan Conference, November 5, 1895.

REVEREND and Lay Brethren, I offer you a hearty welcome to our Fourteenth Diocesan Conference, and I trust you will find it as interesting and useful as it has been in former years. Our subjects have been carefully chosen by a Standing Committee freely elected by all the Rural Deaneries. They are subjects which are coming to the front in the present day, and it is well to hear what can be said about them, and try to make up our minds. When a whole Diocese assembles, as ours does for only two days in a year, time is too precious to spend on matters of second-rate importance.

I. *Our Own Diocese.* The story of our own Diocese during the last twelve months I must pass over rather briefly, for want of time. I need not remind you that things have happened since we last met in this room, of unspeakable importance to Church and State—things which few expected, things which will make history for our children's children, things which demand the serious attention of all Churchmen who are awake and know their duty. About some of these things, as your Bishop, you have a right to expect me to speak. In the meantime I will review the annual history of our Diocese as shortly as I can.

We have lost two of our incumbents by death since our last Conference—Mr Barton of Rainhill and Dr Knowles of Lydiate.

Three have resigned—Canon Fergie of Ince, Mr Everard of St Andrew, Southport, and Canon Livingston of Aigburth. Our entire staff of clergy at the present time consists of 205 incumbents and 213 curates, 90 more curates and 25 more incumbents than I found here when this Diocese was formed in 1880, giving an average of 6,000 people to each parochial district, and a singularly large proportion of curates. It is needless to say that such a provision is utterly inadequate to the spiritual wants of a new Diocese of 1,200,000 souls. Our good ship is thoroughly undermanned, and we cannot overtake either the pulpit or pastoral work that ought to be done. We do our best, and are working on. But it is rather trying to patience to be continually asked by strangers, and even by men who are not strangers, 'When are you going to build a cathedral?' No doubt a grand cathedral, like some which I could name, would be an ornament to Liverpool, and a beautiful luxury. A day may possibly come when some Lancashire man will come forward with an offering of half a million, and build and endow one. But in the meantime more clergy and more churches, within easy reach of every family, are a positive necessity in many of our overgrown parishes, and until they are provided it is waste of time to talk of a cathedral.

To the list of personal losses and changes in the last year, I must be allowed to add one name which I cannot pass over in silence. I refer to that honoured Christian layman, Mr Edward Pemberton Parry. As Chairman of two most important Institutions the Scripture Readers' Society and the Diocesan Church of England Temperance Society—he was probably known to many. For depth of religious character, consistency of life, wisdom in counsel, firmness in maintaining the Protestantism of the Church of England, readiness to give money to every good cause, I have found few lay Churchmen like him since I became Bishop of Liverpool. Quiet and unobtrusive as he was, his removal has made a wide gap in our ranks, and Liverpool is poorer by the departure of Mr Parry.

Church building has made comparatively little progress in our Diocese during the last year. St Gabriel, Huyton, is the only new church which I have been asked to consecrate. The old Parish Church of Farnworth has been reopened after a restoration so thorough and complete that it has cost at least £4,500. A better restoration, next to Ormskirk, I have never seen, and it is one which does infinite credit to the incumbent and his parishioners, as well as to the architect. St Simon and St Jude in Walton is rapidly approaching completion, and will be consecrated about the end of this year. Christ Church, Waterloo, in the new Rural Deanery of Bootle, and Trinity, Formby, are almost finished, and want little but more money to make them ready for consecration. A scheme for a large new parish church at North Meols has been launched, and is in hands which are not likely to let it drop. In fact, the foundation is laid. More churches are still greatly needed in some districts, where the population is continually growing; and I know it well. Blundell Sands; St Luke, Walton; St John's, Bootle; and Kensington Fields, are examples of what I mean. If the Established Church will not provide means of grace for the inhabitants of such districts, we must not be surprised if they join the ranks of Dissent. I have no great Church building Fund in my hands, as some suppose, in order to meet our wants. I can only look on with anxiety, and long for the return of days when Liverpool merchant-princes used to come forward and build churches themselves, like some men whom I could name. To tell us, in the meantime, that some of our existing churches are half empty, and we need no more, is a very weak and ignorant argument. Any intelligent Churchman understands why this state of things exists. As a general rule, a right man in the pulpit, and diligent, wise, and loving house-to-house visitation in the parish, are the cure for empty churches.

School building and school improvement, I am glad to say, have made great progress during the last year. In order to meet the heavy demands of the Education Department, and to prevent an increase of School Boards, our Diocese has made noble exertions, and raised very large sums of money. I cannot sufficiently thank the clergy and laity in some parts of our district for the gallant manner in which they have risen to the occasion, and shown a determination to retain the education of the Church's children in the Church's hands. At Wigan, at St Helen's, at Warrington, at Southport, at Walton, a generous liberality has been exhibited, without which we could not have held our ground. I trust that ground will be maintained, however great the struggle may be. The last words of Sir Henry Lawrence to his successor, before he died of his wounds at the siege of Lucknow, should not be forgotten: 'Never, never surrender!' In saying all this, I disclaim the least idea of enmity to Board schools. Here in Liverpool, as well as in London, they are a positive necessity. Without them, in many districts the children would grow up perfect heathens or infidels. Here, at any rate, I gratefully acknowledge that they provide a large amount of religious instruction. But I must prefer schools in which boys and girls are distinctly and regularly taught such doctrines as the Incarnation and Divinity of Christ, the Personality of the Holy Ghost, and the Atonement. Of such schools I hope the Diocese of Liverpool will never fail to keep up a supply, and I wish they could be found in every parish.

Concerning the general machinery for carrying on the work of the Diocese, I shall say very little this year, because I have not time. Our Diocesan Institutions continue to receive very slender support, and of course can do very little for those who apply to them for grants and aid. It is a state of things not in the least peculiar to our own district. All over England, Churchmen seem unwilling to support great common funds; they prefer giving money to objects near their own doors. I only wish the clergy of the Diocese would understand this, for at present many seem unable to do so. They have a vague impression that our Institutions have very large funds to dispose of; and when they apply for help, and get a very small grant, they are displeased, and think themselves unfairly treated. Once for all, let it be remembered that our Committees can only give what they have received; and if the Diocese gives little, they can give little in return. Those admirable Societies, the Liverpool Scripture Readers' Society and Diocesan Temperance Society, continue to do a large amount of useful work. The Mersey Mission to Seamen, the Girls' Friendly, and the Bible Women's Society, in their respective fields of labour, are most helpful to the cause of pure and undefiled religion. The newly-formed Mothers' Union is little known at present, but I believe it deserves very active support. The Sustentation Fund continues its valuable work, and, in my opinion, is far more likely to prosper on Diocesan than on National lines. On each and all of these agencies I could say much, if I had time.

I cannot close the report of our Diocese in the last twelve months without mentioning three things which appear to me to give cause for much thankfulness. These three are, the success of the general Mission in Liverpool last winter, the poll of Churchmen at the School Board election, and the demonstration in defence of the Welsh Church at the Philharmonic Hall, when Lord Cross, Mr Boscawen, and Alderman Phillips, came down to visit us. On each occasion I believe we might have done far better. But on each, I must frankly say, the result far surpassed my expectations. The Church of England gave some proof of her power, if she will only rise to the occasion, come forward and use it, as our Nonconformist brethren and the Roman Catholics always do. Churchmen this year, and especially at the School Board election, have exhibited a capacity for organized co-operation and active assertion of their just position, which I began to think they did not possess. In Liverpool they have shown that they are finding out their strength, and are beginning to use it. Far more might be done all over England at educational, municipal, and political elections, if all Churchmen would only awake, turn out, and vote on every occasion, instead of sitting lazily at home, and saying, 'It is no affair of mine.' For a reviving interest in public affairs in

1895 I am deeply thankful. I only hope it will continue, and we shall not go to sleep again.

II. *Social Problems.* From this brief sketch of things within our own Diocese I must now turn to matters of far more public and far-reaching importance. I refer to the new and critical position in which the Established Church has been suddenly placed by the recent Parliamentary election; and I feel it a plain duty, as your Bishop, to invite your attention to the consequent duties which are likely to devolve upon us as Churchmen.

I need hardly remind you that the reins of power have been placed in the hands of a Government which commands the largest majority in the House of Commons which any English Government has had since the Reform Bill of 1832.[1] Nor need I remind you that a large proportion of that majority consists of men who are likely to support the Church of England, and not allow it to be disestablished and disendowed without very good reasons. Now, what is this new Government likely to do? This is the point to which I propose to direct your attention.

We are told by men of 'light and leading' and influence, that plain social problems, not sweeping revolutionary changes of the British Constitution, will receive the special attention of the new Government, and that active efforts will be made to solve them. I am not surprised to hear this. We are in a critical position about social subjects in the present day, and I am sure that they demand the special attention of our rulers. Let me try to explain what I mean.

Every observing man knows that during the last sixty years there has been an immense increase of wealth among the upper ranks in England, and, at the same time, a comparatively small improvement in the pecuniary circumstances of the working classes, and a consequent tendency to estrangement and want of harmony between the two bodies. No doubt this is partly accounted for by the altered conditions under which much work

[1] In June 1895 Lord Salisbury formed his third (Conservative) Government.

is now done. Formerly, business was carried on by men of small capital, who employed small numbers of workmen and knew every one whom they employed. Now it is carried on by great companies of employers on a large scale, who cannot possibly know all whom they employ. One result is, that the gulf between masters and men is much wider than it was in the days of our grandfathers, and the relations between employers and employed have gradually become less friendly and intimate than they used to be.

Under these circumstances, you cannot find fault with the formation of Trade Unions in the present day. For anything I can see, they are likely to do good and promote peace, provided they are reasonably conducted, and do not interfere with the liberty of those who object to join them. So long as business is conducted on the vast scale of modern times, the working classes must not be blamed if they co-operate, combine, and endeavour to protect their interests and defend their rights in every legal way. But it is vain to shut our eyes to the fact that a new and very delicate condition of things has now been created, in which there is continual danger of friction between masters and men, which requires the vigilant attention of a wise Government, in order to secure justice to both sides. How to lessen that friction is one of the great social problems of our times, and demands the thoughtful notice of every Englishman.

We in Lancashire, at any rate, ought to help forward all efforts to bridge the gulf between employers and employed, and to promote friendly relations between them. We should strive to get disputes settled by Boards of Conciliation and Arbitration. We know by bitter experience the untold misery which trade disputes and strikes and lock-outs are continually bringing into our parishes, and the hindrances which they cause to the pastoral work of a clergyman. I am sure that any legislative measures for the promotion of temperance, purity, and thrift, and to secure the possession of healthy dwellings, plenty of good water, reading-rooms, and recreation grounds, ought to receive the active support of all clergymen who want to work their parishes with comfort. These things, of course, are not the gospel, and will not save souls. But they are helps and aids, and ought not to be despised.

One thing, however, we must never forget—no legislation, however clever and well-meant, will ever make all men rich and leave nobody poor. As long as the world stands, and human nature is unchanged, there will always be a vast amount of inequality. The Bible says, 'The poor shall never cease out of the land' (Deut. 15:11). Some men will be wise and some foolish, some will work hard and some will be lazy, some will be intemperate and some will be sober, some will be strong and some will be weak. This is a state of things which no laws and no Government can possibly prevent, and forgetfulness of such simple truths is one fertile source of our present-day social troubles. To meet the wave of unhealthy Socialism which is spreading over the country, and to promote the growth of a really healthy Socialism by bringing classes and masses more together, should be an object which all Churchmen should keep before them if they want to strengthen the Church of England. I earnestly hope that every wise pastor of a Lancashire parish will not forget this. The working man needs to be reminded that labour cannot do without capital, any more than capital can do without labour; that you cannot command crops and weather and markets, and prevent occasional depression of trade and excessive competition; that it is impossible to keep wages and supply of work at one uniform level; and that it is quite possible to frighten away capital and drive it into foreign countries. The rich employer, on the other hand, needs to have continually pressed on him the important duty of taking more personal interest in those whom he employs, the duty of going among them from time to time and seeing them face to face, the duty of dealing with them as those who have feelings and hearts and souls, as well as hands to do his work and fill his pockets. If there was more of this sort of thing, and more practical sympathy among employers, we should hear less of strikes among the employed. I have immense faith in the power of sympathy and kindness in dealing with the British workman. If the House of Commons will do its duty by wise social legislation, and the clergy will back it by kind house-to-house visitation, I believe there would be a great increase of 'sweetness and light' in Great Britain.

I cannot, however, leave this part of my address without making one remark which, at first sight, may appear strange. It is my deliberate opinion that the root of many of our social troubles in these days is the absence of a sufficiently high standard of Christian ethics throughout the land, and of plain Christlike teaching about every man's duty to his neighbour. We have certainly had a great revival of doctrinal teaching through missions. We have had a great revival of Catholic and Church teaching, so called. I must think that we need a great increase of thorough, searching teaching about the simple duties of charity, love, kindness, and sympathy among all classes, from the highest to the lowest. Of course such teaching alone will not save souls. It is not the famous three Rs: ruin, redemption, and regeneration. But we have no more right to neglect it than justification by faith or the Ten Commandments. It is my firm conviction that if more was heard from all our pulpits about such simple topics as brotherly love, consideration for one another, good nature, good temper, unselfishness, and readiness to be helpful and make the best of one another, it would go far to make the machinery of our social system work more smoothly than it does now. In short, England would be a happier country if there was more of the Sermon on the Mount and the 13th chapter of the First Epistle to the Corinthians in all churches.

I leave the thorny question of social problems by repeating my opinion, that an immense amount of good might be done if the heads of great Concerns in the manufacturing and colliery districts would take up the practice of going occasionally among their *hands* and talking with them face to face. To visit some of the houses in those long, dreary, monotonous lines of cottages, which are so often found near coalpits and cotton mills; to shake hands with the dwellers, and sit down, and exhibit a kindly interest in the births and deaths and marriages and sorrows and joys of the family—all this would cost little, but would do much. It would do more to bring master and man together than fifty Acts of Parliament. We are all of one blood, whether rich or poor. We are all travelling to the same long home, and shall need the same atoning blood at last. These things ought never to be forgotten. 'Am I my brother's keeper?' was the selfish saying of the first murderer, Cain.

III. *Church Reform.* Next to social problems, I hope that our new Government will not refuse to consider the very serious subject of Church Reform. I know that this is a wide, vague-sounding topic, and many shrink from it as useless and unpractical. But we may go too far in this direction. Events move very rapidly in these days, as they did when the Irish Church was disestablished in 1869. I think it wiser to face the subject betimes, and I propose to direct your attention to it today.

Some people, I know, will tell me that no one wants Church Reform. Such objectors cannot have noticed the speeches made in every part of the country during the recent campaign in defence of the Welsh Dioceses of the Established Church. I have read many of them carefully, and I have been greatly struck by the repeated declaration, 'We *must have our Church reformed as well as defended*.' No less a person than the Archbishop of Canterbury has reminded us in the words of a Prayer-book Collect, that our Church needs to be 'cleansed as well as defended.'

Some people will tell me that no Church Reform is needed. I think such objectors cannot have considered what they are saying. There have been hardly any changes in our good old Church for 230 years. During that long period most of our institutions have been so changed, altered, and reformed that we are like a new nation. Reason and common sense point out that our great ecclesiastical machine must need repairs, alterations, and adaptation to the times. To tell me that it is perfect, and needs no change, is like telling me that which is contrary to the experience of every human institution. The wear and tear of 230 years has done its work, and the machine is capable of improvement.

The field of Church Reform is so wide and varied that I have not the least idea of discussing everything which it includes.

I shall not touch the subject of liturgical revision. Our good old Prayer-book is not perfect, for it was compiled by uninspired men. But I see no minds in any of our schools of thought capable of mending it. Moreover, one set of revisers would want to throw overboard the Creeds and Articles as useless lumber, while another would want to bring back the very defective First Liturgy of Edward VI.

I shall not touch the subject of reunion with our Nonconformist brethren. I regard it as a beautiful castle in the air, and, until the nature of Englishmen alters, utterly impracticable. Keep the walls of separation as low as possible, and shake hands over them as often as you can. But do not dream that you will ever get the walls down. It is too late. It has been hopeless since the unhappy Act of Uniformity in 1662.

Finally, I shall not touch the subject of reunion with the corrupt Church of Rome. The very proposal is monstrous. It would be a disgraceful desertion of the principles of the Protestant Reformation, and an insult to the men who laid down their lives to procure for us the priceless privileges of an open Bible and a pure Gospel. A reform of this kind would be enough to make Bishop Jewel's bones turn in his grave under the floor of Salisbury Cathedral. It would be a base attempt to return to Egypt, and would ruin the Church of England.

I shall simply content myself with mentioning four practical points which appear to my eyes to deserve serious consideration.

Three of them I shall touch very briefly. The fourth and last will necessitate handling at some length.

(1) We need *reform of the Lower Houses of Convocation*, in the representation of the parochial clergy, both in the Province of Canterbury and of York. The population of the whole country has grown immensely during the last 230 years, and especially in the North. The number of the parochial clergy is probably ten times what it was in the reign of Charles II. But all this time the proctors[1] of the parochial clergy are pretty much what they were—excepting, of course, the addition of those returned by the new Dioceses. This cannot be right, and the parochial clergy have a just cause to complain. If this proportion of representation was right in the days of the Stuarts, it must be wrong in the days of Queen Victoria.

(2) We need *reform of our Ecclesiastical Courts*, and a revival of order and godly discipline in matters of doctrine and ritual. At present such order appears almost extinct. The stupid maintenance of the barbarous penalty of imprisonment for contumacy makes legal proceedings for disorder practically impossible. A clergyman has only got to be put in prison to make himself a popular martyr. The result is, that every clergyman does what is right in his own eyes, and liberty of ritual as well as doctrine is threatening the disruption of the whole Church of England. To go on year after year proclaiming to mankind that British wisdom cannot devise some reform of the Ecclesiastical Courts is a sad reflection on British common sense.

(3) We need, thirdly, a *reform and reconstruction of our Canons*. At present they are practically useless, and many Churchmen know nothing of their existence, and, of course, know nothing of their contents. Yet other Churches, beside their great Confessions of faith and doctrine, have codes of rules and regulations about minor matters, and it is hard to see why the Church of England

---

[1] Proctors—persons managing causes (in this case ecclesiastical) in courts administering canon law.

should not have hers. At present not a few of our Canons are obsolete, and some of them superseded and abrogated by the law of the land. In fact the whole body of Canons is like a stuffed beast in a museum, a venerable curiosity, but of no practical benefit to the Church. Surely the time has come for a change. The Northern House of Convocation has made a move about the matter, and I trust it will not come to a standstill.

(4) The fourth and last subject about which Church Reform is needed is one of such serious importance that I shall be obliged to handle it at some length, and perhaps startle you by saying some very strong things, and perhaps things with which many will not agree. That subject is the very *unsatisfactory position of lay Churchmen* in the present day, and the absolute necessity of some clear recognition of their rights in the management of the Church's affairs.

I will begin with a definition. *When we talk of the laity of a Church, what do we mean*? We mean, of course, all within her pale who are not ordained to any ministerial office. We mean the people of the Church, and especially the communicants, in contradistinction to the *clergy*. How immensely important a body they are, it is needless to say. It would be a waste of time to dwell long on such a point. Without the lay members a Church can hardly be said to exist. No doubt the old saying is true, '*Ubi tres, ibi ecclesia.*'[1] But a general without an army, a colonel without a regiment, or a ship-captain without a crew, are not more useless and helpless than a Church consisting of clergy without laity. In the Church of England at any rate there is at present no lack of laymen. There are probably five hundred lay members in proportion to each clergyman. In point of numbers alone, therefore, apart from all other considerations, the laity are a most important part of the Church of England.

I will next inquire, *What was the position of the laity in New Testament Churches*? This is an inquiry which demands special

---

[1] 'Where three (come together), there is the church.'

notice, and deserves special attention. I am much mistaken if a close examination of this point will not astonish some people, and make them open their eyes. I can hardly find an instance in God's word in which the ministers *alone* are ever called 'the Church,' or ever act for the Church without the laity uniting and co-operating in their action. Are the deacons appointed? The Twelve recommend it, 'but the multitude' choose (Acts 6:5). Is a Council held to consider whether the heathen converts should be circumcized? The decision arrived at is said to come from 'the apostles, and elders, and brethren' (Acts 15:23). Are inspired Epistles written by St Paul to particular Churches? In eight cases they are addressed to the 'Church—the saints—the faithful brethren' and in only one case (the Epistle to the Philippians) is there any mention of 'bishops and deacons' in the opening address, and even there they come in at its end. That there was to be a distinct order of men to minister to the Church is, to my eyes, most plainly taught in the New Testament. But that 'the Church' in every city or country meant *the laity*, and especially the communicants, and the ministers were only regarded as the 'servants of the Church' (2 Cor. 4:5), seems to me as clear as the sun at noonday. As for a Church in which the clergy acted alone, settled everything, decided everything, judged everything, and managed everything, and the laity had no voice at all, I cannot find the shadow of such a thing in the Acts or Epistles of the New Testament. I trust that Churchmen who remember the Sixth Article of our English Church will not fail to observe this.

I will now proceed to examine *the present position of the laity in the Church of England*. It is a position which falls very short of the New Testament standard. It is vain to deny that in the actual working machinery of our Church, in its arrangements, plans, schemes, and normal organization, the lay members have comparatively no place at all! Do the Bishops meet in solemn conclave at Lambeth Palace to consider the state of our Zion? There is no place for the laity. Does Convocation hold its annual debates?

There is no representation of the laity. Has a vacant Living or Incumbency to be filled up? The appointment is generally made without the slightest regard to the opinion of the parishioners. I state simple facts. I defy anyone to deny their correctness.

With every desire to make the best of our Church and its Constitution, I cannot avoid the conclusion, that in the matter of the laity its system is at present defective and infra-scriptural. I cannot reconcile the position of the English lay Episcopalian in 1895 with that of his brother in any apostolic Church eighteen centuries ago. I cannot make the two things square. To my eyes, it seems that in the regular working of the Church of England almost everything is left in the hands of the clergy. In all this there is no intentional slight. Not the smallest reflection is implied on the trustworthiness and ability of the laity. But from one cause or another they are left out in the cold, passive recipients and not active members in a huge ecclesiastical corporation; sleeping partners and not working agents in an unwieldy and ill-managed concern. In short, in the normal action of the Church of England, lay Churchmen have been left on a siding. Like soldiers not wanted, they have fallen out of the ranks, retired to the rear, and sunk out of sight.

What is *the true cause of this anomalous state of things*? It is one which may easily be detected. The position of the English laity is neither more nor less than a rag and remnant of Popery. It is part of that '*damnosa haereditas*'[1] which Rome has bequeathed to our Church, and which has never been completely purged away. Our Reformers themselves were not perfect men, and the characteristic Tudor jealousy of Queen Elizabeth prevented their perfecting the work of the English Reformation. Among other blots which they left on the face of our Church, I must sorrowfully admit that neglect of the interests of the laity was not the least one. To make the clergy mediators between Christ and man, to exalt them far above the laity and put all ecclesiastical power into

---

[1] An inheritance entailing loss.

their hands, to clothe them with sacerdotal authority and regard them as infallible guides in all Church matters—this has always been an essential element of the Popish system. This mischievous element our Reformers, no doubt, ought to have corrected by giving more power to the laity, as John Knox did in Scotland. They omitted to do so, either from having been originally brought up under the Romish system, or from want of time, or from want of Royal permission. The unhappy fruit of the omission has been that gradually the chief authority in our Church matters has fallen almost entirely into the hands of the clergy, and the laity have been left without their due rights and powers.

What are *the consequences of this unsatisfactory state of things*? They are precisely what might be expected—evil and only evil. Departure from the mind of God, even in the least things, is always sure to bear bitter fruit. Lifted above their due position, the English clergy have always been inclined to sacerdotalism, and an overweening estimate of their own privileges and powers. Fallen below their due position, the English laity, with occasional brilliant exceptions, have taken little interest in Church matters, and have been too ready to leave everything ecclesiastical to be managed by the clergy. In the meantime, for three centuries the Church of England has suffered great and almost irremediable damage.

Seldom considered, seldom consulted, seldom trusted with power, seldom invested with authority, the English lay Churchman, as a rule, is ignorant, indifferent, or apathetic about Church questions. How few laymen know anything about Church work in their own Diocese! How few care one jot for Convocation! How few could tell you, if their lives depended on it, who are the Proctors of their own Diocese! How few understand the meaning of the great doctrinal controversies by which their Church is almost rent asunder! How few exhibit as much personal interest or anxiety about them, as a Roman spectator would exhibit about the fight of a couple of gladiators in the arena of the Colosseum!

How few could tell you anything more than this, 'that there is some squabble among the parsons; and they don't pretend to understand it'! This is a melancholy picture; but I fear it is a sadly correct one. And yet who can wonder? The English laity have never yet had their rightful position in the management of the Church of England.

You may lay it down as an infallible rule, that the best way to make a man feel an interest in a business is to make him a 'part of the concern.' The rule applies to ecclesiastical corporations as well as to commercial ones. The Scotch Presbyterians, the English Nonconformists, the Irish and American Episcopalians, the Colonial Episcopalians, all realize the importance of this principle, and take care to carry it out. The Established Church of England alone has lost sight of this principle altogether. The laity have never been properly employed, or trusted, or considered, or called forward, or consulted, or placed in position, or armed with authority, as they ought to have been. The consequence is that, as a body, they neither know, nor care, nor feel, nor understand, nor think, nor read, nor exercise their minds, nor trouble their heads as much as they ought to do, about Church affairs. The system under which this state of things has grown up is a gigantic mistake. The sooner it is cut up by the roots and turned upside down the better. If we want to remove one grand cause of our Church's present weakness we must completely alter the position of the laity. On this point, if on no other, there is great need of Church Reform.

But what are the reforms that are needed? Grant for a moment that we have at length discovered that our lay Churchmen are not in their rightful position. What is the remedy for the evil? What is the change that is required? What ought to be done?

The reform I plead for in the position of our laity is simply this. I plead for the general recognition of the mighty principle, that *nothing ought to be done in the Church without the laity*, in things great or in things small. I plead that the laity ought to have a part and voice and hand and vote in everything that the Church says and does, except ordaining and ministering in the congregation. I plead that the voice of the Church of England ought to be not merely the voice of the bishops and presbyters, but the voice of the laity as well, and that no Church action should ever be taken, and no expression of Church opinion ever put forth, in which the lay communicants have not an equal share with the clergy. They have a voice in all our Colonial Churches. They have a voice in the Irish and American Episcopal Churches. I fail to see any good reason why they should not have a voice in all the affairs of the Established Church of England. Such a reform would be a return to New Testament principles. Such a reform would increase a hundredfold the strength of the Church of England.

(1) In my opinion, *no English Convocation ought ever to be gathered together without an equal representation of the laity.* The existing Convocations of Canterbury and York sometimes discuss measures of self-reform. They may spare themselves the trouble of incubation unless they are prepared to throw open their doors, and admit to their counsels the laity. No mere clerical Parliament, however rich in deans, archdeacons, canons, and parochial clergy, will ever possess the country's confidence, or be regarded with much interest, or command much attention. The laity must have a voice and place in Convocation, if the laity are to care for Convocation's proceedings. Once let them in, and recognize their title to sit on equal terms with the clergy, and Convocation debates would soon be diligently studied, and become a different thing. A well-selected body of sensible lay Churchmen would never allow long weary speeches about the 'reserved sacrament,' or let union with decayed and unsound Churches be discussed, while Protestant Nonconformists are completely ignored.

(2) In my opinion, *no parochial clergyman ought ever to attempt the management of his parish or congregation without constantly consulting the laity.* If he does not like to have anything so stiff and formal-sounding as a 'parochial council,' let him at any rate often

confer with his church-wardens and leading communicants about his work. Especially let him do nothing in the way of changing times and modes of worship, nothing in the matter of new ceremonials, new decorations, new gestures, new postures, without first taking counsel with his lay people. The church is theirs, and not his; he is their servant, and they are not his, they have surely a right to be consulted. Who can tell the amount of offence that might be prevented if clergymen always acted in this way? No people, I believe, are more reasonable than lay Churchmen, if they are only approached and treated in a reasonable way. Above all, let every parochial incumbent make a point of teaching every communicant that he is an integral part of the Church of England, and is bound to do all that he can for its welfare. On this point, I grieve to say, the Methodists and Dissenters beat Churchmen hollow. With them every new member is a new home missionary in their cause. Never will things go well with the Church of England until every individual member realizes that he is 'a part of the concern,' and has a duty to do to his Church, and keeps that duty continually in view.

(3) In my opinion, *no appointment to a living or cure of souls ought ever to be made without allowing the laity a voice in the matter*. This is a strong opinion, I know; but it is one which I have deliberately formed. Our present system is a total mistake, and a grievous abuse. Clergymen are constantly thrust upon unwilling parishes and disgusted congregations, who are entirely unfit for their position. The parishioners are consequently driven away from Church, and the Establishment suffers irreparable damage. It is high time to give up this system. I have no faith in Diocesan Patronage Boards. I doubt extremely if they would work well and give satisfaction. I believe they would either be divided among themselves, or else would fill the Church with weak, colourless clergymen. By all means keep patronage where it is at present, divided, and not in any one set of hands. But let every patron, or body of patrons, be required to send the name of the clergyman

whom it is proposed to nominate to a vacant living, to the church-wardens, one month before the name is presented to the Bishop. Let the name of the proposed new incumbent be publicly read out in church, and affixed to the church doors on four Sundays consecutively, and let anyone be invited to object if he can. Let the objector be obliged to satisfy the Bishop that there are good reasons, whether doctrinal or practical, for his objections; and let the Bishop have power, if satisfied, to refuse the patron's nominee, with liberty to the patron to appeal. Of course such a safeguard as this might often be ineffectual. The parishioners may pay no more attention to a 'si quis'[1] about the appointment of a new incumbent than they do to a 'si quis' about the squire's fox-hunting son, who proposes to be ordained and to change a red coat for a black one. The Bishop may find himself sometimes in a very disagreeable and troublesome position, and make great mistakes. But there is nothing new in that. No Bishops are infallible. The objections to the nominee may often be frivolous or incapable of proof. But at any rate *a principle* would be established. The laity of a parish could no longer complain that they are perpetually handed over to new parsons without having the slightest voice in the transaction. One right the laity possess already, I remind them, which I heartily wish they would exercise more frequently than they do. They may effectually prevent young men being ordained who are unfit for orders, by objecting when the 'si quis' is read. Well would it be for the Church of England if the laity in this matter would always do their duty!

Such are the reforms I suggest in the position of lay Churchmen. They are no doubt very wide and sweeping, and bristle with difficulties. But I have yet to learn that they are not most desirable in the abstract, and imperatively required by the times. They will bring down on me a host of objectors. For this I am quite prepared.

[1] 'If anyone' (has objections to offer).

'Sacrilegious reform!' some will cry. They think it downright wicked to let the laity have anything to do with spiritual matters. They wish them to be nothing but Gibeonites, hewers of wood and drawers of water for the clergy.

Well! I reply, look at the Irish Church, and learn wisdom. If Disestablishment comes, and come it may, you will be obliged to cast yourselves on the aid of the laity, whether you like it or not. Even if it does not come, you will never be really strong unless you place the laity in their rightful position. As to the vague talk about sacrilege, it is all nonsense. Touch the idea with the Ithuriel[1] spear of Scripture, and it will vanish away.

But 'it is a dangerous reform,' some men will cry. 'The laity will take the reins into their hands, and lord it over the consciences of the clergy.' Such fears are simply ridiculous. There is far more real danger in letting the laity sit idle, and giving them no active interest in the Church's affairs. I have a better opinion of the laity than these alarmists have. The new ecclesiastical machinery may work awkwardly at first, like a new steam-engine, when its joints are stiff and its bearings hot. The laity may kick over the traces at first a little, and not understand what they have to do. But give them time, give them time. Show them that you trust them, and make them see what is wanted, and I have no doubt the laity would soon settle down in their place, and work with a will.

I leave the subject of Church reforms at this point. I shall never live to see them myself. Church work is particularly slow work, and reform-works slowest of all. I can only commend them to your serious attention. They will all come to the front sooner or later; and before the next attack on the Establishment comes (and come it will), I hope Churchmen will set their house in order, and boldly amend the things that are wanting. It is useless to flatter ourselves that there are no weak points in our line of Church defence. The

---

[1] In Milton's *Paradise Lost*, Ithuriel was one of two angels sent by Gabriel to search for Satan after his entry into Paradise. He was armed with a spear, the slightest touch of which exposed deceit.

recent campaign in defence of the Welsh Dioceses has shown that there are not a few, and it will be judicial blindness to ignore them.

IV. *Our Divisions.* The last and most sorrowful subject which I propose to handle in this Address is the continuance of *our unhappy divisions.* I do not see at present the slightest symptom of their abatement. On the contrary, they seem to my eyes to increase, harden, and crystallize. So long as the mass and the confessional and Mariolatry are tolerated, permitted, and let alone in every direction, so long a large number of the clergy, and a still larger proportion of the laity, are vexed, uneasy, and dissatisfied, and are beginning to say, 'What is the use of the Established Church of England?' It is a state of things which cannot last for ever. A house divided against itself cannot stand.

Remedies and healing medicines at present I can see none. Our ecclesiastical horizon is dark and gloomy in every quarter. Unity no doubt is an excellent thing, and many seem ready to sacrifice precious truth in order to obtain it. But to my eyes unity among Churchmen seems as far off as ever. It will never be obtained by holding meetings, and making fine speeches about it, and wailing over our divisions, while nothing practical is proposed. Such mere talk of the lips reminds me of a baby crying in the dark. It will never be obtained by trying to make all preachers avoid disputed subjects, and be content with a vague, dead-alive, pointless, toothless, negative theology. I look with amazement at the simplicity of those amiable people who dream of unity on such lines, and forget that nothing does good in a fallen world except a full outspoken statement of the whole Gospel of the grace of God.

However, if you wish to know my opinion about the *roots* of our troubles, you shall have it. I am convinced that much of our division is traceable to two grave defects in the Churchmen of this day. I will state them briefly and commend them to your thoughtful attention.

(1) For one thing, I believe there is everywhere in this day a most serious diminution of the good old custom of *private reading*

of the Bible. Between the growth of periodicals and the mischievous influence of what is called 'Higher Criticism,' I have a strong impression that Bibles are not read as much and as carefully as they were two hundred years ago. Men 'err, not knowing the Scriptures.'

I am well aware that there are more Bibles in Great Britain at this moment than there ever were since the world began. There is more Bible-buying and Bible-selling, more Bible-printing and Bible-distributing, than there ever was since England was a nation. There is a general and righteous determination to have the Bible read by children in our schools. But all this time I fear we are in danger of forgetting, that to *have* the Bible is one thing, and to *read* it privately ourselves quite another.

I am afraid that the Bible of many a man and woman in Great Britain is *never read at all*. In one house it lies in a corner, stiff, cold, glossy, and fresh as it was when it came from the bookseller's shop. In another it lies on a table, with its owner's name written in it, a silent witness against him day after day. In another it lies on some high shelf, neglected and dusty, to be brought down only on grand occasions, such as a birth in the family, like a heathen idol at its yearly festival. In another it lies deep down at the bottom of some box or drawer, among the things not wanted, and is never dragged forth into the light of day until the arrival of sickness, the doctor, and death. These things are sad and solemn. But they are true.

I am afraid that many in Great Britain who read the Bible, *do not read it aright*. One man looks over a chapter on Sunday evening, but that is all! Another reads a chapter every day to his servants at family prayers, but that is all! A third goes a step further, and hastily reads a verse or two in private every morning, before he goes out of his house. A fourth goes further still, and reads as much as a chapter or two every day, though he does it in a great hurry, and omits it on the smallest pretext. But each and every one of these men does what he does in a heartless, scrambling, formal kind of way. He does it coldly, as a duty. He does not do it with appetite and pleasure. He is glad when the task is over. He forgets it all when the book is shut. This is a sad picture. But in multitudes of cases, oh, how true!

But why do I think all this? What makes me speak so confidently? Listen to me a few moments, and I will lay before you some evidence. Neglect of the Bible is like disease of the body. It shows itself in the face of a man's conduct. It tells its own tale. It cannot be hid.

I fear that many neglect the Bible, *because of the enormous ignorance of true religion which everywhere prevails.* There are thousands of professing Christians in this country who know literally nothing about the Gospel. They could not give you the slightest account of its distinctive doctrines. They have no more idea of the meaning of conversion, grace, faith, justification, and sanctification, than of so many words and names in Arabic. And can I suppose such persons read the Scriptures? I cannot suppose it. I do not believe they do.

I fear that many neglect the Bible, *because of the utter indifference with which they regard false doctrine.* They will talk with perfect coolness of others having become Roman Catholics, or Socinians, or Mormonites, or Deists, or Agnostics, as if it did not signify much, and was all the same thing in the long run. And can I suppose such persons search the Scriptures? I cannot suppose it. I do not believe they do.

I fear that many neglect the Bible, *because of the readiness with which they receive false teaching.* They are led astray by the first false prophet they meet with who 'comes in sheep's clothing,' and has a pleasant voice, a nice manner, and a gift of eloquent speech. They swallow all he says without inquiry, and believe him as implicitly as papists do the Pope. And can I suppose such persons search the Scriptures? I cannot suppose it. I do not believe they do.

I declare my firm conviction, that an idle neglect of the Bible is one cause of the ignorant formal Christianity which is so widely prevalent in these latter days, and one root of our unhappy divisions and disunion.

(2) But neglect of private Bible-reading is not the only defect among the Churchmen of the present day. I suspect there is a growing disposition among the clergy *to disregard the Thirty-nine Articles*, and to ignore their teaching on many important points. I need not remind you that those Articles are practically the Church's Confession of Faith. The preface to them in the Prayer-book distinctly asserts this, and you cannot repeal or abrogate them without pulling to pieces the Church of England. Moreover, every clergyman, when he is instituted to a living, must publicly read them before his congregation, and solemnly declare his assent to their contents. What then are we to say when a clergyman, after this serious public act, proceeds continually to teach doctrines which cannot be reconciled with the Articles, and especially with the Articles about the Lord's Supper? What indeed are we to say? I cannot answer. It exhibits a most unhealthy and dangerous condition of things within our Church, and makes me tremble for the ark of God. Our forefathers used to think that subscriptions and declarations meant something, and that it was not honourable to ignore them, or teach what they were intended to condemn. But the old order seems to have changed. I make no attempt to explain it, and can only look on with sorrow and amazement.

Nothing, however, I am satisfied, will ever make the majority of intelligent lay Churchmen in this day believe that the Thirty-nine Articles were meant to be a dead letter, or that the many ritual novelties in public worship which are to be seen all over the land were ever intended by Parker, Jewel, Grindal, Whitgift, and the other Elizabethan Reformers, to be Church worship. Nothing will ever make them believe that sacerdotalism and sacramentalism are the true doctrine of the Church of England. Nothing will ever make them believe that the Articles and Prayer-book give any sanction to the mass, auricular confession, prayers for the dead, invocation of saints, and an *ex opere operato*[1] view of the

---

[1] *Lit.* 'from the work performed.' The view that the sacraments yield their benefits by the mere outward act of administration.

sacraments, as if they conferred grace on all who receive them, while the Articles distinctly say, 'in such only as rightly receive the same, they have a wholesome effect and operation.' They are watching, waiting, and wondering whereunto this state of things will grow. The Upper Ten Thousand, and many ecclesiastics in high position, appear to my eyes like men in a balloon, and not to realize what is going on upon earth among the laity. I have no doubt the English layman is a patient creature, and will stand a good deal. But there is a limit to patience. I believe that any attempt at this moment to prohibit evening communion, or to enforce the eastward position on every clergyman, would create a most serious disturbance in thousands of parishes, endanger the very existence of the Established Church, and set people thinking about secession or disruption. There are breakers ahead, and it is the duty of wise pilots not to disregard them.

Some men, I know, laugh at the idea of the Church being in danger. They point to the recent elections, and victories at the polling booths, and tell us that the Church was never so strong as she is just now. I cannot agree with them. To my mind it seems foolish to talk of the Church's strength when such painful divisions exist in our Church's ranks. I am afraid there is silently growing up among our middle-class laity, and the intelligent artisans, a strong feeling of dislike to the Romanizing tendency of the last fifty years, and the morbid hungering of many of the clergy for more Romish novelties in our worship. They are offended, irritated, and annoyed, and mischief is being done. The voting power at Parliamentary elections is in their hands, and unless there is a change for the better, they will use it one day. I have grave doubts whether some of our lay Churchmen will continue to defend our Establishment if another attack is made, unless they can have some assurance that its Protestantism is to be fully and honestly maintained. At present their confidence is greatly shaken. They will defend a Protestant Establishment, but not a semi-Popish one. They will fight to the bitter end to maintain the Church of the Reformation, but they will not lift a finger to support a weak imitation of the Church of Rome. The Church's dangers, I firmly believe, are more from within than without.

My reverend and lay Brethren, we are drifting, drifting, drifting, and what the end will be no man can tell. In the meantime, we must cultivate meekness, kindness, good temper, charity, and patience, and work together, when we can, and while we can, and where we can. With God nothing is impossible Our grand old Church has survived many storms and trying seasons. Who can tell that there may not be 'a good time coming,' and she may yet begin the next century in a healthier and more united condition than that which she is in just now? For this, let us agree to pray. Let us daily pray that the Reformed Church of England may be so 'guided and governed by the Holy Spirit, that all her members may be led into the way of truth, and hold the faith in unity of spirit, in the bond of peace, and in righteousness of life.'

14

ABOUT OUR CHURCH
IN 1896

An address given at the fifteenth annual Liverpool Diocesan
Conference, at St George's Hall, November 3, 1896.

REVEREND and Lay Brethren, once more, for the fifteenth time, I am allowed to preside at our Annual Diocesan Conference, and I offer you a hearty welcome. We are gathered together at a somewhat critical period in the history of the Established Church of England. Questions seriously affecting its interests, and of peculiarly grave and delicate character, are continually coming to the front, and demand the thoughtful attention of all loyal Churchmen. Two of them have been wisely selected by your Standing Committee for discussion this week. I refer to Church Reform and Anglican Orders.

Unhappily these two questions do not stand alone. There are others demanding solution, of no less importance, which are being pressed on our notice in these days, both in Parliament and in the Press, which I propose to consider in this Address. About them all a Diocese has a right to expect its bishop to express an opinion. Without further preface, I proceed to do so this morning. I shall try first to handle the Church's Present Problems and then the Church's Present Position.

I. The first and far the most important subject which demands your attention is *Disestablishment*. I need hardly remind you how much we heard of this matter a year ago. The bold attempt of the recent Government to disestablish and disendow the Church in Wales,[1] to dissolve the union of Church and State, and to deprive the Welsh clergy of their incomes, aroused an unexpectedly strong feeling throughout the land, and made thousands of sleeping Churchmen sit up and open their eyes. The attempt you will remember, failed so completely that it is hard to understand why it was ever made. The enemies of the Church entirely miscalculated their own strength, and the defenders were no less surprised by the amount of support which they received in almost every quarter, from north to south and from cast to west, and nowhere more than in Lancashire.

But have we done with Disestablishment? Is the subject shelved and buried for ever? Is it an old fossil for which there is no resurrection? I warn you not to give way to the thought. The doors of the temple of Janus[2] are not yet closed. This is not the time to lay down our arms and go to sleep, but rather to keep awake and be on our guard. Disestablishment has been once accepted by the House of Commons within the last four years. Will anyone undertake to say what the next Parliamentary election will produce? Political power in this day is very much in the hands of the working classes, and the upper ten thousand are comparatively a small minority. The pendulum may take a violent swing in an anti-Church direction. Once let the voters get into their heads the notion that all clergymen are narrow-minded sacerdotalists and want to Romanize the Church of England, and Disestablishment will come. The battle is not yet over, whatever we may think of the last election. The working classes will not vote to maintain a semi-Romish establishment, and if the Church loses their confidence, she will be ruined.

The length and breadth of the harm which would be done by Disestablishment and Disendowment it would be hard to estimate. The one would certainly accompany the other. It is foolish to

---

[1] In March, 1895, H. H. Asquith (Home Secretary in the Rosebery Government) had introduced a Welsh Church Disestablishment Bill in the House of Commons.

[2] The Roman god of transitions, i.e. the beginning and end of all things.

suppose that the Church will be allowed to dissolve partnership with the State and walk off with all her income. In the agricultural districts, hundreds of Churches would have to be closed. Farmers and labourers alone could not support a minister. Services would have to be given up, and people left like sheep without a shepherd. Even in towns the hands of the Church of England would be greatly weakened, foreign and home missions would be sadly crippled, and every philanthropic agency would receive diminished support. Of course the good old Church of England would still live and not die, but she would live with immensely lessened powers of usefulness; and with Disestablishment and Disendowment would come Disruption. No doubt some thoughtless Churchmen may fancy that separation of Church and State would be an unmixed benefit and a blessing. I take leave to doubt this. The weak points of an Established Church no doubt are many, but the weak points of voluntary Churches are neither few nor small.

The present duty of Churchmen, I believe, is very clear, if the Disestablishment controversy returns. We must keep our powder dry, and be prepared to fight to the bitter end if need be. We must constantly expose and answer the ridiculous slanders and misrepresentations of those who envy our comparative prosperity, and hunger and thirst for a sweeping change.

It is not true, for example, as it is sometimes asserted, that clergymen, as a body, are all sacerdotalists, and want to Romanize the Church of England. There are thousands of clergymen in this day who dislike sacerdotalism and Romanism in every form, and are as sound Protestants as any liberationists in the land.

It is not true that the bishops and clergy of the Established Church are rolling in wealth, and could spare half their incomes. Thousands of the clergy in rural districts are almost ruined by agricultural depression. Even in towns I suspect that many leading Nonconformist ministers receive more pecuniary support than our own parochial clergy. As for the bishops, many of them find it hard to make both ends meet, with the incessant demands made upon their purses. The late Archbishop Longley used to say that he got on pretty well when he was Headmaster of Harrow School, but began to grow poor when he became Bishop of Ripon, got poorer still when he was made Archbishop of York, and was poorest of all when he was Archbishop of Canterbury.[1]

It is not true that the Prayer-book is a mere Popish compilation. The greater part of it is taken out of the Epistles, Gospels, and Psalms. The prayers, as a whole, will bear a favourable comparison with most of the extemporaneous supplications and intercessions in non-episcopal places of worship.

Ignorant statements, such as those I have just mentioned, have been far too often made in the last two or three years, and ought to be boldly and firmly contradicted and corrected on public occasions. Unhappily they are greedily believed, and swallowed, and circulated among the enemies of the Established Church. 'Slander,' says a Chinese proverb, 'is an insect which has long wings but no feet. It cannot stand, but it can fly.'

The printing press, as well as the pulpit and the platform, should be diligently used in resisting the Disestablishment movement. Cheap and simple literature should be widely circulated, and especially literature which gives a plain, honest account of the history of the Church of England during the last three hundred and fifty years. Few Churchmen have a very clear knowledge of the enormous debt which we owe to the Reformation, and of the immense mass of error and superstition from which it delivered us. Not a few have imbibed the stupid idea that our Church was in a dark state before Archbishop Laud arose, and are totally ignorant of the good work done by Parker, Grindal, Whitgift, Jewel, and Hooker. To spread useful knowledge and let in light on blind eyes, is one great business which the friends of the Establishment should take in hand, if they want to repel the attacks of our foes.

---

[1] The appointments listed cover the period 1829–68 (Longley was also for four years Bishop of Durham).

I leave the subject of Disestablishment with one sorrowful reflection. I cannot refrain from expressing my firm conviction that some of the most efficient helpers of the movement are within the pale of our own Church. That large and influential body of clergymen and upper-rank laymen, which appears determined to Romanize the Protestant Church of England, is gradually shaking the confidence of many Churchmen, digging the grave of the Establishment, and making work for the next Parliamentary election. I warn you once more that the middle and working classes have now got immense political power in their hands, and are determined to use it. I am certain they will not elect a House of Commons which favours sacerdotalism, the mass, and the confessional. They will refuse to support the Church at the polling-booth, if they do not feel confidence in Church candidates; and then will come Disestablishment. I am too old to see it. But remember my words: It will come.

II. The second subject to which I propose to call your attention this day is the very important one of *Elementary Church Education*.

This, I need hardly say, is a very difficult and thorny question, and contains knots which the ablest statesmen find it hard to untie. The roots of the difficulty, in my opinion, may be traced to two huge political mistakes from which we are suffering to this day. One of those mistakes was made in 1870, when the Board School system was called into existence. If at that date the Government had boldly insisted that the Bible, the Creed, the Lord's Prayer, and the Ten Commandments, should form part of the religious instruction given to every child in schools helped by the State, unless a parent conscientiously objected, I doubt if one person in twenty throughout the land would have opposed the plan. I believe it was a terrible omission to make the Bible optional to every Board, and to leave out the Creed altogether. The other mistake was made only a few years ago, when the 'Free Education' Act was passed under the vain idea that it was necessary, and would be popular.[1] A greater blunder, in my judgment, was never made. Nobody really wanted 'Free Education.' Nobody asked for it. Nobody said 'Thank you' for it. When it came, the income from school pence in many cases was destroyed, and some three millions of money were recklessly thrown away and not saved, while labourers at ten shillings a week in Suffolk were as willing to pay for their children's schooling as for their children's clothes or food. However, these two mistakes have been made, and are not likely to be given up or repealed. Political clocks are never put back. The result is a perpetual grievance about *religion* in Board schools, and a perpetual worry about *money* in Church schools.

The position of the great question of education at this moment is a very anxious and critical one. The Government, you will remember, brought into the House of Commons last session a huge Bill which proposed to deal with the whole subject. It was much too large a mouthful for any modern British House to swallow. It was a long, complicated, sweeping measure, which, after an immense amount of weary discussion, was withdrawn, and has come to an end. We are promised another Bill in the next session, but at present no one can tell us what it will be like. Will it be long or short? Will it be simple or complicated? Will it contain many provisions of the old Bill which foundered—fished up and re-adapted—or a brand-new measure? All these are inquiries which I cannot answer; and, as Faraday used to say, it is best to keep our minds in a state of judicious suspense.

There are, however, three points about which Churchmen should put down their feet very firmly, and should not hesitate to tell the Government what they expect any new Education Bill to provide. I will tell you what they are. One is the abolition of the objectionable 17s. 6d. limit.[2] Another is the entire exemption from taxes of all schools and school buildings. Another is the just

---

[1] 1891. The Act made the great majority of elementary schools free, and reduced the charge in the remainder.

[2] 17s. 6d. had been made the maximum annual grant of state aid per child at school.

right to claim from Government a reasonable annual support for all elementary Church schools, inasmuch as they educate half the children in the land, and in many cases freely. On these three points I hope all Churchmen will stand together, leave no stone unturned, and, if needful, fight to the last.

There are, however, three points in the Education campaign before us which I frankly admit are disputable, and concerning which I can understand a good deal being said on both sides. I hope I am willing to preserve an open mind about them. At present, however, I hold rather decided opinions about all the three, and I will state them as briefly as I can.

(1) For one thing, I certainly prefer Rate aid to State aid. A fixed State aid per head would be very satisfactory in some schools, but very unsatisfactory in others. The Rate aid would be managed far better by County Councils and Corporations, who would apportion it according to the need of each school, giving more to some and less to others. I am not so much afraid of the management of Church schools falling into bad hands under Rate aid as some appear to be. I have great faith in the fairness and common sense of the English laity, and I do not believe they would ignore the judgment of Church school managers by interfering needlessly with religious teaching or teachers. My heaviest objection to State aid is my strong belief that it would be utterly inadequate and insufficient. I have not forgotten that four shillings a head was all that was proposed in the recent departed Bill,[1] a sum that would do very little for Church schools in the north, whatever it might do in the south. This, too, you will remember, was offered in a Session when a modest proposal to give a little State aid to the depressed agricultural interest, raised a storm in the House of Commons, and was carried with difficulty. After all, there is one very awkward point about State aid which ought never to be forgotten. If words mean anything, 'State aid' means an annual vote of money in the House of Commons for the maintenance of

---

[1] That is, 4s. over and above the previous 17s. 6d. limit.

Church schools. Can anyone doubt that such a vote would bring on an annual fight like the famous Maynooth Grant in days gone by?[1] I dread such annual fights, and I must object to State aid, whatever my excellent brethren in the south may say. If they like State aid, let them allow us, at any rate, to have Rate aid in the north.

(2) For another thing, I must plainly say that I fail to see the wisdom and expediency of allowing ministers or members of religious bodies outside the Church of England to go into Church schools and give religious instruction to their own young people. I cannot believe that the idea, however liberal and good-natured it may sound in theory, would work out satisfactorily in practice. In hundreds of schools no separate accommodation could be provided, unless a room is to be specially provided for the purpose. In many others it would be impossible to ensure the regular attendance of a competent teacher, as he would probably have other demands on his time. The result would be, that the unfortunate nonconformist children would receive less religious teaching than the children of the Church, together with the heavy risk of friction when a Church teacher saw some of his scholars constantly withdrawn from him, as if he was not fit to teach them. I may be wrong, and I lay no claim to infallibility; but my present impression is that the proposed scheme, however well meant, would never work.

(3) One more thing about which I am not convinced at present is the proposed federation of schools. I am not sure that I fully comprehend the meaning of the expression. If it only means the union of all Church schools within a certain district, enabling them to have one banking account, one correspondent with the Educational Department, and one architect to superintend all building alterations, I believe it would be very useful. It would promote economy, prevent overdrawing at banks, and check

[1] In 1845 Sir Robert Peel got Parliament to give Maynooth R.C. College (Dublin) an annual grant of £26,360.

unwise expenditure on bricks and mortar. But if federation means besides, that good schools are to pay down hard money to enable bad schools to stand on their legs, I cannot say that I approve the idea, and I cannot think it would succeed.

We all know that there are schools and schools; schools which are well managed and well worked, and schools which are comparatively let alone, seldom visited by the clergy, and nothing done to cheer, encourage, and stimulate the teachers. In cases like these I do not believe that the managers of one class of schools would like to hand over any part of their income to support other schools, which are weak and languishing because they have done little or nothing to deserve success. There is a good deal of human nature in school managers, teachers, and clergy; and if this is what federation means, I do not like it. However, I am willing to admit there may be something about it which I do not understand.

I cannot leave this part of my address without urging on every clergyman who has an elementary day school, the immense importance of doing everything in his power to keep up every part of the instruction to the highest standard of excellence. I have been pained to observe on some occasions, at the annual great meetings of our Education Council, that the Board schools carry off a much larger proportion of prizes and honours than the Church schools. Of course, I know that there is a competition in which most of our Church schools are very heavily handicapped, and, with limited means, find it hard to hold their own. But I want them to be second to none, and I urge every clergyman who has a Church school to strain every nerve in the great educational race. The frequent visiting of your school, and showing a friendly face and keeping a friendly eye on its work, if only for a few minutes, not so much to teach yourself as to see that the teaching is real and efficient, has a great influence. When I first came to Liverpool, sixteen years ago, I remember walking alone into a large school unexpectedly, and asking the headmaster how often the clergyman of the parish came to visit him, and I received the painful answer, that 'no clergyman had been inside the school for three years!' I need not say that such a neglected school was not likely to prosper. I am certain, after long experience, that kindly attention to teachers, from the highest to the lowest, friendly interest in all they do, and pleasant, genial notice of the children, are things that always pay. They cost little, but they are worth much.

I leave the thorny question of education at this point with much anxiety. The outlook before us is eminently gloomy and uncertain. If, on the one hand, the Government resolves to give real adequate aid to Church schools, whether it be State or Rate aid, I believe they will be able to hold their own, however furiously the aid may be opposed by the Church's enemies. If, on the other hand, the Government refuses to give sufficient aid to Church schools, the weakest and poorest of them must go to the wall, will ultimately be starved to death, and have to be closed and replaced by Board schools. The consequences of this would be most disastrous. There would be a great expenditure required of public money in order to buy up or replace the closed schools starved to death. There would be much murmuring and dissatisfaction among the working classes when they found their children driven into Board schools, where, in many cases, they would not be taught that Christ is God. Above all, there would be created a deep and abiding sense of injustice among the general body of Churchmen. These are very tough knots, and I shall not attempt to untie them.

III. The next general subject to which I think it my duty to call your attention, is one which has come to the front very much during the last two years. I refer to Church Reform. In the course of the recent campaign in defence of the Establishment, we have been told repeatedly, both in the press and on the platform, that we must amend abuses and throw lumber overboard if we mean to beat to quarters and prepare for action. In short, it has become a kind of proverbial saying, that the best Church Defence is Church Reform.

Now, I shall handle this wide subject very briefly today, for two very sufficient reasons. One of them is, that two very important branches of it will be discussed in our present Conference at one of our sessions, and I am extremely glad that they will be introduced by two laymen. For obvious reasons, the clergy ought to be glad to know what the laity are thinking about them and their position. The other reason why I shall be brief is the simple fact that Church Reform formed a large portion of a long Conference address which I delivered in this room a year ago, in which I handled the whole subject pretty fully and exhaustively. Few people, however, seem to have noticed what I said at the time, and a large-type letter of three columns in the *Times*, of last September 8, totally ignored all my statements, and told the public that the Bishop of Rochester stands alone on the Episcopal Bench in recognition of the Reform League. This, however, does not surprise me. I have long observed that things spoken by Churchmen in the Northern province attract little attention in the South. You, at any rate, who were in this room last November, will perhaps remember that I gave you at least half an hour about Church Reform. For this reason, I repeat, I shall not go over the ground again, and the more so as the question is coming up for public discussion.

I cannot, however, pass away from this great subject, and leave it untouched, without two cautions.

On the one hand I advise the friends and advocates of Church Reform to keep a vigilant watch on the proposed *Benefices Bill*, which was left in suspense and did not become law in the last session of Parliament. Undoubtedly it is a move in the right direction, and contains the elements of much usefulness. At present it is a grievous evil that bishops should be obliged frequently to institute men to livings who are physically, or mentally, or doctrinally, unfit for them. But, at the same time, the power of refusing a nominee ought to be carefully safe-guarded, and the just rights of patrons protected, and the feelings of congregations considered. Above all, where the bishop's decision is disputed, and a legal inquiry demanded, a bishop should be bound to have the assistance of a competent legal assessor. But it remains yet to be seen whether the Benefices Bill will be brought in again, and if so, in what form, and with what amendments.

On the other hand, I advise the advocates of Reform not to forget that in giving the laity a voice in the selection of a minister for a vacant church they must carefully consider what they mean by *the laity*. However right and good the principle, it involves very grave difficulties, and will require great wisdom in order to meet them. No man of common sense, I fancy, would like clergymen to be chosen by popular election, whether by the ratepayers, or by the mere churchgoers, or by the communicants. In every such election you would almost always create two parties in the congregation, and have a disappointed minority. Nor can we suppose for a moment that the Crown, the colleges, and the bishops, to say nothing of the great landowners, would consent to give up all their rights as patrons. All these are difficult points, and require very delicate handling. At present I only say that I hope we shall get more light upon them from discussion. The practice of the Disestablished Church of Ireland about filling up vacant livings, and the results of the system, deserve careful investigation.

IV. The fourth and last public subject which has been pressed on the Church's attention during the last few years is the reunion of Christendom. It is one which I shall handle very briefly.

Unity among Christians, it is needless to say, is a most desirable thing. It is one of the four topics named by our Lord in his wonderful last prayer before crucifixion, in the 17th chapter of St John. The want of it is the weakness of the Church and the favourite weapon of the infidel. It is vain to expect much of it in the great visible Catholic Church, in which the various branches differ widely, both in ritual and doctrine, and where the evil are always mingled with the good. You must look for it in that Holy Catholic Church which, as our Prayer-book says, is 'the mystical body of Christ, and the blessed company of all faithful people.'

This, as that great man Isaac Barrow says, is 'the society of those for whom Christ did pray that they might be one.' Yet even among them it is very imperfect, and will be till we get to heaven. Here below there is often unity without uniformity, and uniformity without unity. As to the reunion of all Christendom, it is a mere castle in the air.

Can there be any reunion between the Church of England and other bodies of Trinitarian Protestant Christians in Great Britain? I answer decidedly, that it appears to me hopeless. It might have been possible in the reign of Queen Elizabeth, if that autocratic Tudor sovereign had allowed Parker and Jewel to complete the work of the Reformation. But, unhappily, she pulled them up sharply and snubbed them in every direction, and the seeds of a crop of nonconformity were sown broadcast. The reigns of James I and Charles I only made matters worse, and the Church policy of that unhappy, overpraised man, Archbishop Laud, laid deep the foundations of English dissent. From Laud's time down to the present day the current of events has always been one way, deeper and wider disunion every century. The wretched conflicts of the Commonwealth times, the suicidal ecclesiastical measures of Charles II, the weak attempts at improvement in William III's days, the blind inability of the English bishops to understand or utilize the Methodist movement a hundred years ago, and last but not least, the Romeward tendencies in some parts of the Church of our own times—all these things, I believe, have dug a huge gulf between Church and Dissent which never will be bridged over or filled up—never, never, never!

Can there ever be any reunion between the Church of England and the Church of Rome? I answer without hesitation, that the very idea is monstrous, and reflects no credit on the common sense of those who have launched it in these latter days. I care very little for the Pope's recent decree about Anglican orders.[1] I am quite content to know that our own are perfectly valid, and

---

[1] Pope Leo XIII's 'Apostolicae Curae' of 1896 rejected Anglican orders as invalid.

I never doubted it. But our conception of a Christian minister's office is very different from that of the Pope's. On the one side, the clergyman of the Roman Church is a priest, whose great business is to offer the sacrifice of the Mass. On the other, the clergyman of the Anglican Church is not a priest at all, though called one, and only a presbyter, whose chief business is not to offer a material sacrifice, but to preach the word of God and administer the sacraments. My main reason for objecting to reunion with Rome is the broad fact that her distinctive doctrinal principles are utterly irreconcilable with our own. If the recent decree of Rome had formally announced to the world that the Pope admits the validity of our orders, and recognizes all Anglican clergymen as Catholic priests, it would not make a jot of difference to me. It is doctrine, doctrine, and not orders, which makes the insuperable objection to reunion with Rome. So long as subscription to the Thirty-nine Articles is required from every English clergyman before he can have a licence or be instituted to a living; so long as nine of those Articles are not repealed or tampered with, and distinctly condemn certain Romish doctrines and practices, and especially and particularly the Mass; so long it appears to me a childish waste of time to talk of reunion. That able man, Dr George Salmon, the Provost of Trinity College, Dublin, says in his book on Infallibility: 'As the Roman Church is at present disposed, there can be no union with her except on the terms of absolute submission; that submission, moreover, involving an acknowledgment that we, from our hearts, believe things to be true which we have good reasons for knowing to be false.'[1] I agree with him entirely, and I cannot believe that English Churchmen will tamely consent to submit to such an abject surrender as reunion would require.[2]

I refrain from saying more than a few words about a very painful subject affecting the Church which was brought before the House of Lords last session. I refer to the Bill in which it was

[1] Salmon: *Infallibility of the Church*, Preface v.
[2] See appendix, chapter 14, note 1, pp. 435-36.

proposed to legalise marriage with a deceased wife's sister, which was unhappily carried by a large majority in the Upper House, but happily never reached the House of Commons. It is a disagreeable question, about which there is a curious diversity of opinion, and I shrink from saying much on it when so many ladies are present. Diocesan engagements made it impossible for me to be present at the division in Parliament. But I think it due to myself and to my diocese to say that I should certainly have voted with the minority against the Bill. The proposed change of the law seems, to my eyes, likely to create an immense amount of social discomfort and unhappiness, and I deeply regret the success of the Bill in the House of Lords.

From the difficult problems which I have been trying to discuss, I must now turn to other matters of equal if not greater importance. We are drawing near to the end of another century. Many of you in all probability will live to see AD 1900, if I do not. Let me, as an old man, try to put before you the present position and prospects of the Established Church of England, and offer a few words of practical advice.

I. If we compare the condition of the Church of England in 1896 with the condition in 1796, I have no hesitation in saying that *we have very great cause for thankfulness* to Almighty God. The state of things ecclesiastical a hundred years ago was so entirely different from what it is now, and so eminently unsatisfactory, that I wonder the Church was kept alive and survived the deadly contagion of the first French Revolution. The improvements, reforms, alterations, and changes for the better which have taken place are so numerous that we seem to have had a second Reformation. Within the sixty years of our gracious Queen's reign, not a few of our grand old cathedrals have been thoroughly repaired and preserved from ruin, hundreds of our old parish churches have been restored, and many more hundreds of new churches, especially in the manufacturing districts, have been built. On building, restoring, and renewing churches, it is reckoned that nearly forty millions of pounds have been voluntarily raised and expended. During the same period, glaring abuses of all kinds, such as non-residence and pluralities among the clergy, have been completely suppressed. At the same time, thousands of scriptural schools have been built all over the land. Our great religious Societies for promoting missions abroad and at home have been called into existence. Parochial machinery of every kind has been created and set to work. The standard of preaching and living among the clergy of all schools of thought has unmistakably improved. The number of drones in our hive is decidedly less than it was. Scores of philanthropic agencies of all sorts have been set on foot in every part of England. In spite of all our faults and divisions, the Established Church, as a body, is not asleep, but awake. Her worst enemies must admit that she is not dead, but alive. For all these things I maintain firmly, we ought to be deeply thankful.

Whether, at the same time, there are not some causes for grave anxiety in our Church's condition, I am obliged to say, appears to me rather doubtful. Side by side with an undeniable increase of outward religion, I am afraid that the standard of practical Christianity is not so high as it ought to be, and is rather on the down grade. The painful quantity of Sabbath breaking and neglect of worship, the growth of gambling and racing, the increase of a very loose style of literature, the extravagant love of pleasure and amusements, the continuance of drunkenness, and the annual expenditure of one hundred and forty millions on intoxicating liquors, the half of it not necessary—all these things are rather black clouds on the horizon of our Church, and deserve the watchful attention of all who love her. We may depend on it, an increase of practical godliness is the only sure test of a Church's health and prosperity.

II. The darkest cloud on our horizon, however, is *the continuance and increase of our unhappy divisions*, and especially, I grieve to say, our divisions about the blessed sacrament of the Lord's Supper.

The threatening dangers from these divisions I believe to be very great. I know not whether the coming Lambeth Conference will ignore them as it did in 1887, in spite of my own feeble protest at the end. But if they are ignored and let alone, I believe our Church will receive immense damage. A house divided against itself cannot stand.

With every feeling of respect for the late lamented Archbishop of Canterbury,[1] I have never been able to see that the famous Lincoln decision did anything to lessen or heal our divisions, whatever others may please to say. To my eyes it left things much as they were, and proved the uselessness in these liberal days of all prosecutions about ritual and doctrine, when everybody is right, and nobody is wrong.

Let me once more, and probably for the last time, say a few plain things about the painful subject of our divisions. You all know perfectly well that in the present day strange and apparently Romish views of the Lord's Supper are preached, taught, and put in practice by thousands of clergymen, which Jewel and Hooker and Hall and Usher and Davenant and Beveridge, and a host of other departed divines, never sanctioned for a moment; and that a fog of novelties has arisen and spread over the whole land, and becomes thicker every year. At the same time, we cannot deny that many who advocate or practise these novelties are amiable, zealous, hardworking, self-denying, devout clergymen. Whatever their principles may be, their lives are exemplary and blameless. They profess to love the Church of England quite as much as any of their brethren, and yet, on the doctrine and ritual of the Lord's Supper, the two parties are as the poles asunder.

They cannot work together comfortably. They rarely worship with one another. They support, on every subject, two different Societies, and each thinks their own the right one. In short, there are within our Church two opposing views of the Lord's Supper, and I fail to see how they can be reconciled. It is useless to appeal

---

[1] Edward White Benson (1883–96); for Lincoln decision, see fn. 1, pp. 282.

to Old Church Courts about them, because their decisions are not obeyed. It is useless, apparently, to expect New Courts, as there is no attempt to create them. Hope deferred makes the heart sick. Ecclesiastical discipline seems to have died out, and in place of it there is such a reign of anarchy, chaos, and confusion that every clergyman does what is right in his own eyes. Such are the days in which your lot is cast. I need not tell you that these sad divisions are a cause of great weakness, and terribly damage the Church of England.

Now, I am not going to weary you with long, well-worn statements about the Romish view of the Lord's Supper, such as the cardinal errors of the Mass, Transubstantiation, the Real Corporal Presence, and the Sacerdotal Office. But I do feel it a plain duty to raise a warning voice about a few things which appear to me to be doing special harm in this day, and I must use great plainness of speech.

(1) I hear with deep regret that many clergymen all over the land hold and teach that it is useful, edifying, and desirable to receive the Lord's Supper fasting. I fear there are many strange views in some minds on this subject. You will distinctly understand that I have not the least objection to early administrations, if people prefer them. That is not the question. The ground I take up is of a very different kind.

I contend that the practice of fasting communion is neither commanded nor recommended in Scripture. It is perfectly clear that at the first institution of the sacrament, the apostles could not have received the elements fasting, because they had just eaten the passover. There cannot, therefore, be anything very important in this point, and every believer may use his liberty, and do what he finds edifying to himself, without condemning others. But it may be feared that there lies in the minds of many who attach immense value to fasting communion, a vague belief that the consecrated bread and wine which we receive are in some mysterious way not real bread and wine, and ought not therefore to be mixed with other food in our bodies! Such a belief cannot be praised. Moreover, those who teach that fasting communion is a rule obligatory on all persons, take up a position which is not only unscriptural, but even cruel. To go fasting to an early morning communion is likely to cause the death of delicate persons.

I invite your attention to the weighty words of Bishop Samuel Wilberforce on this very subject, and I ask you to remember that he was always a decided High Churchman, and I did not agree with him on many points. They were spoken a few days before his death. He says:

> It is not in a light sense that I say this new doctrine of fasting communion is dangerous. The practice is not advocated because a man comes in a clearer spirit and less disturbed body and mind, able to give himself entirely to prayer and communion with his God; but on a miserable, degraded notion that the consecrated elements will meet with other food in the stomach. It is a detestable materialism. Philosophically it is a contradiction; because, when the celebration is over, you may hurry away to a meal, and the process about which you were so scrupulous immediately follows. The whole notion is simply disgusting.[1]

(2) I hear, again, with deep regret, that many zealous clergymen are recommending non-communicants to remain in church and be present at the administration of the Lord's Supper. Some of you may hear of this with surprise, and some may ask in their simplicity 'Where is the harm?' I believe it is a growing evil, and a thing that ought to be firmly resisted. It originates in the mischievous idea that the Lord's Supper is a sacrifice offered up by a priest, and not a commemorative ordinance of which all present ought to partake. In short, it is a direct step toward the Romish sacrifices of the Mass, of which your Thirty-first Article declares that they are 'blasphemous fables and dangerous deceits.' That there was nothing of the kind at the first institution, that

---

[1] J. W. Burgon: *Lives of Twelve Good Men*, vol. 2, p. 56.

all present were communicants and all received the bread and wine, that none were merely spectators, that there is not a jot of evidence in the Acts or Epistles that non-communicating attendance was recognized or permitted—all these things are as clear as noonday, and I will not waste your time by dwelling on the subject. Well and wisely says the Homily of the Sacrament, 'We must be ourselves partakers of this table, and not beholders of other.'

But I ask you again to mark the words of Bishop Samuel Wilberforce. He says:

> Non-communicating attendance brings us back to the great abuse of coming to the Sacrament to non-partake instead of partaking: and so we have the condition of things arising in our Communion which already prevails in the Church of Rome...That this custom is creeping into our Church is not an accident; neither is it brought in for the purpose of making children better acquainted with our service. It is, remember, under quite a different impression. It is with the idea that prayer is more acceptable at this time of the sacrifice; that you can get benefit from being within sight of the Sacrament when it is being administered. It is the substitution of a semi-materialistic presence for the actual presence of Christ in the soul of the faithful communicant. It is an abomination, this teaching of non-communicating attendance as a common habit.[1]

To this testimony I will only add the words of a greater bishop still, I mean Bishop Jewel. He says in the *Apology*:

> If anyone, before the private Mass was introduced, would only be a spectator, and would abstain from the Holy Communion, the Bishop of Rome in the primitive times, or the ancient Fathers, would have excommunicated him as a wicked man and a pagan; nor was there any Christian man in these times who communicated alone in the presence of spectators.[2]

---

[1] Burgon, *ibid.*, vol. 2, p. 57.
[2] John Jewel: *Apology*, chapter 2.

(3) I hear again, continually, and I hear it with deep regret, that many hold and teach that it is wrong, improper, and undesirable to celebrate the Lord's Supper in the evening. This is a point, you all know, about which there is an amazing difference of opinion. Some men almost lose their tempers about it, use violent language, and denounce evening Communions as wicked, irreverent, profane, and of evil tendency! Yet, after all, what saith the Scripture? I declare I see no disputed point in connection with the Lord's Supper on which the arguments and evidence are so entirely on one side.

It cannot possibly be sinful to follow the example of Christ and his apostles. Every reader of the New Testament must know that the institution of the Lord's Supper took place in the evening. It is certain that no special hour is recommended to us in the Acts or Epistles. The Lord's Supper at Troas must have been in the evening. This even Mr Sadler admits, in his book on the Acts. It is equally certain that the Prayer-book leaves the matter to the discretion of every clergyman, and allows him to do what is best for his congregation, and wisely lays down no hard-and-fast rule about the time. To forbid evening Communions would completely shut out many persons in large town parishes from the Lord's table. The mothers of many families among the working classes cannot possibly leave home in the morning. The very name 'Supper,' which our Church Catechism especially uses, seems to point to the evening of a day rather than the morning. In the face of these facts, to denounce evening Communions as irreverent, wicked, and profane, is neither reasonable nor wise. I cannot advise any of my brethren who find them useful to give way to pressure from any quarter, and give up the practice.

(4) I hear again with great pain, as well as regret, that many clergymen all over England are continually teaching that it is necessary, and desirable, and useful for communicants to confess their sins privately to a clergyman, to receive absolution before they come to the Lord's table, and afterwards to keep up the habit of confession. That this practice has crept into our Church in

these latter days, and is spreading extensively, there is too much reason to believe. I regard it as so deeply objectionable that I cannot altogether pass it by.

I maintain there is not a single verse in the New Testament to show that the apostles recommended private confession, or that the first Christians practised it. Desirable or useful it certainly is not. The habit of private or auricular confession to a minister, under any circumstances, is one of the most mischievous and dangerous inventions of the corrupt Church of Rome, and has been the cause of enormous immorality and wickedness. Moreover, it is expressly condemned in the 'Homily of Repentance.'

Of course, I am aware that habitual confession is thought by some to be sanctioned by the exhortation in our Communion Service, in which the minister says: 'If any of you cannot quiet his own conscience, but requireth further comfort or counsel, let him come to me, or to some other discreet and learned minister of God's word, and open his grief, that by the ministry of God's holy word he may receive the benefit of absolution.' I reply to all who use this argument, that it is impossible with any fairness to extract auricular confession and sacramental absolution out of this passage. The simple meaning is, that people who are troubled in mind with some special difficulties of conscience are advised to go to some minister and talk privately with him about them, and to get them cleared up and resolved by texts of Scripture, that is, 'by the ministry of God's word.' This is what many clergymen, conducting mission services in the present day, do with those who wait for an 'after meeting' at the end of the sermon. But this is as utterly unlike the mischievous practice of habitual confession and constant confession before communion, as wholesome medicine is unlike opium-eating and water is unlike poison. As to the well-known words used in the Prayer-book at the ordination of a priest, they are simply an authoritative commission to declare publicly, as the apostles did, whose sins are forgiven and whose are not. This is exactly what St Paul did in the Acts.

I must be allowed once more to support what I have just said on this point by the words of Bishop Wilberforce. I take them from the last address which he ever delivered, only a few days before his sudden death. Bishop Wilberforce says:

> This system of confession is one of the worst developments of Popery. In the first place, as regards *the penitent*, it is a system of unnatural excitement, a sort of spiritual dram drinking, fraught with evil to the whole spiritual constitution. It is nothing short of the renunciation of the great charge of a conscience which God has committed to every man, the substitution of confession to man for the opening of the heart to God, the adopting in every case of a remedy only adapted to extreme cases which can find relief in no other way...In *families* it introduces untold mischief. It supersedes God's appointment of intimacy between husband and wife, father and children; substituting another influence for that which ought to be the nearest and closest, and producing reserve and estrangement where there ought to be perfect freedom and openness. Lastly, as regards *the priest* to whom confession is made, it brings in a wretched system of casuistry. But far worse than this, it necessitates the terrible evil of familiar dealing with sin, and especially the sin of uncleanness.[1]

I can add nothing to that. I only express my unmixed astonishment that English husbands and parents can allow wives and daughters to go to private confession, and I publicly declare my entire disapproval of the whole practice.[2]

I pause here, and will go no further. I might easily name other things which I regret, and regard as dangerous innovations in this day. Such things are lighted candles on the holy table at communion by daylight, incense, the mixed chalice, ceremonial ablution, and the use of mischievous catechisms for children, teaching Mariolatry, and seven sacraments instead of two. I pass them all by, because in the present state of ecclesiastical

[1] Burgon, *ibid*, vol. 2, p. 55.
[2] See appendix, chapter 14, note 2, pp. 436-37.

discipline, where absolute liberty seems the only rubric, it is waste of time to do more than express regrets. Some people, I know, regard these things as trifles. I cannot see with their eyes. They are very mischievous trifles. They are just the kind of things which in the present day are gradually sapping the foundations of the Church of England. They irritate and annoy the middle and lower classes, who cannot find them in the very Prayer-book which from childhood they have been urged to value and treat with veneration. They are regarded as an attempt to unprotestantize the Establishment. If they continue to increase, and are not checked, the end will be disestablishment, disendowment, and disruption. This, at any rate, is my deliberate opinion.

III. I conclude by saying a few words about what I believe was intended to be the real and true *comprehensiveness* of the Church of England. If anyone supposes, from what I have just said, that I am a narrow-minded Churchman, and that I can see only one school of thought within our pale, he is totally mistaken. I hold strongly, and always have held from the time of my ordination, that there are three different schools in our Church—the High, the Low, and the Broad. The 'no-party' men, who have no distinct opinions about anything, I pass by altogether. These three schools have existed for three centuries, and may possibly exist till the end of this dispensation. The Church has always found room for all honest and reasonable members of these schools, though they may occasionally squabble and grumble, and snarl, and growl at one another. Each probably thinks it could improve and amend the Church a little. Each school has its own special nostrums and medicines, which it believes would improve the Church's health, if taken. But by letting them all work in their own way, the Church has managed to get on hitherto for two hundred and fifty years. This is what I mean by comprehensiveness.

But are there no *limits to the comprehensiveness* of the Church of England? This is a very delicate question; but I am prepared to look it fully in the face. It is one of such vast importance, in a day of abounding liberalism, that it seems very desirable to lay down one or two leading principles on the subject.

There ought to be some limits to the comprehensiveness of every Church, for the sake of order. Reason and common sense point to this conclusion. Order is heaven's first law. There was order in Eden before the Fall. There will be perfect order on earth at the restitution of all things. A Christian Church utterly destitute of order does not deserve to be called a Church at all. A Church, like every other corporation on earth, must have definite terms of membership. It must have a creed, and certain fixed principles of doctrine and worship. Its members have a right to know what its ministers are set to teach. A Church which is a mere boneless body, like a jelly-fish, a colourless, bloodless, creedless pantheon, in which every one is right and nobody is wrong who is in *earnest*, and in which it does not matter a jot what is preached and taught, so long as the preachers are *sincere*—such a Church is an unpractical absurdity, and the baseless fabric of a dream. The Church which abandons all 'limits,' and will not proclaim to mankind what it believes, or would have its members believe, may do very well for Cloudland or Utopia; but it will never do for a world where there are tears and crosses, troubles and sorrows, sickness and death.

The member of the Established Church of England has a just right to expect one general type of teaching and worship, whether he goes into a parish church in Truro or Lincoln, in Canterbury or Carlisle. Different shades of statement in the pulpit he may find himself obliged to tolerate. But he may justly complain if the doctrine of one diocese is as utterly unlike that of another as light and darkness, black and white, acids and alkalies, oil and water. 'Liberty of prophesying' and free thought, in the abstract, are excellent things. But they must have some bounds. Just as in States the extreme of liberty becomes licentiousness and tyranny, so in Churches it becomes disorder and confusion. The Church which regards Deism, Socinianism, Romanism, and Protestantism with equal favour or equal indifference, is a mere Babel, a 'city of confusion,' and not the city of God.

Now, I contend that the National Church of England has set up wisely-devised 'limits' to its comprehensiveness. Those limits, I believe, are to be found in the Articles, the Creeds, and the Book of Common Prayer, which you cannot get rid of without a revolution. These well-known documents, I maintain, provide limits wide enough for all reasonable men who do not object *in toto* to liturgies and Episcopacy. They are documents, no doubt, which all do not interpret alike. As long as the world stands, and as long as language is what it is, you will never get men to place precisely the same meaning on theological phrases and words. But however variously we may interpret the Articles, Creeds, and Prayer-book, they are unmistakable limits, fences, and bounds within which the National Church requires its ministers to walk, and I am bold to say that he who flatly rejects them, denies them, contradicts them, and transgresses them, is in his wrong place inside the Church of England.

(1) If, for example, on the one hand, a man calling himself a Churchman deliberately denies the doctrine of the Trinity, or the proper deity of Christ, or the personality and work of the Holy Ghost, or the atonement and mediation of Christ, or the inspiration and divine authority of Scripture, or justification by faith, or the inseparable connection of saving faith and holiness, or the obligation of the two sacraments, I cannot understand what he is doing in our ranks. Of course, as an Englishman, he may come into our places of worship. But common sense seems to me to point out that he cannot conscientiously use our Prayer-book, and that he has certainly no right to occupy our pulpits and reading-desks.

(2) If, on the other hand, a minister of the National Church maintains and teaches those distinctive doctrines of the Church of Rome which are plainly named, defined, and repudiated nine

times over in the Thirty-nine Articles, and, ignoring the public declaration which he made on taking a living, deliberately teaches transubstantiation, the sacrifice of the mass, purgatory, the necessity of auricular confession, and the invocation of saints, I contend that he is transgressing the liberty allowed by the Church of England. He may be zealous, sincere, earnest, and devout, but he is in the wrong place in a Protestant communion. He has stepped over the just limits of the Church's comprehensiveness, and is occupying an untenable and unwarrantable position.

Of course, the things I have just said appear very narrow and illiberal to some minds. There are many nowadays who are so enamoured of liberty that they would throw down all theological 'limits,' fences, and restrictions, and leave the platform of our Church as bare as a common. They tell us the only way to save the Church from shipwreck is to pitch overboard all Articles and Creeds as useless lumber, and to assign no bounds to her 'comprehensiveness' so long as her ministers are earnest and sincere. I am utterly unable to see with the eyes of these people. I believe that it is miserable policy to try to purchase unity and peace and charity at the expense of faith and hope and truth. I contend that a rejection of Deism and Socinianism on one side, and a rejection of Romanism and superstition on the other, form 'just and reasonable and fair limits to comprehensiveness,' and that our Church does well and wisely in requiring her ministers to walk within them.

But I go further than this. I contend that the maintenance of certain well-defined 'limits to comprehensiveness' is absolutely essential to the welfare of a Church, and that without such limits it is vain to expect any blessing from God. I think I could name some Churches yet in existence which have fallen into decay, and become lightless lighthouses, in consequence of giving up Creeds and Confessions of Faith. In the vain pursuit of liberty they have sacrificed vitality, and casting overboard distinctive doctrine have committed suicide. They continue to this day, and have a name and place in the earth, but, like extinct volcanoes, they have neither heat, light, nor fire. Nor yet is this all. I fail to see in ecclesiastical history a single instance of good being done to souls except by the agency of men who adhered strictly to positive doctrinal 'limits,' and preached and taught positive distinctive truths. Weigh and analyse the teaching of any English divine who has shaken the earth from the time of the Reformation down to the present day. Tell me, if you can, of any clergyman of any school, who ever roused consciences, awoke the sleeping and revived the dead, who did not hold and proclaim a well-defined and limited theology. Show me, if you can, a single 'master of assemblies,' from Latimer down to the most popular mission-preacher of this day, from Liddon to Spurgeon, who ever wrought deliverance on earth, and turned the world upside down by a mere colourless gospel—a gospel without the Trinity, without the Atonement, without the blood of Christ, without the Holy Spirit, without justification, without regeneration. No! you will never find one—never, never! Grapes will not grow on thorns, nor figs on thistles. The Church which allows its ministers to teach a vague gospel of *earnestness and sincerity*, instead of distinctive Christian doctrine, may get the reputation of being very liberal and tolerant in these latter days, but it will never convert and satisfy souls. A Church must have some 'limits' and bounds to its 'comprehensiveness,' if it desires to do good.

And now let me conclude with an earnest appeal to my brother Churchmen, by way of application. For the sake of peace, for the sake of truth, for the sake of the Church of England, for the sake of Christ, let us strive and pray that we may hold fast both the principles referred to in the subject of this part of my address, the principle of 'comprehensiveness' and the principle of 'limitation.'

(1) Let us endeavour to be of *a comprehensive spirit*. Let us not exclude from the Church those whom the Church has not excluded, nor boycott and ostracize and excommunicate everyone

who cannot pronounce our Shibboleths, or work exactly on our lines. I am a thorough-going Evangelical Churchman, and I am not a bit ashamed of it. I will never give place by subjection, and admit that anyone is a better Churchman than myself. But I have no sympathy with those who advocate a rigid, unbending, cast-iron uniformity within our pale, and want all Churchmen to be, like the rails round Hyde Park in London, of one unvarying mental colour, height, shape, and thickness. If any man asks me to cast out of the Church of this day men of the type of Andrews and Sanderson and George Herbert; or of Burnet and Tillotson and Whichcote; or of Bishops Blomfield or Thirlwall; or of Bishops Wilberforce or Selwyn; I tell him plainly that I will not do it. No doubt I could not preach very comfortably in the pulpits of such men, nor they in mine. I could not take them as curates, nor could they take me. I prefer to support my own favourite religious Societies, and they prefer theirs. But if any Evangelical Churchman wants to thrust these men out of the Church of England, because, like Apollos, they do not seem to him to know the 'way of God perfectly,' I will not lift a finger to help him. I will tolerate them, on my principle of 'Church comprehensiveness,' and in return I expect them to tolerate me.

(2) On the other hand, let us neither be ashamed nor afraid of having limits to our *comprehensiveness, even the limits* of our mother, the Church of England. Let us not overstrain the quality of liberalism so far as to sanction theological licentiousness. Let us be as broad as the Articles and Creeds, but not one inch broader. If any one tries to persuade me that I ought to smile and look on complacently, with folded arms, while beneficed or licensed clergymen teach Deism, Socinianism, or Romanism, I must tell him plainly that I cannot and will not do it. He may tell me that I am a 'troubler of Israel,' and a bitter controversialist; but I repeat that, when truth is in danger, I cannot and will not sit still. At this rate the apostles ought to have left the world alone eighteen centuries ago. They ought to have been satisfied

with the teaching of Socrates and Plato, and were fools to attack heathenism, and live and die preaching Christ crucified. At this rate the English Reformation was a huge schism and mistake, and Ridley and Latimer ought never to have resisted Rome and gone to the stake. No, indeed! I love my own Church too well to tolerate either scepticism on the one hand or Romanism on the other, and I think I am only doing my duty to my ordination vows in trying to 'drive both away.'

But, after all, it matters little what bishops and clergymen may think or do. The question before us is rapidly getting out of clerical hands. There are handwritings on the wall, which it needs no Daniel to interpret. I know something of the laity, and especially in the middle classes, in this country, and I am certain they will never tolerate and support a National Church which desires to return to Rome, or has no theological 'limits,' and holds no distinctive doctrines. They do not want the Established Church of England to be narrow, illiberal, party-spirited, and exclusive. But in a weary, working, sorrowful world, the laity will not put up with a religion either of negations or superstitions. They want bread, and they will not be content with stones. Once let the English laity see that a reign of complete latitudinarianism has begun, that the old landmarks are thrown down and that the National Church does not care a jot whether her ministers preach Deism or Bible Christianity, Protestantism or Popery, but gives equal favour to all—once, I say, let the laity see this, and they will desert the National Church and leave it to perish. Give the laity the old paths of the Bible, and the well-defined limits of the Articles and Creeds and Prayer-book, and they will stand by the Church to the last. Destroy those limits, or refuse to enforce and maintain them, and they will soon cry, 'Let us depart hence'; our candlestick will be removed, and the Church will die for want of Churchmen. In short, there is no alternative. The question is one of life or death. The English Church must either have doctrinal 'limits,' or cease to exist.

15

THOUGHTS FOR THINKERS

*An address given to the sixteenth Liverpool Diocesan Conference,
in St George's Hall, November 2, 1897.*

REVEREND and Lay Brethren, I give you a hearty welcome to
our Sixteenth Diocesan Conference, and I am glad to see so
large an attendance of members. At the same time I must honestly
say I wish the attendance was larger. At present not half the Clergy
of this Diocese ever put in an appearance at these important
Annual Gatherings, while the proportion of the laity who accept
our invitations, and exhibit any interest in our proceedings, is
painfully small. This is not a healthy state of things: but I fear
it is the same in every Diocese in the land. In this respect the
Presbyterians and Wesleyans completely out-distance us. It looks
as if the Church of England was not half awake.

(1) The yearly history of our own Diocese is seldom very
eventful. The Diamond Jubilee of our gracious and beloved
Sovereign, Queen Victoria, has naturally over-shadowed all other
events in 1897, and absorbed all men's attention. Two things
however have occurred in the last twelve months which deserve
special notice.

One of these things is the successful passage through
Parliament of the Liverpool City Churches' Act, an Act of which
the importance was strongly urged on me by the late Mr Whitley,
M.P. for this City, when I first became your Bishop. After sixteen
years this Act has been obtained, and nine old Churches in
Liverpool are now set free for ever from dependence on an annual

payment from the Corporation, and will receive instead a fixed Income from the Ecclesiastical Commissioners. For this most desirable purpose a lump sum of £95,000 has been paid down by the Municipal Body, in commutation of the endowment of the nine livings, and the vested interests of the patrons and officials. Two of the churches, St George's and St John's, will be taken down, and money sufficient to build at least two other churches will, we hope, be provided. The terms on which the whole arrangement has been effected have been the subject of very careful calculation, and, in my judgment, are equitable and fair. I believe that neither of the parties to this very important transaction has any right to complain: and I am convinced that the whole result will be useful, and make for peace.

(2) The other exceptional event in the Diocesan history of the last twelve months is the launching of the ambitious scheme of a Church House for the Diocese of Liverpool. The unsuccessful attempt to provide a Cathedral worthy of our new diocese at the beginning of my episcopate, and the many weary Committee Meetings at the Town Hall about the subject, are now matters of ancient history, and many people seem totally ignorant of them. I take occasion to remark that I was present at all those Meetings, and the common slanderous report that the Bishop took no interest in the subject, and did not wish a Cathedral to be built, is destitute of a grain of truth. But those Committee Meetings finally convinced me that there was no prospect of agreement among the inhabitants of Liverpool about the site of a Cathedral, and not the least likelihood of half a million being raised by the Diocese in this generation for the building and endowment of a suitable metropolitan Church. From that time I resolved to promote the erection of a Church House, and after long delay, caused by bad times, I have lived to see the keel laid. Of the great usefulness of such an Institution I need say nothing, and I have never had any doubt about it. It will strengthen the Church of England in many ways which I need not describe today, promote unity,

bring the clergy together, and facilitate every kind of Diocesan business. I am very thankful for the acceptance and the large measure of support which the scheme has already received, and for the excellent site in Lord Street, which has been secured. But I must remind you emphatically that much more money will yet be required before the Church House can be built, and I must frankly confess, that I have little hope, at my advanced age, that I shall ever sit down within its walls. Money for church purposes is not so easily raised in this Diocese as dwellers in other parts of England seem to suppose. But I do not despair.

(3) Concerning matters of general interest to our Established Church which have come to the front during the last year, there are two principal ones which demand your attention.

One of these is the Education Act (1896), which, after long and weary discussion in Parliament, has become the law of the land.

About this Act you have all heard enough and perhaps too much, and I shall only make a few brief remarks upon it. It is the well-meant effort of a friendly Government to assist necessitous Voluntary Schools by a new further grant of 4/- a head, an effort rendered necessary by that useless, needless, thankless measure, the Free Education Act. Such grant is to be given primarily to poor schools, and is to be managed by organized federations or associations of schools all over the country, while poor Board Schools in rural districts are also to share in its benefits. Whether the Act will work well remains to be proved, but the mere fact that it is called 'tentative' in high quarters shows plainly that some difficulties are expected. I do not wonder. So long as human nature is what it is, I do not expect the principle of 'federation' will ever be popular. I only hope that in our own Diocese there will be as little disagreement as possible, and that School Managers will remember that in this world we cannot always have everything our own way, and must put up with a certain quantity of concession and compromise on all sides. The great statesmen of the Six Powers of

Europe have not found it easy to work together comfortably about Greece and Turkey, and we must not be surprised if we find at first some educational friction in Lancashire. I trust, however, that in all Committee meetings and discussions about the new Act there will be a maximum of light and a minimum of heat.

(4) The other great event affecting the Church of England which has come to the front during the last twelve months, is the Lambeth Conference, or Decennial Meeting, of Bishops of the Anglican Communion from every part of the world. About this I shall say very little, because I was not present at it, in consequence of a troublesome cold and doctor's advice, which, at eighty-one, a Bishop cannot afford to neglect. I know nothing of the proceedings, which were all held in private and in camera. But the results of the discussions are published by the Christian Knowledge Society, and may be read by any one.

I have nothing to say against the subjects which were discussed, or the conclusions which have been put forth by the various Conference Committees, or the great final Encyclical. They are all more or less instructive reading, good, and useful so far as they go. But I cannot refrain from expressing one general opinion. I must deeply regret that the Lambeth Conference completely ignored and passed over the 'unhappy divisions,' both about doctrine and ritual, of the Church of England in the present day. They are divisions which threaten to undo the work of the Reformation, and are gradually rending the Established Church into two distinct parties, and destroying the peace of families, parishes, and congregations. No doubt a cautious policy of silence in the Conference about these divisions saved much trouble, prevented awkward collisions, and made things work smoothly. But with all respect to the managers of this great Synod, I cannot refrain from saying, as an individual Bishop, that in my opinion this policy of 'silence' was not really wise. When I see the immense damage that is being done continually to the Church of England by the tolerated increase of Auricular Confession, and

Mariolatry, and imitations of the Romish Mass, I think the silence I have referred to will do *harm*, and certainly not promote unity. There was no such 'silence' in the 'Official letter of the Lambeth Congress of 1878' and I do not think we are in a more healthy state now. I believe the best friends of the Church had a right to expect at least some expression of regret about our divisions, and I think the conspicuous absence of any expression of opinion about the critical condition of the Establishment will cause much pain and disappointment. The often repeated cry for Unity seems a waste of time in the present state of our Church, and reunion with Methodists or Presbyterians appears impossible. Protestant Nonconformists in England will never join a Church so seriously divided as our own; and I cannot wonder. I believe they would swallow a good deal for the sake of peace; but I do not believe they would swallow sacerdotalism.

I turn from this delicate and unpleasant subject to some other matters which appear to demand your thoughtful attention in the present day. I say 'thoughtful' emphatically and purposely. A Diocesan Conference like ours has no legal power whatever, and I am glad that it has not. But if it is to be of any use it ought to stir men's minds, and set them thinking. Thought is the mother of action, and if we can wind up the clock of Churchmen's minds every year, and send them home to think about matters affecting the Church and the Diocese rather more than they do, we shall do them good, and not meet in vain.

(5) In looking back over the sixteen years of my episcopate I see many causes for thankfulness; but I see one serious exception. On the side of thankfulness I will name several things. The Walton Vicarage Act, which placed the See of Liverpool on a level with other Sees; the 'Turner Pension Fund' created by the princely generosity of one Christian lady; the successful progress of our Diocesan Sustentation Fund; the City Churches' Act; the building and consecration of forty-two new Churches, and the opening of forty-eight licensed Mission Rooms; the large increase

in the number of Incumbents, Curates, and Confirmations; and though last, not least, the hopeful launch of a Diocesan Church House—all these are bright spots in the retrospective history of our Diocese. I began my episcopate with 170 Incumbents; there are now 205. I began with 120 Curates; there are now 220. In my first year I had 4,500 young persons presented to me for Confirmation. In 1896 I had 8,300. I should be very ungrateful if I did not thank God every day for these undeserved mercies.

But there is one unsatisfactory point just now in our Diocesan position to which I feel it necessary to request your thoughtful attention. The point I refer to is the financial condition of our Diocesan Institutions. Their annual income altogether, when the Diocese was created in 1880, was £1,900. Since that year it has annually fallen and declined, and is now no more than £900. In plain words the Diocese only gives half as much to the Societies for Church building, Church Aid, Augmentation of Endowments, and Education, in 1897, as it did in 1880. This is a state of things which ought not to be. A Diocese is not called into existence to be a collection of separate independent parishes, but a united body of Churchmen who bind themselves to support in every way the Church of England, as a corporate whole, within the geographical boundaries of the See, and to maintain Diocesan Institutions for the good of the whole body. We fail entirely to do this at present. Year after year parochial collections are dwindling away, and in a large number of parishes there are no collections at all. I do not like this, though I know the money given to Diocesan Institutions does not at all represent the amount of money given to Church purposes in the Diocese. But I cannot think it is right; and I feel it my duty to call the attention of the Clergy and laity of the Diocese to it.

If it is a wrong thing to have Diocesan Institutions, and every parish is to think of itself alone, and say of its neighbours, 'Am I my brother's keeper?' I wish men would speak out plainly and say so. But if it is a wise and prudent thing for every Diocese to have a common fund for Church Building, or Church Aid, or Education, to which any Clergyman wanting assistance may apply, and by which the strong may help the weak, I do not think our own Diocese is doing its duty. I commend the whole matter to the thoughtful consideration of the Conference. There ought to be a change. At the rate things are going we shall reach the bottom before long, and shall be obliged to give public notice that there are no longer any common Diocesan Funds from which grants can be given, and that all parishes in our Diocese which want assistance must in future shift for themselves. I hope I need not tell this Conference that to have no Diocesan Institutions at all would not be creditable to our new See, and would place us in an exceptional position. The plain truth is that we want more new subscribers, to take the place of old friends who have passed away. I trust that many will come to our aid.

(6) I turn from the comparatively tame subject of our Diocesan Institutions to a matter of far more public importance. I refer to Church Reform. This is a subject which is coming to the front more and more every year, and demands the careful notice of all who really love the Church of England, and wish to keep her healthy and strong. It is useless and too late to say that no reforms are needed, and that the good old ship requires no repair. All ancient man-made machines and instruments have a tendency to wear out and decay, and all as a rule are capable of improvement. From this universal law our Established Church can claim no exemption.

The subject is continually cropping up every year, whether we like it or not, in some shape or another. The Benefices Bill of last Session, the comparatively recent formation of a House of Laymen in each of the Provinces of Canterbury and York, the increasing demands of congregations, when livings are vacant, to have some voice in the selection of a new minister—all these things show plainly that 'Church Reform' is in the air. I wish today to impress on the members of our Conference the absolute necessity of looking seriously at it, and making up our minds as far as we can. Education is changing the character of the country, and laymen of all ranks and classes are no longer illiterate dummies, but think for themselves. To tell Churchmen in this day to sit still, shut their eyes, trust the bishops, and be content with machinery and arrangements which satisfied our grandfathers, is as senseless as it would be to send the Guards to garrison Gibraltar, and arm them with flint-locks or long-bows. No! my brethren, 'Church Reform' is sure to come. Its topsails are already on the horizon, and before long it will be alongside. Unless we want our good old Church to be disestablished, we should try to set our house in order while we can, and consider carefully what is really wanted. What is practicable and what is impracticable? What is possible and what is impossible? What would do good and what would do harm? These are questions which we ought to look in the face, and prepare to answer.

It is needless to tell you that Church Reform is a very wide subject, and greatly complicated by the connection of Church and State. Nevertheless there are some branches of it which appear to me quite within reach, and if Churchmen would only awake and take them up, I believe no Parliament would refuse to sanction them.

(i) We need a Reform about the sale of Livings. It is a crying scandal that the spiritual oversight of souls should be the subject of buying and selling, like a flock of sheep or litter of pigs, and the sooner the whole system is declared illegal the better it will be for the Church.

(ii) We need Reform of our Ecclesiastical Courts both in cases of false doctrine, and immorality. At present their modes of proceeding are expensive, cumbrous, tedious, and dilatory, and their penalties most unsatisfactory. To imprison a clergyman for holding fake doctrine is to go back to the dark ages.

(iii) We need a Reform about the power of Bishops in the matter of institution to vacant benefices. At present a Bishop has no power to refuse any incumbent presented to him, who satisfies certain legal requirements, though he may be inwardly convinced that the man is sometimes mentally, physically, and intellectually unfit for the post he seeks to fill. The English Bishops, I am aware, are no more infallible than the Bishop of Rome. But they ought to have some discretion.

(iv) We need a Reform about the voice of the laity being heard in some way about the manner of the services in the Parish Church, and about the selection of ministers for vacant livings. I frankly confess that this is a very difficult and delicate question, and I doubt whether the laity who take it up realize all that it involves. Does any one wish every ratepayer and parishioner to have a vote for a new incumbent? I cannot believe it. Is the choice to be left to those who attend the church, or to those only who are communicants? These are knots which are not easy to untie, and I commend them to the serious consideration of those worthy people who are fond of writing to the press whenever a living is vacant. The opinion of the congregation, if you give it a voice, should surely be expressed by some wise and carefully chosen Committee.

(v) We need a Reform about all Church patronage. I frankly admit that I mention this with much hesitation. At present there is a good deal to be said for the existing system of wide variety. The Crown, the Bishops, the Lord Chancellor, the Colleges, City Companies, Cathedral Chapters, private patrons, bodies of trustees, all are continually filling up vacancies, and all, no doubt, are continually making mistakes. But I am not quite convinced that the old system can be very much mended. It is easier to find fault with it than to improve it. To sweep away and disfranchise all patrons, and substitute Diocesan Boards of Patronage, such as the Irish Church has, appears to many the right solution of the problem. But I cannot feel satisfied that it would work well. Such Boards could only be formed by placing on them representatives of all schools of thought in the Church. Their appointments could only be made by a great deal of concession among themselves, and by constantly giving way to one another. The whole result would be that strong powerful men of light and leading would generally be passed over for the sake of peace, and, in order to obtain agreement, milk-and-water men of no decided views would be preferred. I doubt extremely whether such Diocesan Boards would do better than the existing system. At any rate I feel no strong confidence in them. I believe they would gradually fill Dioceses with tame, no-party, colourless men without brains, teeth, or claws, who have no distinct opinions about anything at all, and would do no good. However, so long as the Union of Church and State continues, there is no chance of the present system being given up; and the prohibition of sale of livings would stop half its mischief.

(vi) The last but not the least Reform needed is a Reform of Convocation. Of course I need not remind you that the defective representation of the parochial clergy, compared to that of the Deans and Chapters, is most unsatisfactory. In the lower House of Canterbury, the simple fact that two Proctors represent all London is a glaring scandal. The Reform that is really wanted is the admission of the laity in both Houses. I do not forget that 'Houses of Laymen' for Canterbury and York have been called into existence. I have not forgotten it, but I cannot admit that these Houses meet the wants of our times, or carry much weight in the country. We want picked, capable, elected, representative laymen who shall sit in the same House with the clergy, take part in all their debates, and meet them on terms of equality about all subjects. Until the laity have a proper place and voice and vote in the proceedings of our Church assembly I believe that Convocation will never enjoy the full confidence of the country, and few Englishmen will care for its debates. Legislative powers such a Reformed Convocation certainly ought not to have. England would not stand two Parliaments. But if the opinions and wishes of Convocation came to Parliament from a body consisting of able laymen as well as clergymen, I am convinced that they would receive far more respectful attention in the House of Commons than they do now. The thing has been tried in the Colonies and in the Episcopal Church of America with success, and I fail to see why it should not succeed here. At all events I am not afraid of the consequences. I have a strong conviction that in any mixed Convocation the most moderate, conservative, and cautious part of the Assembly would be the laity. I have heard on very good authority that it certainly has been found so in Australia.

I leave the wide subject of Church Reform at this point. There are branches of it which I decline to discuss because they appear to me utterly impracticable. I do not expect the Curates' League will persuade people that seniority entitles a man to promotion rather than gifts or grace. I shall say nothing about liturgical revision, that darling project of some zealous souls. So long as our 'unhappy divisions' exist, I see no likelihood of our venerable Prayer-book being cast into the furnace of reform, and especially when some persons want to go behind the Reformation, put the clock back, and return to the First Prayer-book of Edward VI. I shall not therefore waste your time in attempting to discuss that subject. I do not believe that the financial position of the clergy would ever be cured by seizing and dividing all the large livings, and giving every incumbent, out of the spoil, a dead level income all round of a bare £250 a year, making the clergy all paupers together. I do not think it would answer to make every official position the subject of election, and to throw open every Bishopric, Archdeaconry, Rural Deanery, Deanery, and Canonry to a contest and a poll in the Diocese. Such castles in the air you will allow me to leave alone, until they have got their feet on the ground.

The whole subject bristles with difficulties, and I doubt if many of you will live to see the 'things that are wanting' amended, unless there is some great political Revolution. Church work is notoriously slow work. It is well known that the House of

Commons dislikes to be troubled with Church subjects, and is overwhelmed with secular matters. There is a terrible scarcity of men in the Lords and Commons who have the ear of the House, and are ready and willing to take up Church Reform. If I saw some ecclesiastically-minded man of the calibre of John Bright or Richard Cobden, who would come forward with eloquence, wisdom, power, and pertinacity, and compel a hearing, I should be more hopeful. At present I look in vain for such men. However, I cannot forget that the party is still alive which recently made a deliberate attempt to disestablish the Church in Wales, and the next election may alter the whole political situation, and give churchmen a rude awakening. In the meantime I want to set men thinking. Sooner or later Church Reform will come, and I only hope it may not come to a church disestablished and in ruins. The Welsh campaign tells a plain story. It calls on us to reform our church while we can and while we may. As Rudyard Kipling says in his grand Diamond Jubilee Hymn: 'Lest we forget; lest we forget.'

(7) I must now try to wind up this long address, by some remarks about one very unhealthy and painful symptom which seems to me to characterize the age in which we are living. The symptom I refer to is the increasing indifference to all distinctive doctrines and opinions in religion, in every part of the land. I say emphatically *Increasing Religious Indifference*.

In saying this I ask you not to mistake my meaning. I have not in view those huge masses of people in London and our large towns, who worship nowhere, and appear to have no religion at all. I refer to those myriads in this age who are to be found in all our churches, who are not communicants, and never exhibit any interest in vital religion. I do not forget that man is by nature a poor fallen creature. I do not expect all who profess and call themselves Christians to be angels. But I declare my belief that the size and rapid growth of the school of indifference is one of the most dangerous signs of the times at the close of the 19th century.

The multitude who belong to this school are not open opponents of the faith and Christ's cause; but they simply sit still and do nothing for religion at home or abroad. Ask any good clergyman who works his parish, and visits his people, and knows their characters, what is the chief difficulty he has to contend with? I am certain he would tell you that it is neither Romanism, nor extreme Ritualism, nor Erastianism, nor Broad Churchism, nor systematic Scepticism, nor any other 'ism,' but a half-dead torpid *indifference* about any sort or kind of religion.

(i) You may see the danger I speak of in the vastly altered tone of public feeling about Romanism which has appeared in the last fifty years. There is no longer that general dislike and aversion to Popery which was once almost universal in this realm. The edge of the old British feeling about Protestantism seems blunted and dull. Some profess to be tired of all religious controversy, and are ready to sacrifice God's truth for the sake of peace. Some look on Romanism as simply one among many English forms of religion, and neither worse nor better than others. Some try to persuade us that Romanism is changed, and not nearly so bad as it used to be. Some boldly point to the faults of Protestants, and loudly cry that Romanists are quite as good as ourselves. And yet the two great historical facts (1) that ignorance, immorality, and superstition reigned supreme in England 400 years ago under Popery, (2) that the Reformation was the greatest blessing God ever gave to this land—both these are facts which no one but a Papist ever thought of disputing fifty years ago! In the present day, alas, it is convenient and fashionable to forget them!

No doubt this altered tone of public feeling has been furthered immensely by the proceedings of one extreme party in the Church of England, which has gradually familiarized people with every distinctive doctrine and practice of Romanism—the real presence, the mass, auricular confession and priestly absolution, the sacerdotal character of the ministry, the monastic system, and a histrionic, sensuous, showy style of public worship. And the natural result is, that many simple people see no mighty difference between the Church of England and the Church of Rome. The spurious liberality of the day we live in helps on the reaction of feeling. It is fashionable now to say that all sects should be equal, that the State should have nothing to do with religion, that all creeds should be regarded with equal favour and respect, and that there is a substratum of common truth at the bottom of all religions, whether Buddhism, Mahommedanism, or Christianity! The consequence is, that myriads of ignorant folks begin to think there is nothing peculiarly dangerous in the tenets of Papists, any more than in the tenets of Methodists, Independents, Presbyterians, or Baptists, and that we ought to let Romanism alone, never expose its unscriptural character, and avoid controversy. One thing at any rate is patent and obvious to every observing eye. Whatever the cause may be, public feeling in England is strangely altered about the Church of Rome, and it is a very painful feature of our times.

(ii) You may see the danger again in the widely spread disposition to make cleverness and earnestness the only tests of orthodoxy in religion. Thousands of professing Christians nowadays seem utterly unable to distinguish things that differ. If a preacher or lecturer is only clever and eloquent and earnest, they appear to think he is right, however strange and heterogeneous his sermons or lectures may be. Popery or Protestantism, an atonement or no atonement, a personal Holy Ghost or no Holy Ghost, future punishment or no future punishment, High Church or Low Church or Broad Church, Trinitarianism, Arianism, or Unitarianism, nothing comes amiss to these people if it is clever. They can swallow all if they cannot digest it! They seem to regard doctrine as a matter of no importance, and to think everybody is going to be saved and nobody going to be lost. Their religion is made up of negatives; and the only positive thing about them is, that they dislike distinctness, and think all extreme and decided and positive views are very naughty and very wrong. They are content to shovel aside all disputed points as rubbish, and if you charge them with indecision they will tell you, 'I do not pretend to understand controversy; I decline to examine controverted points. I daresay it is all the same in the long run.' Who does not know that such people swarm and abound everywhere? And who does not know that any one who denounces this state of things, and insists that a clergyman should be loyal to the Articles of his Church, is regarded as a narrow, party-spirited, ungenerous person, quite unsuited to the nineteenth century.

(iii) You may see the danger again in the demand which many are loudly making for the adoption of a general policy of toleration and forbearance within the pale of the Church of England. Such a policy, we are gravely told, is the true remedy for 'the present distress.' Every clergyman is to be allowed to hold and teach and do what he likes. No one is ever to be called to account, either for his ceremonial actions at the Lord's table or his sermons in the pulpit. Every school of thought, however extreme, is to be tolerated. No prosecutions in any Court, whether spiritual or secular, are to be permitted, since the Lincoln case.[1] The model for the Anglican Church is to be Israel in the days of the Judges when 'Every man did that which was right in his own eyes' (Judg. 21:25).

The mere fact that such a monstrous policy as I have described finds acceptance with many Churchmen is, to my mind, one of the greatest perils of the Church of England, and its adoption could only have one result. That result would ultimately be disruption, disintegration, and disestablishment. You could not possibly have two or three distinct churches within one communion. It is amazing to me that the advocates of this notable policy of universal toleration do not see that it would infallibly end in our Church being broken to pieces.

No doubt, at first sight this policy of universal toleration looks very specious. It suits the temper of the times. What more likely

[1] See p. 282.

to provide peace and stop quarrelling than to declare the Church a kind of Noah's Ark, within which every kind of animal, and every opinion and creed, shall dwell safe and undisturbed, and the only terms of communion shall be willingness to come inside and let your neighbour alone? Nevertheless, I must confess my utter inability to understand how this policy could ever be carried out without throwing overboard all Articles and Creeds, without doing away with all subscriptions, in short without altering the whole constitution of the Church of England.

(iv) Finally, you may see the growing danger of indifference which I speak of in the painful increase of Sabbath-breaking in the land. In town and in country, in Belgravia and Bethnal Green, the state of things is the same. Full Churches are the exception on Sunday, and half-empty Churches the rule. A religious census of any large population tells the same story. The Fourth Commandment of the Decalogue seems to be left out in the cold and ready to die. Partly from the spread of infidelity, that old enemy of the Lord's Day; partly from the morbid love of liberty, and letting everyone do as he likes; partly from the exaggerated love of pleasure which marks this age; partly from the facilities afforded by railways for Sabbath travelling, of which our fathers knew nothing, and got on well enough without them; partly from one cause and partly from another, the devil is just now getting more help in his favourite campaign against the Lord's Day than he has done since the Reformation. You may see what I mean, in the persistent attempts now made to throw open places of amusement, aquariums, museums, picture galleries, and such-like places, under the plausible pretence of 'affording recreation to the working classes.'

I have no hesitation in saying that this unmistakable increase of Sabbath neglect is one of the worst symptoms of the increase of indifference to vital religion in our days. There is an insepa-rable connection between the observance of the Lord's Day and the prosperity of true religion. Voltaire was quite right when he said he could never succeed in destroying Christianity unless he destroyed Sunday. Whether Englishmen know it or not, their Sabbath has been one of their richest possessions, and the grand secret of their position in the world. Of it the famous words may be truly used, that 'it is the cheap defence of a nation.'[1] It is the English Sunday which has made England what it is. It is a simple fact that wherever spiritual religion in a Church is strong and vigorous, the honour of Sunday goes up, and wherever it decays, Sunday ceases to be well observed. In a word, Sunday is the barometer of every so-called Christian nation. Tell me how Sunday is kept in a land, and I will tell you what the Church of the land is.

I leave the whole subject here, and close my address with one sorrowful remark. If open sin and dissipation, and drunkenness, and love of the world, are ruining thousands of Churchmen, I am sure that utter indifference about religion is ruining tens of thousands.

Now is there no remedy for this state of things? Is there no cure for this terrible plague of the Church in these latter days? Amidst the endless strife of Church parties, the weary, unprofitable controversies about the sacraments, the ministry, and the ceremonials of worship, the only party which seems to me to grow and increase annually is the huge party of 'religious indifference.' Can nothing be done to check the progress of this party, and restore health to our Zion? I answer, nothing, in my opinion, but an outpouring of the Holy Spirit. More schools and universities will not set us right. They touch heads but not hearts. Spiritual is the disease, and spiritual must be the remedy. In plain words we need among us more of the 'real presence' of the Holy Ghost. For this let us all pray and besiege the throne of grace continually.

I cannot forget that the early Christians of the first four centuries turned the world upside down with their doctrine, emptied the heathen temples of their worshippers, stopped the

---

[1] Edmund Burke: *Reflections on the French Revolution*.

bloody gladiatorial combats, confounded the Greek and Roman philosophers, gave a new position to women and children, and raised the moral standard of all Europe. And yet they had none of our many advantages; no printed books, no Cathedrals or grand churches, no Religious Societies and no subscription lists! But they had that which we seem to lack in 1897, the real presence of the Holy Spirit in their work, their preaching, their characters, and their lives. This was the secret of their power! That is what we want among us at the end of the nineteenth century, more prayer, closer union with Christ, more of the real presence of God the Holy Ghost!

Happy would it be for this country if a cry went up daily from every Christian family and every parish and congregation in the land: 'Come from the four winds, O breath, and breathe on the Church of England, that she may awake to a sense of her danger, shake off her growing indifference, do her first works and be alive.' Men and brethren, I say once more, the true medicine that we need is the 'real presence' of God the Holy Ghost. For that presence, when we leave the Conference of this week, let us resolve to pray, and never to cease praying.

> Hear we the Saviour's voice,
>   Pray, brethren, pray!
> Would ye his heart rejoice?
>   Pray, brethren, pray!
> Sin calls for ceaseless fear,
>   Weakness needs the Strong One near;
> Long as ye struggle here,
>   Pray, brethren, pray![1]

---

[1] Quoted from 'Hark, 'tis the Watchman's cry,' a hymn from 'The Revival,' 1859.

16

THE PRESENT DISTRESS

Part of an address given at the seventeenth Liverpool Diocesan Conference, November 1898.

MY Reverend and Lay Brethren, from diocesan subjects I turn to four others of far more gravity, subjects in which I think every Churchman ought to take a very deep interest in the present day. I shall make no apology for handling them in order, and asking you everyone to look steadily at them. Those subjects are—Church Reform, Church Defence, Church Divisions, and Church Toleration.

(1) I shall begin with *Church Reform*. This is an old and wide subject, which is rapidly becoming one of grave importance. I can remember the time, seventeen years ago, when some members of this Conference smiled at those who brought it forward, as amiable enthusiasts. They would not smile now, if they were alive. The Benefices Bill, and the fierce debates which accompanied that measure, have made the House of Commons sit up and have compelled attention. In every part of the land men are awake and alive about Church Reform. Committees and Societies for obtaining it, with active members of every rank, are coming to the front everywhere.

It is useless to say that Church Reform is not needed. After two centuries and more the grand old ship, which has stood so many battles and breezes, requires not a few repairs and amendments. Reason and common sense point out that there is a continual increase of defects in all human handiwork, and a gradual tendency to decay. The progress of knowledge, science, and education brings to light weak points requiring improvements of which our forefathers never dreamed. Church Reform is rapidly becoming a necessity if our Church is to live and not die.

The subject is continually cropping up every year, whether we like it or not, in some shape or another. The mere fact that a Reform League with many influential supporters has been lately called into existence, is a fact which alone speaks volumes. The repeal of the Corn Laws, we should remember, began with a League.[1] The Benefices Bill of last Session, the comparatively recent formation of a House of Laymen in each of the Provinces of Canterbury and York, the increasing demands of congregations, when livings are vacant, to have some voice in the selection of a new minister—all these things show plainly that Church Reform is in the air. I wish today to impress on the members of our Conference the absolute necessity of looking seriously at it, and making up our minds as far as we can.

It is needless to tell you that Church Reform is a very large subject, and greatly complicated by the connection of Church and State. Nevertheless there are some branches of it which appear to me quite within reach, and if Churchmen would only unite in trying to obtain them, something might be done. Though I shall go over old ground, which I have surveyed more than once, I will mention Reforms which seem to me urgently needed.

(i) We need reform of our Ecclesiastical Courts, both in cases of false doctrine and immorality. At present their constitutions are defective, their modes of proceeding expensive, cumbrous, tedious and dilatory, and their penalties most unsatisfactory. To imprison a clergyman for holding false doctrine is to go back to the dark ages.

(ii) We want a new set of Canons for the regulation of all the proceedings of the Church of England. Those that we have

---

[1] The Anti-Corn Law League, founded by Cobden and Bright in 1839. The Corn Laws were repealed in 1846.

at present are many of them practically useless, and little more than curious fossils rendered needless by alterations of law. In this matter we might learn a few things from the new Canons of the Disestablished Church of Ireland.

(iii) We need a reform about the voice of the laity being heard in some way, both about the manner of the services in the parish church, and about the selection of ministers for vacant livings.

(iv) We need a reform about all Church patronage. I frankly admit that I mention this with much hesitation. At present there is a good deal to be said for the existing system of wide variety. But I am not quite convinced that the old system can be very much mended. It is easier to find fault with it than to improve it. However, so long as the union of Church and State continues, there is not much chance of the present system being given up; and the prohibition of sale of livings would stop half its mischief.

(v) The last but not the least reform needed is a reform of Convocation. The reform that is really wanted is the admission of the laity in both Houses. Until the laity have a proper place, and voice, and vote in the proceedings of our Church assembly, I believe that Convocation will never enjoy the full confidence of the country, and few Englishmen will care for its debates. Legislative powers such a reformed Convocation certainly ought not to have. England would not stand two parliaments. But if the opinions and wishes of Convocation came to Parliament from a body consisting of able laymen as well as clergymen, I am convinced that they would receive far more respectful attention in the House of Commons than they do now.

(2) From Church Reform I turn to *Church Defence*. It is my firm belief that as a body there are no Christians more ignorant of the principles and history of their own community than English Churchmen, and I believe the time has come when a strenuous effort ought to be made to increase the knowledge of distinct doctrine and historic Christianity throughout the land. I should like the clergy to preach and explain more frequently the Creeds

and Articles, and make men understand clearly what a Churchman ought to know and believe. I should like the leading events in the history of our Church during the last three centuries to be made quite familiar to our people, so that they may be able to answer the enemies who make erroneous assertions and reckless statements about us. It is time to awake out of sleep. The Disestablishment campaign may be upon us again before long. We must be prepared to defend as well as to cleanse the Church.

But systematic pulpit instruction is only part of what is needed in order to meet the ignorance of the times. We ought to organize a supply of information about English Church history. We ought to provide a qualified body of lecturers whose whole business shall be to visit every diocese, and tell people what the story of the Church of England really is. One caution only must be remembered. The lecturers must be thoroughly impartial, and not one-sided men. If, for example, they went about telling people everywhere that Archbishop Laud was a blessed martyr, and saying nothing about Ridley and Latimer; or if they praised James II, and abused the Puritans; such lecturing would do more harm than good. However, I trust these doubts and fears would prove groundless. I believe that an honest, capable body of lecturers would spread much light, and dispel a vast amount of ignorance which now exists. After all, I must express my firm belief that the best defence of the Church of England in the present day is more attention to the pastoral work of the clergy.

We want more house-to-house visitation, more direct personal dealing with the souls of the people, more kindly, friendly, evangelistic aggression. The whole style of clerical work is greatly altered. Multiplied Services and Communions absorb a vast amount of time and attention. But I have grave doubts whether our Church would not be much stronger if there was more old-fashioned pastoral visitation.

I have a firm conviction that the sympathy and confidence of the working classes are the chief defence of the Church of

England at this crisis of her history. This sympathy and confidence, I believe, the clergy will find no difficulty in getting if they go to work in the right way.

I assert confidently that the English working man is peculiarly open to sympathetic attention, and the clergyman has peculiar opportunities of showing it. The working man may live in a poor dwelling; and after toiling all day in a coal pit, or cotton mill, or iron foundry, or dock, or chemical works, he may often look very rough and dirty. But after all he is flesh and blood like ourselves. Beneath his outward roughness he has a heart and a conscience, a keen sense of justice, and a jealous recollection of his rights as a man and a Briton. He does not want to be patronized and flattered, any more than to be trampled on, scolded, or neglected; but he does like to be dealt with as a brother, in a friendly, kind, and sympathizing way. He will not be driven to attend daily services, or early communions, and indeed has no time for such things. He will do little for a cold, hard formalist, however correct he may be in ritual. But give him a clergyman who really understands that it is the heart and not the coat which makes the man, and that the guinea's worth is in the gold, and not in the stamp upon it; give him a clergyman who will not only preach Christ in the pulpit, but come and sit down in his house, and take him by the hand in a Christ-like, familiar way during the week; give him a clergyman who realizes that in Christ's holy religion there is no respect of persons, that rich and poor are 'made of one blood,' and need one and the same atoning blood, and that there is only one Saviour, and one fountain for sin, and one heaven, both for employers and employed; give him a clergyman who can weep with them that weep, and rejoice with them that rejoice, and who feels a tender interest in the cares and troubles, and births and marriages and deaths of the humblest dweller in his parish; give the working man, I say, a clergyman of that kind, and as a general rule, the working man will come to his church. Such a clergyman will not preach to empty benches. Such a clergyman is the best and most efficient defence of the Established Church of England, and will have a congregation who will be her best guards and supporters.

(3) I turn next to the painful subject of *Church Divisions*. It is needless to tell most of you that our Church has never been free from divisions ever since the days of that unhappy man, Archbishop Laud. I know it is the fashion to admire him in the present day, and I have seen book after book written to show how much the Church of England is indebted to Laud. I cannot agree with the writers of these books, and I shall always regard Laud as the real founder of English dissent. But the divisions of the present day are far the most serious that have ever troubled our Church, and demand our most serious consideration. When that great organ of public opinion, *The Times* newspaper, throws open its columns to lengthy controversial correspondence about such subjects as auricular confession, and gives the public powerful articles discussing religious points in dispute, it is high time to rub our eyes and ask ourselves what it all means. How are we to account for the agitation and excitement, unrest and disquiet, and disturbance about religion which is heard of in every part of the land? I shall offer an answer to these questions. I point to *extreme ritualism*.

In saying this, I ask you not to misunderstand me. There are Ritualists and Ritualists. There are some who, with many errors, are loyal and faithful men at heart; there are others who hold such strange and heterodox opinions, that it is hard to understand why they remain inside the Church of England at all. These are the troublers of our Israel. These are what I mean by extreme Ritualists.

I am firmly persuaded that the root and cause of the present state of things is the strong conviction of many lay Churchmen that it is the secret intention of not a few of the clergy to undo the work of the Protestant Reformation, and to re-introduce into England the erroneous doctrines and worship of the Church of Rome. Rightly or wrongly, they look upon the movement of the extreme Ritualist body with suspicion, and regard it as the highway to Popery. Some of them no doubt have read English history, and know something of the reign of James II. They do not forget the unhappy efforts of that misguided monarch to suppress Protestantism, and bring back Popery into the land, which cost him his own crown, drove him into exile, and caused the Revolution of 1688. They remember those things, and resent the slightest appearance of a return to Romanism in 1898.

The laity throughout the land complain justly about the ceremonial novelties which extreme Ritualists have thrust into our Church worship during the last forty years. They have all been in one direction, whether of dress or gesture or posture or action or anything else. They have been as un-Protestant as possible. They have been borrowed or imitated from Popery. They have exhibited one common bias and animus, an anxious desire to get as far as possible from the ways of the Reformers, and to get as near as possible, whether legally or illegally, to the ways of Rome. They have shown one common systematic determination to un-Protestantize, as far as possible, the simple worship of the Church of England, and to assimilate it, as far as possible, to the gaudy and sensuous worship of Popery. A short catalogue of specimens will show what I mean.

(1) Our Reformers found the sacrifice of the Mass in our Church. They cast it out as a 'blasphemous fable and dangerous deceit,' and called the Lord's Supper a sacrament. The extreme Ritualists have re-introduced the word sacrifice, and too often glory in calling the Lord's Supper a Mass.

(2) Our Reformers found altars in all our churches. They ordered them to be taken down, cast the word 'altar' entirely out of our Prayer-book, and spoke only of the Lord's table and the Lord's board. Even one hundred years after the Protestant Reformation, when our Liturgy was finally revised and placed on its present basis, in the reign of Charles II, the Revisers did not attempt to

bring back into our Communion Service the word 'altar.' The extreme Ritualists delight in calling the Lord's table the 'altar,' and setting up altars in all their churches.

(3) Our Reformers found our clergy sacrificing priests, and made them prayer-reading, preaching ministers—ministers of God's word and sacraments. The extreme Ritualists glory in calling every clergyman a sacrificing 'priest.'

(4) Our Reformers found the doctrine of a real corporal presence in our Church, and laid down their lives to oppose it. They would not even allow the expression 'real presence' a place in our Prayer-book. They distinctly repudiated alike both Romish transubstantiation and Lutheran consubstantiation. They declared in their 29th Article that faithless communicants are 'in no wise (nullo modo) partakers of Christ.' The extreme Ritualists have re-introduced the doctrine, and too often honour the consecrated elements in the Lord's Supper as if Christ's natural body and blood were in them.

(5) Our Reformers found in all our churches images, rood screens, crucifixes, and holy places, and indignantly cast them out. The extreme Ritualists are incessantly trying to bring them back.

(6) Our Reformers found our worship stuffed with processions, incense-burning, flag-carrying, candles, gestures, postures, flowers, and gaudy sacrificial garments, and ordered them all to be put away. The extreme Ritualists are too often labouring to re-introduce them.

I pause here, and will go no further. I might easily name other things which I regret, and regard as dangerous innovations in this day. Such things are lighted candles on the holy table at Communion by daylight, incense, the mixed chalice, ceremonial ablution, holy water, and the use of mischievous catechisms for children, catechisms teaching Mariolatry, and seven sacraments instead of two, and worst of all, enforced auricular confession. I pass them all by, because in the present state of ecclesiastical discipline, when absolute liberty seems the only rubric, it is waste of time to do more than express regrets.

I can only look on and grieve. Some people, I know, regard these things as trifles not worth attention. I cannot see with their eyes. They are very mischievous trifles. They are just the kind of things which in the present day are gradually sapping the foundations of the Church of England. They irritate and annoy the middle and lower classes, who cannot find them in the very Prayer-book which from childhood they have used, and been incessantly urged to value and treat with veneration. They are regarded as an attempt to un-Protestantize the Establishment. If they continue to increase, and are not checked, the end will be disestablishment, disendowment, and disruption. This, at any rate, is my deliberate opinion.

The plain truth is that extreme Ritualism, with its many novelties, seems to be gradually alienating the middle classes and lower orders from the Church of England. These have now the voting power in their hands, and are pretty sure to use it at the next election, and to leave the upper ten thousand in a minority. Thousands of tradesmen and farmers and artisans have an instinctive horror of Popery. It is not wise to sneer at them as unlearned and ignorant men, as some do. They may not be very intelligent or deeply read in theological matters, but they are determined not to put up with Popery. They cannot draw nice distinctions: they are apt to call a spade a spade, and to give things their right name. They may not be able to speak like John Bright, or write like Macaulay, but they have heads on their shoulders, and can and will think. And if they see the slightest attempt to re-introduce Popish ceremonies into our parish churches, their suspicions are roused, they will walk off to Chapel. The Churchman who allows these suspicions to be roused may be earnest, well-meaning, innocent-minded, and zealous, but he is no true friend to the Church of England.

Once for all, I must honestly avow that my chief fears of extreme Ritualism arise from the effect which it has on the minds of the lower and middle classes. They do not like it. They will not have it. They call it Popery.

It is my own belief that the strength of the extreme Ritualists lies chiefly among the upper classes. Members of the English aristocracy who like ornate services with much music and singing and little preaching and prayer; half-instructed people who have gradually seceded from Evangelical families; idle young ladies and thoughtless young men who seldom read their Bibles and like lively, sensational worship, and dislike anything which seems plain and dull—these, and such as these, in the present day are continually falling away and proclaiming that they are *not satisfied* with old-fashioned Protestantism. They are like children who admire poppies more than corn, and like babies who care for toys more than food. But extreme Ritualism does not meet the wants of the hard-working, the hard-headed, the hard-handed masses of the great middle classes and intelligent artisans, the brain and muscle of England. These men want food for their souls and rest for their consciences. They find life too hard and heart-wearing to be content with trifles and toys in worship. If the Church will not provide them with the plain bread of the pure Gospel unadulterated and unmixed, they will leave her and pitch their tents elsewhere.

What the end of our unhappy divisions and the present distressing state of things is likely to be, it is impossible to say. I do not wish to be a black prophet. I have great faith in our Church's tenacity of life. She survived the temporary suppression of Protestantism in the reign of 'bloody Mary.' She survived the overthrow of Episcopacy and the proscription of the Liturgy in the days of the Commonwealth. She survived the expulsion of 2,000 most able clergymen in 1662, many of them learned and excellent Fellows of Colleges, by the Act of Uniformity. She survived the secession of the non-jurors when William III came to the throne. She survived the loss of the Methodist body in the last century. She has survived the departure to their own place of Manning, Newman, Oakley, Faber, the two Wilberforces, and many others in our own day. If she is faithful to the grand old principles of the

Protestant Reformation, I believe she will yet live and not die. But at present I am firmly convinced that the huge divisions caused by the movement called Extreme Ritualism are seriously endangering the life of the Church of England.

(4) The last subject which I propose to handle in this Conference paper is 'Church Toleration.' Toleration, up to a certain point, will always be one mark of a healthy Protestant Church. As long as human nature is what it is, it is useless to expect all Christian people to see all things, both great and small, in exactly the same light and to require from them a Chinese uniformity. Common sense tells us that Churchmen ought to tolerate diversities in matters indifferent about which both Scripture, Prayer-book, and rubrics are all silent, and no question of doctrine is involved. There are a good many small points of this kind, as we must all be aware. To condemn men as heretical and unsound because they do not agree with us about these small points appears to me the height of narrowness and intolerance. We may think our brother very stupid for not seeing things as we do; but in the absence of Bible and Prayer-book argument he has as much right to have an opinion as ourselves.

But toleration must have limits; and this is precisely the point at which I see danger ahead in the present day. That danger consists in the growing demand which many are making for the toleration of every kind of religious opinion and ritual practice within the pale of the Church of England. Such a policy, we are gravely told, is the true remedy for 'the present distress.' Every clergyman is to be allowed to hold and teach and do what he likes. No one is ever to be called to account either for his ceremonial actions at the Lord's table or his sermons in the pulpit. Every school of thought, however extreme, is to be tolerated. No prosecutions in any Court, whether spiritual or secular, are to be permitted. The model for the Anglican Church is to be Israel in the days of the Judges, when 'Every man did that which was right in his own eyes' (Judg. 21:25).

The mere fact that such a monstrous policy as I have described finds acceptance with many Churchmen is, to my mind, one of the greatest perils of the Church of England; and like extreme Ritualism its adoption could only have one result. That result would ultimately be disruption, disintegration, disendowment, and disestablishment. You could not possibly have two or three distinct churches within one communion. It is amazing to me that the advocates of this notable policy of universal toleration do not see that it would infallibly end in our Church being broken to pieces.

No doubt, at first sight the policy of universal toleration looks very specious. It suits the temper of the times. What more likely to provide peace and stop quarrelling than to declare the Church a kind of happy family or Noah's ark, within which every kind of opinion and creed, and every animal, shall dwell safe and undisturbed, and the only terms of communion shall be willingness to come inside and let your neighbour alone? Nevertheless, I must confess my utter inability to understand how this policy could ever be carried out without throwing overboard all Articles and Creeds, without doing away with all subscriptions, in short, without altering the whole constitution of the Church of England.

Whether this state of things will ever be sanctioned and allowed I cannot tell. Nothing in these days is impossible. Nothing is too absurd to concede and allow in the present mania for complete freedom of thought, and absolute liberty of opinion. I will only ask my hearers to consider carefully what the practical working of the new system would be.

What would be the position of the laity? At present the English lay Churchman, wherever he lives, or moves to, in England, may justly expect to find a certain degree of uniformity in the services and sermons of the parish church. No doubt he may find more singing and surplice-wearing and outward ceremonial in one place than another. One clergyman may give more prominence to one set of verities than another. But on the whole the diversity is generally within limits. There will be an end to all this when the reign of universal toleration begins. He will be startled to hear from one pulpit that much of the Old Testament is defective and uninspired, or that there is no such person as the devil, and no future punishment. If he moves to another parish, he may be astonished to see the Lord's Supper administered with a sacrificial dress, and accompanied by incense and lighted candles in broad day, and adoration of the consecrated elements. If he dislikes all this he must not complain! However much aggrieved, he will be told that this is the famous brand-new policy of toleration, and that he must submit! Will the laity be content and satisfied with this state of things? I doubt it extremely. There would be general grumbling all over the country. Myriads of the middle class would leave the Church and become Dissenters.

What would be the position of the English clergy? At present, in spite of much friction and jarring, the great majority of the three schools of thought—honest High, Low and Broad, with the exception of violent and extreme men—manage to get on pretty amicably, and respect one another, especially on such matters as education, temperance and missions. There is a common bond of union in loyal love to the Church of England, and a cordial desire to hand her down uninjured to their children. There is a common determination to abide within the limits of our creeds and formularies, and not to transgress them. There is a common dislike of the furious zealots who are striving by addition or subtraction or alteration to depart from the old paths. There will be an end of all this when the reign of universal toleration begins! When the Mass on one side, and avowed scepticism on the other, are formally sanctioned by authority, it is vain to suppose there would not be a large secession of some conscientious clergy from our communion. Others who did not secede would draw together for protection, and crystallize and solidify their own peculiar views, and refuse to recognize any others. In short, there would be a multiplication and increase of our 'unhappy divisions,' which would endanger the existence of the Church of England and shake it to the very centre.

What, above all, would be the position of our English Bishops? At present they make a solemn promise at their consecration, that they will be 'ready, with all faithful diligence, to banish and drive away all erroneous and strange doctrine contrary to God's word, and both privately and openly to call upon and encourage others to do the same.' Once let the much praised policy of universal toleration be accepted and formally authorized, and I fail to see the slightest use in this promise. Some of a Bishop's clergy will hold a Romish view of the Lord's Supper, and openly call it the Mass. Others will be content with the views of the Prayer-book, and indignantly repudiate incense, the chasuble, a material presence, an altar and a sacrifice. Some of his candidates for ordination will hold broad and liberal doctrines which cannot, by any ingenuity, be reconciled with the Articles, and will write them down in their examination papers. Others, with equal coolness, will offer sceptical statements about inspiration and the atonement. What then, is the unhappy Bishop to do? He will be able to do nothing at all. He must become an 'honorary member of all schools of thought.' He will be obliged to smile on all with equal complacency, and to license, institute, and ordain anybody or everybody, without asking any questions at all or requiring any declarations, promises, vows, oaths, or subscriptions. If the Church of England long survived such a chaotic state of things it would be a miracle indeed. When there are no laws or rules, there can be no order in any community. When there is no creed or standard of doctrine, there can be no church, but a Babel. Let men say what they please. A ship without a compass, a lighthouse without a lantern, a locomotive express engine without a fire, would not be more useless than a Church would be without Creeds, Articles, or Rubrics, and sailing under the flag of universal toleration.

I bring my annual address to a conclusion at this point ... Whether Parliament is going to interpose and help us I cannot tell. I see little hope of deliverance from any other quarter. There are handwritings on the wall which it needs no Daniel to interpret. There is a current setting in towards the disestablishment of all national Churches, and it is a question whether we are not already in it. We are daily drifting downward, though some may neither feel nor perceive it, and in a few years, unless we exert ourselves, we shall be over the falls. In a day like this every loyal Churchman should be ready to do his duty, and determine, by God's help, to hand down the pure faith of the Reformation to his children's children.

17

FAREWELL TO THE DIOCESE

REVEREND and Dear Brethren, almost the last words of the great Apostle to the Gentiles are before the eyes of my mind today: 'I have finished my course; the time of my departure is at hand.' After filling unexpectedly the office of your Bishop for nearly twenty years, I am about to resign a post which years and failing health at the age of eighty-three told me I was no longer able to fill with advantage to the diocese or to the Church of England.

I have resigned my Bishopric with many humbled feelings. As I look back over the years of my episcopate, I am conscious that I have left undone many things which I hoped to have done when I first came to Liverpool. I am equally conscious that the many things I have had to do with—meetings, ordinations, confirmations, and consecrations—have been done very imperfectly. I only ask you to remember that I was sixty-four, and not a young man, when I first came here, and to believe that, amidst many difficulties, I have tried to do my duty. But I am thankful that our God is a merciful God.

Before I leave you I ask you to accept a few parting words from an old minister who has had more than fifty-eight years' experience, and during that time has seen and learned many things. It is written, 'Days should speak, and multitude of years should teach wisdom' (Job 32:7). Let me, then, charge all the clergy whom I am about to leave behind me never to neglect their preaching. Your districts and population may be comparatively small or large. But the minds of your people are thoroughly awake. They will not be content with dull, tame sermons. They want life, and light, and fire, and love in the pulpit as well as in the parish. Let them have plenty of it. Never forget that a lively, Christ-exalting minister will always have a church-going people.

Last, but not least, cultivate and study the habit of being at peace with all your brother ministers. Beware of divisions. One thing the children of the world can always understand if they do not understand doctrine. That thing is angry quarrelling and controversy. Be at peace among yourselves.

May God bless you all.

To the many lay Churchmen whom I shall leave behind in this diocese (knowing far less of them than I should have done if I had come among them a younger man), I can only send my best wishes, and add my prayers that this diocese may have God's blessing both in temporal and spiritual prosperity. Cling to the old Church of England, my lay brethren, cling to its Bible, its Prayer-book, and its Articles. Let no charitable institution suffer. Consider the many poor and needy. Support missionary work at home and abroad. Help the underpaid clergy. Never forget that the principles of the Protestant Reformation made this country what she is, and let nothing ever tempt you to forsake them.

In a little time we shall all meet again; many, I hope, on the King's right hand and few on the left. Till that time comes I commend you to God and the word of his grace, which is able to build you up, and give you an inheritance among them that are sanctified. I remain, your affectionate Bishop and lasting friend,

J. C. LIVERPOOL.
The Palace, Abercromby Square,
February 1st, 1900.

APPENDIX

CHAPTER 1

1. 'The composition of a purely ecclesiastical tribunal to be substituted for the present 'Court of Appeal' in cases of heresy, is a problem beset with such complicated difficulties, as to render it almost hopeless that any scheme will ever be derived for its solution, which would give general satisfaction; even if there were not so many who would reject it for the very reason that it appears to recognize a principle, the mystical prerogative of the Clergy, which they reject as groundless and mischievous.' *Bishop Thirlwall's Remains*, ii. p. 135.

'That the members of the judicial committee would ever consent, or be permitted, to renounce their supreme jurisdiction, and exchange their judicial functions in this behalf, for a purely ministerial agency by which they will have passively to accept, and simply to carry into effect, the decision of a clerical council, this is something which I believe is no longer imagined to be possible, even by the most ardent and sanguine advocate of what he calls the inalienable rights of the Clergy, so long as the Church remains in union with the State on the present terms of the alliance. But if they do not take up this subordinate position, the principle of the ecclesiastical prerogative in matter of doctrine, which to those who maintain it is probably more precious than any particular application of it, is abandoned and lost. The Church will, in their language, continue to groan in galling fetters, and an ignominious bondage.' *Bishop Thirlwall's Remains*, ii. p. 137.

2. The following evidence was deliberately given by that well-known Clergyman, the Rev. W. J. E. Bennett, Vicar of Frome, before the Royal Commission, on Ritual:

'2606. "Is any doctrine involved in your using the chasuble?" "I think there is."

'2607. "What is that doctrine?" "The doctrine of the sacrifice."

'2608. "Do you consider yourself a sacrificing priest?" "Distinctly so."

'2611. "Then you think you offer a propitiatory sacrifice?" "Yes, I think I do offer a propitiatory sacrifice."'

3. 'We cannot but respect the courage and openness with which the leaders of the Ritualist movement avow their designs, and disclose their plan of operation. They inform us that their party is engaged in a "crusade against Protestantism," and aims at nothing less than "re-Catholicizing the Church of England, and that, with a view to this ultimate object, they are agitating for disestablishment." After this, it must be our own fault if we are not on our guard. But when the same persons put in a plea for toleration, I do not know how to illustrate the character of such a proposal more aptly than by the image suggested by one of themselves, of "two great camps." It is as if one of these camps should send to the other some such message as this: "We are on our march to take possession of your camp, and to make you our prisoners; but all we desire is, that you should let us alone, and should not attempt to put any hindrance in our way."' *Bishop Thirlwall's Remains*, ii. p. 307.

CHAPTER 3

TABLE I.

The following is a summarized Statement, carefully drawn up from Visitation Returns, of the Total Expenditure in each Rural Deanery in the Diocese of Liverpool, on building, enlarging, or restoring Churches, on building or enlarging School-rooms, and on building Mission Rooms or Parish Rooms, during the three years ending October 1884:

Rural Deanery of		North Liverpool	£20,302	15	5
,,	,,	North Meols, and Ormskirk,	20,379	15	2
,,	,,	Walton,	7,500	18	3
,,	,,	Wigan,	21,047	10	0
,,	,,	Childwall,	16,371	16	2
,,	,,	South Liverpool,	5,341	19	3
,,	,,	Prescot,	14,225	9	3
,,	,,	Toxteth,	29,905	6	9
,,	,,	Winwick,	10,310	0	0
		Total	£145,385	16	2

TABLE II.

The following is a summarized Statement, carefully drawn up from Visitation Returns, of the money contributed and expended in each Rural Deanery in the Diocese of Liverpool, for Parochial Charities, Diocesan Institutions, Home Missions, and Foreign Missions, during the three years ending October 1884:

Rural Deanery of		North Liverpool	£16,164	16	2
,,	,,	North Meols, and Ormskirk,	14,118	0	0
,,	,,	Walton,	9,080	0	0
,,	,,	Wigan,	4,638	0	0
,,	,,	Childwall,	12,861	0	0
,,	,,	South Liverpool,	12,025	0	0
,,	,,	Prescot,	7,417	0	0
,,	,,	Toxteth,	20,770	0	0
,,	,,	Winwick,	1,698	0	0
		Total	£98,771	16	2

I think it right to say that the sum total in each of these Tables does not represent the whole amount of money actually expended and contributed. But unhappily the returns from some Parishes, in reply to my 37th and 38th Articles of Inquiry, are very incomplete.

J. C. LIVERPOOL.

CHAPTER 4

The schemes which some politicians gravely propose in the present day are so amazingly unreasonable, unpractical, and useless, that I think it well to say a few words about one of them, in order to prevent simple-minded people being deceived.

I remark, then, that some tell us that the cure for all the poverty and social depression of the lower classes is to give them land. 'Give every man three acres of British soil,' they say. 'Create an immense class of peasant proprietors, and there will be an end of complaining, destitution, and pauperism.' How this notable plan could be carried into effect without forcibly depriving the present landowners of property most of them have honestly bought, and do not want to part with, I fail to see. Moreover, whether there is sufficient land worth cultivating in Great Britain to provide every man with three acres is more than doubtful. However, these are little difficulties which I am willing to pass by.

The point which I wish to urge on the consideration of all sensible readers is simply this: the mere possession of three acres of land without capital, to nineteen men out of twenty, would be perfectly useless. It would do them no more good than the gift of a white elephant. One really might suppose, on reading the speeches of some modern political orators, that land produces crops without labour, and that the working man has only to strike his foot on the soil, and bread and meat and potatoes will at once start up before his eyes! But every practical farmer or agricultural labourer could tell us that this is ridiculous and absurd. There is no profession in which skill, diligence, and constant attention are more necessary, if success is to be obtained, than in that of the cultivation of land. And if any one thing has been found out by long experience, it is this, that a man cannot live with comfort, and bring up a family, if he has only three acres of land, and nothing else to depend on. It is too much land to leave him time to attend to any business. It is too little to make him as well off as a steady London or Birmingham artisan who has regular employment.

I may be allowed to speak pretty confidently on this subject. I have passed forty years of my ministerial life in agricultural parishes. I have had more opportunities than most men of observing the condition of farmers, both great and small, and of agricultural labourers. I have not the slightest hesitation in saying that, as a general rule, the occupiers of three or four acres of land are in a most miserable condition, and are not nearly so well off as the labourers around them, who are regularly working for the farmers at twelve or fourteen shillings a week, paying a fair rent for a cottage and half an acre of allotment land, but not possessing a foot of soil of their own. If the owner and occupier of three or four acres is a strong man, living close to a town, with two or three sons to help him, and knows what can be done with land, and is never idle, or drunk, and has a succession of good seasons and good prices, I have observed that in some rare exceptional cases he can get on pretty well for a few years. But I repeat that, as a general rule, such a man is sure to come to grief at last I am therefore quite certain that the idea of improving the condition of London or Birmingham artisans, who know nothing of farming, by giving each man three acres of land, without capital to farm it, is a complete delusion, and would infallibly lead to bitter disappointment. He must begin his first year with borrowing, and we all know the old proverb, 'He that goes a-borrowing goes a-sorrowing.' I advise those who are not satisfied with what I have just said, to study an admirable book lately published by Lady Verney, entitled *Peasant Properties*. If that book does not show the utter fallacy of the vaunted three-acre remedy for the wants of the working classes, I am greatly mistaken.

After all, the grand error which lies at the root of half the wild schemes for ameliorating the condition of the lower orders is forgetfulness of the great Bible doctrine of the fall, and the consequent corruption of human nature. So long as men and women are what they are, no laws or enactments of Parliament will ever produce a dead level of equality, or prevent some being rich, and others very poor, just as it was in the golden days of Solomon. So long as human nature remains unchanged, some men will be industrious and some will be lazy, some will be stupid and some will be clever, some will be intemperate and some will be sober, some will be thrifty and saving and some will be extravagant and wasteful, some will be strong in body and some will be delicate and weak. So long as this is the case it is utterly impossible to prevent immense difference in the circumstances of men. No doubt it is quite right to provide bridges and steps by which men in a lower position may raise themselves to a higher one, to supply the poor with the cheapest and best education, to encourage those who are disposed to emigrate to seek a new position in Colonies where land and food are cheap and labour is highly paid. But those many political philanthropists who are now proclaiming from the house-tops schemes and nostrums by which everybody is to be well off, and nobody is to be poor in a fallen world, are only wasting their time, deluding ignorant hearers, raising expectations which can never be fulfilled, and exhibiting their own want of common sense.

CHAPTER 6

The following are the churches which I have consecrated since I became Bishop of Liverpool:

1. St John the Evangelist, Walton; 2. Maghull Parish Church; 3. St Ambrose, Farnworth; 4. St Andrew, Wigan; 5. St Luke, Southport; 6. St Cyprian, Edge Hill, Liverpool; 7. St Stephen, Crown Street, Liverpool; 8. All Saints, Toxteth Park, Liverpool; 9. St Gabriel, Toxteth Park; 10. St Agnes, Toxteth Park; 11. St Bede, Toxteth Park; 12. St Chad's, Everton; 13. St Polycarp, Everton; 14. St Benedict, Everton; 15. St Athanasius, Kirkdale; 16. Aspull, Wigan; 17. St Paul, Widnes; 18. St Mary, Waterloo; 19. St Philip, Southport; 20. Crossens, Southport.

St Lawrence, Kirkdale, and St Philip, Shiel Road, Liverpool, are opened, but not consecrated for want of an endowment fund.

Three large new churches are being built, and approach completion, one at Earle Road, Liverpool, one at Woolton, and one at Ince, near Wigan.

TABLE I.

The following is a summarized Statement, carefully drawn up from Visitation Returns, of the Total Expenditure in each Rural Deanery in the Diocese of Liverpool, on building, enlarging, or restoring Churches, on building or enlarging School-rooms, and on building Mission Rooms or Parish Rooms, firstly, during the three years ending October 1884, and, secondly, during the three years ending October 1887:

Rural Deanery of—	1884			1887		
North Liverpool,	£20,302	15	5	£14,550	5	5
North Meols, and Ormskirk,	20,379	15	2	26,992	4	7 ½
Walton,	7,500	18	3	35,417	6	10
Wigan,	21,047	10	0	19,803	0	0
Childwall,	16,371	16	2	29,200	10	8
South Liverpool,	5,341	19	3	6,846	3	1
Prescot,	14,225	9	3	22,444	18	11
Toxteth,	29,905	6	9	36,253	12	3 ½
Winwick,	10,310	0	0	6,313	18	0

TABLE II.

The following is a summarized Statement, carefully drawn up from Visitation Returns, of the money contributed and expended in each Rural Deanery in the Diocese of Liverpool, for Parochial Charities, Diocesan Institutions, Home Missions, and Foreign Missions, firstly, during the three years ending October 1884, and, secondly, during the three years ending October 1887:

Rural Deanery of—	1884			1887		
North Liverpool,	£16,164	16	2	£17,741	10	7
North Meols, and Ormskirk,	14,118	0	0	16,649	16	5 ½
Walton,	9,090	0	0	8,194	0	11 ¼
Wigan,	4,638	0	0	6,173	9	1
Childwall,	12,861	0	0	14,444	9	2
South Liverpool,	12,025	0	0	17,085	18	1 ½
Prescot,	7,417	0	0	8,518	11	8
Toxteth,	20,770	0	0	27,102	5	11
Winwick,	1,698	0	0	1,598	8	6 ½

I think it right to say that the sum total in each of these Tables does not represent the whole amount of money actually expended and contributed. Unhappily the returns from some Parishes are rather incomplete. But on the whole there is a very satisfactory increase during the second period of three years.

J. C. LIVERPOOL.

CHAPTER 9

Some readers may think the statement of this paragraph extravagant and overdrawn. I request them to read the following passages from a statement recently made by the Roman Catholic Bishop of Salford, Manchester:

ENGLAND'S CONVERSION NO DREAM

I hear some one whisper: you are dreaming, you are raving; to talk of the conversion of England is childish babble. You are not two millions out of twenty-seven millions of the population. You lose thousands of your poor through the workhouse system and by proselytism for hundreds you gain in the upper classes. You misunderstand the English race, you misread their strong Protestant character, if you expect their conversion to Catholicism.

THE PENAL TIMES

To this I reply: compare the attitude of England during the last three hundred years towards the Catholic Church with her attitude today. For three hundred years Catholics were socially and civilly proscribed. They lived, or rather groaned, under all manner of disabilities. It was a crime to profess the Catholic religion, to hear Mass, to harbour a priest, to possess beads or medals blessed by the Pope, to communicate with Rome, to perform any act of the Catholic religion. The legal penalties were fines, confiscation, imprisonment, banishment, torture, and death, and they were all applied with a remorseless hand. No Catholic could hold a commission of the peace, a commission in the army or navy, or any civil position of trust and responsibility. Catholic education was proscribed, so that the children of Catholics had to grow up in ignorance, or to pass the seas if they would obtain education. Even the fathers of men now living remember the time when the only safe way for a Catholic to retain his estates was by legally conveying them to a Protestant, and when a Catholic could be compelled by any stranger on the road to give up his horse for a five pound note. Not only were the laws of the land directed against Catholics, but for nigh three centuries the whole literature and the social and public life of the country seemed to combine with the Legislature for their degradation and utter extinction. But what is the attitude of England towards Catholics today?

ENGLISH CATHOLIC TODAY

They are in honour equal with their fellow-countrymen. They fill all posts of trust and honour save only the highest: they are viceroys, governors of colonies, lord-lieutenants, privy councillors, members of parliament, cabinet ministers, chairmen of county councils, and magistrates. They are generals in the army, admirals of the fleet, judges of the land. There is no path of civil or public service which is not now open to them, and in which they are not welcomed. Once and again there has been a brief outburst of the old Protestant fear and bigotry, as forty years ago, when it is thus that a Protestant contemporary writes: 'Liberals and Conservatives vied with one another in uttering furious nonsense, and the whole heart of the nation went with them. But the legislative results were a miserable penal law, which was never put in force, and was repealed a few years ago with every expression of contempt.' Now put this change down to whatever cause you please, to communication with the Continent, contact with Catholics, the abolition of class privileges and ascendency, indifference in matters of religion, the spread of education among all sections of the people, the decay of prejudice, critical research, which is causing the history of England to be rewritten—whatever be the causes, the result, the change is undeniable.

CHANGE IN THE ESTABLISHMENT

Nor is this all. Not only has the attitude of the population changed, but the very Establishment which was set up in rivalry to the Church, with a Royal supremacy triumphantly pitted against a Papal supremacy, this very Establishment has changed its temper and attitude. Its Bishops, ministers, and people are busily engaged in ignoring or denouncing those very Articles which were drawn up to be their eternal protest against the Old Religion. The sacramental power of orders, the need of jurisdiction, the Real Presence, the daily sacrifice, auricular confession, prayers and offices for the dead, belief in Purgatory, the invocation of the Blessed Virgin and the saints, religious vows, and the institution of monks and nuns—the very doctrines stamped in the Thirty-nine Articles as fond fables and blasphemous deceits—all these are now openly taught from a thousand pulpits within the Establishment, and as heartily embraced by as many crowded congregations. Even the statue of the Blessed Virgin Mary has been set up with honour over the principal side entrance to Westminster Abbey, and she has been recently enthroned upon a majestic altar under the great dome of St Paul's.

I give this passage without comment. If it does not open men's eyes to the danger in which the Reformed Church of England stands at this moment, I fear nothing will. Unhappily none are so blind as those who will not see.

CHAPTER 14

1. What says the Nineteenth Article? 'The Church of Rome hath erred, not only in their living and manner of Ceremonies, but also in matters of faith.'

What says the Twenty-second Article? 'The Romish doctrine concerning Purgatory, Pardons, Worshipping and Adoration, as well of Images as of Reliques, and also Invocation of Saints, is a fond thing vainly invented, and grounded upon no warranty of Scripture, but rather repugnant to the word of God.'

What says the Twenty-fourth Article? It forbids the Romish custom of having public prayers and ministering the sacraments in Latin, as 'repugnant to the word of God.'

What says the Twenty-fifth Article? It declares that the five Romish sacraments of Confirmation, Penance, Orders, Matrimony, and Extreme Unction, are not to be accounted sacraments of the Gospel.

What says the Twenty-eighth Article? It declares that 'Transubstantiation (or the change of the substance of bread and wine) in the Lord's Supper, cannot be proved by Holy Writ, but is repugnant to the plain words of Scripture, overthroweth the nature of a sacrament, and hath given occasion to many superstitions.' It also declares that 'the sacrament of the Lord's Supper was not by Christ's ordinance reserved, carried about, lifted up, or worshipped.'

What says the Thirtieth Article? 'The cup of the Lord is not to be denied to the lay-people.'

What says the Thirty-first Article? 'The sacrifices of masses, in the which it was commonly said that the priest did offer Christ for the quick and the dead, to have remission of pain or guilt, were blasphemous fables and dangerous deceits.'

What says the Thirty-second Article? 'Bishops, priests, and deacons are not commanded by God's law either to vow the estate of single life, or to abstain from marriage.'

What says the Thirty-seventh Article? 'The Bishop of Rome hath no jurisdiction in this Realm of England.'

2. The following report of the Committee of the Upper House of Convocation of the province of Canterbury, being a Committee of the whole House, appointed on the 9th of May last, to consider and report on the teaching of the Church of England on the subject of Confession was laid on the table by his Grace the Archbishop of Canterbury on July 23, 1873:

'In the matter of Confession, the Church of England holds fast those principles which are set forth in Holy Scripture, which were professed by the Primitive Church, and which were re-affirmed at the English Reformation. The Church of England, in the Twenty-fifth Article, affirms that penance is not to be counted for a Sacrament of the Gospel; and, as judged by her formularies, knows no such words as 'sacramental confession.' Grounding her doctrines on Holy Scripture, she distinctly declares the full and entire forgiveness of sins, through the blood of Jesus Christ, to those who bewail their own sinfulness, confess themselves to Almighty God, with full purpose of amendment of life, and turn with true faith unto him. It is the desire of the Church that by this way and means all her children should find peace. In this spirit the forms of Confession and Absolution are set forth in her public services. Yet for the relief of the troubled consciences, she has made special provision in two exceptional cases.

'(1) In the case of those who cannot quiet their own consciences previous to receiving the Holy Communion, but require further comfort or counsel, the minister is directed to say, "Let him come to me, or to some other discreet and learned minister of God's word, and open his grief, that by the ministry of God's holy word he may receive the benefit of absolution, together with ghostly

436

counsel and advice." Nevertheless, it is to be noted that for such a case no form of absolution has been prescribed in the Book of Common Prayer; and further, the Rubric in the first Prayer-book of 1549, which sanctions a particular form of Absolution, has been withdrawn from all subsequent editions of the said Book.

'(2) In the order of the Visitation of the Sick, it is directed that the sick man may be moved to make a special confession of his sins if he feel his conscience troubled with any weighty matter, but in such case absolution is to be given when the sick man shall humbly and heartily desire it. The special provision, however, does not authorise the ministers of the Church to require from any who may repair to them to open their grief in a particular or detailed examination of all their sins, or to require private confession as a condition previous to receiving the Holy Communion, or to enjoin or even encourage any practice of habitual confession to a priest, or to teach that such practice of habitual confession, or the being subject to what has been termed the direction of a priest, is a condition of attaining to the highest spiritual life.'

—*Times*, July 24, 1873.

INDEX